# ONE DAY, ONE TRUTH

Zak Malerich

# Introduction

**An everyday walk with the LORD...** With each new day that the Lord so graciously gives you, there comes a new truth from God's Word; God inspired words to begin your discussion with the One who took your place by dying on the Cross. Jesus did this so you could be set free from the sin and evil powers that has enslaved this world—to break you out of the prison of darkness that this fallen world embraces and hates the very name of Jesus. The Lord has shined His Light on you so you would learn the Truth about who the Living God is, who you were created to be, and why you were created. This fallen world brain washes the people who happen to make it out of the womb. And living in this world's dark and misguided ways always leaves us unsatisfied and wanting more, and this life always ends in eternal death when we die in darkness. Living and loving in the ways of this world is evil and wicked in the eyes of the Lord. This fallen life lived apart from Jesus has no lasting value and makes you an enemy of God. But when you are humble enough to admit you are not God and confess your rebellion against the Author of Life, you will be given another chance—a new life-journey—one where you can clearly see the right path that lies before you and where it leads. The Father always knows best; the Son has paved the Way to Heaven, and the Holy Spirit is here to guarantee your eternal future. With the Lord your victory is certain, because through the death and resurrection of God the Son, there is the eternal life that you were meant to live.

# Preface

# *"A Life Redeemed; One Day, One Truth at a Time"*

Before I began my redeemed life-journey in Christ Jesus at age 55, I was so deep into the darkness of sin and rebellion against our Holy God, that I did not care whether I lived another day or not. Although my life looked good and pretty normal on the outside, I was trapped in a very dark place on the inside. There were a lot of troubling questions that I longed to know the truth about; questions that tormented my heart and soul; questions that went unanswered in all of my failed attempts to find them. I searched my past, my mind, the world's array of secular minds, religious minds and the Catholic Church. But the results always left me feeling the same; dissatisfied, empty and wondering if there was any truth to this life at all. And with my emptiness came the hopelessness, and with this combo, the darker my world became. Although my search for the truth continued, I decided to make the best of this life and went with the flow of the world to pursue success, hoping there was more to this life than meets the eye. On occasion, I would seek the LORD but only half halfheartedly, because I wasn't really sure that God cared about my life or what goes on in this hard and crazy world.

As for my meager beginnings; I was born into a dysfunctional family with alcoholic parents and a pedophile for a father. From my youth I found myself discouraged and depressed, yet I hope that this life was not in vain. After a bloody year in the hell of Vietnam, I came home even more discouraged and depressed, and added lost and confused to my condition. But still hoping there was something left for me. I went to college on the GI Bill and started my career in the nursery and landscape business. I got married, raised a daughter, and then the bottom dropped out of my life and I was swallowed up by the darkness that rules this evil world. I ran away from my family, my home, and my career. My life, as I knew it to be, came crashing to the beginning of the end. It was time to wallow in self-pity and then check out. There was no more of me left to give. It was time to wash my hands of this life that was not worth the trouble it caused. After a near fatal overdose of wine and antidepressants, I married again for all the wrong reasons, and with my new wife in tow moved from the west coast to the east coast, running as far away from my past as I could drive. I ended up in Florida and settled down in dysfunction, where I commissioned myself as a drunk on a mission of slow death. I reasoned that if God would not let me end my life quickly, I would do it slowly, one drink, one day at a time. And so my life became one drink, one lie at a time. My one drink led to another drink to another drink and the more I drank the more my existence became a lie. I had become so ashamed of myself that my entire life became a lie. And the bigger the lie, the more I hated this life. And the more I hated this life, the more I hated who I was. And the more I hated who I had become, the more beer I drank to ease the pain and hopefully put an end to my darkness filled with guilt and shame and hopelessness.

And so my existence went; from one drink to another until in one of my drunken stupors an ex-con tried to end my misery, but failed. And when I woke up from a coma three days later in the hospital, all that was left was a broken mess of flesh with a concussion, a shattered jaw with metal plates, and a few loose teeth that were ready to fall out. I realized then, that I just existed in a broken body with a dead spirit. But still the LORD kept me alive in my sin and utter brokenness. It was after this near death experience that I decided to run away again and as far away from Florida as I could drive and ended up back where I came from. And once again my existence became waking up, drinking, and passing out. Until finally my plan of slow death began to pay off. My physical health began to decline as my mental health had, and with that decline the darker my darkness became until I was begging God to send me to Hell where I belonged. I turned the hatred I had for living inward that resulted in a self-loathing so strong I could not look at myself in the mirror. I isolated myself, disconnected my phone, locked my doors , hiding in my dark world of drinking, self-loathing, pornography, and depression.

But one day while I was wallowing in a self-loathing, drunken stupor, I received a card and short note from a long lost girl friend from my days before Vietnam. She was someone I was very close to and someone I had befriended during a very difficult time in her life. We had fallen in love and talked about getting married if I survived Vietnam. But the ways of war took its toll on my already lost and confused life. I came back deeply depressed, guilt ridden, and confused even more about this life and the God whom I thought cursed me with it. I was angry at God for allowing so much horror and blood and death and terror and the waste of so many human beings for no reason. I came back addicted to pot and opium, and was called a baby killer in the eyes of my country that I fought for. But it was on that day in July of 2004, almost 40 years after Vietnam, that the mailman delivered a message from God that saved a broken man's life that was so lost in his own darkness that he was on the verge of exiting this world for the real darkness of the eternal abyss. On that day, a speck of hope arrived to one who had lost all hope. It was as if an angel was reaching out to me and it lit a spark of light in my soul. Unbeknownst to two long lost teenage lovers, God was beginning a journey for two people who were destined to travel together on a journey that would change both of their lives forever. It was through the plan of our Almighty God and Savior that we married in 2009. It was through that one simple message of outreach that many lives were changed forever. The Lord woke me up. I found a Christ centered recovery program, and Jesus led me to Beaverton Foursquare Church, which became my family. And it is where I ended up working, went to a Bible College, and started becoming the man that God had intended me to be. The transformation began and is still being done today, and will one day be completed when I see my Savior and God face to face.

I can remember vividly, how the New Life Recovery Bible that Sherry sent me, started to make real sense for the first time in my life. I could understand the words that I was reading and could put it to work in my life. The Lord Jesus Christ, the Good Shepherd of my soul, healed the wounds of my past. He gave me the peace about this life that I had long been searching for. But most of all, He gave me hope; that this difficult, most confusing life is not lived in vain when you know the Truth and follow the Way. I became so excited about discovering the Truth that from the very beginning I wrote it down on paper and shared it with anyone who would read it. And thus, an idea was born and God put it on my wounded but healing heart to share it with the world. And so this is its beginning.

The world we live in is not any easy place to live in. It is hard to survive. It is hard to find peace when everything is crumbling around you. It is a dangerous world that we live in and it is getting more dangerous as the days and nights go by. Our dark world is filled with all kinds of evil and wickedness and it is not Christ friendly. The ruler of this fallen world is Satan and his aim is to take as many people as he can into the eternal burning Lake of Fire. The Devil has tried his best to defeat the God who created him, but has failed. He knows his time on earth is coming close to its end. He knows he has lost and his reign is almost over. But until it is, this world will continue to decay before it gets better. The worst is yet to come and that comes straight from the mouth of the Living God, who defeated the sin and death that Satan brought into our world. God's Plan for Man and all of creation is closing in to its completion. The time to choose is drawing dangerously close to running out. Don't miss out on the undeserved gift of forgiveness and redemption and eternal life.

My deepest prayer for both those who are searching for the Truth and those who are discovering the Truth, is that these Holy Spirit inspired words from my finger tips, when read each day, will bring you hope, peace and eternal joy. But even deeper in my prayers is that when you open the Book of God's Story that it speaks to your heart in ways that will bring you the Wisdom of God and everlasting life; that the Holy Spirit will open the eyes of your heart so you can experience the LORD our God, Savior, and Helper like never before. We are all created in the image of our gracious and merciful God and we have within our very makings the desires to know Him and to know the Truth. This fallen world tries to convince us otherwise, but you can look at the state our world is in to see where its ways lead. The LORD has a mighty plan my friend, and you are a part of His Plan. He does not force anyone to follow His Plan, but our Lord God and Savior, Jesus Christ, is in Heaven right now as your Advocate, defending your fallen state. He has sent the Holy Spirit to guide and teach you. He is doing everything short of snapping His fingers to make you His. He is calling you and His Still Small Voice will tell you one Truth; one day at a time!

# From My Heart

I would first like to thank my beautiful wife, Sherry, for putting up with my many hours of isolation with the Lord as I wrote and re-wrote what the Holy Spirit was directing. It was not easy for her as a new wife, for I was determined to follow God's calling. She stood by me and didn't strangle me. Thank you, my earthly angel. I would also like to thank my good friend and mentor, Pastor Harry. He was the first person that the Lord put in my new life of seeking the Truth. He stood with me, unafraid and held me accountable in my recovery. He not only shared His knowledge and wisdom with me, but he took me into his family. Thank you, my friend. I would also like to thank our Senior Pastor, Randy Remington, for bringing me so many truths that I had longed for for most of my life. His messages from the LORD were critical in saving my life. For this new life-journey in our Lord and God Christ Jesus, I knew, was my last and final chance to escape the horrors of Hell. Thank you Pastor Randy. You are truly a Spirit filled Shepherd and a man of the Living God. I owe much of my godly knowledge to you. You are God's voice for many and a blessing for this dark world. I also want to thank all my professor's at Multnomah Bible College now "Multnomah University". I wanted to dig deep into God's Word and the Truth, and you all came through with flying colors. What I learned is priceless and I will use it to the best of my ability to shine God's Truth on the people of this fallen world who are without hope or deceived. And last but not least, I want to thank the entire staff of my eternal family at Beaverton Foursquare Church. They joyfully took me under their wings and helped nourish my spiritual health and well being. They showed me what it is like to be Spirit filled and at peace. There are always people in our church hallways and common areas praying, laughing, crying, healing, teaching, comforting, and living and loving like Jesus. You are all very much appreciated, for I feel your love, respect, and gratitude for all the work I have done beautifying our campus. I did it for you. You deserve a beautiful place to work in. The ministry that you all dedicate yourselves diligently to, reaches throughout our city, state, country, and around the entire world. Well done, dear saints. You make a difference in a world that is confused, uncertain and fearful about tomorrow. And it is not the kind of difference that fades in the sunset or dissipates in doubt, but change that has eternal value, and glorifies the Living God—the Way, the Truth, and the Life. Jesus Christ is our Creator, Provider, and our only Savior and you are all unafraid and faithful to live for Him. What our world needs is more saints like you, my dear friends and colleagues in Christ Jesus. You were carefully knit by the hands of God and it clearly shows. Thank you all!

# Dedication

I dedicate this long suffering book to the Lord, My God and Savior, and to my beautiful wife, who was inspired by the Living God to search and find a long lost soul, so she would point me to the Savior of our souls, Jesus Christ. Even though I owe the Lord much more than I can ever give in return, I owe my wife, Sherry Lyn, my full gratitude for being instrumental in saving my human life, so I could receive the gift of eternal life. Sherry was called by God to find me and she did. But what she found was not the person she remembered, but a man beaten up by this life—a mere shell clothed in shame, guilt, self loathing, and a disdain for living—a broken man soaked with sin and depression, who thought dying was the best answer to a way out. I had a death wish and was well on the way of destroying myself and ridding the world of just another disheartened soul.

I thank you my earthly angel for seeing the man that God wanted me to be. Thank you for sticking it out. You sacrificed much in the name of love and companionship. Without you and your faith in the power of God the Holy Spirit to transform my life, and without your perseverance of a saint called by God, I can now share with confidence, the Truth of who our LORD God is and what He can accomplish in anyone's life no matter how deep they have been sucked into the darkness of sin and Satan. From the glorious saving Light of King Jesus that pours out of my soul, I say I love you and I dedicate this book in the spirit of what you gave and gave up for me.

Zak Malerich has been a patient of mine for the last 10 years. He has developed in that time a peaceful and fulfilling life which is well-reflected in his daily devotionals he has created over the last few years. His desire to bring guidance to others has inspired his daily offerings and his helpful ministrations to others around him who might be in need. This change in his life has emerged from the black hole of despair which characterized his former life into a new place of peace and joy for him and the people his life touches. It has been a privilege to share his journey with him.

Ward T Smith MD

I'm amazed at how often the Holy Spirit will touch a current need in my life through the reading of the day in this inspiring and challenging devotional. There's a voice in these pages -- it's the Father's voice -- a gracious wooing, but also an urgent and penetrating call to discipleship. I think just what we need to hear to be faithful, obedient, and joyful followers of Jesus in these trying times.

Keith Reetz<br>Assistant Pastor

Zak has written a book that characterizes his life-devotion to God, the Word, and right living.

Patti Fletcher, Librarian,<br>Beaverton Foursquare Church

I was so thrilled to hear that our friend Zak was going to publish the Bible studies that we as a church staff have been privileged to get in our email boxes over the past few years. Great nuggets of truth, supported by God's Word—always encouraging and directing us to a God who loves us, forgave us and for Whom nothing is impossible. Zak has an unique gift of communicating the truth of our awesome God. I always come away having my faith strengthened by his words of wisdom.

Dawn Scott<br>Operations /HR Dept.<br>Beaverton Foursquare Church<br>Beaverton, Or.

Jesus once responded to Peter with the words, "Blessed are you, Simon Bar-Jonah, for flesh and blood has not revealed this to you, but My Father who is in heaven" (Matthew 16:17). I think that Jesus could say the same thing to Zak, that the Father has taught him truths through His

Word that have gone beyond mere human instruction. When the Father reveals something to you, it becomes part of your life in a profound and transformative way.

I have had the joy of not only reading much of what Zak has written, but I have had a front row seat in watching the Word incarnated in Zak's life on a daily basis. As a master gardener, Zak understands something about planting a seed and nurturing it as it grows unto full fruition. What a perfect metaphor for a man who has grown and become fruitful through the planting of the Word in the soil of his own heart. I consider it a joy to be Zak's friend and Pastor and commend the words of this book because they have been forged in the garden of his life journey with Jesus through the living Word of God. The message is credible, but so is the messenger.

Randy Remington, Sr. Pastor,
Beaverton Foursquare Church

Zak Malerich and his writings have been a great encouragement to me over the years. He is a man who loves Jesus Christ and lives to glorify His Name. Zak's devotional messages are Spirit led, concise, and boldly address all aspects of our daily walk as Christians.

You will be strengthened and encouraged in your everyday walk, gleaning food for thought and prayer each day, as you read through Zak Malerich's devotional messages.

Ken Fletcher
Pastor
Beaverton, Oregon

The prophet Jeremiah writes that the mercies of the Lord are new each morning (Lamentations 3:22-23). In his book, One Day One truth, Zak Malerich demonstrates a profound trust that those mercies are to be found in God's Word. He takes his readers there every day, and he does so with a sense of gratitude for God's mercies that fairly drips from his pen. If you want a trusted guide who will lead you into the arms of a loving and merciful God, I can think of none better than Zak. He has tasted and seen that the Lord is good.

—Steve Mitchell, Communications Director, Beaverton Foursquare Church

# Foreword

I first met Zak about ten years ago. I was the Pastor on duty that day; in other words, I got to talk with anyone who walked through the door of our Church. The Zak who came through the door that day was a mess. The years of self-hatred were written all over his face. He was deeply discouraged and very depressed. There had been some seeds of the gospel planted in him years before, but they had not taken root. We got to talk that day about the great love of the Savior for him. Over the years our friendship has grown and I have had the privilege of watching him grow in his love for Jesus Christ, and in his understanding of the Word of God. These writings well reflect the hope he has in the Lord our God. It is my joy to see Zak move forward from the very dark place he was in, to standing firmly in the grace of God.

It is our prayer that you, too, will be moved closer to the Lord God our Savior, Jesus Christ, as you read this book; that He would draw you higher on solid ground and find yourself firmly in His grip.

Abundant blessing to you!

"For the grace of God has appeared that offers salvation to all people. It teaches us to say 'no' to ungodliness and worldly passions, and to live self-controlled, upright and godly lives in this present age, while we wait for the blessed hope—the great appearing of the glory of our great God and Savior, Jesus Christ, who gave Himself for us to redeem us from all wickedness and to purify for Himself a people that are His very own, eager to do what is good." Titus 2:11 (NIV)

Harry Falkner
Assisting Pastor
Beaverton Foursquare Church
Beaverton, Oregon

# January

# "Mighty in Strength"

**Psalm 27:1**
The LORD is my light and my salvation; whom shall I fear?
The LORD is the strength of my life; of whom shall I be afraid? (NKJ)

Trusting and believing in the sovereignty of God is the only way we can maintain the staying power it takes to survive the onslaught of attacks from the Enemy of God and this fallen world, and do it with fearless joy in our hearts and the hope for better days ahead. The powerful forces of evil that are consuming our world are much too strong for mere human strength alone. And sadly, for many of us when our human strength is not enough, we turn to alcohol, drugs, sex, money, gambling, working, shopping, and many other kinds of worldly gods that only numb the pain of our failures and give us a false sense of courage to face another day and the hopelessness it brings. It is our fallen human nature to first search the world for things that can satisfy our deepest human longings, often ignoring our Creator who is the only One that can deliver us from our fears.

Whenever I ponder the awesome power of God, it always amazes me that we have this incredible power readily available to give us the winning resources we need that will win the everyday battles for our hearts and souls. It is only because of God's unconditional love and His mercy and grace that gives us the chance to overcome the dark forces of this world that want to defile God's glory, one person at a time. Trusting and relying on the Lord God to lead your life-journey will give you the strength and wisdom to fight the Enemy of your soul. My dear friends, our awesome God created us in such a way that we would always need to depend on Him for all your needs, and once you understand and believe this truth, you can boldly face each and every new day with both confidence and peace that the victory is yours. For you are living in Christ Jesus the Lord and Savior of the world; the One who conquered sin and death for you.

## A Whisper of Hope

**Walk with Me...**dear child, in this new year, for when you do you will have all you need for living in this uncertain and difficult world. I will fill you with strength, wisdom, and the power of the Holy Spirit for this new adventure into unknown territory for you. Do not cling to the old sinful ways you have, instead, seek My new and holy Way.

**Job 9:4**
For God is so wise and so mighty.
Who has ever challenged Him successfully? (NLT)

**Do not be grieved, for the joy of the LORD is your strength.**
(Nehemiah 8:10)

# "Victory Is Yours"

**1 Peter 2:11**
Dear brothers and sisters, you are foreigners
and aliens here. So I warn you to keep away from
evil desires because they fight against your very souls. (NLT)

Since the fall of mankind, people have struggled to survive against the evil forces of this world that continue to attack us in our most vulnerable weaknesses. For most people every day is a battle for both our physical lives, as well as our spiritual lives. From the dawn of time this sin filled world has bombarded us day in and day out with many pleasures of the flesh that Cause us to sin. And the only break we seem to get is when we sleep, but even then our dreams may be filled with the desires of the world that leave us craving for more. This fallen world has always tried to lull us into believing that because this life is so short and the only life we have, that it's all about indulging in the pleasures that make us happy, and they can help us escape the chaos around us. But the truth is, my friends, no matter what we indulge in, the chaos remains.

Knowing the absolute Truth about this life and seeking the Living God, Jesus Christ is the only way we will ever find the peace that will help us persevere the terrible chaos that will, one day, end in victory for all those who put their hope and trust in the Lord their God. Until that day, we must prepare ourselves by living in God's Light, learning the absolute Truth, and trusting in our Savior to help us fight the good fight. We need to be strong and live our lives in confidence, knowing that even though we will lose a battle or two along the way, when it's all said and done we will stand in victory with the Lord our God!

## A Whisper of Hope

**Come into My Presence, child...**do not believe the lies of the Enemy. Instead, focus your thoughts on Me—your Wisdom and Strength. Let Me direct your paths so you won't be led astray. Focus not on the pleasures of this world, but on my Presence; then each day you will be able to face the temptations with victory.

**Ephesians 6:12-17**
For we are not fighting against people made of flesh and blood, but against the evil rulers and authorities of the unseen world, against those mighty powers of darkness who rule this world, and against wicked spirits in the heavenly realms. Use every piece of God's armor to resist the enemy in the time of evil, so that after the battle you will still be standing firm. (NLT)

**But thanks be to God, who gives us victory through our Lord Jesus Christ.**
(1 Corinthians 15:57)

# "Grace and God"

**Psalm 145:17**
The LORD is righteous in all His ways, gracious in all His works. (NKJ)

The way I see the grace of God is "His Divine Favor" for the people He created in His image, because without His gracious favor we would all perish in our weakness and sin. Our Creator not only chose to share His eternal glory with us, but He also made us with many of His own attributes. When I finally began to understand these things about our God, I finally recognized that my life really had a purposeful meaning, that my life actually mattered to God, and I had a specific part of His great redemptive plan for mankind. And now I can be confident in the face of this fallen world because I know I have the One Sovereign God; the same One who created the world and then saved it personally cares about my meager existence in the vast scheme of His perfect plan.

God's grace is amazing towards the rebellious people of this wicked world and it's a pure and precious gift that is given in unconditional love. But even knowing this, we still sometimes question why a God who is so filled with love, mercy and grace lets all the pain and suffering continue to devastate the people of our world. I believe we all wrestle with this question at some time in our lives, and this is why we must live by our faith in Christ Jesus. We must believe and trust that our Creator is perfectly holy and just, and His plan for mankind is flawless. The Lord knows why we cling to our lives even when they are filled with pain and sorrow and struggling just to survive. He knows firsthand the hardships of this life, and this is why the Lord graciously provided the Way, the Truth, and the Life. The sin that Satan brought into our world is the reason we live with so much pain and suffering and turmoil. But there is coming a day when the Lord God will put an end to Satan, his evilness, and all unrepentant sinners. He will then create a new Heaven and Earth where His children will live perfect lives forever. This is why the Lord wants us to know the Truth, for when we know the end of the story; we can find peace in amidst the chaos.

## A Whisper of Hope

**My dear child...**It is by grace that you have been saved from the destruction that this fallen world will one day face. It is by grace that you have life and all that you have. I Am with you at all times and in every circumstance. Bathe in the presence of My Saving Light and I pull you out of darkness that consumes this world. You will find my grace when you need it, and it's sufficient in all circumstances.

**Ephesians 2:8**
For by grace you have been saved through faith;
and that not of yourselves, it is the gift of God. (NKJ)

**God is opposed to the proud, but gives grace to the humble.**
(James 4:6)

# *"Trusting Jesus"*

**Psalm 146:7, 8**
The LORD frees the prisoners.
The LORD opens the eyes of the blind.
The LORD lifts the burdens of those bent beneath their loads. (NLT)

Only God can set us free from the power of sin, restore our broken lives, and transform us into the likeness of His Son. But in order for this to happen we must humbly live our lives in repentance, accept His forgiveness, and believe He is the Sovereign God who keeps His every promise. There is always hope when we trust the Lord with our lives, for He is all powerful and all knowing. He provides all that we need and protects us from being destroyed by the Enemy of our souls. The Lord loves us even when we don't love Him and He is always faithful even when we are not. His abiding love is unconditional and He is over flowing with amazing grace and mercy.

Why not step out of your comfort zone and let the Savior of the world take you on an eternal life-journey unlike anything the world can offer you. Who better to trust than the One True God who always has been and always will be—the One who created us? Our Creator knows everyone completely and far better than we know ourselves. Most of us have made a real mess out of our lives by trusting this fallen world and relying on our own limited abilities to find truth and purpose to this life. When we learn about the incredible attributes of God and His absolute truths about life and death, the best option we have is trusting in our Creator— the One who saved us from eternal condemnation by hanging naked, nailed to a wooden cross. You can fully trust in your Lord God and Savior, Jesus Christ, because He is the Way and the Truth to eternal life.

## A Whisper of Hope

**Learn to say...** "I trust in You Jesus" whenever you find yourself in dire need. Take a moment of time to ponder the awesome power I have and know the depth and the breadth of My Love for you. This simple practice will help you in every situation. By acknowledging My sovereignty you will view your circumstances in a new light. By trusting Me, your fear and uncertainty loses its grip on you.

**Isaiah 58:11**
The LORD will guide you continually, watering your life when you are dry...
You will be like a well-watered garden, like an ever-flowing spring. (NLT)

**Therefore if the Son makes you free, you shall be free indeed.**
(John 8:36)

# "Having Faith"

**Romans 1:17**
This Good News tells us how God makes us right
in His sight. This is accomplished from start to finish
by faith. It is through faith that a righteous person has life (NLT).

Every person born into this world lives by faith, because no matter what our beliefs are, we live each day as if there will be a tomorrow and the day after and so on. Every day we get out of bed and go to work with faith that we will return home. We turn on the coffee maker in faith that it will give us a cup of coffee. We start our cars in faith that it will work and not blow up. Every day we entrust our lives to so many people we don't really know; people working in a hospital, or the pharmacy, or a restaurant, or when we get on an airplane. So why then do most of us have trouble trusting in the One who created us and this beautiful world to sustain us? Why is it so hard for us to believe and trust in the Living God who gave us His Life and the promise of salvation?

Our Almighty God lovingly created us to depend on Him for life, but when the first people Adam and Eve sinned, we became separated from our Creator. Mankind began to depend on this fallen world, rather than God--so God sent His Son to pay the final price for our rebellion and we can now come back into the Holy Presence of the living God. We can trust Him to take excellent care of us. The Lord has not only given us the opportunity to humble ourselves and admit our dependency on Him as our Good Shepherd in this unpredictable and harsh world, but He has also given us His life, which if accepted, gives us everlasting life in Heaven as well. When we walk through our life-journey in faith that God is who He says He is, and that He will do what He promises He will do, we walk in confidence knowing we are safe. Our loving God is the only One you should trust with your life. So take a leap of faith my friend, and step up to take the hand of God! You'll be so glad you did.

## A Whisper of Hope

**Trust in Me, dear child...**by relinquishing control of your life-journey into My hands. Let go, and realize that I Am God. This is My world. I made it and I control it. You can achieve a life worth living by living in faithful dependence on Me. So live in Me and I will fulfill the desires of your heart.

**Romans 5:1-2:**
Therefore, since we have been made right in God's sight by faith,
we have peace with God because of what Jesus Christ our Lord has
done for us. Because of our faith, Christ has brought us into this place
of highest privilege where we now stand, and we confidently and joyfully
look forward to sharing God's glory. (NLT)

**So you see, it is impossible to please God without faith.**
(Hebrews 11:6)

# *"Knowing God"*

**Hosea 6:3**
Oh, that we might know the LORD!
Let us press on to know Him. Then He
will respond to us as surely as the arrival of
dawn or the coming of rains in early spring." (NLT)

The best way to know and understand the LORD our God is by spending some alone time in His Holy Presence, reading His Word, and waiting quietly for Him to speak to your heart. By doing this you are inviting Him into your life and you will discover the Truth about who God is, who you are, and why He has given you the life you have. The Lord wants to draw you close to Himself so He can provide what you need for living a righteous life that will honor Him and you. When we develop a loving and personal relationship with our Saving God, He blesses our lives with the wisdom and power to not only persevere this difficult life with peace and thanksgiving in our hearts, but to trust Him so our fears and doubts will begin to lose their mighty grip on us. It is so important my friends, that we spend personal time with God everyday so we can confess our sins and ask Him for His forgiveness—to thank Him for all He does and to share our deepest thoughts and concerns with Him. Then we can ask for His boundless mercy and grace to guide us in all Truth and Wisdom.

Christ Jesus is the only Living God and He can be trusted to get us peacefully through our days with His perfect guidance. The Lord is not only your Source for salvation, but He is also the best Guide for our life-journey here on earth. Living in fear, doubt, uncertainty, and sinfulness is not the way God wants you to live your life in this world. He is your Heavenly Father; the One who made you in your mother's womb. He loves you and He wants you to love Him in return. You must learn to trust God with all things because if you depend on anyone or anything else, you will lose the most precious gift of all; eternal life as it was meant to be.

## A Whisper of Hope

**Trust and rely on Me, My child...**and you can count on Me to be with you always, especially in your times of great need or trouble. I keep the best for all those who put their trust in Me, for the more you trust in Me, the more I enable you to do. Learning to trust Me with your life will take some time. Start by trusting me with those everyday problems that arise, and then when a fearful and turbulent storm comes your way, My grace will be sufficient to see you through to victory.

**Isaiah 26:3-4**
You will keep in perfect peace all who trust in You,
whose thoughts are fixed on You! Trust in the Lord
always, for the LORD GOD is the eternal Rock. (NLT)

**"Blessed is the man who trusts in the LORD, and whose Hope is the LORD.**
(Jeremiah 17:7)

# "Discover Joy"

**Psalm 16:11**
You will show me the way of life, granting me the joy of
your presence and the pleasures of living with you forever. (NLT)

I t is the eternal hope and peace, which our Lord promises, that we are able to fully trust our amazing Creator and Savior to guide and provide our lives with true purpose and the moral values that brings the joy of the Lord while living in a dark world filled with pain—a world that takes pleasure in robbing us of our joy. Without a personal relationship with our Lord God and Savior and without His direction, the purpose of life will always fall short of the goodness that God intended, and this life would end up quite futile. For if this short life is it, how could we ever find the peace and joy that our hearts truly long for? What on earth would make this difficult life truly worth living? Is it worth all the pain and disappointment and discouragement?

Without the hope that Jesus' death and resurrection brings, this life would be nothing but a struggle to survive with a lot of sorrow and pain, discouragement, dead ends, dissatisfaction, confusion, uncertainty, doubt, fear, disappointment, a moment or two of gladness, many days of unhappiness, regrets of days gone past, living with unbearable guilt and shame, and finally dying in the darkness and God knows what else. Not a pretty picture, nor one to be excited about. Without God directing your life-journey there is absolutely no logical rhyme nor reason for living in this world. Without the Light of the World to brighten this dark and difficult life there would be no hope for anyone at any time. Without the Creator and Light of the world Jesus Christ, there would be absolute darkness. Your life is no accident, my friend, God created you for a reason—a good and honorable reason, not to make you unhappy and confused, and certainly not to let you suffer and just die. That is the Devil's plan for you, not God's.

## A Whisper of Hope

**Let Me bless you, My child…**with the peace and joy that only comes through knowing Me. Open your heart to receive all that I have for you. Do not focus on just the temporary joy that this fallen world offers, for it will leave you emptier than before and wanting even more. Rather, look beyond this world and find a life worth living in Me.

**Isaiah 49:13**
Sing for joy, O heavens! Rejoice, O earth!
Burst in song, O mountains! For the Lord has comforted
His people and will have compassion on them in their sorrow. (NLT)

**Do not sorrow, for the joy of the LORD is your strength.**
(Nehemiah 8:10)

# "The Way"

**Psalm 119:105**
Your Word is a lamp to guide my feet,
And a Light for my path. (NKJ)

In this brief leg of our life-journey there are many paths before us. When we are born into this world, the paths that we follow are chosen for us because we are unable to provide for ourselves. When we come of age and live somewhere where we are able to decide on a path, most of us chose a path that seems right with good rewards. Some of us choose to follow a safe path that someone else has paved before them. And some of us choose a path that is both adventurous and dangerous—one that brings excitement into our lives. But whatever path is taken, there is only One Guide who will lead you on a life-journey that will fill your heart with everlasting joy and peace, one that will sustain you in the trials and tribulations that living in this fallen world always brings. It's the only path that leads to godly living and everlasting life in the Light of God's glory.

This incredible, eternal path my friends, will take you on a life-journey unlike anything this world has to offer. It is a glorious journey that is good for us and good for the world, and it just keeps on getting better. And unlike the many paths of this fallen world, when you allow the Creator of Life to direct your path, your life-journey will be blessed with the promise that no matter what obstacles stand in your way, or how dark it becomes, or how many wrong turns you make, your Sovereign Guide will never abandon you nor will He ever forsake you. The first leg of this life-journey is never easy, but a God-driven journey will get you Home safely.

## A Whisper of Hope

**Let Me guide your way, dear child…**for I will lead you safely Home. Walk with Me and learn to live above your circumstances, for My glorious Light shines brightly on those who follow the righteous path of eternal life. Chose the perfect Guide and the path to Heaven, and you will find peace.

**Proverbs 3:5-6**
Trust in the LORD with all your heart, and lean not on your own understanding;
In all your ways acknowledge Him, and He shall direct your paths. (NKJ)

**He guides me in the paths of righteousness for His name's sake.**
(Psalm 23:3)

# "God's Peace"

**Psalm 4:8**
I will lie down in peace and sleep,
For You alone, O LORD, will keep me safe. (NLT)

There is no better way to live this difficult life than turning it over to the Lord our God, and trusting Him to guide you in all circumstances. We were not created with enough ability to deal with and overcome every circumstance that is put before us, especially those circumstances that are beyond our control. Humbly admitting that we are not in control is never an easy thing for most people, because we like to think we are in control even when we are not. And when all that we know how to do fails, we tend to lose hope and at the end of our frustrating day we cannot sleep. And when we cannot sleep, our health will fail, which causes anxiety and depression to set in. But when we give our lives to the Lord, we are asking Him to personally guide us through our life-journey, and we learn to trust Him, for He is our life-line.

It was only after I turned my decaying life over to God that I was able to get up in the morning without dreading the days outcome, because I knew that no matter what the day brought, that the Lord would be with me and my life was safely in His hands. When we rely on the Author of Life to guide us through all of our circumstances, it will lighten the burdens we bear so we can move through the day with confidence. And at the end of our day we are able to sleep in peace knowing that the Lord is watching over us. But even though we are safely in His care, life in this fallen world will continue to be hard and unpredictable until He takes us Home. The greatest Hope we have, whether we wake up to face another day or not, is that we will be in the presence of the Living God.

## A Whisper of Hope

**Rely on Me in faith, My child...** so you can travel your life-journey safely in My hands. This day was graciously given to you. Rejoice in it, refusing to worry about what lies ahead. Pray in faith and I will keep you safe.

**Philippians 4:7**
And the peace of God which surpasses all comprehension,
will guard your hearts and your minds in Christ Jesus. (NASB)

**Now may the Lord of peace Himself continually grant you peace in every circumstance.**
(2 Thessalonians 3:16)

# "The Message"

**1 Timothy 2:3, 4-6**
Our Savior who wants everyone to be saved and to understand the Truth.
For there is only one God and one Mediator who can reconcile God and people.
He is the man Christ Jesus. He gave His life to purchase freedom for everyone.
This is the message that God gave to the world at the proper time. (NLT)

This message from our Lord God is a message of incredible Good News and it is for the entire world. It's a message of hope and salvation that is available for every living person—a message of eternal life. Our Savior wants no one to suffer the eternal condemnation that sin brings. Because God is love, He despises the eternal consequences that sin brings to the people He creates. So God sent us Hope in a Redeemer; the Savior of the World—the Son who reconciled the relationship between God and man. Because we are all natural born sinners, we fall short of the holy standard God sets for us. Sadly, ever since the Devil deceived the first man and woman into disobeying God, this fallen world reeks of sin and thrives on everything wicked and evil.

There are many of us, including myself, who go through most of our lives unaware that we are living in sin. And because of the abounding mercy and grace of our loving God, He pulls us out of the muck and mire of our sins and teaches us how to live a godly life. How awesome it is that we have a Redeemer and a Savior, who invites us to be cleansed and forgiven so we can live in fellowship with God. And it is only by living in Christ Jesus, that you will no longer be controlled by the power of sin—sins that lead to eternal darkness and death. Living in the Light of Jesus Christ exposes the lies and deceit that has enslaved our world in sin. Live in the Light my friends; be freed from the power of sin.

## A Whisper of Hope

**I Am Truth...**my child, the only One who cannot lie. I do not change the truth to meet My needs like this world does. Although the world is under the sedge of deception, where sin is pleasure and evil is good, there is Hope for those who hunger for the Truth. And this hope is found in Me.

**Isaiah 33:21-22**
The LORD will be our Mighty One. He will be like a wide river of protection
that no enemy can cross. For the LORD is our judge, our lawgiver, and our King.
He will care for us and save us. (NLT)

**If you do this, you will experience God's peace.**
(Philippians 4:7)

# *"Hope in Christ"*

**Revelation 7:16-17**
"They will never again be hungry or thirsty; and they will never
be scorched by the heat of the sun. For the Lamb on the throne
will be their Shepherd. He will lead them to springs of life-giving
water. And God will wipe away every tear from their eyes." (NLT)

There is no better promise than these prophetic words spoken by the risen Jesus to the apostle John while he was a prisoner exiled on the island of Patmos. There is nothing in this world that can offer us this kind of hope for the future, because King Jesus will return in glory to judge and rule His Kingdom on earth forever. It is our God-given nature to look ahead and hope for better days, especially for those of us who find ourselves struggling just to keep our heads above water. But unfortunately, there are those who are experiencing the better days of prosperity now, which leaves them addicted to the pleasures of this sinful world and fighting to get more before they die. And in this fallen state of immediate pleasure, these misguided people will almost always end up wondering if their pleasure is all there is to this very short life that ends in death and nothing else.

It was not until I understood just how fleeting this worldly life is without Jesus that I realized how my life-style was nothing more than a nightmare that had no end. But now I know and believe in the Truth of God's Word—the promise of a new and better life and the hope for a wonderful future that can neither be taken away nor will it ever end. The hope that our Lord God, Christ Jesus has been promising throughout the ages has changed my life of hopelessness, doubt and meaningless despair into a life of joy-filled truth with eternal purpose. The world now has the Good News that saves, my friends. Believe and trust in His Promise of eternal life, because Jesus came to give us life, not to take it away.

## A Whisper of Hope

**My Promise of Peace and Joy…**is yours, My child; Promises that you can build a good life on.
I purchased this promise for you with My blood and by suffering beyond anything that you can
imagine. You receive this promised gift by trusting and believing in Me.

**John 6:35**
And Jesus said to them, "I am the Bread of Life.
He who comes to Me shall never hunger, and he
who believes in Me shall never thirst." (NKJ)

**The Lord is my Shepherd; I have all that I need.**
(Psalm 23:1)

# "Our Protector"

**Psalm 125:2**
Just as the mountains surround and protect Jerusalem,
So the LORD surrounds and protects His people, both now and forever. (NLT)

When we entrust our lives to God, He never lets our circumstances or our temptations become so great that we cannot endure or overcome them. Living in this fallen world will never be free from pain, suffering, heart break, sorrow, confusion, deception, fear, or doubt, but by having the faith to trust that our awesome God is who He says He is, and that He will do what He says He will do, we become His protected children. Persistent perseverance of faith is what defines us as His children. The spiritual discipline we learn to develop in the midst of all the challenges that we face daily is priceless. This discipline not only strengthens our faith and courage, but it also plays an important role in shaping our moral and spiritual character. Temptations and trials are necessary in order for us to develop and live by the godly characteristics that were given to us by our Lord God, Jesus Christ.

So be encouraged and find comfort my friends, in knowing that our Savior left His Home in Heaven to endure the same kind of hardships and temptations that we all must face in this difficult and evil world. Jesus did this to not only to save us, but to teach us how to live a solid godly life. Our Lord courageously set an excellent example for us to live by—one of endurance and perseverance in the face of persecution. God will never allow anything in the lives of His children that they cannot deal with. We have a Sovereign Savior we can fully trust to be our everlasting Protector.

## A Whisper of Hope

**Rely on Me, dear child...**to be both your Guide and Protector. It is through your trials that I am able to build a godly character in you. I will equip you with everything you need in order to persevere and win the battles against the evil forces that want to enslave you and then destroy you. You cannot do it alone. With Me, you will travel your life-journey safely in the shadow of My wings.

**1 Corinthians 10:13**
The temptations in your life are no different from what others experience.
And God is faithful. He will not allow the temptation to be more than you can
stand. When you are tempted, He will show you a way out so that you can endure. (NLT)

**When your endurance is fully developed,
you will be strong in character and ready for anything.**
(James 1:4)

# "Learning His Way"

**Psalm 25:5**
Lead me in Your truth and teach me,
For You are the God of my salvation. (NLT)

I began to believe and trust in the Lord God when the Holy Spirit revealed just what it was that our Savior, Jesus Christ did for me personally, not to mention what He accomplished for the entire world. The Holy Spirit helped me understand the pain and suffering that Jesus volunteered for and fully accepted on our behalf. Whenever I meditate on what our Lord gave up to come live in this sin infected world as the final sacrificial Lamb of God, I experience an awesome peace knowing that I am safely in God's hands. We may not fully understand what the Lord puts before us, but we can fully trust that whatever it is, it will transform your life, and give you the strength to persevere the world.

It is not easy to trust, especially if this life has brought us a lot of pain, suffering, unhappiness, and disappointment. As a new Christian, I found it extremely hard to trust in someone I could not see, touch, or audibly hear. But as I began to learn and understand the nature of God, I slowly began to learn how to trust Him one circumstance at a time. Trusting in Jesus, my friends, is a life-saving, life-changing decision. It's hard to describe the joy and peace that this one decision has given me, but I can tell you that Jesus pulled me out of the darkness and hopelessness that I had been trapped in most of my life. And now, my new life in Christ Jesus is a life that is truly worth living.

## A Whisper of Hope

**It is possible; My child...**to find the true peace and joy even in the midst of the darkness that has consumed this world. In fact, My Light shines the brightest when your life is filled with suffering and pain, or stress and frustration, or discouragement and doubt. Lift up your empty hands in faith and I will fill them with My Hope.

**1 John 2:27**
But you have received the Holy Spirit, and He lives within you,
so you don't need anyone to teach you what is true. For the Spirit
teaches you all things, and what He teaches is true—it is not a lie.
So continue in what He has taught you, and continue to live in Christ. (NLT)

**He leads the humble in doing right, teaching them His way.**
(Psalm 25:9)

# *"No More Shame"*

**Psalm 32:5**
Finally, I confessed all my sins to You and stopped
trying to hide them. I said to myself, "I will confess my
rebellion to the LORD." And You forgave me! All my guilt is gone. (NLT)

There are many people who are loaded down with enough guilt and shame that it would easily bring an elephant to its knees. There was a time in my life when I understood very little about the nature of sin or did I realize its negative effect on our character and the dire consequences it has on our lives. Although God built into the fibers of our being the moral differences between right and wrong, we are nonetheless, natural born sinners who cannot control nor overcome our sinful behavior on your own. And because of our weakness to refrain from sin many people succumb to the battle and medicate the pain of their failures with more sin. There are still others who take pleasure in their sinful rebellion, defying the authority of God and are proud about it. And so it continues; the stumbling about in the darkness of ignorance or the blatant pleasure of it. Either way, the consequences are never good.

What an amazing miracle it is that we have a Savior who left the glory of Heaven to touch us in such an unconditional and forgiving way that your guilt and shame and bondage to sin can be removed forever, so we can live this life with purpose and joy. Because of the blood of Christ Jesus our sins are forgiven and the guilt and shame of our past is nailed to the Cross of Christ. God has given you His Word and His Spirit to help you heal from your dark past of wicked deeds so you can start a relationship with the Lord God who created us and saved us.

## A Whisper of Hope

**Be not afraid, my child...**for there is nothing that you have done or said that I don't already know. Be not anxious or worried when you come to Me, for I Am a forgiving God, One whose nature is to forgive and save that which is lost. Let Me fill you with My life saving power so I can heal your wounded heart and give you hope—hope that will set you free from the bondage of sin so you can live with peace and joy!

**1 John 1:8-9**
If we say we have no sin, we are only fooling ourselves
and not living in the truth. But if we confess our sins to Him,
He is faithful and just to forgive us our sins and to cleanse us from all wickedness. (NLT)

**Oh, what joy for those whose rebellion is forgiven.**
(Psalm 32:1)

# *"His Grace"*

**Psalm 34:22**
The LORD redeems the soul of His servants,
And none of those who trust in Him shall be condemned. (NKJ)

With every breath we are dependent upon the grace of God. Just the fact that we wake up each morning is because we have a loving and gracious God. Even though we are a prideful and rebellious people who love our sin, God is always faithful to forgive us when we ask. We have an awesome Savior who volunteered to take the punishment for our sins that were justly due. The Lord is the One who holds the universe in perfect order so our world can exist. He provides everything we need to live a good life. Everything we have comes from our Creator. He has given us a beautiful world filled with wonderful things that give us pleasure and bring us happiness, because He wants us to enjoy life.

The Lord graciously offers us knowledge and wisdom through His Word. He died the sinner's death, so He could offer us forgiveness and salvation. He gives us the Holy Spirit to help us live a righteous life and love others. When we decide to accept Jesus as the Lord over our lives, He will provide the Way. God gives us exactly what we need at exactly the right moment. As a child of the Living God, you can be sure in His sovereignty—that He hears your every cry and He sees your every trouble. He is a saving God who is filled with unconditional love. This life is Filled with pain, suffering, heartache, failures and all kinds of trouble, but when we run to our Provider and Savior, we are headed right into the gracious arms of the Almighty God.

## A Whisper of Hope

**My grace is sufficient, child...**to help you in your times of need—to refresh your weary soul and lighten your heavy loads. This life-journey is much too difficult for you to live on your own. Do not be ashamed or afraid of your weariness or weakness. Instead, see it as an opportunity for Me to take charge of your life. Start where you are, at this very moment and let Me help you get through this one day, one step, and one moment at a time.

**Ephesians 2:8**
For by grace you have been saved through faith,
and not of yourselves, it is the gift of God. (NKJ)

**My grace is sufficient for you, for My strength is made perfect in weakness.**
(2 Corinthians 12:9)

# "Peace in God"

**Habakkuk 3:18-19**

I will rejoice in the LORD. I will be joyful in the God of my salvation.
The Sovereign LORD is my strength! He will make me as surefooted
as a deer and bring me safely over the mountains. (NLT)

No matter how difficult our circumstances may be and no matter how unfair this world treats us, there will always be reason for believers to rejoice in our Lord God and Savior, Jesus Christ. Because of His great love and compassion for us, the Son of God has made it possible for anyone to come into the very presence of the living God. The salvation of mankind is a gift from God; one that is graciously offered to anyone, no matter what our past mistakes have been. Without the Robe of Christ covering our sinful flesh it would be impossible for any human being to stand blameless before our Holy God.

It is because of the Lord God's unchangeable attributes that we can fully trust Him with our lives, even when we are deeply trapped in the chaos of darkness that engulfs this world. The better you know the Lord Jesus Christ, the better you will understand your personal circumstances and the more peace you will have about them. And even though there will be times when it is hard to understand why God allows bad things to happen, we can be confident that He will guide us safely over the rugged peaks of our life-journey at the proper time and according to His good will. To receive the promise of God's gift of salvation is a great event to celebrate and praise our awesome God for. And always remember my friends, that having the power of God behind you is having a secure and rewarding life-journey that will take you Home where you belong.

## A Whisper of Hope

**Be glad, My child…**that your life-journey is not in vain. It is a learning process that will teach you the glories of life even though you must suffer for awhile. I came to snatch you from the grips of Satan and his fallen world and to lead you on the only path that leads to an everlasting life with Me. This is My promise; I give you My Word.

**Ephesians 2:4**

But God is so rich in mercy, and He loved us so very much,
that even while we were dead because of our sins,
He gave us life when He raised Christ from the dead.

**His peace will guard your hearts and minds in Christ Jesus.**
(Philippians 4:7)

# *"Call Me Hope"*

**Lamentations 3:24**
The LORD is my portion, says my soul,
Therefore I have hope in Him. (NKJ)

The biggest influence in my life that caused me to lose heart and assume a defeated position was the futility I felt in relying and hoping in this world to satisfy my needs, because it is unstable, out of control, and in flux—here today and gone tomorrow. When I finally accepted that this life had no lasting value, I decided to escape into the darkness and hide in my depression and defeat. I now understand that Lord God allows many of us to reach that point of hopelessness in order to set the stage for His redeeming Truth that is desperately needed in our world. And as I began to understand the absolute Truth about this life and its final outcome, it was obvious that my only hope was trusting in the Way that God provided for us through His Word, and the death and resurrection of Jesus Christ. Our infinite Savior is the only One who can save us from the dark endings of this wayward world.

Traveling through this life-journey by trusting in the absolute principles of our Lord God is the only Way to live in this short life. But there is one absolute principle that stood out and gave me the most hope in my hopelessness, and it was knowing that nothing would ever separate me from God's love. Once you know and believe in God's unchanging Truth, my friends, your life-journey on this earth will no longer be lived in vain, instead, you will enjoy a God-driven, purpose-filled life with glorious meaning and eternal value. The living God is your best and only Hope, because He has prepared an awesome eternal life-journey for all those who Call Him their Hope.

## A Whisper of Hope

**Put your Hope in Me...**For when you do I will reside in the depths of your heart. It is then that My Hope will begin to reign in you. You will not find an ounce of lasting hope, or peace in the world around you, in the circumstances you create, or in any human relationships you may acquire. I Am your Hope.

**1 Peter 1:21**
Through Christ you have come to trust in God.
And you have placed your faith and hope in God,
because He raised Christ from the dead and gave Him great gloryand live your life-journey as God. (NLT)

**I Am the LORD and I do not change!**
(Malachi 3:6)

# "In Glory We Stand"

**Isaiah 60:19**
No longer will you need the sun to shine by day,
nor the moon to give its light by night, for the LORD
your God will be your everlasting light, and your God will be your glory. (NLT)

I t is an awesome feeling knowing with certainty that you, a mere human being who has made many mistakes through ungodly choices, will one day share in the glory of God. For me, just thinking about that day gives me a peace in my heart that is unlike any peace that this fallen world has to offer. Knowing that our Creator and Savior provided the way for us to have the opportunity to share in His eternal glory always puts new life and new hope in our hearts! Even as this world continues spinning out of control, those who belong to God are safely in the hands of our Lord God and Savior, Jesus Christ. The Lord not only provides us with the strength to persevere when this difficult life is getting the best of us, but He also gives us the wisdom and the willingness to help and comfort those who have given in to the darkness of this fallen world and are succumbing to their pain and hopelessness.

But the Good News is our Savior, Jesus Christ has overcome this evil world, and no matter how hard or difficult this fallen world makes your life, the hope you have in Jesus will be your Rock and your Refuge; a place where you can find rest for your weary soul so you can stand strong and steadfast in your faith that God is God and the everlasting hope He promises cannot be taken away. This incredible inheritance is both a privilege and an honor and a gift that was dearly paid for.

## A Whisper of Hope

**Be still, My child…** and know that I AM God. There is absolutely nothing in this universe that is more powerful nor more gracious than I Am. One day you will discover how wide, how long, how high and how deep My Love is, but until that day you must trust in My Word.

**Psalm 62:5-8**
Let all that I am wait quietly before God, for my hope is in Him.
He alone is my Rock and my salvation, my Fortress where I will
not be shaken. My victory and honor come from God alone. He
is my refuge, a Rock where no enemy can reach me. (NLT)

**For as the waters fill the sea, the earth will be filled with
an awareness of the glory of the LORD.**
(Habakkuk 2:14)

# *"Our Best"*

**Isaiah 49:6**
He says, "You will do more than restore the people
of Israel to me. I will make you a Light to the Gentiles,
and you will bring My salvation to the ends of the earth." (NLT)

From the beginning God has been our Provider and Redeemer. He promised to send a Savior who would bring salvation to all people of this fallen world, and He sent His Son to do just that. Our Creator knows us completely. The Lord knows our every weakness and He also knows what our strengths are.  He knows everything we need and don't need. Because our Almighty God is sovereign over every detail of His creation, He knows how dependent we are on Him as our Provider and Protector. We have an awesome God who never gave up on the human race. He took matters into His own hands and rescued us from the selfish, sinful desires that lead to self-destruction—desires that lead us into to eternal death and darkness.

Our Lord God is both gracious, merciful, and His lovingkindness reaches to the ends of the Earth. And the better we understand this, the more sense it makes to keep our focus on Christ Jesus, our Lord God and Savior. As you focus on the Lord and all that He is to us, it becomes natural to praise and exalt Him as the Lord Most High. And the higher you exalt God, the more you will praise Him, and the closer He draws you to Himself. By knowing the Infinite God who created you and what He voluntarily endured for you so you could escape the dark pits of Hell, you should never let a day go by without thanking Him from the depths of your heart. He deserves no less; He deserves our best.

## A Whisper of Hope

**I am the Resurrection and the Life…**Most people search for life in all the wrong places. They chase after fleeting pleasures by accumulating possessions and wealth, not thinking of the inevitable. Unlike the world, I freely offer to all people an abundant Life that never ends, especially those who are overwhelmed, weary, lost and hopeless.

**1 Samuel 2:1**
My heart rejoices in the LORD;
My strength is exalted in the LORD.
I smile at my enemies, because I rejoice in Your salvation. (NKJ)

**You will keep him in perfect peace, all who trust in You.**
(Isaiah 26:3)

# "Words of Life"

**Colossians 3:16**
Let the message about Christ, in all its richness, fill your lives.
Teach and counsel each other with all the wisdom He gives. (NLT)

The Word of God is at the heart of human life. It is only through the Living Word of God that anyone can find the kind of peace that helps us persevere the worst this world can dish out. God's Word is for anyone who can humble themselves enough to accept the Truth about who they are, who God is, and what God has done and planned for mankind and His creation. The Light of God's Truth has exposed the evil that lurks in the darkness of this fallen world, and the only Way we can find our way out of its evil grip that leads to death is by following the Light that God has given us. And this Light for the world is Jesus Christ, our Lord and Savior.

Jesus is the only One who has the power to lead is out of the fear, anxiety, and uncertainty that is darkening this world as it heads into destruction. I have learned over the years that there are billions of little gods on this earth who think they are the center of the universe—that life revolves around them. But this is not the truth, because our lives are all about the glory of God. Only by learning the absolute truths that God has so graciously shared with us, will we find any peace within the dark circumstances that surround us on every side. The lies that have gripped the people of this world are all from the father of lies, the Devil, who prowls around in the darkness looking for someone to devour. The Truth that brings life to its fullest is found only in the Light of God's Truth. When Jesus shines His Light upon the paths of this difficult journey, you will see the Way, learn the Truth, and live your life-journey as God created you to do.

## A Whisper of Hope

**Learn to live, My child…**above your circumstances, always looking up for answers. This requires focused time with Me, the One who has given you life. Troubles, worries, and anxiety are woven into the very fabric of this perishing world, and only My Words of Life can empower you to face the endless assaults of this fallen world and then give you the Light to escape. As you sit quietly in My Presence, I will shine My Light into your troubled heart and fill you with My everlasting Peace.

**John 8:12**
"I am the Light of the world, he who follows Me
shall not walk in darkness, but have the Light of Life." (NKJ)

**"You have sorrow now, but I will see you again; and no one can rob you of that joy!"**
(John 16:22)

# "Walk of Faith"

**Romans 3:22**
We are made right in God's sight when we trust in Jesus Christ
to take away our sins. And we all can be saved in this same way,
no matter who we are or what we have done. (NLT)

Having faith that Jesus Christ is our Lord God and Savior, is the only lasting hope we have in this life and the next. Trusting that our Lord God is who He says He is, gives us a new lease on this life that carries on into the next. Believing in the promises of our Savior brings us both courage and perseverance in the face of impossible odds. As it is for all believers, it was only when the Holy Spirit opened my eyes to the Truth that I could put my faith in the Lord and find peace in my life. With all the uncertainty and turmoil and catastrophes that confront our world everyday—circumstances beyond our control—we must depend on our Creator, for it is only our Lord God and Savior who can rescue and save us from the destruction that is coming to this fallen world in the near future.

When you reject the Truth and ignore God's saving grace and His future plans for you, you will live in darkness that will, if continued, forever separate you from the goodness of God. But when you humble yourself before the Lord and admit your powerlessness against the unseen forces that consume and control the world, He will deliver you from your bondage to sin, free you from the fear of death, and begin a healing process that will transform your life no matter how deep into the darkness you are. And once this happens, dear friend, you will begin to learn what it really means to live, and do it with joy and faith. And when it becomes your nature to trust and live by faith in Christ Jesus, you will experience the true peace of God; that the Lord is with you wherever you go.

## A Whisper of Hope

**Walk by faith, My child...**and not by sight. And as you take your first step of faith, learn to lean on Me when you trip, for I will teach you, step by step, what you need and when you need it. Step out in faith and experience the redeeming work of My hands. For when I give you My Spirit, this empowers you to live beyond your natural ability and strength.

**Habakkuk 2:4**
"Look at the proud! They trust in themselves,
and their lives are crooked, but the righteous
will live by their faith. (NLT)

**So now, through faith in Christ, we are made right with God**.
(Galatians 3:24)

# "A Peace of God"

**Philippians 4:6-7**
Don't worry about anything; instead, pray about everything. Tell God
what you need, and thank him for all he has done. If you do this, you will
experience God's peace, which is far more wonderful than the human mind can
understand. His peace will guard your hearts and minds as you live in Christ Jesus. (NLT)

The peace that God delivers to those who step out in faith to live a righteous and holy life is so much more than the temporal peace that this fallen and misguided world can come up with. God's promised peace is a peace that can never be taken away from you, because it is everlasting and true. God's amazing peace will never let you down nor will it ever disappoint you. His "perfect peace" will give you both the confidence and the comfort that will calm any of life's most turbulent storms that blow your way. God's peace is a sovereign peace that will give you the courage to stand strong and confident in all situations. God's awesome peace will help you overcome the many fears that come with living in this unpredictable world. God's loving peace will shine so brightly from your life that others will see the "Light of Peace" in your eyes and they, too, will want what you have, because the darkness that is consuming our world is threatening to swallow them up . But the most beautiful reality of God's amazing peace in my life was when I truly became an open recipient to it, for I found the courage to face each day. I knew that no matter what this world dumped on me that day, I was safely in His hands and with this kind of peace I received the day with gladness in my heart, thanksgiving on my lips, and God's peace in my heart—a peace that this ungodly and violent world cannot take away!

## A Whisper of Hope

**My Dear Child…**let thankfulness temper all of your thoughts. Begin and end each day that I give you with thanksgiving and praise. Have a thankful heart in all circumstances and stay close to Me so that I can bring you My Peace. There are many who complain and curse Me for their troubles, but My peace in your heart will protect you from this deadly sin!

**John 14:27**
"Peace I leave with you. My peace I give to you; not as the world gives
do I give to you. Let not your heart be troubled, neither let it be afraid." (NKJ)

**You will keep in perfect peace all who trust in You,
all whose thoughts are fixed on You.**
(Isaiah 26:3)

# "Trust in Truth"

**John 12:44-45**
Jesus shouted to the crowds, "If you trust Me, you are really trusting
God who sent Me. For when you see Me, you are seeing the One who sent Me." (NLT)

Y ou must truly believe with all your heart, mind, and soul these words from our Lord God, for they are spoken in pure truth, especially if you want to experience a renewed life in this world, and a glorious resurrected life in the new world to come. I say this because if you refuse to believe in the Gospel of our Lord God Jesus Christ to follow the man made truths of this fallen world, you will not only experience the emptiness and futility that comes with trusting in false hope, but you will also experience a very dark resurrection to spend an eternity wishing you could truly die. As finite human beings, we will never comprehend the full extent of what Jesus accomplished by dying on the cross, but what we do know from Scripture is that upon His death, Jesus took the full punishment for mankind's sin and rebellion against the righteousness of God throughout the ages.

If people would just open their hearts and minds to the facts of God's glorious redemptive plan and what He had to do to make it possible for anyone of us to share in His eternal inheritance, they would experience the many blessings of joy and peace that He pours out on His children. Whenever I think of how small and insignificant my life is, compared to the vastness of the universe and God's complete redemptive plan, it boggles my mind to think that the Creator, who holds the entire universe in perfect unison, left the glory of heaven to save such a proud and hateful people from the dire consequences that our detestable, godless behavior towards Him deserves. God has given us all the living proof we need—proof that He has defeated both sin and death—proof that He can make us new and fill us with joy. Trusting in the Truth, my friends, will not only bring you peace, joy and rest during your weary laden journey in this frustrating world, but He will also reward you with a glorious eternal future as well.

## A Whisper of Hope

**I Am your God...**the One who gives and keeps on giving. When I died for you on the cross, I bought your freedom and gave you eternal life that keeps on giving. I poured out My Life's blood like a drink offering, just for you--that is My nature; that is who I Am. Remember, dear child, that My death and resurrection was My victory for you.

**Colossians 1:3**
For He has rescued us from the one who rules
in the kingdom of darkness, and He has brought us
into the Kingdom of His dear Son. God has purchased
our freedom with His blood, and has forgiven all our sins. (NLT)

**"I have told you all this so that you may have peace in Me."**
(John 16:33)

# "Sorrow for Joy"

**Jeremiah 31:13**
For I will turn their mourning into joy. I will comfort
them and exchange their sorrow for rejoicing. (NLT)

W hat incredible joy there is when we know this Truth from our LORD God, even in
the midst of our darkest moments. No matter how difficult our circumstances may be,
joy can always be found when we stop focusing on our troubles and take some time to focus
on the Lord and His promises. We have a loving God, my friends, who watches over and cares
about every detail of our lives. I know that it can be quite difficult at times understanding why
God would allow all the pain, suffering, and sorrow that most of us go through while living in
this world, but the one thing that will give you hope and the peace about your circumstances,
is the promise that one day the Lord our God, Christ Jesus will return to make all things right
for those who love, know, and obey Him faithfully.

Unfortunately, the Devil has deceived much of this world into believing that the Christian's
hope is only for the poor and weak and only the strong survive, because they believe their destiny lies in the strength of their own makings. But fortunately, by the mercy and grace of our
righteous and loving God we have the Truth that will set us free from the lies that this world
embraces and lives by. Our Creator has given the peoples of this world the Living Light that
exposes all the deceit and darkness of the Devil. God's eternal Light brightens the only path
that leads to the everlasting joy of living, whether it's in this life or in the next. Put your hope
in the promises of our Lord God, Jesus Christ, my friends, and you will not only experience
real joy in your troubled life now, but you will also gain a renewed heart and mind that will be
at peace with the world around you. Let the true Savior of the world lift you up in joy so that
the entire world will know that you belong to Him and that He lives in you.

## A Whisper of Hope

**Trust Me, dear child...** for there is no need to live in fear and uncertainty. There will be times
when your life-journey is dark and spinning out of your control, but this is when you must be
still and know that I Am God. Let Me pull you from the darkness and set you on the Rock
that is much stronger than any of your circumstances. Then take refuge from the heat in the
shadow of My wings!

**Isaiah 61:10**
I am overwhelmed with joy in the LORD my God!
For He has dressed me with the clothing of salvation
and draped me in a robe of righteousness. (NLT)

**In Your presence is fullness of joy.**
(Psalm 16:11)

# "One Who Saves"

**Psalm 138:7**
Though I walk in the midst of trouble, You will revive me.
You will stretch forth your hand against the wrath of my enemies.
And Your right hand will save me. (NASB)

We happen to live in a beautiful but fallen world, where everyday life finds us surrounded by troubles and uncertainties. If you want to grasp the true reality of the troubles our world is faced with, all we must do is turn on the news, or in many cases just look out your window. Trouble and uncertainty are facts of life for every living creature, no matter where they live on this planet. It has been this way since the fall of mankind and it will continue this way until the end of time.

So is there any hope for our world? Is there anyone or anything that can really give us hope? Is there any real hope or are we just waiting to die? Or are we just living in denial in order to mask the hopelessness that has overwhelmed us? How many of us have cried out to God during impossible odds, begging Him for deliverance, only to continue suffering at the hands of this world?

O, my friends, there is real hope and that Hope lies at the foot of the cross of our Lord God and Savior, Jesus Christ. I know because I can now look back on my life and see how the hand of God was protecting, providing, and giving me chance after chance to come to Him. If you are now where I was, desperately trying to survive with purpose in this storm filled life, and being coerced by the Enemy to believe all is hopeless; it is not, for there is always hope when you belong to God. It is vital for our survival that we understand and believe in God; that His Plan is for everyone who humbly admits there many sins against God's holy ways. For then, in those times of seemingly utter hopelessness He will "stretch out His hand" and if you chose to grab hold in faith, He will turn your hopelessness into joy and give you His peace. It never ceases to amaze me what our gracious God can accomplish in the lives of His people when we live a faith filled life of trusting in Him. Our Lord Jesus has freed you from the final wrath of God if you choose, which is unimaginably far worse than anything the world can put you through. And it is for this reason that you should repent and rejoice. We have a God who saves any life, anywhere, and at any time.

## A Whisper of Hope

**Fear not, My child**...for I Am always with you. I will never leave you, nor will I forsake you! Let this assurance soak into your heart and soul, until you overflow with My peace and joy. The world around you is relentlessly pursuing your demise. Take refuge in Me—the One who saves.

**Isaiah 33:2**
But Lord, be merciful to us, for we have waited for you. Be our strength
each day and our salvation in times of trouble. (NLT)

**"The LORD God of your fathers has spoken to you; do not fear or be discouraged."**
(Deuteronomy 1:21)

# *"Heart and Soul"*

**Joshua 22:5**
"But be very careful to obey all the commands
and the law that Moses gave to you. Love the LORD
your God, walk in all His ways, obey His commands, be
faithful to Him and serve Him with all your heart and all your soul." (NLT)

O ur hearts and souls are the deepest parts of our very existence—the essence of who we are. And the only One who knows what truly lies in the depths of our most inner being, is the One who created us; our Lord God and Savior, Jesus Christ. We often hide our true feelings by the external things that we say or do, but it is only God who really knows what is in our hearts and souls. When I first began to believe that there was absolutely nothing hidden from the eyes of God, it gave me enough fear and reverence for the Lord to change my thoughts, words, and actions, because I not only feared the final wrath of God, but I wanted to also please Him. And as I began to grow in faith and my knowledge of the attributes of our Sovereign God's incredible and unchanging character, it became a blessed check and balance for me. I became less afraid of Him, more willing to follow His will, and the desire to express my gratitude and love for Him. Once I figured out how frivolous it was, trying to hide the dark things in my life from the Lord God, I began to enjoy living in the Light of God's Truth, and the difference was much like night and day.

Living a new life-journey in the Light of God's Truth is never an easy task for any of us, but the Lord will take your hand my friend, like He did for me, and gently guided you back into the land of the living—one step, and one day at a time. Learning how to live a godly life is not only a life-changing lesson that you will never regret in this lifetime, but it is also God's way of preparing you for the eternal life to come. Once you have the Promises of God written on your heart and buried into your soul, this life will become more enjoyable than you ever thought possible!

## A Whisper of Hope

**Don't hide in the dark, My child…**For I can see and hear all things visible or invisible. There is nothing that you do that causes Me to love you less. You cannot surprise Me, nor can you shock Me, for I have seen it all. And has you move through your day, fix your eyes on Me. Gaze upon your Creator with love in your heart and I will refresh your soul.

**Jeremiah 24:7**
Then I will give them a heart to know Me,
that I am the LORD; and they shall be My people,
and I will be their God, for they shall return to Me with their whole heart. (NKJ)

**Incline your ear, and come to Me. Hear, and your soul shall live.**
(Isaiah 55:3)

# "In God's Light"

**Psalm 119:105**
Your Word is a lamp to my feet And a light to my path. (NKJ)

For me, as it has for countless others, living in God's Light has been the most enlightening, life changing experience I have ever known. The Lord God, Christ Jesus came into this world to expose the evil things hidden in the darkness of Satan—a darkness that is destroying the lives of many lost and wandering souls. The Light that shines from Heaven, allows us to see this world as it really is; a world that is ruled by deception and many false gods who are leading multitudes of people away from the Truth and into certain death and eternal destruction. I was one of those drawn into the darkness by the many lies of the world; lies that caused me to hate the very God who created me and the One who loved me unconditionally even though I lived as if He didn't exist. I lived in my dark world filled with doubt, confusion, and totally unaware of my demise into the abyss of Hell. Stumbling through this life-journey in darkness is rather unsettling, especially when you have no idea where your next step will take you. I spent the majority of my life drifting deeper into the darkness of Satan until I finally succumbed to the hopelessness and gave up searching for that one thing I had always longed for and so desperately needed.

But praise the Lord, because if it had not been for His lovingkindness, I would have blindly fallen into the deepest depths of Hell, forever separated from the love and joy and goodness of God. Unlike so many other deceived souls that are lost in the darkness of Satan's world, I can now proclaim the glory of God's Light, for He has reached down from Heaven and plucked me out of the darkness that I was so hopelessly trapped in and shined His light of Truth upon my life—Truth that set me free from the chains of bondage that held me captive. Let Jesus break the chains that hold you in bondage, my friends and let Him lead you out of the darkness of this fallen world—darkness that will eventually consume you with the deepest darkness you can't even imagine—forever separated from the glorious Light of the Living God.

## A Whisper of Hope

**Receive My Light…**dear child, and bathe in its Truth. Don't walk through your life-journey in bondage to the darkness that leads into the pits of Hell. Let Me lead you into the Light of My Truth, where you will find peace and joy in knowing Me. I Am always nearer than you think. Never fear the darkness when it tries to consume you, for I Am your Ever Shining, Everlasting Light—the One you can always trust. Walk in My Light and sleep in peace my child—for all is well.

**Psalm 56:13**
For you have rescued me from death; you have kept my feet from slipping.
So now I can walk in Your presence, O God, in Your life-giving Light. (NLT)

**For you were once darkness, but now you are light in the Lord. Walk as children of Light.**
(Ephesians 5:8)

# "Victory Deeds"

**Deuteronomy 32:4**
He is the ROCK; His deeds are perfect. Everything He does is just and fair.
He is a faithful God who does no wrong; How just and upright He is! (NLT)

There is absolutely no Rock more solid than the LORD our God. There is no stronger foundation in which to build our lives upon than the Rock of our salvation, Christ Jesus. And because of the solidness of the Rock, when we tap into His wisdom and power, it enables us to withstand the onslaught of temptations and trouble that Satan controls the world through. The Rock gets us over the many hurdles that are a part of living in this imperfect world. We are God's creation and cannot exist without Him. We cannot fight and win the battles for our hearts and souls without the sovereign strength and wisdom of God. There are times when our circumstances are beyond human control and they cause us a lot of anger, resentment, or hopelessness that turns into frustration, confusion, and not knowing which way to turn or what to do. And it is these kinds of obstacles in living that leave us exhausted and feeling ashamed because of our inability to fix it.

Our Creator is our Rock and Savior and He not only knows and understands the human nature completely—our strengths, our weaknesses, our frustrations, and even our deepest and most inner feelings, but He also knows everything about everything, and how to fix things. The Rock of our salvation has everything we need to help us through any kind of circumstance that comes our way—good or bad. Our Sustainer and Provider, Christ Jesus, is the best option you and I have, my friends, especially when we humbly surrender to His will and sovereignty. He is always available and ready to help resolve what you are faced with. He is also able and willing to direct the path of your life-journey that will lead you safely Home. The Rock is the greatest Helper, Healer, and Provider you will ever have, and He will do for you what no one else can do; you can be victorious in the battles of life with honor and dignity and eternal rewards—a victory that the Lord will gladly celebrate with you!

## A Whisper of Hope

**Always come to Me first, dear child...**in anything you need help with. Accept them for what they are—the reality of living in a fallen world. You can let them destroy you or you can rely on Me to bring you victory. I Am the Way, the Truth, and the Life. Come to your Rock and sit quietly in My Presence and know that I can do all things!

**2 Samuel 22:31**
As for God, His Way is perfect; The Word of the LORD is proven;
He is a Shield to all who trust in Him. (NKJ)

**He alone is my rock and my salvation, my fortress where I will never be shaken.**
(Psalm 62:2)

# *"His Glory"*

**Isaiah 53:2-9**

My Servant grew up in the LORD'S presence like a tender green shoot, sprouting from a root in dry and sterile ground. There was nothing beautiful or majestic about His appearance, nothing to attract us to Him. He was despised and rejected—a man of sorrows, acquainted with bitterest grief. We turned our backs on Him and looked the other way when He went by. He was despised, and we did not care.

Yet it was our weaknesses He carried; it was our sorrows that weighed Him down. And we thought His troubles were a punishment from God for His own sins. He was beaten that we might have peace. He was whipped, and we were healed! All of us have strayed away like sheep. We have left God's paths to follow our own. Yet the LORD laid on Him the guilt and sins of us all.

He was oppressed and treated harshly, yet He never said a word. He was led as a lamb to the slaughter. And as a sheep is silent before the shearers, He did not open His mouth. From prison and trial they led Him away to His death. But who among the people realized that He was dying for their sins—that He was suffering their punishment? He had done no wrong, and He never deceived anyone. But He was buried like a criminal; He was put in a rich man's grave. (NLT)

P raising the Lord Jesus Christ, our Creator, Redeemer, and the Lover of our souls should come with every breath we take. I cannot imagine starting the day without acknowledging the glory and majesty, the mercy and grace, and the unconditional love and forgiveness that makes up the essence of our Great Sovereign God and Savior—the One who provided the Way for all of us to escape the decadence around us that is driving this fallen world into a horrible and terrifying end. This gracious provision of unearned salvation gives witness to who our awesome God really is and all He has done. Every morning when I sit in God's presence, filling my heart with the warmth of the Son, it awakens my soul to bathe in the glory of His Light. And I urge you, my dear brothers and sisters, to join in and bathe in the Son's Light—for when you do, the fog will clear and you will be able to see and soak in the Son who willfully gave you an awesome reason to have joy and purpose in your life.

## A Whisper of Hope

**Be filled with My Presence…**when you sit quietly with Me, My child. For in this fallen world you need the Light of the Son to lead you out of the darkness and into the Land of the Living. And it is in My Presence that you will find the strength and wisdom and courage to face the uncertain day before you and the Hope for a glorious tomorrow.

**1 Corinthians 10:31**

Therefore, whether you eat or drink, or whatever you do, do all to the glory of God. (NKJ)

**And let the whole earth be filled with His glory!**
(Psalm 72:19)

# *"Alive in God"*

**Deuteronomy 30:20**
"That you may love the LORD your God, that you may obey His voice,
and that you may cling to Him, for He is your life and the length of your days." (NKJ)

Apart from the love of God there is only disappointment and darkness, and it matters not how rich or famous, or how poor or unknown you may be, because living without God is not living at all. Without the Lord the universe and everything in it would be nothing but endless chaos—no life. No sunrises or sunsets, no oceans or mountain streams, no lush forests teaming with wildlife, nor any fragrance or colors to pleasure our senses. There would be neither gentle breezes nor refreshing rains. No music, no joy, no laughter, no children, no love, and no hope. Without our amazing God there would be absolute nothingness. And without God's unconditional love, mercy and grace, life on this earth would not be very pleasant; it would be nothing more than a dark and painful struggle to survive—a struggle that no one would survive. When you chose to live your life without acknowledging there is a God, you are living in denial; not wanting to admit your weakness, believing you are the one in charge and this life is all about you.

When you choose the world over God you are living the life of a fool, because living apart from the Creator will ultimately lead to some very dire and very long lasting consequences. When people rely solely on the physical world and others, this life becomes rather frivolous because the earth and everything in it will one day pass away. The only thing to be gained by living and dying apart from the living God of Creation is eternal darkness, forever separated from the Light to live in an all consuming darkness with much pain and suffering and no chance to escape. If you have not chosen to live in the Way of the Lord, there is no better time than now to connect with Christ Jesus, your Lord God and Savior. Surrender to Him and He will give you a new and better life—one that is truly alive and one that is everlasting. Now is the time, because tomorrow may be too late!

## A Whisper of Hope

**I Am...**the Way, the Truth, and the key to eternal life. Without Me, your life-journey in this world will not end well, my child. Life without the Living God is no life to live, for it becomes all about everything that will one day disappear. I created your life to be eternal, and apart from me there is no joy, nor will you find any peace. The world tries to draw you away from Me, but do not be fooled, for this life is but a breath; eternity is forever!

**Matthew 16:25-26**
If you try to keep your life for yourself, you will lose it.
But if you give up your life for Me, you will find true life.
And how do you benefit if you gain the whole world but lose
your own soul in the process? Is anything worth more than your soul? (NLT)

**For You are the Fountain of Life, the Light by which we see!**
(Psalm 36:9)

# *"Heaven Rewards"*

**1 Peter 1:3-4**
Now we live with a wonderful expectation because Jesus Christ
rose again from the dead. For God has reserved a priceless inheritance
for His children. It is kept in heaven for you, pure and undefiled, beyond the
reach of change and decay. And God, in His mighty power, will protect you until
you receive this salvation, because you are trusting Him. (NLT)

From the moment sin entered into our world, life has become an everyday struggle just trying to stay alive, leaving little time for anything else, because there are just too many unplanned difficulties and hardships that seem to take the joy out of living. Disasters are always lurking around every corner, whether they are natural disasters, manmade disasters, or self-inflicted disasters. And every day we face the realities of sickness and death; two realities that are common in this world and no one is spared. Life is hard and difficult for most, and yet, we do whatever it takes to hang on just one more day. I have often wondered what it is about this difficult life filled with so much misery, that makes most people want to hang on to it. The world is not a friendly place. It does its best to beat us down and take what little joy we can find. There are a couple of main reasons why people cling to this life. The first being that God designed into the very fiber of who we are, the desire to live forever and enjoy it. The second, being a bit bleaker, is it's our fallen human nature to fear the unknown—that this life may be the only life we have--or even worse, will we suffer the final consequences for our bad behavior?

The Lord masterfully created life on earth and it was good. But because of one bad angel and one man's disobedience, all of creation paid the price. And so it is that sin and death are now an imminent part of living in this world that cries out for justice—cries that the Lord has heard and answered. For when our Savior returns to the earth the second time, He will get rid of the bad and make all things new. He has promised to create a New Heaven and earth as it was intended to be—perfect in every way; void of pain and sorrow and the stench of death. When you truly believe in God's eternal plan for you my friend, you will long to be with Jesus and will no longer live in fear of death, because you will know that all your hardships and struggles, your pain and sorrow, and all your fears and failures will not have been in vain.

## A Whisper of Hope

**Remember My child...**that you live in a fallen world where nothing is as it was created to be. Much frustration and failure will result from your seeking perfection in this life. There is nothing perfect about this world but Me. This is why your closeness to Me not only satisfies the deep eternal yearnings you have, but it will also fill your troubled life with joy and peace.

**1 Peter 1:13**
Look forward to the special blessings
That will come to you at the return of Jesus Christ. (NLT)

**Take delight in the LORD, and He will give you your heart's desires.**
(Psalm 37:4)

# February

# "Purpose Not Chaos"

**Isaiah 45:18**
For the LORD is God, and He created the heavens and earth and put
everything in place. He made the world to be lived in, not to be a place
of empty chaos. "I am the LORD," He says, "and there is no Other." (NLT)

B efore I knew who our Almighty God was and how my life fit into His plan, the total sum
of my life-journey was a lot of unhappiness, confusion and a futile purpose. There seemed
to be little reason for my existence. As a matter of fact, I found little reason for anything, especially human life. And as for my own existence, there had been too much pain for much too long
for anything to make sense. I found no joy in living, nor did I believe it would ever change. But
when I thought my life was over, my futile view of life came to an abrupt end when the Lord
finally opened my eyes and softened my heart to His Truth. When I began to learn and understand why this life was so difficult and why it was so hard for me to cope with it, I experienced
a resolve so deep that I felt as if my life had just began.

We will never fully understand why God allows bad things to happen while we are on this
side of heaven, but what the Lord has made clear to me, is that in the end everything will come
together perfectly for His glory and His eternal Kingdom to come. I have learned through
many years of living apart from God that it is far better to live with Him than not, because with
the pain there comes relief, out of chaos comes purpose, and out of emptiness comes fullness
and Life. When we live in the Light of God's Truth there is forgiveness and hope. When we
are one with our Savior there is life not death. Our Living God has overcome the world, my
friends and we, too, will follow suit when we believe and surrender our broken lives into His
care and control.

## A Whisper of Hope

**I Am the LORD your God**...the Shepherd of your soul. And because I AM, I can remove all of
your sins and cleanse you as white as snow. I will set you free from the grip of Satan and his dark
and evil world, for when you live in Me, I live in you and in the chaos you will find true purpose.

**Micah 6:8**
O people, the LORD has told you what is good,
and this is what He requires of you: to do what is right,
to love mercy, and to walk humbly with your God. (NLT)

**Blessed are all those who put their trust in Him.**
(Psalm 2:12)

# "True Light"

**Psalm 43:3**
Send out Your Light and Your Truth! Let them lead me. (NLT)

There is no One more capable or more willing to help us in our times of need than the Provider in Chief; our Lord God and Savior, Jesus Christ. This simple, yet profound truth that was penned by a lost and struggling soul thousands of years ago, is still heard and acted upon by the Lord everyday it is spoken in prayers of petition and thanksgiving. When you put your hope in the God of salvation, He always does what is perfect for your life, especially when you wait patiently in faith and live in His Light. The One who created you for Himself is always watching over you and He will never lead you astray, because He is always faithful and trustworthy even when you are not.

Our gracious God has given us His Truth because He wants to save us from the self-destruction that our sin-filled, rebellious life-style brings. It is life changing my friends, when you choose to live in God's Light, rather than self-destructing in the darkness that this fallen world embraces. When we rely on the One who formed us in our mother's womb, we can be sure that He knows how to provide our every physical and spiritual need. When we live without God's sovereign help and instead, rely on the temporary things of this world, we are left empty, confused and wishing there was more to life. We end up disappointed, unhappy, and forever regretting the choices we made in this brief life. When you choose God over the world, His Light exposes the lies of the Devil and you will be set free from this fallen world that holds you hostage to sin and death. Never doubt for a moment the Power of God that will get you safely Home to Heaven.

## A Whisper of Hope

**My Light, dear child...**will definitely guide you Home. It matters not how long you have walked in darkness or how many wrong paths you have taken, for what truly matters is that you come to Me when I call. I will forgive and forget your sinful past, give you eternal purpose and bring you Home.

**Philippians 4:6-7**
Don't worry about anything; instead, pray about everything. Tell God what you need, and thank Him for all He has done. If you do this, you will experience God's peace, which is far more wonderful than the human mind can understand. His peace will guard your hearts and minds as you live in Christ Jesus. (NLT)

**"Awake, O sleeper, rise up from the dead, and Christ will give you Light."**
(Ephesians 5:14)

# *"Rocky Road"*

**Isaiah 48:17**
The LORD your Redeemer, the Holy One of Israel, says:
"I am the LORD your God, who teaches you what is good
and leads you along the paths you should follow." (NLT)

We find comfort in the fact that God's Word will never lead anyone astray. His Word is the absolute Truth and the Final Authority—for the Creator cannot be otherwise, for if He were anything less, He would not be God. We can trust our Redeemer to show us the Way that leads to righteous living, when we surrender to His will and wait on Him to be our Teacher and Guide and our Shepherd and Savior. The Lord tells us: "I will be your God throughout your lifetime—until your hair is white with age. I made you, and I will care for you. I will carry you along and save you" (Isaiah 46:4).

Our Lord God and Savior deserves our every thanks and praise for His abundant mercy and amazing grace, but most importantly, for His unconditional love and total forgiveness. The unconditional Love of God never changes even when we reject Him, ignore Him, and rebel against Him. Our goodness cannot increase God's love for us, nor can our sinfulness diminish it. Our steadfast faith does not earn His love any more than our stupidity jeopardizes it. He does not love us less if we fail, nor does He love us more when we succeed. God's love is not a human emotional kind of love, because it's not dependent on us. When you let God reign over your life my friend, allowing Him to direct the paths of your life-journey, you will discover that His Way is never the easy way, but the end results will be well worth the rocky road you travel on through this difficult life of calamity.

## A Whisper of Hope

**Find comfort, dear child…**in knowing Me, for My peace is so unlike the world's peace. By following My Perfect Plan, I will change the way you think and feel. I will prepare you for the road ahead and beyond. When you trust in Me, you will learn how to overcome the Enemy and the lies of this fallen world. I will guide you away from the smooth paths of pleasure and onto the rocky road that leads to your redemption and eternal life.

**1 Timothy 4:8**
Physical training is good, but training for godliness is
much better, promising benefits in this life and in the life to come. (NLT)

**Lead Me in Your truth and teach me, for You are the God of my salvation.**
(Psalm 25:5)

# "Soul Food"

**Isaiah 55:2, 3**
Listen, and I will tell you where to get food
that is good for the soul. Come to Me with your
ears wide open. Listen, for the life of your soul is at stake. (NLT)

Our loving God is a gracious Provider; One who gives us every good and healthy thing. He is continually seeking to save our souls from the Destroyer of souls, the Devil. Satan cleverly disguises his sin and when you eat from his plate, it not only speeds up your destruction in this life, but it will also destroy the glorious eternal life that God has planned for you as well. Satan and this world are relentless when it comes to offering us the kind of food that is poison to our minds and hearts, and deadly for our souls. The Devil's food is bad for both the body and the soul, because it always leads to death and decay. But the special food of the Good Shepherd is so heavenly nutritious that it extends our lives indefinitely.

The Lord God, Jesus Christ, never grows weary in His search for those who are lost and gorging on the Devil's food, because God knows that a life void of heavenly nutrition will weaken and deteriorate the precious life He has created. Whatever the worldly source you are feeding on my friend, it's time to change your diet and feast on the Word of God, the Perfect Nutritional Plan for healthy living. You don't want your heart to become so poisoned that you slowly die the death that is without end. Call on the Lord while you can, and ask for some of His delicious soul food while He is still serving, because His food for your soul gives everlasting vigor and joy.

## A Whisper of Hope

**Ask Me, dear one...**and I will give you food for your soul. I Am the One and only God, the Shepherd of your life, and your well being is dependent upon the Health Plan for Living I have created for you. Trust Me My child, and I will give you the Bread of Life; a heavenly food designed for a healthy life-journey that is without end.

**John 6:33, 35**
"For the bread of God is He who comes down from heaven and
gives life to the world. And Jesus said to them, "I am the Bread of Life,
He who comes to me shall never hunger, and he who believes in Me shall never thirst. (NKJ)

**Seek the LORD while He may be found, call upon Him while He is near.**
(Isaiah 55:6)

# "Call on God"

**Psalm 28:1**
To You I call, O LORD my Rock; do not turn a deaf ear to me.
For if you remain silent, I will be like those who have gone down to the pit. (NIV)

My journey through this life has taught me some very hard lessons; that living apart from God is a life lived in vain. Living without God is living a lie. It's living in darkness that is filled with shallow hope at best, because you believe that no matter what you do or what you gain, it will always come to an end as if it had never happened. Without our Lord God and Savior, Christ Jesus, there would be no eternal hope, for there would be no forgiveness, only condemnation. There would be no joy or lasting purpose—only death and more darkness. Without Jesus as our Advocate, our cries for mercy and grace would fall on deaf ears. If God the Holy Spirit was not living and actively working in this fallen world, it would be a living hell for everyone, for there would be no grace—only the luck of the draw.

Christ Jesus is the only true and living God we have, and He is the only One who can keep us from the death and destruction that awaits this world and all those who belong to it. If you can picture a world without Christ and His Church, you would picture a dark and brutal life, for it would be nothing but empty chaos and misery with no escape other than dying! God hears all the cries of His suffering people, who are blindly grasping for answers and a hope for the future. And if they would only set aside the madness of this fallen world and call on God, quiet their hearts, and listen for His Still Small Voice, He would answer. And when you wait in faith, the Lord will do what He always does best, which is bringing everlasting hope and blessed salvation.

## A Whisper of Hope

**Take heart, My child…**For I have overcome this dark and evil world. I know just how cruel and difficult this world can be, for it put me to death. This is why I died for you; to give you a hope and a future that will be filled with joy forever!

**Jeremiah 10:10**
But the LORD is the only true God,
the living God. He is the everlasting King. (NLT)

**Life itself was in Him, and this life gives Light to everyone.**
(John 1:4)

# "Deeply Rooted"

**Jeremiah 17:7-8**
"But blessed are those who trust in the LORD and have made
the LORD their hope and confidence. They are like trees planted
along a river bank, with roots that reach deep into the water. Such
trees are not bothered by the heat or worried by long months of drought.
Their leaves stay green, and they go right on producing delicious fruit." (NLT)

These words are from the mouth of God, words of wisdom in their purest form—bringing simple truth that is easily understood and life changing as well. For when we follow God's well designed plan and draw from His infinite resources, our lives will not only flourish in good season, but when periods of drought or violent storms threaten to destroy or uproot us, we will find ourselves firmly grounded in the Word of Life that sustains our physical and spiritual lives. God gave us His written Word and His Holy Spirit so we would learn how to live righteous and holy lives that would glorify Him and produce in us a healthy, heavenly fruit that this sin diseased world is in so dire need of.

When we are growing in God's Truth, feeding on His every Word, we develop a strong and hardy root system that provides us with the strength and courage to weather the storms and droughts that are inevitable in this dangerous world. Allowing the Infinite Gardener to tend your life will in due time, produce a life-saving fruit that you can share with those who are starving for truth and dying in the storms of ungodliness that are wreaking havoc upon our world. For when God's fruit is digested, it will save you from being discarded and thrown into the fire. Being deeply rooted in the Word of God, my friends will grow you strong and vigorous and nothing of this world will ever destroy you!

## A Whisper of Hope

**Grow strong and healthy, My child...**for you have the world's best Gardener to feed you with His Word and to prune you so that you are healthy and fruitful. When you remain connected to Me, you will produce the most needed fruit in the world—the fruit of salvation and peace, for there are many starving people who are slowly dying from their poisonous diet of sin and decaying morals.

**John 15:4**
Remain in Me, and I will remain in you.
For a branch cannot produce fruit if it is severed
from the vine, and you cannot be fruitful apart from Me. (NLT)

**People need more than bread for their life;
real life comes by feeding on every word of the LORD.**
(Deuteronomy 8:3)

# "Power and Grace"

**Jeremiah 32:17, 18, 19**
"O Sovereign LORD! You have made the heavens and earth by your strong hand
and powerful arm. Nothing is too hard for You! You are the great and powerful God,
the Lord of Heaven's Armies. You have all wisdom and do great and mighty miracles. (NLT)

For people who make mother earth their god and rely solely on her as their source for life, there is a Truth that must be heard and understood while there is still time for them to hear it. This dying world and most of its people have been duped by the lies of the Devil and it's drawing them away from their Creator, Provider, Protector, and Savior. The Lord has been calling out to the deceived people of this world for thousands of years, trying to rescue them from the darkness so they can live in the Light of His Truth. Our Sovereign God knows how futile it is to live apart from Him, for without His power and grace to sustain us, the Devil and this fallen world will devour us. When we depend solely on the world to meet our needs, it is not only a foolish choice, but it is also wasting a precious life, because loving this world is living a death sentence—a life that is lived in vain and without hope.

Our Lord wants every person He creates to rely on Him in trust, believing He will supply them with everything they need to live a righteously good life—a life filled everlasting joy and the hope of Heaven as their peace. When most of us take the hand of God, He drags us out of our sin screaming and kicking, but He eventually sets us down firmly in the Light that leads to everlasting life. And along the way you will gain the wisdom to accept the hardships of life as the pathway to peace. When you rely on the Lord, He is always with you and guiding your journey Home. But if you deny the Lord and refuse to take His hand, the day of reckoning will come like a thief in the night, and you will beg God for another chance only to be denied because you denied Him.

## A Whisper of Hope

**I Am your Creator...**the One who knows you best. I know everything that you will ever need for life, from the smallest to the greatest. You must not worry yourself dear child, for I will give you exactly what you need when you need it. Trust and rely on Me to be your Provider, because I gave My life to save you. I will never forsake you nor will I ever abandon you.

**Hebrews 4:16**
So let us come boldly to the throne
of our gracious God. There we will receive
His mercy, and we will find grace to help us when we need it. (NLT)

**How blessed are the people whose God is the LORD!**
(Psalm 144:15)

# "Peace of Heart"

**John 14:27**
"Peace I leave with you, My peace I give to you;
not as the world gives do I give to you. Let not your
heart be troubled, neither let it be afraid." (NKJ)

Because we live in a fallen world there will always be difficult days and devastating times when most believers will question God's authority or motives, even when they believe He is sovereign over all things. Whenever this cruel world deals us a crummy hand, I believe the Devil is right there doing his best to convince us that God is either cheating us out of something we think we deserve, or He is simply punishing us. The Devil is crafty and deceitful and always busy trying to belittle God in anyway he can. And no matter where we may be in our faith walk with Christ, we will always be fighting against the evil forces that dominate this humanistic world, because this world and all who follow it are always ready to fight against the very fiber of God's Divine Plan.

Until Jesus' return there will always be difficult times when we find ourselves in situations that seem impossible to change no matter how much we trust God with our lives. But one of the most valuable lesson I have learned in my faith walk with Christ, is that no matter how uncertain and fearful I am in my uncomfortable circumstances, when I read God's Word and listen for His Voice, I always find the peace I need for my troubled heart. And in this peaceful state of mind, I always find the courage and hope to move forward in my faith and trust in Jesus to do what no one else can do. All things are possible when we live in Christ Jesus our Lord God and Savior. Who better is there than our Lord God, Jesus Christ? Our Savior is the only One who can save us from our troubles and give us the true and lasting hope that gives us the peace of God—the very peace that our weary hearts and souls long for!

## A Whisper of Hope

**Let My Peace, dear child**...bring comfort and healing to your wounded, skeptical heart. Do not listen to any other voices but Mine. I Am the Word of Life. Let the truth of my words be written on your heart, because the dark forces of this broken world will never cease trying to lead you away from Me. .

**Jeremiah 29:11**
"For I know the plans I have for you," says the LORD.
"They are plans for good and not for disaster, to give you a future and a hope. (NLT)

**You will keep in perfect peace all who trust in You,
whose thoughts are fixed on You.**
(Isaiah 26:3)

# *"Safe Refuge"*

**Psalm 34:21-22**
Calamity will surely overtake the wicked, and those who hate
the righteous will be punished. But the LORD will redeem those
who serve Him. No one who takes refuge in Him will be condemned. (NLT)

This heartfelt psalm written thousands of years ago is a clear message from a troubled, yet trusting servant of God. It's an easily understood message that everyone should pay very close attention to and take heed. For these two verses are a short and to the point summary of the life God has given us; that whosoever turns their back on the Lord will suffer the consequences. This dying world can only offer us temporal things at best; things that lead us away from our only Refuge; things that satisfy our longings for the moment and they're gone. What good are all the worldly things we can gain today when we know they will be gone tomorrow? Are a few short years of earthly pleasure worth the loss of your soul?

Sadly, there are many prideful people in this world who scoff at Christian living because they have been lied to by the greatest deceiver of all time, the Devil. These misguided, unhappy people usually have a disdain for the Christian, because those who belong to Christ Jesus, even when they have little, remain joyful in their faith while they wait on the Lord to bless them in the age to come—blessings beyond our limited imaginations—blessings that have no end. Don't be a duped, self-serving follower of the world, one who enjoys the moment and worries about dying later. This is not a wise way to live, my friend. God has given you this gift of life to glorify Him in the way you live; ways that will prepare you for the glorious eternal life to come. For what you see now as excellent and good, is nothing compared to the glory that awaits all those who find refuge in the Lord. You can hide in the darkness of this world and die forever, or run to the Lord and live forever. With God you are safe!

## A Whisper of Hope

**This world is not safe, My child…**it reeks of death and decay. I, on the other hand am a Safe Haven for those who serve Me faithfully. I Am their Protector and Provider. When you run to Me for refuge from this evil and dangerous world, you will find eternal life no matter what this world does. Look to Me, your eternal Refuge.

**Isaiah 51:6**
Look up to the skies above, and gaze down on the earth beneath.
For the skies will disappear like smoke, and the earth will wear out
like a piece of clothing. The people of the earth will die like flies, but
my salvation lasts forever. My righteous rule will never end! (NLT)

**LORD, You are my strength and fortress, my refuge in the day of trouble!**
(Jeremiah 16:19)

# "Soul Keeper"

**Psalm 121:5, 7**
The LORD is your keeper;
The LORD shall preserve you from all evil;
He shall preserve your soul. (NKJ)

In my life-journey with the Lord, it became extremely reassuring and quite comforting knowing that the One who suffered and died to save the life of my soul, was carefully watching over my everyday life, especially with all the chaos and evil impacting the lives of everyone in this chaotic world. Once I began to develop a personal relationship with our gracious and loving God, it enabled me to move forward in my life-journey of recovery without the usual fear of failure. I knew that even though I would experience some defeat and failure in my new life, I could rely on the Lord to help me use my failures as an opportunity to grow in His grace and gain confidence in His saving works.

This is how our incredible God works in the lives of those who belong to Him. No matter who we are or how spiritually mature we think we are, we all get discouraged and disappointed by our mistakes and failures. But when you know that the Lord God is always close and watching over you, rather than throwing in the towel and condemning you, you will be able to move forward knowing you have been forgiven. We have a loving God, my friends, but even though He is gracious and merciful and all forgiving, He allows us to fail, because it is by His redeeming work of our failures and mistakes that His glory is proclaimed. For when He pulls us out of the muck of our discouragement and sets our feet back on solid ground, we know that our life is safely in His hands and we will shine brightly in the Light of the Keeper of our souls.

## A Whisper of Hope

**You can sleep in Peace...**My dear child, for I Am your Keeper who never sleeps. My watchful eye is always open and I see all that goes on. I Am always aware and hear your every sigh. You are never left alone in the battles for your soul, and as long as you have the One who is your Strength and your Shield, you will find victory both now and forevermore!

**Psalm 33:18-22**
Behold, the eye of the LORD is on those who fear Him,
on those who hope in His mercy, to deliver their soul from death,
and to keep them alive in famine. Our soul waits for the LORD; He is our
help and our shield. For our heart shall rejoice in Him, because we have trusted
in His holy name. Let Your mercy, O LORD, be upon us, just as we hope in You. (NKJ)

**The LORD will provide.**
(Genesis 22:14)

# *"Trusting God"*

**Jeremiah 39:18**
"For I will surely deliver you, and you shall not fall
by the sword; but your life shall be as a prize to you,
because you have put your trust in me," says the LORD.' " (NKJ)

It was not easy for me to learn how to trust God with my life, because after years of trusting the world and others, I was quite leery in the trust department, especially when I could not see or touch the One I was trusting. When the Lord rescued me from my self-destructive life-style, I was numbing the pain of the past and the hopelessness of the future. My living apart from God and in the world not only made me skeptical and wary of people, but it also caused a deep sadness that was dragging me down into the darkness. For me to learn how to trust the God that I thought dealt me a crummy hand, I had to believe that I truly mattered to Him and that He was not mean and out to do me in. I also had to earnestly believe His Word was the Absolute Truth and He had a meaningful purpose for me. I had to learn how to live God's Way rather than my old misguided ways and that of the worlds.

The holy quest that God calls us on is a difficult road to follow, because the righteous standards that He calls us to live by go against everything this fallen world stands for and teaches us; it's a war for our hearts, minds, and eternal souls—a war against the most powerful Enemy of God; a dangerous foe we cannot see. But the news is good, because Jesus has already won the war for us. The not so good news is there are still many difficult battles to come and many hard lessons to be learned. And even though our old ways and sinful habits are difficult to change, we have the Lord with whom all things are possible. For encouragement when the battle is tough, I look back on my miserable life without the Lord, and compare it to my present life with the Lord and the difference is totally amazing; like night and day!

## A Whisper of Hope

**Trusting Me, dear one...**to guide your life-journey is not always an enjoyable adventure, but the destination is. You must learn from your mistakes, because then, it will become much clearer to you that My Way is not only the best way, but it is also the Only Way. So, let not your heart be troubled, for you are precious to Me, and I would never lead you astray.

**2 Samuel 22:2-4**
The LORD is my rock, my fortress and my deliverer;
The God of my strength, in Him I will trust. (NKJ)

**"With men this is impossible, but with God all things are possible."**
(Matthew 19:26)

# "The Search"

**Psalm 63:1**
O God, You are my God. I earnestly search for You.
My soul thirsts for You, my whole body longs for You
in this parched and weary land where there is no water. (NLT)

Like many before me, I had wandered deep into the wilderness of life, where I found myself hopelessly lost, desperately thirsting for Truth, and searching for a way out. Then the Lord plucked me from the grips of death, graciously took me into His arms, and gave me a drink of living water that gave me a new life and a new heart. We have a Good Shepherd who searches for those who are wandering in the wilderness, hopelessly lost, and slowly dying. I had, like so many lost and thirsty people, found myself drinking from the wrong cups, never satisfied, and sensing there was something missing and terribly wrong. And I, like many others, learned the hard way, because no matter how much I consumed, it always left me empty and wondering why.

When we surrender to the Lord He teaches us the Truth; that this fallen world cannot satisfy the true longings of our hearts and souls. There is only one Way and only One God who can satisfy what we truly long for—He is our Lord God and Savior, Jesus Christ. The world was not created to satisfy our every need, my friends. What the fallen people of this world have created for our pleasure is not good for the eternal life of our souls. The world can only satisfy our carnal flesh; it cannot satisfy God's anger against our sinfulness, only the Savior can do that. And that's what truly matters, because without Jesus there is only condemnation. Without Jesus there can be no eternal life.

## A Whisper of Hope

**Search for Me, My child...**I Am the Bread of Life. From My Word flows the living water that quenches your thirst and brings eternal life. Drinking from the world's cup of poison will bring you nothing but darkness and death. Drinking from the cup of life that I offer will satisfy your deepest longings and give you eternal life.

**Isaiah 58:11**
The LORD will guide you continually, giving you water
when you are dry and restoring your strength. You will
be like a well-water garden, like an ever-flowing spring. (NLT)

**"I am the Bread of Life; he who comes to Me will not hunger,
and he who believes in Me will never thirst."**
(John 6:35)

# "You're Safe!"

**Psalm 130:7**
O Israel, hope in the LORD, for with the LORD
there is mercy and with Him is abundant redemption. (NKJ)

Just as the people of Israel found hope, mercy, and redemption in the Lord God, so too, can every person who walks upon this earth. The only true hope that we have is found only in our Lord God and Savior, Jesus Christ. The Lord's mercy never changes and His unfailing love for us remains the same, regardless of our rebellious past and in spite of future failures. The Lord's gift of forgiveness and salvation is for everyone. This cruel and unforgiving world is relentless in battering its people into submission and destroying their lives. But it doesn't have to be this way, because our sovereign God is always searching for those who are in need of His sovereign help, especially those who humbly admit their need for forgiveness and redemption.

If you want to experience any real peace or joy in this life, you must first know the Truth about the One who created you and the life He created you to live, because it's the Truth that will set you free from the deadly power of sin and your fear of the unknown. When you live in the Way of God's Truth, you will have a lasting purpose that is safely in the protection of God. Since the day death entered into our world because of sin, this life has been just one storm after another, never knowing when they will strike or what damage they will do. Many people view these storms as punishment from God, and in some cases they very well may be, but most of them are simply the consequences of living in a fallen world and making bad choices. But with God guiding the Way, you will get through the storms and be stronger and wiser and better prepared for the next one knowing you are safe.

## A Whisper of Hope

**Your life is safely in My Hands, dear child…** You need not worry about the storms of today, nor should you live in fear of the storms of tomorrow. For when you trust Me, the victory will indeed be yours! When you allow Me to walk you through the storms that can destroy you, you will not only find the best way to survive them, but you will benefit richly from them as well. My Hope is sure, My mercy is perfect, and My Redemption is priceless.

**Isaiah 49:26**
"All the world will know that I, the LORD,
am your Savior and Redeemer, the Mighty One of Israel." (NLT)

**Jesus Christ is the same yesterday, today, and forever.**
(Hebrews 13:8)

# "True Wisdom"

**Psalm 111:10**
Reverence for the LORD is the foundation of true wisdom.
The rewards of wisdom come to all who obey Him. (NLT)

The word reverence can be translated as fear, which in both cases means that we should not only fear the LORD because of His sovereign power and authority over His creation, but we should also honor and respect Him in awe because He is our infinite Father. We would be wise to know and fear the consequences that sin brings into our lives, because Hell is not a place that you want to spend eternity in. It is healthy for us to love, honor and respect the Lord God for sending the Holy Spirit into our lives to help guide us in a righteous way while we are living in this difficult world and to give us the strength to persevere in faith. Without the gracious wisdom that our Lord God and Savior, Jesus Christ, has shared with us, no one would escape the horrors of Hell.

As God fearing people who belong to the Lord, we should begin each day with thanksgiving and renewed reverence for the LORD, because our moment to moment lives depend on His amazing grace. We must read His Word daily and pay close attention to what God wants us to know. We must know who God is, why He created us, and what lies beyond this life. Without God's wisdom we could not survive the onslaught of troubles that hit without warning. The Lord tells us to focus on the eternal things of life, rather than just living for the moment. When you know God, you will fear and respect Him and when you put this short life into its godly perspective, it will give you an everlasting peace that the world cannot give, nor take it away. Reverence for the One who created you, my friend, and accepting His authority over your life, is wisdom at its eternal best.

## A Whisper of Hope

**Fear is a good thing, My child...**for it brings you understanding that will save your eternal life. For fear and respect is the Way to have everlasting peace. By fearing God's condemnation that sin brings, holds you accountable and prepares you for the wonderful joy to come.

**Hebrews 12:28**
Since we are receiving a Kingdom that is unshakable,
let us be thankful and please God by worshiping Him
with holy fear and awe. For our God is a devouring fire. (NLT)

**"The fear of the LORD is true wisdom; to forsake evil is real understanding."**
(Job 28:28)

# *"God's Glory"*

**1 Corinthians 10:31**
Whatever you eat or drink or whatever you do,
you must do all for the glory of God. (NLT)

For Christians, this simple truth gives our lives a meaningful purpose that is easy to understand and beneficial in all that we do. When we are living in the Light and reading God's Word, it holds us accountable to all our thoughts and actions, which makes our life-journey a lesson worth living. It causes us to think before we do anything that can hurt our relationship with God and other people. Since the Lord has graciously given us the Way to escape eternal condemnation and live a godly life, is it not right that we honor and glorify Him? Of course it is, because God delights when we make Him the reason for living. Now that we have been justified in the death and resurrection of Christ Jesus, we should make every effort to live for God, because He paid a hefty price for our salvation.

The Lord knows how we struggle with our sinful, fallen nature. He knows how weak and vulnerable we are in the hands of the Enemy and his fallen world. The Lord knows the weaknesses of our flesh and He knows firsthand, the temptations we face. But through the indwelling of the Holy Spirit, we receive the wisdom and strength to overcome those sinful things that draw us away from God . And I assure you, my friends, that whenever anyone overcomes the clever temptations of the Devil, God's glory will shine for the world to see.

## A Whisper of Truth

**Glorify Me, dear child...**for this is the reason I created you. It is not easy to do in this sinful world, but when you commit your life to Me, I will show you how and give you the strength to pull it off. By living for Me you will find the Truth and the Way to eternal life.

**1 Corinthians 6:20**
For you were bought at a price;
Therefore glorify God in your body
and in your spirit, which are God's. (NKJ)

**Give unto the LORD the glory due to His name.**
(Psalm 29:2)

# "Priced for Life"

**Isaiah 43:1-3**
"Do not be afraid, for I have ransomed you. I have called you by name;
you are mine. When you go through deep waters and great trouble, I will be
with you. When you go through rivers of difficulty, you will not drown! When
you walk through the fire of oppression, you will not be burned up; the flames will
not consume you. For I am the LORD, your God, the Holy One of Israel, your Savior." (NLT)

Learning and accepting this wonderful and encouraging Truth about the LORD our God
has been a revelation that has changed my life in ways that I could have never foreseen
without the saving grace of our Lord God and Savior. Knowing there is a real and living God
who cares about every aspect of my life in detail, and the One who has called me to be His very
own child is an awesomely, heartfelt feeling like no other I have ever experienced. Knowing
these kinds of things about God has given me the confidence to put my hope and trust in the
Living God, because I know and believe He will always get me through the storms of this difficult life-journey that seems to blow in one troubling storm after another.

When living with the Savior as our Guide and Teacher we are not only able to survive the
storms of life, but we will emerge on the other side with a stronger faith and commitment to the
Lover of our souls, Jesus Christ. You have an awesome God and Savior my friends, for you can
always rely on Him to give you hope in your times of discouragement and hopelessness; joy in
those times of despair and desperation, but most of all, you can be absolutely sure of His forgiveness and redemption, because He paid a great price for your life—you are priced for eternal life!

## A Whisper of Hope

**I paid a hefty price for you,** My child; a price that makes you Mine for eternity. I did this to
save you from the hands of the Enemy—the hater of God and all righteousness. And because
you belong to Me, you have all you will ever need for everlasting life. Never fear this world dear
child, for the plans I have for you are far above this fallen world.

**Hebrews 10:39**
But we are not like those who turn
their backs on God and seal their fate.
We have faith that assures our salvation. (NLT)

**I am the LORD, and there is no other Savior.**
(Isaiah 43:11)

# "Perfect in Me"

**Isaiah 51:6**
Lift up your eyes to the heavens, and look on the earth beneath.
For the heavens will vanish away like smoke, the earth will grow old
like a garment, and those who dwell in it will die in like manner; but My
salvation will be forever, and My righteousness will not be abolished. (NKJ)

Because we live in the age of technology, most people can gaze upon the entire world and see much of what is happening with just the touch of a button. For thousands of years God's plan for mankind has been unfolding, but for the first time we can actually see the events which are shaping things foretold many years ago by the prophets of God. Our gracious and loving God has put the plan into words so we could look into the future and be ready for what lies ahead. We can look back in history and see how mankind has always failed when trying to create the perfect world order, much like he is still trying to do today, but now the global effect of these failures are causing unprecedented chaos like we have never seen before. It has become pretty obvious that the entire earth and everything in it is growing old and tired and groaning for the redemption of God's healing touch. And one day soon the Lord of hosts will order His angels to pour out His wrath upon this fallen world that has turned away from God and persecuted His children.

The revelation of our Lord Jesus Christ concerning the end of the church age is not a pretty picture, but one that everyone needs to ponder. For those of us who believe in the inerrant, infallible truth of God's Holy Word, we have a free ticket out of this world before the Lord unleashes His anger against those who love sin more than Him and hate righteousness. The Church of Jesus Christ are the true repentant sinners who have put their hope and trust in the Good News, and they will escape the wrath of God and be taken into Heaven for a seven year honeymoon with Jesus while total chaos engulfs those left behind. Don't be one of those left behind, my friend, instead live for the Living God who provided you with the Way to escape the decadence of this dying world and its final condemnation—the Way that will bring you joy and peace in this ungodly world.

## A Whisper of Hope

**Know Me and you know the Truth, dear child…**the truth about the world you live in and where it's headed. I will free you from the sin and fears you have about death and the destruction around you. I give real Hope and keep My promises, not meaningless hope and frivolous promises like that of the world's. What I promise you is an escape route out of the reign of terror that is to come and the promise of an everlasting life as it was created to be—perfect in Me.

**Revelation 16:1**
Then I heard a mighty voice shouting from the Temple to the seven angels,
"Now go your ways and empty out the seven bowls of God's wrath on the earth." (NLT)

**"Yes, Lord God Almighty, Your punishments are true and just."**
(Revelation 16:7)

# "Merciful Grace"

**2 Corinthians 1:3**
All praise to the God and Father of our Lord Jesus Christ.
He is the source of every mercy and the God who comforts us. (NLT)

The more we learn about our gracious and merciful God, the easier it is to trust and rely on His sovereign power, infinite wisdom, and undying faithfulness, especially when we find ourselves in circumstances that are not only anxiously difficult, but seemingly hopeless as well. In spite of the many difficulties that we are faced with in just trying to survive in a world that is rapidly decaying, God has given us the ability to reflect and focus on His goodness and blessings, rather than on our struggles and discouragement. Although God has allowed some tough circumstances to develop during my life, I can look back and see His mercy and grace at work, which helps me better understand how God protects and provides for us throughout our entire life-journey.

I have come to that place in my life where I can truly see and understand how our broken lives bring glory to God when He pulls us free from the grips of Satan and out of the darkness that this world embraces. Being in the arms of the Savior is reason to rejoice. Our saving God laid down His life in order to defeat the sin and death that holds us captive. This single fact alone gives us more than enough reason to sing and celebrate our lives no matter how difficult they may be—no matter how painful they are. When you start feeling as if the darkness is threatening to consume and take over your life, you should reach out and take the saving hand of God, but do it with gladness in your heart, thanking Him for all He has done. For you will never find a better Source for comfort in the entire universe than in the amazing mercy and grace found in the arms of God!

## A Whisper of Hope

**Trust Me, My child...** with gladness in your heart. For I Am the One who can rescue you from your pain and suffering so you can be redeemed. This dark and difficult world, ruled by Satan, will never cease trying to drag you down into its pits of despair and hopelessness. But amidst the onslaught of trouble and temptation, there is hope, and I Am your Hope.

**Psalm 13:5-6**
But I trust in Your unfailing love; my heart rejoices in Your salvation.
I will sing to the LORD, for He has been good to me. (NLT)

**Grace and truth came through Jesus Christ.**
(John 1:17)

# *"Greater is He"*

**Isaiah 59:1**
Behold, the LORD's hand is not so short that it cannot save;
Neither is His ear so dull that it cannot hear. (NASB)

There are a couple of facts about God in this verse that are absolute in their truth and they are this; God can do anything at anytime, and He hears everything all the time. The Lord our God is aware of everything going on in the world. He sees how easily we slip into the sin and evil that controls our world. God knows everything about everybody He creates and He sees the suffering and pain we all experience. And this is why the Creator has intervened on our behalf. He suffered and died and rose again to send His Holy Spirit into the world to guide us in all truth and righteousness and to protect us from the evil one. Those who are reborn of God are a new creation, and become a part of His Body, the Church, and we can always depend on His faithful, sovereign help, especially in our times of trouble.

By accepting God's gift of forgiveness and redemption, and by allowing the Holy Spirit to transform my life and soften my heart, I have discovered what it means to truly live in trust. He may not always answer me when I want or how I want, but because He responds in some way, the Lord has taught me to trust and be patience. Unbeknownst to me, Satan and his dark ways had succeeded in dragging me down that path of self-destruction that leads to death, but when the time was right, our Savior stepped in and rescued me before this fallen world could take me down for the count. Thanks be to our Sovereign God—the Savior who sees and hears all things and can do all things. The redeemed can find peace and resolve amidst the darkness, knowing that the Hand of our Mighty God is always poised to help, especially when we are trusting Him in faith.

## A Whisper of Hope

**Be at peace, My child...**because there is nothing so big that I cannot overcome for you, nor is there anything so small that I cannot detect. Knowing and believing these two things about Me will comfort your weary soul. With the peace I give you, you will be able to face this difficult life with confidence, for I Am Faithful and True and I AM always there for you!

**Isaiah 61:10**
I am overwhelmed with joy in the LORD my God!
For He has dressed me with the clothing of salvation
and draped me in a robe of righteousness. (NLT)

**He is my Shield, the strength of my salvation and my Stronghold.**
(Psalm 18:2)

# "Reach for God"

**Hosea 6:3**
"Oh, that we might know the LORD! Let us press on to know Him. Then He
will respond to us as surely as the arrival of dawn or the coming of rains in early spring." (NLT)

Pressing on to know the LORD our God has become a wonderful, eye opening experience
that has given me a new lease on life—one that has finally given me a true and lasting purpose—one that has given me hope for a future that will not suddenly come to an end. Pressing
on with the knowledge and understanding that the Lord God has so far graciously given me,
I have found a message of hope for everyone; a message that gives clarity in a foggy world that
is crying out in desperation—a world buried deep in darkness. There are so many lost and
hopeless people in this dark world who don't even know they are lost and hopeless. And then
there are those who think they have found the way, but they, too, are lost and don't know it.
Most people are just too busy with the world to find the time or take the initiative to discover
the real Truth and they will miss out on an opportunity of an eternal life time. The Lord God
has made it possible for us to personally know Him and one day meet Him Face to face. Most
people will never experience His unconditional love or His amazing grace, nor will they get to
share in His infinite Wisdom and glorious blessings.

Sadly, most of the world will never know God or the wonderful plans He has for them—
plans that would have given them a true and meaningful purpose for life. Instead they will rely
on this decaying world led by Satan, who promises nothing but meaningless hope that leads to
eternal darkness and condemnation. But our God and Savior Jesus Christ, can always be trusted
to deliver everything He promises, if only they would soften their hardened hearts enough
to let Him in, so they could learn and know the Truth. For when we discover what our true
options are, the choices we have are simple and easy to understand—life or death—Heaven or
Hell—God or the Devil. Reach out, my friends, and take hold of your Creator's hand, for He
will never lead you astray or let you down.

## A Whisper of Hope

**Reach for Me...**dear child, for I hold your life in My hand. I Am the Truth and I keep My Word.
Do not let the darkness of this world deceive you into believing the lies of the Enemy; lies that
maim and destroy this life, and then kill your eternal soul. Knowing Me is to have peace and
joy and eternal life.

**John 12:46**
"I have come as a Light to shine in this dark world, so that all
who put their trust in Me will no longer remain in the dark." (NLT)

**Teach me Your way, O LORD; I will walk in Your truth.**
(Psalm 86:11)

# *"Light in the Son"*

**Psalm 84:11, 12**
For the LORD God is a sun and shield; the LORD gives grace
and glory. No good thing will He withhold from those who walk
uprightly. O LORD of hosts, how blessed is the man who trusts in You! (NKJ)

I have learned that walking in the Light of the Son, which the Lord has so graciously called me to do, has given my life-journey a new meaning and a new way of living. I have discovered what it means to walk uprightly in the Lord and what a humbling experience it is. I have also come to realize that the LORD God provides us with everything we need to live a righteous life while basking in the Son Light of Life, which shines brighter than all the suns in the universe put together. And in His Light we find the Lord's Sovereign Power, which is far greater than all the power that makes up this vast universe, as our source for protection. We all need God's power and grace as we struggle to live in a world that is cursed with sin—a troubled world filled with murder and chaos, death and destruction—a world that cries out for some blessed hope that can save lives, make a lasting difference, and bring about a lasting peace.

That Hope my friends, is found only one Way and in One Person, and it is through the Cross of our Lord God and Savior, Jesus Christ. Because of His redemptive death on the Cross, the Lord promises everyone forgiveness, total cleansing, and everlasting life. You can find joy in this dangerous life, but only in the Lord of all creation, because He brings hope and resolve to even the most skeptical of hearts. By faithfully walking upright in the Light of the Son, you will not only find your way out of the darkness that surrounds you, but the Son will also light the path before you to keep you upright and moving in the right direction. Ask God for the Son Light if you haven't already done so, because it will save your life and bring you peace. Find the Son's Light while you still can, because once the Son sets on that final day, the darkness will swallow you up forever!

## A Whisper of Hope

**I Am your Light...**in a world clothed in darkness; the Light that will lead you out of the darkness and into My glory. As Lord of Heaven's army I will protect you and keep you in My Light for safety. Bask in Me, My child, and you will find the Way. Follow My Light and it will lead you into Heaven's glory forever. You will find no better offer than in the Light of the Son.

**John 8:12**
"I am the Light of the world; he who follows Me
will not walk in the darkness, but will have the Light of life."

**O taste and see that the LORD is good;**
**How blessed is the man who takes refuge in Him!**
(Psalm 34:8)

# *"Heart of Wisdom"*

**Psalm 90:12**
So teach us to number our days, that we may gain a heart of wisdom. (NKJ)

What the LORD is trying telling us through this prayer of Moses, is to use the short time He has given us to learn His infinite wisdom on life. It is true that we don't always need God to remind us how short our lives are, because the older we get the more aware we are of its shortness. But what we do need are frequent reminders not to waste our lives in the foolishness of this fallen world. When reflecting on the brevity of time, God's wisdom tells us to live for the eternal things in life, rather than just focusing on the pleasures of this wicked world for immediate gratification. As mortal human beings it becomes quite humbling to look into the grave that will one day be our bed, because many of us have spent a good portion of our lives living by the foolish wisdom of this fallen world and for what? But sadly, even though living in the foolishness of this world gets us by somewhat, it unfortunately leaves us empty and wanting more of the same, alone, afraid, and feeling betrayed.

My dear friends, with the Lord as your Teacher you will learn the absolute truths about life and death; truth that will bring you wise understanding and long lasting rewards. Reading and studying the wisest Book of all time, the Word of God, is the smartest decision you will ever make, because inside its cover are thousands of words that will tell you everything you need to know in order to live a wise and productive life in a deceitful world filled with many gods and their falsehoods. And unlike the wise people of this foolish world, you will find comfort and peace for your soul and lasting joy in your heart. Having reverence for the Lord and fearing His just wrath is the beginning of all wisdom. And with this wisdom firmly grounded to your life, you will be able to follow God's Way into glory and bring many a lost and foolish soul along with you.

## A Whisper of Hope

**Need wisdom?**...come to Me, the Author of Life. When you need understanding, look to My Wisdom, because it was I who wrote the Book on life. Within its pages you will not only find peace for your soul but you will also find the right way to live a life that is worth living no matter how difficult your circumstances may be. To know Me, is to know Wisdom that is pure and priceless. .

**1 Corinthians 3:18-19**
Stop fooling yourselves. If you think you are wise
by this world's standards, you will have to become a
fool so you can become wise by God's standards. For
the wisdom of the world is foolishness to God. (NLT)

**The wise shall inherit glory, but shame shall be the legacy of fools.**
(Proverbs 3:35)

# "Songs of Praise"

**Psalm 92:1-2**
It is good to give thanks to the LORD, and to sing
praises to Your name, O Most High. To declare Your
lovingkindness in the morning, and Your faithfulness every night. (NKJ)

There are many things about this life that we don't understand. There are many situations that arise which cause us to question both the goodness and fairness of the Living God. There are times when even our own circumstances seem too hard and undeserving. I know from my own experience, that when I gave up on myself and of ever finding the real meaning to life, all I longed for was death; to be rid of this cruel and unfair life that I didn't ask for. I can still recall sarcastically thanking God in my depression and drunken stupor for all the pain and misery I believed He had personally inflicted upon my life, because as far as I could tell, this was the reason He created me in the first place. It's true that we live in a cruel and unfair world, but the darkness that consumes this world is not the result of a mean or unjust God, but from the most evil Enemy of God, the Devil, his band of fallen angels, and his wicked human disciples.

The Lord does not force us to follow His Way. Instead, He gives us a free will to choose the Way out of the darkness, or not. But He knows how weak we are in the face of so many temptations, and many times He will nudge us a bit in His direction, because God loves us and His sovereign power can help us overcome our weakness to sin. Because He knows we will always fall short of His glorious standards, He sacrificed His Son so our nakedness in sin would be clothed in the righteous robe of Christ Jesus. We have in our Savior, my friends, a loving, righteous, and just God who deserves all of our thanks and praise, because without Him we would all be doomed to misery in Hell. I have learned to believe and trust in the Lord Jesus Christ as LORD over all things, and that He can transform any life, and fill any heart with His Truth. It is for this reason that the Lord God deserves to hear our songs of praise. Inner praise is a wonderful way to communicate your feelings to God, but singing them out so all of Heaven can hear them blesses the LORD even more.

## A Whisper of Hope

**Sing to Me, My child…**with thanksgiving and praise. Nature teaches you to sing your gratitude; just as the birds of the sky do—singing songs of praise in the morning and with thanksgiving in the evening. Do this in spite of what your circumstances may be, for when you do, I will be blessed greatly, and so will you.

**Colossians 3:16**
Let the word of Christ dwell in you richly in all wisdom,
teaching and admonishing one another in psalms and hymns
and spiritual songs, singing with grace in your hearts to the Lord. (NKJ)

**"He is your praise, and He is your God"**
(Deuteronomy 10:21)

# *"Life's Battle"*

**Micah 6:8**
He has shown you, O man, what is good; and
what does the LORD require of you but to do justly,
to love mercy, and to walk humbly with your God? (NKJ)

The Lord God never commands us to do the impossible. God knows what our limits are without Him and He knows what we can accomplish with Him. Because of our sinful nature it is not always possible for us to be fair, kindhearted, and humble in every circumstance. And it is for this reason that we need the Lord God to help us in our quest to live and love like Jesus. We have His written Word that tells us how and the Living Word who shows us the Way. We have God's mercy and grace when we fall, and His mighty strength to pull us up. There is nothing too great for our Mighty God, nor is there anything beyond His reach. There is no greater power than the One who spoke the universe into existence, nor is there a love that can compare with the love that our Savior has shown for mankind.

Our human flesh is weak and our spirit is flawed, but when you humbly surrender your life to the Lord, you can trust Him to help you finish this life in victory. With God you have everything you need to fight and win your battles for life—battles that must be fought while living in this fallen world. Everyone in this world is born into a great and mighty war—an everyday battle to survive, and an everyday battle for our hearts, minds, and souls. There is a raging war between God's goodness and the evil of Satan; furious battles that will determine whether you spend eternity with God in Heaven or with Satan in Hell.

## A Whisper of Hope

**Trust Me, dear child...** for I AM the Way, the Truth and the Life. Without Me you have neither the Wisdom to save your soul nor the Strength to fight the Enemy. When you follow My battle plan, it will navigate you through the mine fields of Satan, whose purpose is to maim and kill. You can join My army of saints and live in victory, or surrender to Satan and join him in the Lake of Fire forever.

**Psalm 24:8**
͏ the King of glory?
͏ and mighty,
͏ battle. (NLT)

How we thank God,
ver sin and death through Jesus Christ our Lord!
(1 Corinthians 15:57)

# "Majestic Light"

**Psalm 104:1, 2**
Let all that I am praise the LORD. You are robed
with honor and majesty. You are dressed in a robe of light. (NLT)

The Lord our God is truly an amazing Being; One who deserves nothing less than every ounce of our praise and worship. In all His magnificence, the LORD is worthy of praise for His incredible creative skills, His infinite wisdom and knowledge, and for His awesome power. Our Sovereign God created all things. He is the Author of life and the King of the universe. He does whatever He wants to do without having to ask anyone for their input or permission. His magnificent and majestic glory stretches across the universe and can be seen as far as the eyes of man can reach and infinitely beyond. The extent of His creation is so great and so vast that it is impossible for our finite minds to even comprehend. Since the beginning of mankind, God has been steadily revealing His secrets to us; each more amazing than the last, and it will take an eternity to discover the wonder of it all!

Creation is a mystery that will never be solved by our finite human minds, but we can know enough to stand in awe of and give the Creator the glory that is due. Every person with eyes can see the majestic work of His hands. And I pray, dear friends, that you, too, will begin to discover how incredibly great our awesome God is, for when you do, you will develop an amazing hunger to know just who He is, for He is clothed in magnificence and splendor—a majesty so incredible that you will honor, love, trust, and stand in awe of the LORD, who will one day usher you into His glory.

## A Whisper of Hope

**See My greatness, dear child…**as you gaze into the heavens. Discover My majesty and you will respect My sovereignty. And by learning who I Am, you will discover who you are and where you stand in the great scheme of My plan; for the plans I have for you are also great and glorious!

**1 Chronicles 29:11**
Yours, O LORD, is the greatness, the power,
the glory, the victory and the majesty. Everything
in the heavens and on earth is Yours, O LORD, and this
is you Kingdom. We adore you as the One who is over all things. (NLT)

**The LORD is my Light and my salvation.**
(Psalm 27:1)

# *"Lord of Lords"*

**Habakkuk 3:2**
I have heard all about You, LORD. I am filled with awe
by your amazing works. In this time of our deep need, help us again
as you did in years gone by. And in your anger, remember your mercy. (NLT)

Our God did not create us to survive on our own, nor does He sit on His throne in Heaven and watch us destroy ourselves and do nothing. From the moment God created the first man, He has not only been protecting and providing for us, but He is also very active in our history and redemption, because out of the Lord's heart flows a love for human beings so great that we will never completely comprehend its full measure. It's out of God's abundant mercy and amazing grace that we even exist, and it's truly amazing that throughout human history most people live as if God doesn't exist; that there is no one to hold them accountable for satisfying the hungers of their carnal flesh. And yet, the Lord does not give in and annihilate us because of our evil and rebellion against Him. The lies and deception that Satan uses to blind people from the Truth is running ramped and out of control. But the true Message of God, in all its richness, keep pressing on, changing one heart and saving one soul at a time.

Because we are living in the last days of the Church age, the Good News of salvation through Christ is being spread like never before. The Savior of the world has overcome this dark and evil world by victoriously defeating sin and death so that we, too, could follow suit. This Good News is the only hope we have of surviving this fallen life with our eternal souls safely in the hands of God. The day is coming my friends, when Satan's reign on this fallen world will suddenly end and God's redemptive plan will come into completion. And on this day everyone will be held accountable for how they lived this first leg of their life-journey. Don't wait for that day to fall on your knees and proclaim that Jesus Christ is Lord, for then it will be too late!

## A Whisper of Hope

**Come to Me, dear child…**for only I can save you from the sure death and destruction that will consume this world and all those who belong to it. Never doubt My ability to protect and provide eternal life for you. Ask in faith and it shall be given unto you.

**Philippians 2:9-11**
God raised Him up to the heights of Heaven and gave Him a name
that is above every other name, so that at the name of Jesus every knee
will bow, in Heaven and on earth and under the earth, and every tongue
will confess that Jesus Christ is Lord, to the glory of God the Father. (NLT)

**"Great and marvelous are Your actions, Lord God Almighty!**
**Just and true are Your ways.**
(Revelation 15:3)

# *"Dwelling Place"*

**Deuteronomy 33:27**
The eternal God is your refuge,
and His everlasting arms are under you.
He will thrust out the enemy from before you. (NLT)

Our omnipresent God is with His children 24/7 to be their refuge—a place of safety and a Source for strength in times of weakness. He is not just a place of refuge during difficult times, but He is also our Source for godly living in a godless world. This Satan-directed world and all those who live by its ways believe that Christians are weak and use God and His "book of fables" as an escape from the hard realities of living. Every person born into this fallen world is born with a weak and perishable body—one that is easily destroyed and one that is easily drawn into the bad choices that pull us away from God; who is the only Hope we have in this world that is headed for destruction.

Our Lord God and Savior is very real, and it's the power of His Word and the Holy Spirit that holds the key to our victories over sin and death. In reality, Christians turn to the Lord for their salvation that is found in His unconditional mercy and grace. We also run to God for His comfort, wisdom, and for His mighty strength—not to escape reality, but to gather the tools we need to fight the good fight while we live in this evil world. We need the help of our wise and mighty King if we are to overcome the great deception that rules this fallen world. We need the Living God for His protection, His Light to guide us through the darkness, and His resurrection Power to fight the Enemy. We need God to lead us safely Home where we can live in perfect peace forever. Run to the Lord God for refuge and make Him your dwelling place, because it's the only way Home.

## A Whisper of Hope

**Lean on Me, dear child…**and trust My every Word. I AM your Protector and Provider. I will not let you wander so far away that you cannot be found. I know there will be times when you will slip and tumble downward, but I'm there to pick you up. Dwell in My Presence and I will give you the power to overcome the evil that has consumed the fallen world.

**Psalm 90:1-2**
LORD, You have been our dwelling place
in all generations. Before the mountains were
born, or You gave birth to the earth and the world,
Even from everlasting to everlasting, You are God. (NASB)

**O LORD my God, You are very great!**
(Psalm 104:1)

# *"Incredible Plan"*

**Zechariah 1:3**
"Return to Me," declares the LORD of hosts,
"that I may return to you," says the LORD of hosts. (NKJ)

Although our Sovereign God righteously reigns in judgment over His creation, His character is not that of a dictator, but one of infinite knowledge and understanding, unending love and compassion, and overflowing with mercy and grace—characteristics that we can only begin to understand. And it is because of these perfect attributes that our Lord God and Savior continually searches for His lost ones who are wandering in the darkness of this fallen world. Only the Good Shepherd can rescue us from the evil that lurks in the darkness and bring us safely into His flock, where He not only protects us from the gaping jaws of the Enemy, but He also heals the wounds that living in this fallen world inflicts upon us. Once the Lord God has us under the wings of His protection, He brings comfort to our troubled souls and fills out hearts with an amazing peace that comes when we know and believe that His forgiveness and restoration are both complete and final.

There is only One True and Living God and He is Jesus Christ. He is the only One who can forgive your sins and promise you eternal life. Living this difficult life in Christ is an awesome place to be dear friends, for you will be in the arms of your Savior. When I began to understand enough to put my faith and hope in the promises of God's Word, I was finally able to experienced the kind of peace I had always searched for and failed to find. I found amazing peace in knowing that our God is loving and righteous and that my life truly mattered to Him—that my life was created to be a part of God's incredible Plan. This incredible eternal Plan for a new life, on a new earth is real and it's for anyone who humbly admits their need for Jesus to save them from the consequences of sin.

## A Whisper of Hope

**Never forget, child…**that your only Hope is in My Plan for man. All other ways are both futile and a waste of precious time. It matters not how far you may have strayed from My Presence, because I AM Faithful and True to you. I will heal and protect you. I AM your eternal Refuge and Healer, a Place where you can rest your weary soul in peace and comfort.

**Psalm 57:1**
Have mercy on me, O God, have mercy! I look to You for protection.
I will hide beneath the shadow of your wings until this violent storm is past. (NLT)

**The LORD reigns…He shall judge His peoples righteously.**
(Psalm 96:10)

# "Bread of Life"

**John 6:68-69**
Simon Peter replied, "Lord, to whom would we go?
You alone have the words that give eternal life. We
believe them, and we know You are the Holy One of God." (NLT)

Jesus asked His twelve apostles if they, too, were going to abandon Him for saying He was the Bread of Life; that "All who eat my flesh and drink my blood remain in Me, and I in them (John 6:56). The followers who abandoned Jesus could only see the humanistic, literal meaning of Jesus' words, not the spiritual. Jesus' apostles knew that He was who He said He was; the Son of the Living God. As I look back at the many times I halfheartedly tried to find God to learn the truth about this life, there were just too many things I couldn't understand; things that were so out-of-touch with the world I was struggling to survive in. And with each failed attempt I found myself feeling more empty, more discouraged, and finally so hopeless that I gave up my search for God and gave in to wickedness of this world. I accepted this hard and difficult life as a curse from God, and that my life was not worth living.

There are too many things in this life that our finite minds will never understand this side of Heaven, but I believe that God wants to use our personal failures and the discouragement they bring us to open our eyes to the futility of following the ways of this fallen world. Many times our failures and mistakes will drive us into the mighty arms of our loving God, Jesus Christ. He is not only the Savior of the world, but He is also the Author and Finisher of Life. He opens the eyes of those who cannot see the Truth and mends our broken hearts when we can see. We have a God who knows precisely how desperate we are for Him. We have a Savior who has saved us from Hell. We have a Shepherd that has made it possible for every living person to find peace and everlasting life in Him. What we have in Jesus Christ, my friends, is the True Bread of Life—our lifeline to Heaven.

## A Whisper of Hope

**I AM…**your Source for Life, the only One who can keep you alive. There is a day coming when your earthly life will end, and so will your choices. When you partake of my body and blood, which was given up for you, you will not perish in the eternal darkness of Hell, but live forever in My Glory.

**Matthew 6:8**
Don't be like them, because your Father knows exactly
what you need even before you ask Him! (NLT)

**"No one who comes to Me will ever be hungry again."**
(John 6:35)

# March

# *"Simple Truth"*

**Psalm 119:130**
As Your words are taught, they give light; Even the simple can understand them. (NLT)

When God's words find their way into our hearts and souls, the Light of His Truth will break through the darkness of this fallen world and bring blessed hope to anyone. It is often out of deep desperation that many hopeless people will open up the Bible in search of something they can hold on to, something that would comfort their souls and hopefully bring resolve into their troubled lives. Sadly though, if we do not allow God's Truth to seep deep into our hearts, the Light quickly dims and we are hard pressed to find a way out of the darkness that is consuming us. But when we allow the Truth of God's Word to penetrate the hardness of your hearts, we find its true meaning, because it opens our minds to the life-saving instructions that are clear and concise. The Truth of God's Word is always easier to see when God's Light is shinning upon its pages and into your softened heart.

You cannot just see or hear the words of God's absolute Truth in order to experience the transforming power they bring; they need to penetrate deep into your heart and soul. Mankind has proven over and over again, throughout the ages, that when we are disconnected from our Creator we are oblivious to His Truth, leaving us uninformed, unprotected, and in the grasp of Satan's evil grip, which is causing much chaos and destruction in its wake. Without God's Word and the Holy Spirit dwelling within your heart, this life becomes a very dark and hopeless place. But with God in your heart, His Word in your hands, and His Light showing you the Way, you will find your way out of the dark that promises you nothing but defeat and death. See God's Word—touch it, read it, and feel its power, my friends, for the Light of God's Son will surely shine as the dawns coming light, subduing the darkness so you can see the Way that leads to a glorious eternal Life.

## A Whisper of Hope

**I Am the Light of the world, dear child…** And the Word that brings life. My Truth was revealed so you could find your way out of the darkness of sin that has consumed the world. My Light brightens the paths of your life-journey so you will not fall into the pits of hell. The Light of My Truth will bring you hope, peace, and life, whereas the darkness will only bring you fear, anxiety and death.

**1 John 1:1-2**
The One who existed from the beginning is the One we have heard and seen.
We saw Him with our own eyes and touched Him with our own hands. His is
Jesus Christ, the Word of Life. This One who is life from God was shown to us,
and we have seen Him. And now we testify and announce to you that He is the
One who is eternal life. He was with the Father, and then He was shown to us. (NLT)

**Your Word is a lamp to my feet and a light to my path.**
(Psalm 119:105)

# "Soul Keeper"

**Psalm 121:5, 7**
The LORD is your Keeper. The LORD shall preserve
you from all evil; He shall preserve your soul. (NKJ)

What comfort and peace these words from God can bring to any believing, weary soul who is struggling to survive in a world of incredible turmoil and daily uncertainty. It's not rare that we spend many sleepless nights fearing what the next day or week or month may bring as we fearfully watch the world around us fall apart. There are so many lost and terrified souls who are uncertain about the direction the world is headed in because they either deny Christ or don't know the Truth. When people put their hope and trust in this fallen world there is really no hope at all, for any sane person can see that the world is going nowhere but down. I know from my own past that when I put my hope and trust in the things of this world, I was mostly unhappy, feeling awfully empty, and always searching for something that made sense. When you stand back and take a hard look at how dysfunctional people have become and how deceit is governing the nations, the obvious outcome tends to look rather bleak.

But thanks be to the God of our salvation, who has, for thousands of years, been saving weary and defeated souls who have chosen to put their hope and trust in the Word of Life, Christ Jesus; the One who has defeated the sin and death of this dying world. Our Hope is in the Lord, who will one day return with His army of angels and His faithful followers from ages past to make things right. God's plan of redemption has given His children the strength and wisdom to overcome the fear and doubt that consumes so many—fears that can easily push one's life into the hopelessness of dark defeat. Our only hope is found in knowing the Lord our God and Savior, Christ Jesus has saved our souls. When your weary soul has its true and faithful Keeper, you will have found the Light that brings you Hope in the Truth!

## A Whisper of Hope

**I Am your Keeper...**I vow to keep you safe from the evil one that rules this world. I protect you day and night so that you can walk and sleep in peace. Trust Me, My child, to be your Soul Keeper, and go forth in confidence to spread your hope and peace in Me wherever you go. For there are many whose souls are kept in darkness by the soul killer named Satan.

**Matthew 16:25-26**
If you try to keep your life for yourself,
you will lose it. But if you give up your life
for Me, you will find true life. And how do you
benefit if you gain the whole world but lose your own
soul in the process? Is anything worth more than your soul? (NLT)

**And now we are in God because we are in His Son, Jesus Christ. His is the only true God, and He is eternal life.**
(1 John 5:20)

# "Forgiveness in Fear"

**Psalm 130:3-4**
LORD, if you kept a record of our sins,
who, O LORD, could ever survive? But You
offer forgiveness, that we might learn to fear you. (NLT)

What a profound affect these words of God can have on the life of any hopeless soul who believes they are too bad to be forgiven. Reverent fear of God and humble repentance always works in making us right with God. It took many heart wrenching failures and almost complete mental and physical destruction before I believed that God really does forgive our sins, no matter how wrong we think they are. And His forgiveness is both complete and final— so much so that everyone who experiences it will stand blameless before the Lord our God on Judgment Day. By accepting God's forgiveness for my sinful rebellion against Him, it opened the eyes of my heart so I could see and learn the truth about who God is, and what my part was in His amazing eternal Plan for man. I discovered that to know and fear the living God is to know the One who holds the destiny of every living soul in His hands, and this my friends is the beginning of all true wisdom.

Our sovereign God takes delight in forgiving our sins, because His mercy filled forgiveness saves our lives and gives Him glory. Our Lord God, Jesus Christ is the God of Forgiveness and it is because of His everlasting mercies and grace that anyone can find forgiveness and healing. The Almighty God, the Creator of the universe, does not need us for anything; But it is we, His created people, who need Him for everything. Like the many saints before me, I am relying on God; not the world, not other people, not man made plans or wisdom, and certainly not myself, for I have put my life into the powerful, saving hands of the Living God. And this decision is always available for any and all who will humble themselves before the Living God and accept the forgiveness that is freely given.

## A Whisper of Hope

**Accept My forgiveness, dear child…**for when you do I will show you what it means to "fear" Me, the One who creates and sustains all things. Never allow yourself to become so prideful that you slow down or stop your quest for true wisdom. Nor should you busy yourself in My name in order to gain My forgiveness, for you can do nothing without Me.

**Proverbs 9:10**
"The fear of the LORD is the beginning of wisdom.
And the knowledge of the Holy One results in understanding." (NLT)

**Great is His mercy toward those who fear Him.**
(Psalm 103:11)

# *"Perfectly Just"*

**Malachi 4:1-2**
"The day of judgment is coming, burning like a furnace. The arrogant and the
wicked will be burned up like straw on that day. They will be consumed like a tree
—roots and all. But for you who fear My name, the Sun of Righteousness will rise with
healing in His wings. And you will be free, leaping with joy like calves let out to pasture." (NLT)

To be true followers of the Way, we Christians must build our lives on every Word of God,
believing it is without error and absolutely true. The Lord not only gave us His Word to help
us understand who He is and to instruct us in the ways of righteous living, but to also warn us about
the consequences of our sin and rebellion. Having briefly stated this truth, it would behoove us to
take seriously all of the prophesy found in God's Word. Knowing the future of God's Way is not only
encouraging those who believe, but it's also warning those who refuse to believe. The final judgment
of the Lord is imminent for everyone. For those who have made Christ the Hope of their salvation,
they will be judged according to the good they have done, for all the bad stuff is burned up and
forgotten. But for those who chose to deny the Truth and make the world their god, or those who
believe they are good enough; they will receive full punishment for their disobedience and pride.

The Lord God left the glory of Heaven to save us from the damnation of eternal Hell that
everyone deserves because of sin. Christ Jesus not only paid the full price for our undeserved
redemption with His human life, but He was raised into a perfect glorified body, much like the
one we believer's will receive upon completion of His amazing Plan for man. Our God is merciful
not to give us what we deserve and gracious enough to give us what we don't deserve. But we must
also know that our Holy Lord God is perfectly just in everything He says and does. This is why
God took upon Himself a human body so that He could become the final and perfect sacrificial
Lamb who had to die an unconscionable, excruciating, unwarranted, criminal death nailed to a
wooden cross. God did this so that we, a sinful, broken people would have the opportunity to be
cleansed and forgiven, so we could to live with Him in Heaven for eternity. And this, my friends,
was perfectly just for Him to do.

## A Whisper of Hope

**I Am the Sun of Righteousness…**bringing much needed light into this dark world that is getting
darker by the day. This life-giving Light is not meant to be horded, nor should it be hidden away
and kept secret. Instead, My Light must shine its truth for everyone to see, so they can choose for
themselves, whether they want eternal life or eternal darkness.

**John 8:12**
Jesus said to the people, "I am the Light of the World.
If you follow Me, you won't be stumbling through the
darkness, because you will have the Light that leads to life." (NLT)

**He will bring the people of the world to judgment.**
(Jude 15)

# "Safe Haven"

**Matthew 7:21**
"Not everyone who says to Me, 'Lord, Lord,' shall enter the Kingdom
of Heaven, but he who does the will of My Father in Heaven." (NKJ)

We should never allow ourselves to become so overly comfortable in our salvation that we begin to compromise our faith and take our focus away from the One who has so graciously given us the gift of eternal life. When we surrender our will to the Lord God, He begins to reveal the truth about this misguided world and how easy it is to be duped into believing the lies of Satan—lies that dominate the world around us—lies that will ruin one's life in a heartbeat. We know through God's Word that every person is born with a sinful nature and because of this, we always fall short of God's standard. So no matter who we are or how righteous or good we consider ourselves to be, we must remain alert at all times, keeping our sinful nature in check and looking for the inevitable attacks of the Devil, who is always on the prowl looking for someone to deceive and destroy.

Sadly, there are many who call themselves Christians who pick and choose the kind of God they want in Christ Jesus to be, so they can continue to enjoy the things of this world that gives them pleasure and satisfies their nature to sin. The Lord wants us to find pleasure in the many things He has created, but the hands of Satan perverts them to use us against God. It is for this very reason my dear friends, that we must encourage and pray for one another to remain focused on God's will, to read and study God's Word, and to pray for God's strength and wisdom. Because the more we learn and understand God's plan, the better equipped we become in winning the battles for our hearts and minds, and securing our place in Heaven. God will not invade the inner sanctions of your soul and force you to follow His will, but when you surrender your sinful will life into His mighty hands, you can be sure that the Author of Life will give you safe haven during this difficult and dangerous life-journey. There are indeed many ways and many gods you can choose from in this dark and troubling world, but there is only One Way and only One God who has both the resources and the power to get you Home safely where you belong.

## A Whisper of Hope

**I Am, dear child…**the only One who offers you safe haven in this world that plots your death and destruction. There is only one thing that can take you away from Me, and that is; dying in your sin. So don't believe the lies of Satan or follow other gods, instead, make Me your only God and I promise you a safe and rewarding journey Home.

**1 Peter 5:8**
Be sober, be vigilant; because your adversary the Devil
walks about like a roaring lion, seeking whom he may devour. (NKJ)

**Grow in the grace and knowledge of our Lord and Savior Jesus Christ.**
(2 Peter 5:18)

# *"Lost and Found"*

**Isaiah 1:18**
"Come now let us reason together," says the LORD. "No matter how deep
the stain of your sins, I can remove it. I can make you as clean as freshly fallen
snow. Even if you are stained as red as crimson, I can make you as white as wool." (NLT)

What a profound declaration of the Truth this is from our Holy and Righteous God. What an encouraging promise this is from the Savior who continually pursues the lost so they can be cleansed and made righteous. But make no doubt about it dear friend, just as Christ pursues His lost and wayward people, so too, does the Enemy pursue your soul and will do anything to pull you away from God, hoping to stain you with so much sin that you will believe that God could never forgive you. Do not believe this lie, for God so loved the world that He gave His One and only Son to be the perfect and final sacrificial Lamb of God. This single act of perfect love and justice is the complete atonement of mankind's sin and rebellion. And it's for you as well.

Many lost and wandering souls are led into a life of sin by the likes of Satan and his godless world view, which has no godly purpose or lasting value—it's much like chasing the wind until you run off a cliff. Most of these deceived people pursue things that feel good for the moment, but are unaware of its meaningless, short sightedness, and eternal deadliness. Most of our world operates against the very grain of God's will and many of its people are desperate for something that will fill the empty gap and give them peace. And there is only One Person and One Way to fill that desire; the death and resurrection of our Lord God and Savior, Jesus Christ. He sets us free from the power of sin and the sting of death. He removes the shame and guilt of our sinful past and gives us a new lease on life—an eternal life. The forgiveness and the cleansing power of Christ Jesus is complete, and no one who has the breath of life is ever too lost to be found. Complete forgiveness and redemption, is but a breath away for anyone who truly longs for peace, hope, and forgiveness.

## A Whisper of Hope

**Come to Me...**My dear child, and I will fill the emptiness that only I can fill. This delusional world is filled with false hope and confusion, making it difficult to escape its darkness. But take heart, for I have overcome the world for you and your redemption is but a decision away. I not only bring you salvation, but also My peace and wisdom will weather the storms until the day I bring you Home.

**1 John 1:9**
But if we confess our sins to Him, He is faithful and just
to forgive us and to cleanse us from every wrong. (NLT)

**"Behold! The Lamb of God who takes away the sin of the world!**
(John 1:29)

# *"Fearful and Safe"*

**Isaiah 8:13, 14**
Do not fear anything except the LORD Almighty, He alone is the Holy One.
If you fear Him, you need fear nothing else. He will keep you safe. (NLT)

There are many things about this unruly world that are so out of control that they cause many of us to live in fear of what tomorrow may bring. The chaotic condition that the world is in, is not going to get any better as we draw closer to the Second Coming of our Lord God, Jesus Christ. This privileged planet that was, in the beginning, a display of God's magnificent creative glory is now distraught and groaning desperately for Jesus. The world's view is for some brilliant human leader to rise up and take the steps to bring about world peace, and order to the chaos, saving the planet and creating a utopian life for everyone. But don't be fooled by this humanist foolishness, because it is impossible for imperfect humanism to create anything that is perfect. Only a Perfect God can create perfection. And the only Savior for this world is the Lord Jesus Christ, for He is the only perfect One who can bring peace and order and perfect justice to our world.

Satan is the reason for the fallen state we are living in and one day the Lord of lord's, the King of kings will get rid of him forever putting an end to all evil and sin forever. And then God will complete His plan and make everything new and perfect. When you know the truth about what the future holds and truly believe in the promises of God, you will experience a peace you never thought possible. What our Lord Jesus Christ accomplished on the Cross is beyond our human understanding, but it does remove the power of sin and the fear of death that holds us captive. Fear of the unknown is quite natural for most of us and it robs us of the joy of living. Our Almighty God calls us to fear only Him, for it is only God who holds the power of life or death. Only God can save you from the eternal darkness of Hell. When you fear the wrath of the Almighty God, you are wise. If you scoff at God and His Truth and believe in the humanist way to utopia, you are foolish, and will receive exactly what the foolish deserve. Be wise and believe in God's Plan and He will give you Heaven.

## A Whisper of Hope

**Fear nothing but Me, your God…**trust your Savior to keep you safe. I not only have the power to keep this promise, but I also hold your future in My hands. My love for you exceeds any and all love that you can comprehend. And with Me at your side, Satan and his dark and evil world holds no power over you that you cannot overcome.

**Deuteronomy 31:6**
"Be strong and of good courage, do not fear nor be afraid of them;
for the LORD your God, He is the One who goes with you.
He will not leave you nor forsake you." (NKJ)

**I sought the LORD, and He delivered me from all my fears.**
(Psalm 34:4)

# "Humble Ways"

**Psalm 25:9**
He leads the humble in what is right,
teaching them His way. (NLT)

Humility is never easy for most people, because this humanistic world teaches us that humanism and worldly wisdom is how it is, which is opposite from God's ways, especially when it comes to what is good and what is not. When we rely on our fallen human wisdom the results are always the same disastrous results, because they always led us further from the Truth of God and deeper into the lies of the Enemy. By giving us the wisdom to make the right choices, the Lord has graciously given us all we need to live a righteous spiritually healthy life. The Lord does not force us to choose His true wisdom, but when you choose the wisdom of God, you are choosing life. When you choose the world's wisdom you are choosing eternal death.

Our sovereign and righteous God has given us everything we need to live a good and pleasing live that only get better and will last forever. It is because of God's great love for man that He has given us His written Word for learning the Way, His life to purchase our salvation that we could never earn, and His Holy Spirit to guide and protect us in this dark world that hates God. The Lord does not force His will upon us, but He makes it readily available for anyone who asks. Because for anyone to make sense out of the created order of things we must first know and believe in the infinite Creator, our Lord God and Savior Jesus Christ, and accept His sovereign rule over the entire creation. We must also humbly admit that we are not gods and that we need the True and Living God for everything. If you are hungry for the Truth my friend, then humbly come to the One who created the Truth. It will be the most humbling experience of your life.

## A Whisper of Hope

**Come humbly...**My child, for I know all things, including what is best for you. I will never lead you astray, nor will I withhold My good will from you. I have given you My Word for right living and My Spirit to guide and teach you, for the Enemy of your soul is clever and his ways are deceitful. Hold firm to the Truth and I will guide you safely as you head for Home.

**1 Corinthians 3:18-21**
Stop fooling yourselves. If you think you are wise by this world's
standards, you will have to become a fool so you can become wise by
God's standards. For the wisdom of this world is foolishness to God. (NLT)

**Humble yourselves in the presence of the Lord, and He will exalt you.**
(James 4:10)

# *"Joy in Thanksgiving"*

**Psalm 28:7**
The LORD is my strength, my shield from every danger.
I trust in Him with all my heart. He helps me, and my heart
is filled with joy. I burst out in songs of thanksgiving. (NLT)

Because we live in a world that demands much and thrives on our weakness, we need a Savior who has the Sovereign Power to protect our hearts and minds from being poisoned and our souls from being destroyed by this wicked world. We need a Savior who is True and Faithful, and that Savior is Christ Jesus, our True God and Faithful Lord. Because our God is the Creator and His Divine attributes are perfect, holy, and just, we can faithfully trust Him with our everyday lives knowing that He will keep us safe and on the path to glory—even when we fail, stumble and loose our way. And once we discover how true and faithful our God is, our hearts will be filled with so much joy that we will sing songs of praise and thanksgiving to the only True and Faithful God there is.

Prior to Jesus rescuing me from the darkness I was trapped in, I never knew the joy of anything because my world was too dark and I was too bitter. My heart was hardened by war and my mind poisoned with lies, which left my heart empty and hopeless and I was desperate to pull the plug. I had become so consumed in my own self-loathing and self-destruction that I sank deeper into my miserable existence, working on a free ticket to Hell. But through the love, mercy, and grace of God, I was saved from the clutches of Satan and for the first time in my life, I found hope and peace in knowing my life was safely in the Savior's hands. Now I am singing songs of praise and worship for His great works of creation and His amazing grace, which gives Him great pleasure and glory, because it honors and glorifies His greatness.

## A Whisper of Hope

**It honors Me, My child...**whenever you sing songs of praise and worship to Me as your God. When you honor Me with your praise, I will honor you. When you proclaim My Glory, I will share it with you. I gave it all so you could have it all, so live this life in thanksgiving. When you glorify Me with your thanksgiving, let the world know what they are missing!

**Colossians 3:16**
Let the words of Christ, in all their richness, live in your hearts
and make you wise. Use His words to teach and counsel each other.
Sing psalms and hymns and spiritual songs to God with thankful hearts. (NLT)

**I will turn their mourning into joy.**
**I will comfort them and exchange their sorrow for rejoicing.**
(Jeremiah 31:13)

# *"Saving Grace"*

**Isaiah 12:2**
"Behold, God is my salvation, I will trust and not be afraid; for the LORD GOD is my strength and song. And He has become my salvation." (NASB)

God revealed the coming Messiah to the prophet Isaiah to not only encourage the people of Israel, but unbeknownst to Him, to also encourage all peoples of the world throughout the ages. Jesus is and always will be the only Hope we have for escaping the consequences of sin that this decaying world poisons our hearts and minds with. God sent His Son to destroy the evil power that enslaves us to sin and the fear of death. It is through Christ Jesus that we find truth and purpose to this life and what lies ahead for us in the future. Our Lord God and Savior, Jesus Christ, voluntarily shed His blood upon the earth and died nailed to a wooden cross so the people of this world, who are all cursed with sin, could be saved from the wrath of God that is justly due to everyone.

There is another sacrifice that is needed my friends, that is nailing your old life of sin to the Cross of Jesus to die and then be born again in Him. When you are living anew in Christ, you are surrendering to His care and control so He can replace it with a life that is truly worth living. When you believe and accept the atonement for your sins that Jesus paid for with His blood, you will be overwhelmed with His amazing mercy and grace, because you are shown how undeserving you are. Sinless Christ took the sins of the whole world so we could stand holy and blameless in His Holy Presence. Those of us who belong to Christ, no longer have to live in fear of death or what tomorrow will bring, because we have eternal life no matter what happens in this fallen world. We also have the promised Helper, the Holy Spirit, to comfort us when needed, to teach us God's Ways, and to empower us with His mighty strength to overcome this world. Our Lord becomes our strength in weakness so we can walk fearlessly with Him while we share the Good News of salvation with those who are desperate for some blessed hope in a world that is dying..

## A Whisper of Hope

**Trust Me, dear child...**walk in faith believing I AM who I say I AM, for when you live your life-journey believing in Me, you will have everything you need. Don't put your trust and hope in this fallen world ruled by the Devil, for it will only bring you down. Look to Me for the Way and the Truth, and I will set you free from your bondage to sin and protect you until I bring you Home!

**Titus 2:11-13**
For the grace of God has been revealed, bring salvation
to all men. And we are instructed to turn from godless living
and sinful pleasures. We should live in this evil world with self-control,
right conduct, and devotion to God, while we look forward to that wonderful
event when the glory of our great God and Savior, Jesus Christ, will be revealed. (NLT)

**Let Your unfailing love surround us, LORD, for our hope is in You alone.**
(Psalm 33:22)

# "Fountain of Life"

**Psalm 36:7**
How precious is your unfailing love, O God!
All humanity finds shelter in the shadow of Your wings. (NLT)

What I find so incredible about the Lord our God, is that every person who walks on the face of this earth, no matter who they are or where they live or what they believe in, all have the opportunity to find those strong and faithful, stretched out arms of the Almighty God. He is the only One who has the power and wisdom to protect and fulfill the hopes and dreams of anyone who would just trust and believe in the Way of His Son, Christ Jesus. I know and believe that the Lord has always watched over and protected my life, even though I lived most of it doubting His ways and refusing to rely on Him for anything. Instead, I put my hope in the lies of this world and trusted its ways to meet my needs and to give me the hope of a better and fulfilling life down the road.

Because I chose to live apart from God, I suffered the consequences of my worldly choices, which with time, left me feeling letdown and betrayed. And when I finally crashed, I knew my hope had run out and there was no way out of the darkness that was plotting my destruction. But unbeknownst to me, God was always there making sure I stayed alive, because He loved me enough to save me from dying in my sin. And after this world had chewed me up and spit me out for dead, the Good Shepherd reached out and with His mighty arms pulled me from the grips of Hell and certain death. And it was there in His arms, as He held me exhausted and worn down, that I experienced the incredible comfort and peace of God while He skillfully put me back together again. And then He set my feet firmly on the road to recovery that gave my life a purpose worth living for. We have an awesome God my friends, a Righteous and Loving Savior who is the Fountain of Life and the Light of the world. Run to Him while you can!

## A Whisper of Hope

**I AM always with you...**My child, watching and listening for your cries of help. Never doubt My sovereign abilities to protect and comfort you in the struggles of this difficult life. I AM your strength whenever you are weak. I AM your Healer when you are hurt.. I AM your Shepherd when you are lost. And I AM your Redeemer when you sin. Never doubt that I AM who I AM, your Everything.

**1 Chronicles 29:11**
Yours, O LORD, is the greatness and the power and the glory and the victory
and the majesty. Everything in the heavens and on earth is Yours, O LORD,
and this is Your kingdom. We adore You as the One who is over all things. (NLT)

**For You are the Fountain of Life, the Light by which we see.**
(Psalm 36:9)

# "Faithful and True"

**Isaiah 10:27**
In that day the LORD will end the bondage of His people.
He will break the yoke of slavery and lift it from their shoulders.

After seven years of God's wrath being poured upon the earth, King Jesus will return with His Church to set up His Kingdom on Earth for one thousand years. He will set those who survive the tribulation free from their bondage to this fallen world. On that glorious day the King of Creation will rule and reign over the world and there will be perfect peace among the nations. There will be no more pain or suffering, nor will there be any disease or death. The world will be free from the evil power of Satan, who has from the beginning, corrupted our minds, hardened our hearts and killed our souls. We will no longer have to put up with the deceitful ploys of Satan, because an angel of the Lord will bind him in chains and throw Him into the abyss and seal it tight for one thousand years, and there will be no more war. Everyone will prosper and no one will ever go hungry. The entire world will experience peace and prosperity for the first time. With Jesus physically ruling the world, there will be no lawless criminals running around, for the Lord will quickly remove them forever. In those one thousand years of no death, people will repopulate the world, for during the seven year tribulation two thirds of the world's population will be killed.

All these things sound pretty farfetched to most people, but God's Word tells the whole story from beginning to the end, and it's nothing but the absolute truth. Don't be caught off guard my friends, because before all this happens, those who belong to Jesus will meet the Lord in the sky to spend the tribulation in Heaven. Stay alert and be prepared, because you don't want to be one of the two thirds that pay the ultimate price for rejecting God's Plan; an extremely damning experience with a whole lot a pain for eternity.

## A Whisper of Hope

**Wait faithfully, dear child…**and be patient, for I AM coming soon, just as I have promised. And when I do, hang on for the ride of your life. The plans I have are perfect and true, for I will make all things new!

**Revelation 19:11-13**
Then I saw heaven opened, and behold, a white horse. And He who
sat on him was called Faithful and True, and in righteousness He judges
and makes war. His eyes were like a flame of fire, and on His head were many
crowns. He had a name written that no one knew except Himself. He was clothed
with a robe dipped in blood, and His name is called The Word of God. (NLT)

**The entirety of Your word is truth.**
(Psalm 119:160)

# "In His Grip"

**Psalm 40:2-3**
He lifted me out of the pit of despair, out of the mud and the mire.
He set my feet on solid ground and steadied me as I walked along.
He has given me a new song to sing, a hymn of praise to our God. (NLT)

It is only by the grace of God that anyone is rescued from the grips of evil that consume this fallen world. I, like many others, can testify to the truth of these words written by King David. The Lord is always with His children, fighting for our hearts, minds, and eternal souls. He is forever ready and always willing to help us when we find ourselves stuck deep in the muck of this dark world—when we are trapped in the grips of the Enemy who relentlessly seeks to destroy everything that belongs to God. Satan, once the most beautiful and mightiest of all God's angelic beings, is the god of this fallen world, and He with his band of other fallen angels are much too strong for our limited human strength and abilities. The only hope we have to successfully battle the constant onslaught of enemy attacks is found only in the Power of God. Without His power and grace, no one would escape the fiery pits of Hell.

Whenever we come to the throne of God's marvelous grace, and surrender our lives at the foot of His Cross, we receive everything we need to win the battles of good and evil that have been fighting each other since the dawn of time. When we have the resurrection power of God living in our hearts and the Holy Spirit fighting the battles that we cannot win, Satan loses His grip and we are set free from the darkness that threatens to swallow us up. And once we are out of the pit of darkness that breeds hopelessness and fear, Jesus sets our feet on solid ground for the rest of our earthly life-journey, for we are safely in His grip forevermore.

## A Whisper of Hope

**Live in Me...**and I will live in you. When you are in My grip you remain safe and out of the powerful hands of evil. The forces of darkness are much too strong for you alone, dear child, but with My power in you, you will overcome. Living in Me brings you life to the fullest.

**Hebrews 4:16**
So let us come boldly to the throne of our gracious God.
There we will receive His mercy, and we will find grace to help us when we need it. (NLT)

**Do not tremble or be dismayed, for the LORD your God is with you wherever you go.**
(Joshua 1:9)

# *"Creative Glory"*

**Isaiah 40:28-29**
Have you never heard or understood? Don't you know that the
LORD is the Everlasting God, the Creator of all the earth? He never
grows faint or weary. No one can measure the depths of His understanding.
He gives power to those who are tired and worn out; He offers strength to the weak. (NLT)

There is absolutely no doubt, whatsoever, that we have a Creator, and that Creator is the Almighty God. His power is unmatched (omnipotent) and His knowledge has no limit (omniscient). God is not bound by time or space (omnipresent) and nothing can hide from His view. In other words, the LORD our God is all powerful, all knowing, and is in complete control of everything in His entire creation. Only fools reject this absolute Truth and there are many intelligent fools in the world who not only deny the truth that there is an incredible intelligence behind creation, but they simply deny the existence of God Almighty altogether. The Lord wants us to know and acknowledge that it is He who keeps the universe in perfect working order so that we and our tiny planet can survive. I think it's a whole lot easier to believe in an all powerful God who spoke the universe into existence than it is to believe that everything began with a mysterious Big Bang—that life developed by chance and that human beings where at one time big hairy apes.

The Lord our God and Creator has an awesome plan, my friends and He will bring this glorious plan into completion when the time is perfect. Jesus offers everyone He creates a piece of His glory through victory in Him, but there are far too many hurdles for us to get over without the Power of God helping us. There is also too much pain, suffering and uncertainty for us to endure without the comfort and peace of the Lord to renew us. We live in a world that blatantly denies God and His sovereign Kingship. We live in a world that is governed by the Devil and his dark forces. We live in on a planet that is cursed because of sin. And the only way out of this mess that Satan and fallen mankind has created, is through our faith that God is who He says He is and that He will do what He says He will do. When you believe in the victory of the Lord our God, it will become yours as well!

## A Whisper of Hope

**Believe, My child...**I Am the Creator. I created the universe to house the people whom I created in my image. I created all that is good and I did it for you. I also created the Way, that if you so choose, you could live in the Presence of my Glory forever. I love you and I want you to love Me as well. I AM preparing a special place just for you, dear one, and I have the power to help you get there.

**Colossians 1:15-17**
Christ is the One through whom God created everything in Heaven and earth. He made the things we can see and the things we can't see. Everything has been created through Him and for Him. He existed before everything else began, and He holds all creation together. (NLT)

**Only fools say in their hearts, "There is no God."**
(Psalm 14:1)

# "God of Joy"

**Psalm 47:1-2**
Come, everyone, and clap your hands for joy! Shout to God with joyful praise!
For the LORD Most High is awesome. He is the great King of all the earth. (NLT)

No matter what circumstances God's children are faced with, we have many reasons to rejoice in the LORD our God, for without His amazing grace, incredible mercy, and His unconditional love, this life would be a hopeless mess. I believe the greatest message in God's Word is the Hope we find in knowing the Absolute Truth; that no matter how Satan and this fallen world lashes out against us, the children of God have the Advocate who stands before God the Father as our Defender. Our Lord Jesus Christ, has not only defeated the power that sin has over mankind and the fear of dying that most of us live with, but Jesus has also won the case that the Devil holds against us and bridged the gap that once stood between God and man.

Because of our sinful nature and the decadence of the world that surrounds us, it is rather hard to find something that will bring true joy into our hearts, especially in the midst of our own personal turmoil. The only way any of God's children can find the strength and joy to get past all the suffering and hopelessness that this fallen world inflicts on those who belong to the world, is by directing our focus on the True God of Hope, Lord Jesus Christ. For it is in this Hope, through the gift of salvation, that gives us the strength to share our Hope that this difficult life is not all there is. And by praising our God of Hope for who He is and what He has done and is still doing, will also bring us joy in the purest form while we suffer the hardships of living in this fallen world.

## A Whisper of Hope

**Look to Me, My child…**to persevere with joy in your difficult trip through this life. The impossible circumstances of this fallen life are too much for you to face on your own. I AM the only One who can bring you true joy. This life is a precious gift, even to those who feel it is a curse. Knowing the Truth will bring you joy!

**1 Timothy 2:5**
For there is only one God and one Mediator
who can reconcile God and people.
He is the man Christ Jesus. (NLT)

**Let Your unfailing love surround us, LORD, for our hope is in you alone.**
(Psalm 33:22)

# *"One Who Saves"*

**Isaiah 43:2-3**
When you go through deep waters and great trouble,
I will be with you. When you go through rivers of difficulty,
you will not drown! When you walk through the fire of oppression,
you will not be burned up; the flames will not consume you. For I am
the LORD, your God, the Holy One of Israel, your Savior. (NLT)

God gave this message to His people Israel to give them hope and encouragement. When we choose Jesus Christ as our Lord and Savior, living His Way and loving Him with all our hearts, souls, and minds, this message is for us as well. For we can be confident that our Savior will keep us safe amidst the onslaught of evil attacks from the Devil and his dark world that is headed for destruction. And we can also be sure that the power of God will keep us free from the sin that had once held us captive and on the road to Hell. This fallen world is spinning wildly out of control, and is without mercy, oppressing most of its people, and so it's not hard for us to question God's authority and doubt that He is really in charge. This is why we must hold firmly to the Truth that we have in our Great God and Savior, King Jesus, because when our hearts are being filled with fear and doubt, Satan takes advantage of our these weak moments and we are tempted to lose hope and be discouraged.

But because of the atoning work of Jesus that He paid for on the Cross, we can now come into the Holy Presence of the Living God just as we are, filled with fear and doubt. And it is there in His Presence that we receive God's comfort and peace, because He reaffirms our hope; that no matter what this world does to us, we will only die, but for a moment. And this my friend, removes our fears and renews our faith. And with the renewal of our hearts and minds, comes the joy of knowing the Lord and that He is watching and waiting for just the right moment to bring all things together for the Good of His Glory. With our renewed hope for salvation we can reach out to the many lost and hopeless souls with the Good News Message of eternal life through Christ Jesus— that He defeated sin and death for everyone in the world to embrace.

## A Whisper of Hope

**I Am the Redeemer, child…**the only One who holds your eternal destiny in His hands. When your life is in My hands, no matter what troubles you may face, I am always there to help you overcome. When you trust in My Power of My Word, I will renew your strength and bring you hope. Life in Me is life eternal—life as it was meant to be.

**Psalm 25:5**
Lead me by Your truth and teach me, for you are the God who saves me.
All day long I put my hope in You. (NLT)

**Be strong, and do not fear, for your God is coming to destroy your enemies.**
**He is coming to save you.**
(Isaiah 35:4)

# "Glorious God"

**Psalm 89:8, 14**
O LORD God of Heaven's Armies! Where is there anyone as mighty as
You, O LORD? You are entirely faithful. Righteousness and justice are the
foundation of Your throne. Unfailing love and truth walk before you as attendants. (NLT)

The mightiest weapons of mankind stand puny and useless against the Lord; our Almighty God of Creation and the King of the universe is the Savior of it all. Even the incredible light that pours out from our sun is nothing compared to the Glory of God Almighty. And His Presence is nothing less than pure holiness and perfection; so much so that it is impossible for anyone to stand before Him. He is the One and Only true God; a God of incorruptible justice, and our Loyal Advocate and faithful Mediator. It is because of God's unconditional love for people and His abundant mercy and grace that we are able to exist in this vast universe that could swallow us up in a heartbeat. Our Lord Jesus graciously holds the universe in perfect order so everyone will have the opportunity to receive a glorified body that will spend eternity discovering the wonders of our Glorious God.

It becomes an amazing life-journey when you embrace and believe in the Sovereign Lord of creation, who has paved a saving path for you to travel on in this difficult part of your life-journey—a path that leads straight through Heaven's door and into eternity. Until you know and trust in the Lord who covers you completely, you will never discover the true joy of living this gift of life. Living in this brutal world that has fallen away from the goodness of God is not only painful, but it is unable to offer anything close to the kind of everlasting hope and peace that comes from Heaven. Knowing the Truth and embracing the Savior will cause even the most pessimistic life to change forever. Discovering the Truth about God and His Way to salvation will bring you everlasting peace no matter what this unpredictable world does, for you will have the confidence that God will see you through to the other side. But what I find the most exciting about this gift of life; is I know that there is so much more to come—an eternity of discovering the glory of God.

## A Whisper of Hope

**I AM your life-line, dear child...**Hold tightly to Me and you will live in peace and know My Joy. The day is coming when I will make all things righteous and new for all those who live in My Light and embrace My saving grace. And as you wait, live in patient love for others. Spread the wealth of My glory to the poor in spirit and share the joy of living to the hopeless and lost.

**Deuteronomy 10:17, 21**
The LORD your God is the God of gods and Lord of lords.
He is the great God, mighty and awesome, who shows no
partiality and takes no bribes. He alone is your God. (NLT)

**But He said, "You cannot see My face, for no man can see Me and live!"**
(Exodus 33:20)

# "Firmly Grounded"

**Psalm 105:4**
Seek the LORD and His strength; Seek His face continually. (NASB)

If Christians are to remain confident in the saving grace of our Lord and God, Jesus Christ, and if God's children are to stand strong against the Enemy of our souls and if we want the wisdom and courage to proclaim the incredible message of hope that the Good News of salvation brings, one must, without fail, stay grounded in God's Word. We must humbly come before the throne of God's marvelous grace every day, because without the Lord, we could not carry our cross and boldly live in a world that hates the Holy God of Israel. As bearers of God's Light, we must take the risk and share the Light so others will find their way out of the darkness that is consuming our world. When we fail to stay connected to our Savior through His Word and prayer, we are easy prey for the hungry jaws of Satan who lurks in the darkness ready to devour anything that belongs to God.

When I first became a believer in the Son of God and I put my life into His care and control, I quickly learned how futile it was to successfully fight the battles for my heart and soul without the Power of God. The temptation to sin was much too strong for me to fight on my own, and believe me, I really tried and failed miserably . But because of God's loving grace, my failures drove me back into His strong and forgiving arms, and with renewed hope and strength I was able to press on in confidence that my new life-journey in the Kingdom of God was forever. I can truly testify my friend, just as many have before me, that it is only through the Resurrection Power of Christ that we even stand a chance against the powerful evil forces that are driving this world into the abyss. There are many roads you can take, but only one leads to eternal life with God in Heaven; all others only lead into the deepest pits of Hell where darkness and pain is as good as it gets.

## A Whisper of Hope

**Stay firmly grounded in Me...**dear child, for without it, you stand weak against the enemies of your soul, for they are too strong for you alone. Stay connected to My Power and Wisdom. Stay on the path I have set before you. And stay under the shield of My protection. You will be challenged and lose a battle or two, but don't be discouraged and keep the faith, because I have defeated the sting of death, and so too, will you.

**Ephesians 3:17-18**
And I pray that Christ will be more and more at home in your hearts as you trust in Him. May your roots go down deep into the soil of God's marvelous love. And may you have the power to understand, as all God's people should, how wide, how long, how high, and how deep His love really is. May you experience the love of Christ, though it is so great you will never fully understand it. Then you will be filled with the fullness of life and power that comes from God. (NLT)

**Put on all of God's armor so that you will be able to stand firm
against all the strategies and tricks of the Devil.**
(Ephesians 6:11)

# "God of Creation"

**Isaiah 45:18**
For the LORD is God, and He created the heavens
and earth and put everything in place. He made the
world to be lived in, not to be a place of empty chaos.
"I am the LORD," He says, "and there is no other." (NLT)

The world's view of creation is nothing more than an accident caused by a mysterious big bang—that there is no creator—that living matter formed by some chemical reaction that cannot be explained. There are many lost souls who think there are many kinds of gods for different kinds of circumstances. There are others who believe in a god who created everything, but then abandoned it to evolve and survive on its own. Some believe that everyone is a god. And then there are those who foolishly make whatever suits their fancy the god of their choice. But when you set aside all the utter foolishness of manmade gods and get down to the seriousness of it all, the only thing that makes any sense at all, is that there is not only an intelligent Designer, but One who is a caring, loving, all powerful, and all knowing Creator—a living God who skillfully designed the universe, the Earth, and life. And this incredible Creator is none other than the One Living God of the Bible, the Almighty Lord God, the King of the Universe, our merciful Savior.

The Lord created a Divine Order my friends, and by the power of His Word the universe is held together in perfect harmony; a harmony that reveals the Majesty and Glory of the Living God. We have a triune God in the Father, Son, and Holy Spirit, who knows and cares about the condition of His creation, especially the human beings that He made in His likeness. God knows how easily we can destroy ourselves because of our love of sin, so He has provided the Way for us to avoid the road that leads to Hell. But sadly, most of the people in this world are drifting further and further away from their Creator and Savior to embrace the way of the Devil, who has duped and blinded them from the Truth.

## A Whisper of Hope

**Listen to the Truth, dear child...**it will open your eyes and set you free from the fear of death and the darkness that engulfs this world. I not only made you, but I have also saved you from a world of lies that plots your demise. Remember that the Creator is always greater than what He creates!

**Isaiah 45:5,7**
I am the LORD, and there is no other; there is no God besides
Me. I create the light and make the darkness. I send good times
and bad times. I, the LORD am the One who does these things. (NKJ)

### "I am the LORD, who makes all things."
(Isaiah 44:24)

# "Promise Keeper"

**Psalm 119:49-50**
Remember Your promise to me, for it is my only hope.
Your promise revives me; it comforts me in all my troubles. (NLT)

Before I surrendered my sin-filled life to the Lord, I was taught to put all of my hopes and dreams in the things and ways of the world, leaving God out of the equation altogether. And after many years of working hard and thinking like the world, I discovered that the things of this world could never fully satisfy, nor could they last. Unfortunately, most of us go through a process I call humanistic osmosis; blindly following the world unaware of the dire consequences when this life is over. Like so many, I lived my life believing the way to happiness and contentment was found by traveling the roads that the world paves. And unbeknownst to me, I spent most of my adult life running with the world and feeling short-changed, which left me empty and depressed. Little did I know that God was allowing me to discover the truth about this fallen life the old fashion way of trial and error, allowing me to make humanistic decisions-that lead to failure, hoping I would learn from the consequences.

There usually comes a time when many of us finally realize that the world with all its resources cannot satisfy the desires of our hearts and soul, nor can they fully satisfy the hungers of our sinful flesh. And it is with this discovery that I begin to wallow in my hopelessness, succumbing to the weakness of my sinful flesh, and I began sinking into the darkness of defeat. If ever you find yourself in this dark place, my friends, don't give up or give in to the lies of this wicked world, because there is promised hope in the Savior of the World, Christ Jesus. And when you come humbly to the foot of the Cross and nail your old life of sin to it, you will be given a new life that is right with God and forever lasting. You will experience the promised victory over this fallen world that offers you everything, but delivers only the darkness of death.

## A Whisper of Hope

**I Am, dear child...** the Keeper of promises. I came to save you from this deceitful world that seeks to destroy your heart and kill your soul. The world can promise you nothing that is good or lasting, but what I promise is beyond your imagination and is forever! I promise you a piece of Heaven's glory that I paid for with My blood and death.

**2 Peter 1:3-4**
As we know Jesus better, His divine power gives us everything we need for living a godly life. He has called us to receive His own glory and goodness! And by that same mighty power, He has given us all of His rich and wonderful promises. He has promised that you will escape the decadence all around you caused by evil desires and that you will share in His Divine Nature. (NLT)

**Without wavering, let us hold tightly to the hope we say we have,**
**for God can be trusted to keep His promise.**
(Hebrews 10:23)

# "God Hears"

**Habakkuk 1: 2, 4**
How long, O LORD, must I call for help?
But you do not listen! I cry, but you do not come to save. (NLT)

E vil and the decadence it brings is eating the people of our world alive, causing a lot fear, anxiety, and uncertainty about the future. People are crying out for anything or anyone in this world that would give them some hope. Sadly, their crying out is futile, because nothing from this world is capable of fixing this decaying world—fixes that are too big for human wisdom or power. Most people of this world are either too busy struggling to survive or they are simply too focused on getting all they can, while they can to know about the only One who can fix the problems that the world faces. These lost souls don't know or even seem to care that our Lord God Jesus Christ, will come again to clean up the mess caused by thousands of years of sin and rebellion against the living God. The King of the universe will return with fire in His eyes to destroy all that is evil and those who oppose the Word of God. King Jesus will then rule and reign on Earth where people will live in peace and prosperity. There will be no more war or sickness or death; life will be good for the first time since our falling away from God.

The lost and desperate souls of this fallen world don't know God's Plan because the Devil and his loyal followers have distorted the Truth so much that most people don't know what to believe; they simply go with the flow, live for the moment, and hope for the best end result. The Devil has convinced the world that God is not gracious or merciful and that He doesn't care what happens to us. Many believe that God is off doing other God things and has a deaf ear when it comes to our desperate cries for help. This is not so, my friend, the Lord hears your every cry and He knows how you suffer in this fallen world that groans to be fixed. Our loving Creator cares deeply about each and every one of us. We have a Savior that has defeated death for us. We have a Redeemer who hears our every cry. And one day soon, He will make all things new and no one shall ever cry again!

## A Whisper of Hope

**I hear you...**My child and I know your pain and fear, for I see and hear all things. I came into this fallen world to save my people and give them hope. I came to save you! I AM God your Redeemer and you must trust the plans I have for you, for they are good and true.

**Romans 8:21-22**
All creation anticipates the day when it will join God's children
in glorious freedom from death and decay. For we know that all creation
has been groaning as in the pains of childbirth right up to the present time. (NLT)

**"Fear not, I [God] will help you."**
(Isaiah 41:13)

# "Know the Truth"

**Psalm 139:1**
O LORD, you have examined my heart
and know everything about me. (NLT)

Our Sovereign LORD is as much a personal God as He is Holy and Perfect in every way. He is not a God who stands apart from His creation, but a loving and gracious God who wants only what is best for people. It is so amazing that in the scheme of who God is; the Great and Awesome Creator of an unending universe and life itself, that He takes the time and the resources He created to personally reach out and touch individual people so they can know who He is and what He has planned. He makes every person uniquely different, each with their own personal qualities and purpose—a purpose that is made to fit who we are and what we can manage with God's help. The Lord knows firsthand what it's like to carry the weight of the world upon our shoulders and He knows all of the burdens that we try to manage on our own.

How wonderful it is to have an all powerful God who knows and loves us so dearly that He allowed Himself to be tortured and nailed to a wooden cross by mere mortal men. The Lord knows our pain and the burdens we bear; even the most secret shame and remorse that we carry deep inside our hearts; things we fearfully keep hidden in a darkness so deep that we think God Himself has no idea what they are. You cannot hide anything from the One who created you. And you should never underestimate His power. When you exclude the Lord from your life, the burdens you try to hide and carry on your own will eventually become so great that you will collapse under the weight, much like I did. But as I sunk deeper in my guilt and shame, oblivious to the love and grace of our God and Savior, He reached down just at the right moment and slowly began to remove the burdens that I was not created to bear. When living apart from God, my friends, it is impossible to bear the burdens brought on by this fallen world; we are not gods, merely mortal human beings touched by the decadence of sin and death. But we all have the same merciful God who not only saved the world from destroying itself, but also saves us from the eternal consequences of our sin.

## A Whisper of Hope

**I know you, dear child…** better than you know yourself. I know all the things you try to hide in the darkness and I will forgive you if you ask, for I love you and I want to take your burdens so you can enjoy this life. You can do nothing that surprises or shocks me, for I AM GOD. Do not hide in the dark. Rather, bring your burdens to Me and find My eternal peace for your weary burdened soul.

**Hebrews 4:16**
So let us come boldly to the throne of our gracious God.
There we will receive His mercy, and we will find grace to help us when we need it. (NLT)

**Give your burdens to the Lord, and He will take care of you.**
(Psalm 55:22)

# *"Forgiven and Redeemed"*

**Isaiah 48:17**
The LORD your Redeemer, the Holy One of Israel, says;
I am the LORD your God, who teaches you what is good
and leads you along the paths you should follow. (NLT)

The LORD created us to be able to come into His Presence as Adam and Eve did in the Garden of Eden, but when sin entered into the equation, the relationship was broken and mankind began to depend on themselves and could no longer be in a close relationship or walk in His Presence. But because of God's great love for human beings, He came into this broken world as a man of flesh to remove our sins, take our just punishment, and to reestablish the broken relationship. Our Lord and God not only reconciled the relationship so we could enter into the holy Presence of God, but after ascending back into Heaven He sent the Holy Spirit into the world to help guide and protect us while traveling this difficult journey on the road to Heaven.

When you humbly ask God to forgive all your sins, He will. When you ask Him to make you a new person, He does. When you ask Him to be the Lord over your life and will, He accepts. Christ Jesus chose to pay the ransom that freed us from the power of sin that leads to darkness and death. When you surrender to the One who created you and also saved you, He removes the blinders from your eyes and softens your heart so you can better see and understanding the world around you. He teaches you the Truth—what is right and what is not—what is good and what is bad, because the world teaches you just the opposite. And as you trust the Lord of your life, He provides both the power and motivation to transform your old, sin-filled life of darkness and doubt into a brand new life filled with everlasting hope and peace. Our awesome God and Savior is the Sovereign King of the universe and He invites you to be a part of His holy family as His adopted child, and you will receive the crown of everlasting life, walking and talking with the Author of Life, as you were created to do.

## A Whisper of Hope

**My dear child…**listen closely for My voice, for when you hear Me calling, follow the path that brings you back into My Presence. You live in a dangerous world and you need My Spirit to protect and safely lead you home. Your journey in this fallen world will be hard and exhausting, but your struggles and pain will shape your eternal character and prepare you for a heavenly journey unlike anything you can ever imagine!

**1 Timothy 2:5, 6**
For there is only One God and One Mediator
who can reconcile God and people. He is the man
Christ Jesus. He gave His life to purchase freedom for everyone. (NLT)

**So Christ has really set us free.**
(Galatians 5:1)

# *"Our Provider"*

**Psalm 145:13, 14**
The LORD is faithful in all He says; He is gracious in all He does.
The LORD helps the fallen and lifts up those bent beneath their loads. (NLT)

It has been said that a Christian's faith is nothing more than a crutch to be leaned upon or a cop-out when things get too tough to deal with. What many unbelievers refuse to acknowledge is that we, a very weak and tiny being, live in a dangerously vast universe so big we cannot even imagine its enormous size and we are extremely helpless and vulnerable when compared to the incredible power it holds. We are also incapable of defending ourselves against the unseen forces of evil that hate God and want to destroy all that is His—principalities and powers that exceed any and all human ability. The truth is, my friends, we need someone greater than ourselves, the universe, and Satan to save us from the destruction that is eminent when we stand alone. And that some One is our Creator, Jesus Christ.

The Lord God keeps the entire universe in precise order by the Power of His Word, to protect our tiny planet that houses the most precious of all He has ever created; human life. Mankind would not survive for a moment if it were not for our gracious and Almighty God. We would never survive in this vast universe that is always on the move, nor could we withstand the attacks from Satan's evil powers when they rear their ugly heads. As God's created people, we must depend upon His great power to survive. We need His gracious favor to sustain the bodies we live in, and we need the power of His Holy Spirit to keep our souls alive. It is only because you have a loving, gracious, and merciful God, that you even wake up in the morning or make it through the entire day. Our sovereign God, Creator of everything seen and unseen, has carefully and personally designed us with His mighty skillful hands. The Living God wants only what is best for every person He blesses with the breath of life, and He does this by perfecting in us what we were originally designed to do—to glorify and honor Him by the way we live our lives.

## A Whisper of Hope

**You are, dear child...**the most precious of all My creation and I will care for you above all else. But in order for Me to do this, you must trust Me with your life. Remember that the world hates Me and all those who follow My Way. But fear nothing, for I have overcome the world and will protect you until it is time to come Home. I Am your Provider, Protector, and Redeemer. And even in the midst of your darkest hour, remember; I AM GOD.

**2 Peter 1:2-4**
As we know Jesus better, His divine power gives us everything we need for living a godly life. He has called us to receive His own glory and goodness! And by that same mighty power, He has given us all of His rich and wonderful promises. He has promised that you will escape the decadence all around you caused by evil desires and that you will share in His Divine Nature. (NLT)

**He Himself gives life and breath to everything,**
**and He satisfies every need there is.**
(Acts 17:25)

# *"It is True"*

**Isaiah 35:1-10**
Even the wilderness will rejoice, in those days. The desert will blossom with flowers. Yes, there will be an abundance of flowers and singing and joy! The deserts will become as green as the mountains of Lebanon, as lovely as Mount Carmel's pastures and the Plain of Sharon. There the LORD will display His glory, the splendor of our God.
With this news, strengthen those who have tired hands, and encourage those who have weak knees. Say to those who are afraid, **"Be strong, and do not fear, for your God is coming to destroy your enemies. He is coming to save you."** And when He comes, He will open the eyes of the blind and unstop the ears of the deaf. The lame will leap like a deer, and those who cannot speak will shout and sing! Springs will gush forth in the wilderness, and streams will water the desert. The parched ground will become a pool, and springs of water will satisfy the thirsty land. Marsh grass and reed and rushes will flourish where desert jackals once lived.
And a main road will go through that once deserted land. It will be named the Highway of Holiness. Evil-hearted people will never travel on it. It will be only for those who walk in God's ways; fools will never walk there. Lions will not lurk along its course, and there will be no other dangers. Only the redeemed will follow it. Those who have been ransomed by the LORD will return to Jerusalem, singing songs of everlasting joy. Sorrow and mourning will disappear, and they will be overcome with joy and gladness. (NLT)

The hope and encouragement that this Scripture brings to those of us who believe that the Bible is God's inerrant Words of Truth is priceless. Because in this fallen world that breeds nothing but hopelessness and death, this 2,000 plus year old message from God can light up the deepest darkness and bring life to the dead and lifeless. The Lord our God; the King of the Universe is coming soon my friends, to rightly claim what is His and disregard all that is not. Since God's Word is His Truth, we have no time to waste in sharing this Good News. Jesus brings Light where there is only darkness, and life to those who have lost it. Christ Jesus is the Hope for everyone who is searching for something more than death, who are struggling to just survive, and hoping for some blessed peace in their life. This encouraging and wonderful Hope that we find in our Lord God and Savior, is the only Hope that will help guide us safely Home with joy in our hearts and a smile upon our faces. Come Lord Jesus!

## A Whisper of Hope

**I AM the Truth…**and when you believe in Me and all that I have written down for you, and when you obey My commands, you will have a glorious new and everlasting life, in a glorious new and everlasting body, in a glorious new and everlasting Home.

**1 Thessalonians 5:2-4**
For you know quite well that the day of the Lord will come unexpectedly,
like a thief in the night. When people are saying, "All is well; everything is
peaceful and secure," then disaster will fall upon them…And there will be no escape. (NLT)

**And He who sits on the throne said, "Behold, I am making all things new."**
**And He said, "Write, for these words are faithful and true."**
(Revelation 21:5)

# "One God Only"

**Isaiah 44:6,10**
The LORD Almighty, says: "I am the First and the Last;
there is no other God." "Who but a fool would make his
own god—an idol that cannot help him one bit." (NLT)

I believe the first thing we must do in order to find peace, purpose, and understanding about this difficult life-journey that no one gets to volunteer for, is to believe in the only True and Living God who left the glory of Heaven to live and die so we could die and live. Christ Jesus became a man of flesh and blood to become the final sacrificial Lamb of God who took away the sins of the world. God is not the earth or the moon or the sun or the whole universe or anything else in creation or anything we can create with our hands or minds. Throughout the history of the world, man has foolishly made many different things his god or gods—gods that are all fakes—man made gods that deceive the world in Satan's favor. There are many foolish people who try to replace the Living God with the world's gods, but none of them can give us life, nor can they save us from our sins and the condemnation that is due.

It is not my objective to condemn people for living foolish lives worshiping false gods, because I, too, was once living this life foolishly drinking and smoking the gods that controlled my life. Most people who do not know and love the Lord our God and Savior have probably never really heard or understood the Truth and so they view God and His redemptive plan for mankind and the world as science fiction or simply crazy. Because we love our little gods that give us pleasure, they control the way we live. And even though I spent most of my adult life indulging in the gods of this fallen world, deep in my heart I was searching for the truth about this cursed life that gnawed at my heart and tormented my soul. The world's gods failed to give me the answers that I so desperately hungered for and I, like many, was left empty and hopeless, for there is only One God, One Truth, and One Answer—Jesus Christ!

## A Whisper of Hope

**There is only One God…**My child. I AM He. And I can tell you that all of Heaven rejoices when anyone comes to understand and believe this essential Truth. This deceitful world has filled your mind with too many lies for much too long. But as you learn the Truth, so, too, will you find life in Me.

**John 17:3**
And this is the way to have eternal life—to know You,
the only true God, and Jesus Christ, the One You sent to earth. (NLT)

**But the LORD is the only true God, the Living God.**
**He is the Everlasting King!**
(Jeremiah 10:10)

# *"Truth Be Known"*

**Isaiah 55:6**
Seek the LORD while He may be found,
Call upon Him while He is near. (NKJ)

Although we face many unknowns as we move through this short life, there is One Known that is perfect and true. This Truth never changes, nor does it ever deceive us. This Truth lights our way through the darkness of this wicked world and protects us from our enemies. It is the only Truth that saves innocent lives from the hungry jaws of Satan. Our Lord God and Savior, Jesus Christ is that Truth and it is through our redemption in Christ Jesus that we discover the truth about what is known and what is not; about life and death. It is through God's Word that we learn we only have this present life to decide where we want to spend eternity, because the moment we die, we will either be trapped in the dark pits of Hell or in the Presence of our glorious God. The false truths of Satan have had thousands of years to twist and manipulate God's Truth to the point that most people are so uncertain they don't know what to believe. The Devil has cleverly disguised the truth to fit neatly into all lifestyles and all world views, including the Christian world view.

As a Christian we must always remain alert and ready for anything that the world and Satan throws our way. We must put on the armor of God everyday for protection. We must feed on every word of God to give us the strength and courage to fight the battles for our heart and minds. The Lord wants no one to perish into Hell because of our rebellious nature to sin, because that is why He came and died to save us. Our gracious God is giving us time to choose; Him or Satan; life or death; Heaven or Hell, but the time, dear friend, will soon run out and so will the opportunity of an eternal lifetime. Don't refuse God's gift of salvation, for if you do, you will forever regret it!

## A Whisper of Hope

**Believe Me, dear child**...for My Word speaks nothing but the Truth. It is only through Me that you find life and the way Home. Discover the Truth and you will shine with the goodness of God that points the Way for all to see. Traveling the rough roads of this life-journey in the Truth is never easy, but the final destination is indeed, Heavenly!

**Psalm 33:4-5**
For the Word of the LORD holds true, and everything
He does is worthy of our trust. He loves whatever is just
and good, and His unfailing love fills the earth. (NLT)

**Hold to the truth in love, becoming more and more in every way like Christ.**
(Ephesians 4:15)

# *"Victory King"*

**Psalm 44:4, 7**
You are my King and my God. You are the One
who gives us victory over our enemies. (NLT)

Jesus Christ is the King of the universe and Lord of creation. And it is our victorious King who gives us our victory over sin and death—the two most deadly enemies we have because they take our lives and kill our souls. When we humbly submit our lives to the care and control of our eternal King, He becomes the Lord of our lives and He not only helps us overcome the attacks of the Devil and his evil forces, but Lord Jesus also helps us keep them at bay. It is through God's Word that He opens our eyes to the truth about the most deadly of all wars— the unseen, spiritual war against the Lord God and His Church—evil against godliness, sin against holiness.

When you combine the infinite Wisdom of God with His omnipotent Power, Satan and his evil cronies will crumble at the mention of His Name. But in order to fight the good fight my friend, and stay on top of God's Victory Plan, you must join the King's army and draw from His wisdom and strength, rather than fighting bravely on your own. For when you are one with the King, you will taste victory, for the key to defeating sin and death can only be found in the blood of the Lamb. But until the King returns to put an end to this war forever, the everyday battles will continue to rage on; battles that must be fought one day at a time with the King of Victory covering your back side.

## A Whisper of Hope

**Victory is yours, My child...**when you put your life in My hands. There is no other way to win the battles for your heart and soul but with My help. There is no One greater than I, for I defeated sin and death once and for all. When you follow the victory plan I have for you, you will be victorious.

**1John 5:4-5**
For every child of God defeats this evil world by trusting Christ
to give the victory. And the ones who win this battle against the
world are the ones who believe that Jesus is the Son of God. (NLT)

**How we thank God who gives us victory over sin and death.**
(1 Corinthians 15:57)

# *"Light Rescue"*

**Psalm 56:13**
For You have rescued me from death, you have
kept my feet from slipping. So now I can walk in
Your Presence, O God, in Your life-giving Light. (NLT)

What a profound, life-changing revelation this is, especially for those of us who have journeyed down the dark paths of destruction; those lost and desperate souls searching for something that would relieve the pain and shame. Many of us have found ourselves trapped in a world of deception, selling our souls and walking hand in hand with the Devil—the Destroyer of lives and the killer of souls. This world is manipulated by the lies of Satan, which he uses to draw us into his web of sin and self-destruction. Satan has used his power to convince the world that God is either dead or He doesn't care—that this life is all there is, so we must get what we can while the gettin' is good. But this is not the truth, my friends, for we have a loving and merciful God who knows the mess that sin has created for our world.

Our Lord God and Savior so loved the world that He left the glory of Heaven to save us from the darkness and give us the hope for a bright and glorious future that has no end. He suffered at the hands of mortal evil men and died hanging naked on a tree for the sins of the world. Christ Jesus paid the full price for our salvation. Our Mighty God defeated sin and death so we could escape sins deadly sting. Lord Jesus is the only life-saving Light that rescues us from the eternal grave of darkness that embracing this fallen world brings. By simply knowing and embracing this Truth, my friend, will brighten the path of your life-journey so you can find your way Home.

## A Whisper of Hope

**I AM, the Light of the World...**the only Light that brings you life. When you walk in the Light, dear child, there is no reason to fear the wrath that awaits those who live and thrive in the darkness of this sinful world. The Light from Heaven will keep you safe. My Light is your only Hope!

**Ephesians 5:8**
For though your hearts were once full of darkness, now you are full
of the Light from the Lord, and your behavior should show it. For this
Light within you produces only what is good and right and true. (NLT)

**"I am the Light of the world.
If you follow Me... you will have the Light that leads to life."**
(John 8:12)

# *"Unending Grace"*

**Joel 2:21, 23**
Don't be afraid, my people! Be glad now and rejoice, because
the LORD has done great things. Rejoice in the LORD your God!
For the rains He sends are an expression of His grace. (NLT)

The vast majority of people living on this earth find themselves not only struggling to survive, but a good many of them are allowing their dire circumstances get the best of them. Christians are certainly not immune to the hardships that that come with living in this fallen world, but the difference between Christians and all others, is that God's children know without a doubt that the Lord is in control and they also know what the future holds. A Christian knows that no matter what this fallen world does, they are never left alone to fight the battle, because they have the Word of God and His promise of salvation. Our Almighty God and Savior gives us His Word that He will make all things new and perfect forever for those who are called by His Name. For those who belong to the world, all they know for sure is that their death is imminent and they can only guess at what lies beyond the grave.

The world, in its current state of decay, chews its people up and spits them out dazed and confused, but for the chewed up Christian there is always the hope for a much better tomorrow. This is but one of the reasons that most Christians can rejoice and be glad in their troubles. As new Christians begin to understand their undeserved gift of salvation and eternal life, they begin to focus on the hope they have in the Lord, rather than focusing on themselves and what this dying world can give them. We live in a dangerous world that threaten us every day, but with Jesus living in your heart, your troubles will not keep you discouraged or fearful for very long, because just as the rain God sends to sustains us, so too, do the everyday miracles of the Lord's gracious favor.

## A Whisper of Hope

**Walk boldly with Me, dear child...**for I have overcome this fallen world. Do not be afraid or worried, because they take away your joy in living, and the eternal joy to come. Oh, the plans I have for you, plans that you cannot imagine—plans that have no end!

**Romans 8:38**
And I am convinced that nothing can ever separate us from His love.
Death can't, and life can't. The angels can't, and the demons can't.
Our fears for today, our worries about tomorrow,
and even the powers of hell can't keep God's love away. (NLT)

> **My grace is sufficient for you,**
> **for My strength is made perfect in weakness.**
> (2 Corinthians 12:9)

# *"Right Living"*

**Micah 6:8**
He has told you, O man, what is good; and what does
the LORD require of you but to do justice, and to love
kindness, and to walk humbly with your God? (NASB)

What we have in our Creator is a holy and righteous God—a living God who requires people to be holy as He is holy—to be other than that of the world. He calls us to live righteous lives that are gracious and just and motivated by love. But because of our fallen nature it is difficult for us to act justly and to always show kindness to others. We are a selfish, self-centered, and pride filled people who find it hard to humbly believe that we are not in control and are subjected to a higher being, who is the living God who calls us to obedience—to either live His Way and follow His rules, or suffer the consequences. And until you believe and understand who God is and who you are not, you will live in utter darkness until you wake up in the pits of Hell.

It doesn't take a superior mind of great intellect to comprehend the simple Truth of God, it simply takes a humble and contrite heart. Unfortunately, people who have never accepted the Bible as the inherent Word of God that is absolute in its Truth, believe they are the captains of their souls and in charge of their destiny, and it's the ways of the world that they must submit to. For those who deny the existence of God, it's survival of the fittest that fuels their motivation and unbeknownst to them, the Devil is their god. Satan is the God of this world and his ways are pure evil and wickedness. He is the most powerful enemy of God, and he is directing most of the people in this sinful world away from God. Humanism stands against the very fiber of God's holiness, but when the Holy Spirit of God fills the hearts and souls of human beings, their hardened hearts will soften, and living justly and loving others will be their new way of living—walking humbly with our God and living to please Him.

## A Whisper of Hope

**Listen closely, dear child**...and I will teach you a new Way to live. For the ways of this fallen world are deceiving in their nature and will rob from you the joy of living. Don't believe the lies of the Enemy and his wicked followers, because their lies may sound good in the moment, but they are poison to the mind and deadly to the soul.

**2 Chronicles 30:9**
"For the LORD your God is gracious and merciful,
and will not turn His face from you, if you return to Him." (NKJ)

**The LORD is righteous in all His ways and kind in all His works.**
(Psalm 145:17)

# April

# *"Mighty Salvation"*

**Psalm 62:7**
In God is my salvation and my glory;
The Rock of my strength, and my refuge, is in God. (NKJ)

Much like David the giant killer, who wrote this psalm while he was being hunted down to by King Saul, we too have enemies who are hunting us down; enemies we can see and many that we cannot see. Some are looking for the opportunity to take what they can from us, while others want the life of our eternal souls—those evil enemies who are always on the prowl searching for someone to devour and destroy. These enemies of God are constantly looking for ways to draw us into the world of darkness and away from the protection of God's Light. Our limited human strength is no match for Satan and his evil demons, for they are clever, strong, and very motivated to trap us in darkness of our sin. We cannot successfully battle the ways of the Enemy without the help of our Mighty God and Savior, Jesus Christ. There is no greater Warrior than King Jesus my friends, because He has already defeated the power of sin and the darkness of death. His sovereign powers and wisdom are no match for anyone or anything, visible of invisible.

It is our faith in Christ Jesus, the Word of God, and the help of the Holy Spirit that we can shield ourselves from those fiery arrows of Satan that can pierce our hearts and kill our souls. Satan and His powerful forces of evil are devouring the world and all those who belong to it, because Satan knows his time is running out. Your time is quickly winding down, my friends and so is the opportunity to choose God and eternal life. There is no better time than this very moment to stop what you are doing and embrace the gift of salvation from your Savior, for it will save and preserve the precious life that God has so graciously given you, because when you belong to Jesus you are safely in the hands of God.

## Whisper of Hope

**I Am your Rock and Refuge…**always there to protect and do battle for you. You cannot fight alone and live, My child, for the dark forces that are at work in this world are far too powerful. Be strong and be courageous, because this world is being ravaged by the Enemy and I need you to shine God's Light wherever you go and whatever you do.

**Ephesians 6:10-12**
A final word: Be strong with the Lord's mighty power. Put on all of God's
armor so that you will be able to stand firm against all strategies and tricks
of the Devil. For we are not fighting against people made of flesh and blood,
but against the evil rulers and authorities of the powers of darkness who rule
this world, and against wicked spirits in the heavenly realms. (NLT)

**Guard me as the apple of your eye. Hide me in the shadow of Your wings.**
(Psalm 18:8)

# "All You Need"

**Isaiah 46:3-4**
Listen to Me, all you who are left in Israel. I created you and have cared for you since before you were born. I will be your God throughout your lifetime—until your hair is white with age. I made you, and I will care for you. I will carry you along and save you. (NLT)

These words from the Living God were not only for His people Israel at that time in history, but they were also meant of all of God's children throughout the ages—words that not only encourage those who have already put their hope and trust in the Lord God, but to also reveal His Truth to those who do not know Him. The Lord wants everyone to know where they came from and what they can expect from the One who created them. He wants us to know and believe that everything in the heavens and on earth was created by God and for God. Our Creator and Savior, Jesus Christ sustains the universe and everything in it, and He provides everything that every living creature needs. The survival of creation is 100% dependent upon its Creator, and if you think you can live without God, you are either living in complete denial of the Truth or you are living in the darkness so full of yourself that you cannot see the Truth about your humble existence.

God created the universe and mankind for His glory and good pleasure, not the other way around, and our purpose is to live for God and do it in such a way that it brings Him honor and glory. When we humbly surrender to the Truth, the Lord draws us into His Presence where He can personally teach us who He is and how He loves us. If you live apart from the Living God who saved you, you are controlled by your sinful nature and the darkness of Satan. And if you die apart from God, the darkness will swallow you up forever. Most people who live apart from God, like I once did, believe and trust in the world to satisfy their hunger and thirst for life, but at the end of the day, we are left feeling empty, hopeless and confused. Don't live apart from your Creator my friends, because it will steal the joy of living that God has for you—joy that He went to the Cross to provide for you!

## A Whisper of Hope

**Rely on Me, dear child...**for I will provide abundant blessings when you do. Come to Me for protection and I will keep you from being sucked into the darkness of Satan and his fallen world. Embrace Me as your Lord God and Savior, and you will always sleep in peace.

**Colossians 1:16**
For by Him all things were created that are in heaven and that are on earth, visible and invisible, whether thrones or dominions or principalities or powers. All things were created through Him and for Him. (NKJ)

**Draw near to God and He will draw near to you.**
(James 4:8)

# "Darkness to Light"

**Psalm 146: 8**
The LORD sets the prisoners free.
The LORD opens the eyes of the blind.
The LORD lifts the burdens of those bent
beneath their loads. The LORD loves the righteous. (NLT)

The LORD gives graciously to those who are poor in spirit. He provides everything we need for our physical survival and our spiritual health. He sets us free from our bondage to sin and the fear of death. He opens our eyes to the deceitful ways of this fallen world. He is our Burden Bearer so we can rest in His peace. He gives freely, the gift of salvation and eternal life. Everything living depends on God for its very survival. Without His infinite wisdom the hardships of this difficult life would make us crazy. Without His sovereign strength we would never find our way out of the darkness of this evil world—we would never know the Truth. Without the mercy and grace of God, we would have no hope. Without the love of God there would be no reason to live, for without the Father, Son, and Holy Spirit this world would be in total disarray, engulfed in misery and total darkness. Without Jesus our lives would have no lasting value or purpose.

The Lord did not create us and then leave us to our own demise. He is our Father who provides and protects everything He creates, especially His children. When you honor God the Father, and accept the gift of salvation that God the Son paid for with His life, and then trust God the Holy Spirit to direct your life-journey, you will have found the reason you were created—you will have found what it truly means to live! You are no longer a slave to your sinful nature. You are no longer held captive by the fear of our own mortality. When you give God the burdens that continually wear you down and rob your joy, you will experience the peace of God that will get Home safely.

## A Whisper of Hope

**I AM, dear child...**your Light in this dark world. I AM the only Way out of the evil that has gripped this world. I AM your Savior, Protector, and Comforter. I can bear all your burdens and free you up so you can enjoy the life I have given you.

**Matthew 11:30**
Then Jesus said, "Come to Me, all of you who are weary
and carry heavy burdens, and I will give you rest. (NLT)

**God is Light and there is no darkness in Him at all.**
(1 John 1:5)

# "Holy God"

**Isaiah 57:15**
The high and lofty One who inhabits eternity, the Holy One, says this:
"I live in that high and holy place with those whose spirits are contrite and
humble. I refresh the humble and give new courage to those with repentant hearts." (NLT)

Our Holy God is always faithful to His children. He is the only Father that keeps His every promise. He faithfully watches over His children because He wants to keep them safe from this dark and wicked world that wants only to destroy what belongs to God. And for those of us who have surrendered our lives to the Lord, we belong to Him. When He was murdered and punished for our sins, He defeated the sting of sin and broke its power over us. And when our Savior was resurrected from the grave and ascended back into Heaven, He not only defeated eternal death for us, but He also sent the Holy Spirit to help expose the lies of the world and to help us fight against the enemies of God. We have a powerful Savior, my friends, a gracious and loving God who comforts us when we fail, gives us courage when we are afraid, and strengthens us to fight the everyday battles for our hearts and minds.

It takes a deep desire and a sincere commitment to follow God. It takes a humble and contrite heart to live a holy life. The change from sinfulness to godliness is not an easy one to make, because we enjoy our sin and it's hard to give it up. Changing the way you think and act from a fallen world view to a Christian world view is indeed a difficult road to travel, because the wicked ways that consume this world are a powerful force to be reckoned with, and one that is difficult to sever. But with the resurrection power of God, the victory over sin and death is for anyone who will humble themselves before the Lord and crucify their old life of sin on His Cross!

## A Whisper of Hope

**Hold on to Me...**dear child, because I never fail, and I will never forsake you or let you go. I will give you rest and refresh you, for I know firsthand the weariness that this life-journey brings. Take My hand and I will walk you safely Home where you belong.

**Deuteronomy 7:9**
"Therefore know that the LORD your God, He is God,
the faithful God who keeps covenant and mercy for a thousand
generations with those who love Him and keep His commandments." (NKJ)

**God is our refuge and strength, always ready to help in times of trouble.**
(Psalm 46:1)

# *"Joy In Living"*

**Psalm 30:1, 12**
I will praise You, LORD, for you have rescued me.
You refused to let my enemies triumph over me.
O, LORD my God, I will give You thanks forever!

What an honor and privilege it is to be able to sing this song in truth. What an incredible blessing it is to know that the victory is yours no matter how this fallen world tries to hurt or discourage you. All of God's children have a glorious future ahead of them—one so glorious that our finite minds can't even begin to comprehend. Our God is not only the Creator, but He is our Savior as well; One who loved His creation so much that He had a plan in place before He created the world—one that would save us from the grips of eternal death and damnation, and give us a glorious new life that would never end. Our God is a mighty and gracious Savior, who is our faithful Shepherd, because He neither grows weary or gives up searching for those who are lost and want to be found. And when He finds them, He does whatever it takes to bring them Home safely.

There are many lost souls, like myself, who have had the Enemy come within striking distance of completely destroying our lives, our hope, and our souls. What an amazing joy it brings when you know that all of your sins have been forgiven and forgotten by the God of creation. It is the inner joy of forgiveness and redemption that makes a Christian stand apart from the rest of the world, because just as Christ Jesus was resurrected from the grave and given a glorious new body that is void of pain, suffering, death and decay, so too, will all those who live in His Name. Our eternal new life in the new Heaven on earth will be void of sin and its consequences and everyone will be abundantly happy without tears of frustration and grief. It will be a glorious eternal life because we will be walking hand in hand with God in the light of the Son. There is nothing of this world, nor is there anyone but Christ Jesus that has the ability to fill us with this kind of joy. It is only through the amazing grace and living sacrifice of our Lord God and Savior that we can experience true and lasting joy while living in a world that is consumed with the pleasures of sin.

## A Whisper of Hope

**Shout for joy, dear child...**singing songs of thanks and praise to your Savior. I came to into this dark world, not to judge, but to save. I came to suffer and die so you could escape the decadence and find peace for your soul and joy in your heart. This Good News is for all people, especially for those who are looking for joy in all the wrong places.

**Isaiah 61:10**
I am overwhelmed with joy in the LORD my God!
For He has dressed me in the clothing OF salvation
and draped me in a robe of righteousness. (NLT)

**I will turn their mourning into joy.**
(Jeremiah 31:13)

# "One Voice"

**Zechariah 10:2**
Household gods give false advice, fortunetellers predict only lies,
and interpreters of dreams pronounce comfortless falsehoods. So my
people are wandering like lost sheep, without a shepherd to protect and guide them. (NLT)

Much like it was in Zechariah's day, people are still turning to the many false gods of this fallen world, rather than turning to the only True and Living God. These false gods of Satan's and his band of followers are still at work today, filling hearts and minds with lies that are detrimental to our everyday lives and our spiritual health. There are billions of people today who still rely on fortunetellers, Tara cards, séances, and other such nonsense. Millions of people put their faith in written horoscopes found in daily secular newspapers, and many others join religious cults, rather than seriously looking into the only Reliable Source for the Truth. The Word of God is the only Source for the Absolute truth—Truth that is not twisted and reshaped to fit our sinful lifestyles; Truth that is righteous and just and never changes with the times. The Truth is the only Way to escape the decadence of this dying world to live an eternal life as it was created. The Truth is the Lord our God, Jesus Christ.

The precise balance of creation that makes it possible for our very existence lies in the Almighty hands of the Living God. Every breath we take is at the mercy and grace of our Creator, not by chance. The Lord God is both Creator and the Author of life and His purpose is much greater than just satisfying our selfish human passions. But in order to discover the true purpose for our existence we must turn to our Creator and learn why we were created. This fallen world has an endless supply of falsehoods and frivolous ways to obtain truth, happiness, and peace of mind, but they are all lies and schemes of Satan and he is sucking the life out of this world and dragging it into the depths of darkness. The Devil is leading the lost straight into Hell with his lies and false gods. Don't follow him and this world my friend, instead, follow the Good Shepherd into the safety of His fold, where He will heal your wounds and lead you to better pasture; a real place where you can feed on His every Word of truth and live as you have never lived before.

## A Whisper of Hope

**Listen to My Word...**dear child, for they are the words of life. Don't listen to the many false voices of this fallen world, for they are words of death and will lead you into a darkness you will never escape from. There are many false shepherds whose smooth sounding voices will lead you astray, but My voice will lead you into the glory of Heaven and eternal life!

**Jeremiah 23:30-32**
"Therefore," says the LORD, "I stand against these prophets who get their messages from each other—these smooth-tongued prophets who say, 'This prophecy is from the LORD!' Their imaginary dreams are flagrant lies that lead my people into sin." (NLT)

**Today you must listen to His voice. Don't harden your hearts against Him.**
(Hebrews 3:7)

# "It's God's Glory"

**Malachi 2:1-2**
"And now, O priest, this commandment is for you. If you will not hear, and if you will not take it to heart to give glory to My name," says the LORD of hosts, "I will send a curse upon you, and I will curse your blessings. Yes, I have cursed them already, because you do not take it to heart." (NKJ)

Even though this message from the LORD was given pacifically to the corrupt priests of Judah who were using their influence to satisfy their own greed, I believe it is also for those of us who profess our faith in Christ, because Christians are priests, and we are held accountable in our spheres of influence. This especially holds true for the leaders of the Church, whom the Lord has called to shepherd His flock. Because of the moral decline in America, the Church is also infected and combined they are causing our country to suffer, which is a perfect example of God's judgment. The Lord has exposed many Christian leaders and priests in our country who have defiled God's name by their corruption, immoral living, and false doctrine teaching; ushering in God's curse.

All the turmoil that has engulfed this world are the consequences of moral decay and a worldwide rebellion against the Lord and His Church. This rebellion and its consequences are running their course, my friends, just as God's Word has been telling us for thousands of years. But there is Hope, for we have a Savior in Jesus Christ our Lord. He is our ticket out of this hellish world that is dominated by Satan and those he enslaves. Our Savior will return, not to save us, but to eliminate the evil and all who follow it, ushering in the last age of time. Our King will create a new Heaven and a new earth where we will spend living in the Presence of our awesome God forever.

## A Whisper of Hope

**Honor Me, dear child…**by living a holy life. When you do, I am on your side. When you don't, I am against you. I paid a hefty price to bring you into My Presence and I command you to live in My Way, for it is the only Way to escape the punishment you deserve. Your obedience will not make your journey any easier, but you can be confident in its heavenly destination.

**1 Thessalonians 4:16-17**
For the Lord Himself will come down from heaven with a commanding shout, with the call of the archangel, and with the trumpet call of God. First, all the Christians who have died will rise from their graves. Then, together with them, we who are still alive and remain on the earth will be caught up in the clouds to meet the Lord in the air and remain with Him forever. (NLT)

**And He who sits on the throne said, "Behold, I am making all things new."**
(Revelation 21:5)

# "No Barrier"

**1 Samuel 6:20**
Who is able to stand in the presence
of the LORD, this holy God?" they cried out. (NLT)

There are absolute laws of the universe that God created, which not only hold creation together, but also set the standards for how we should live. All of God's laws are absolute and they will only change if He changes them. We must accept these laws and live by them whether we want to or not, or whether we believe them or not. But there is one absolute that is critical for us to know and believe, because our future is at stake. No sin can be in the Presence of our Holy God—we must be holy and without blemish to be with God, to plead for forgiveness or to simply ask for His help. And it's because of this absolute law that our Lord God left the glory of Heaven to live as a man of flesh and blood to become our sin. Jesus paid the price to bring down the barrier between God and man. Now, we can again be in the Presence of our Holy God at any time or any place. This selfless act of absolute love became the righteous covering for anyone who wants it.

God's standards are high and without Jesus it would be impossible for us to meet those standards. What an amazing, life-saving gift this is my friends, for we were once dead in our sin and separated from God, but we are now alive in Christ and cleansed by His blood. We can now come to God as we are and not be struck down or ignored, but forgiven and loved! The Spirit of God is at work in our world and living in His children. He hears our every cry and feels our every pain. He comforts the uneasy, loves the unlovable, and forgives the unforgivable. We have a gracious God who wants no one to suffer in the eternal darkness of Hell. We have a Father in Heaven, our Savior at His side, and the power of His Holy Spirit to guide us Home. The world tries to convince us otherwise, but only Jesus is the Way, the Truth, and the Life. So enter into Heaven's Most Holy Place with the Most High God, for there is no barrier to keep you from His Holiness because of the precious blood of Christ.

## A Whisper of Hope

**Come into My Presence, dear** child...and let's spend some time together, for your sin is hidden in Me. But one day I will take you into My garden where we can sit and talk Face to face awhile. But until then, you must live this difficult life covered by My blood, trusting in the absolute Truth.

**Hebrews 10:19-20**
And so, dear brothers and sisters, we can boldly enter heaven's Most Holy Place
because of the blood of Jesus. This is the new, life-giving way that Christ
has opened up for us through the sacred curtain, by means of His death for us. (NLT)

**"I am the Way...No one can come to the Father except through Me"**
(John 14:6)

# *"Broken"*

**Psalm 50:13-14**
I don't need the bulls you sacrifice; I don't need the blood
of goats. What I want instead is your true thanks to God; I
want you to fulfill your vows to the Most High. (NLT)

The LORD no longer requires us to kill innocent animals as a sacrifice for our sins because the blood of Jesus was the final sin offering for everyone. But what God requires is for people to nail their old life of sin to the Cross of Christ and be born again to live in repentance and thanksgiving to God. It's far better to put our old life of sin to death and receive the power of the Holy Spirit to help us live in obedience to God, rather than killing animals and relying on our own power to defeat our sinful behavior. All of humanity has a sinful nature and we live in a fallen world that embraces sin and the ways of Satan and combined, they hold us in bondage to sin and death. Only the blood of Christ can cleanse our sin and only the resurrection power of God can keep us clean.

There is only One God and He is the only One who can forgive our sins. There is only one sacrifice for the complete atonement for sin and only one Savior who can fix our broken lives and our broken world, and He is the Author and Finisher of Life, Jesus Christ. Although the death and resurrection of Jesus is ours as well, God does not force it upon anyone; we must make the decision to either live God's way or the world's way. If you choose God's Way and submit your life to God He will direct the rest of your life-journey in ways that may not be the easiest road to follow, but when traveled in faith, will guarantee you a healed heart that is filled with the love of Jesus and honor and thanksgiving to the Lord God who saved your eternal life, and promised a perfect world that is not broken.

## A Whisper of Hope

**I AM the Great I AM**...the Living God. Whenever you exalt My Name above all other names, you have My full attention. Whenever you come to Me as your Savior, you can be sure of My life-saving Power. Fear and doubt and weakness are a part of your fallen nature, but when you sacrifice your old sinful life to Me and live in thanksgiving and repentance, I will direct your path so that you can travel confidently Homeward bound.

**Psalm 51:17**
The sacrifice You want is a broken spirit. A broken
and repentant heart, O God, you will not despise. (NLT)

Obedience is far better than sacrifice.<br>(1 Samuel 15:22)

# "Heart View"

**1 Samuel 16:7**
But the LORD said to Samuel, "Do not look at his appearance or at the height
of his stature, because I have rejected him; for God sees not as man sees, for
man looks at the outward appearance, but the LORD looks at the heart." (NASB)

Because Saul (Israel's first king) had openly defied God's commands, the LORD told Samuel to anoint a new king for His people. And like most humans, Samuel was looking at the outward appearance of the men He had to choose from. Samuel had to go through them all to find God's choice and He was the youngest and the smallest, but David would become a man after God's own heart and Israel's greatest King. We cannot hide or conceal anything from God. He knows everything about us—He knows what we think and He knows what is in our hearts. We can deceive other people by our words, looks and behavior, but not so with God. God knows all of our faults and failures and how wicked and rebellious we are, yet He suffered and died to make us righteous and blameless. Our Savior searches for the many desperate hearts that are lost in the darkness of this wicked world. The LORD reaches into the deepest depths of our being and gives most of us many chances to be rescued, even though most of us don't even realize how desperately we need to be rescued.

As part of our fallen human nature, we are all guilty of judging other people by their appearance or mannerisms before we even have the opportunity to know them. And many times after we get to know them, we like them, and then find ourselves ashamed of how we pre-judged their character. How blessed we are that our Living God is not like us, for if He were, we would not have a chance to be redeemed. If God were to judge us by our looks and actions, we would all be hopelessly lost in the darkness without a clue to our destruction and eternal separated from our awesome God.

## A Whisper of Hope

**Come, My child...**to the only One who knows you completely. I know just what you need and when you need it. I know when you are lost and confused and searching for answers that you so desperately need. I know when you are sad and lonely and in dire need of My peace. I know you inside and out.

**Proverbs 2:6-8**
For the LORD grants wisdom! From His mouth come knowledge
and understanding. He grants a treasure of good sense to the godly.
He is their shield, protecting those who walk with integrity. He guards
the paths of justice and protects those who are faithful to Him. (NLT)

**For You formed my inward parts; You wove me in my mother's womb.**
(Psalm 139:13)

# *"Stand by Me"*

**Psalm 62:5-6**
I wait quietly before God, for my hope is in Him.
He alone is my Rock and my salvation, my Fortress
where I will not be shaken. (NLT)

Because we are a fallen people, it's a struggle for many of us to wait quietly for God; to be patient and confident that the Lord is both willing and able to help, especially when we are on the verge of giving up. As finite human beings we are limited to what we can accomplish, but not so with God, because He has no limits. Many times we can find ourselves helpless against the circumstances of this fallen world, and without God's power and grace we succumb to the pressure and want to just give up. But with God's help and our steadfast faith that God is God, we gain the courage and strength to wait patiently for God's good and perfect will to be done. To have this kind of faith does not come naturally nor does it happen overnight, because it is our human nature to be leery of trusting anyone, especially One that we cannot see, touch, or audibly hear.

The way we grow in our faith and trust in the Lord is by getting to know who He is and what He can do. And the way we do this is by reading the living Word of God and asking the Holy Spirit to reveal its Truth. When you learn and understand the absolute Truth, you will begin to believe in the sovereign power that God has over creation; that the Lord our God and Savior is in charge and directing the events of man to complete His redemptive plan. And His plans are both incredible and out of this world—plans for a perfect future—plans that have no end. When you build your life on God, the solid Rock of our foundation, you will systemically grow in your faith to trust the Lord with all things, especially during the raging storms of this unpredictable life!

## A Whisper of Hope

**Stand by Me...**My child, for I Am the only Solid Rock on which to build your life. A Place of protection; a Safe Haven from this savaged world that wants to kill and destroy you. When you stand by Me, I will direct your life-journey and lead you in all Truth.

**Jeremiah 29:11**
"For I know the plans I have for you," says the LORD.
"They are plans for good and not for disaster, to give you a future and a hope." (NLT)

**Wait for the Lord, and He will save you.**
(Proverbs 20:22)

# *"Peace in Salvation"*

**Psalm 68:19**
Blessed be the Lord, who daily bears our burden,
the God who is our salvation. (NASB)

For Christians who have surrendered their lives to the Lord of Creation and are relying on Him to guide them, it becomes quite natural to give the Lord thanks and praise for all He has done and continues to do, but most pacifically, for the saving grace of salvation that no one deserves nor could ever accomplish on their own. As a believer in the Way and the Truth, we know that Christ Jesus is not only the Lord God and Savior of the world, but He is also our own personal Savior as well. We fully trust in the death and resurrection of Christ Jesus as our own and are cleansed of sin so we can live in His Presence now and forever. Faith in the Cross at Calvary will remove your fears about death and give you the peace to rest in the weariness of living in this cruel and unfair world that is constantly trying to beat you into submission to its dark and evil ways. If you have sincerely accepted the gift of salvation that the Lord God personally paid for with His life's blood, the best you can give Him in return is a life of repentance, always living in thanksgiving and praise. It delights the Lord whenever we surrender to His will and humbly open our hearts to His healing touch.

It honors God greatly and brings glory to His Name when we live in repentance and do it with thankful hearts regardless of our circumstances. By living this difficult life-journey in faith knowing that God is near and protecting you from the evil forces of darkness, you gain a heavenly peace that will enable you to praise God, anytime and anywhere. How blessed we are to have a personal God who walks with His children every day and keeps them safe through the night. How blessed we are to have a Savior who takes us as we are and cleanses us from our sins. We have so many reasons to praise and worship the One True God who formed us in our mother's womb, but it is our salvation from the hellish price of unrepentant sin that we should be most thankful for, because without it, living this life would not be worth the trouble, and it would have a terrible ending as well.

## A Whisper of Hope

**You honor Me, My child…**with a heart of thanksgiving, a moment of praise, and by living a repentant life. Without Me your future would be very dark indeed. But when you embrace My Truth and My Way, your entire life-journey with Me is directed with holy precision. Although the journey is never easy, the rewards for your faith are great and forever.

**1 Thessalonians 5:16-18**
Rejoice always. Keep on praying. No matter what happens,
always be thankful, for this is God's will for you who belong to Christ Jesus. (NLT)

**When a man's ways are pleasing to the LORD,**
**He makes even his enemies to be at peace with him.**
(Proverbs 16:7)

# *"Impossible Prayer"*

**Daniel 2:19-20**
Then the mystery was revealed to Daniel in a night vision. Then Daniel
blessed the God of heaven; Daniel answered and said, "Let the name of
God be blessed forever and ever, for wisdom and power belong to Him." (NASB)

Our Sovereign Lord God is the One who spoke the universe into existence and created all that exists. This same Mighty God also delights and takes a personal interest in the lives of all those who belong to Him and call Him Father. Because of God's greatness, He sees and hears every desperate cry and every whispered plea from the mouths of all suffering people, especially those with a loyal heart for Him. And just as Daniel prayed for deliverance, all Christians everywhere have this same awesome power that prayer in faith can unlock. Our prayers become a mighty tool for all believers who are humble of heart and serve the Lord. For our God can work any miracle at any time for anyone. There is absolutely nothing that our Living God cannot do or control, both in the physical realm as well as in the spiritual realm. And this, my friends, when realized and believed in, can do miraculous wonders for anyone who prays to the Lord in faith.

If God can answer Daniel's impossible request, so too, can God answer your seemingly impossible prayers as well. If it is God's will to do so and it is good for you, He will answer in His own time and in His own way and all you must do is believe. But in the interim we must continue to praise our God with thanksgiving no matter what our circumstances are. The Lord God is our Heavenly Father and our personal Savior who loves and desires the best for you. You can trust the Lord with your life, my friend, because He gave His so you could keep yours. So go to your God and Savior in Heaven while you can, for when you do you can be sure that whatever answer He gives will be forever in your favor!

## A Whisper of Hope

**Talk to Me, My child...** for when you do I will listen, for I want what is best for you. Trust in Me and I will help you find the best answer to your prayer! I will never give you anything that is bad for you, because of My undying faithfulness.

**Jeremiah 32:17**
Ah Lord God! Behold, You have made the heavens and the earth by
Your great power and outstretched arm! Nothing is too hard for You. (NKJ)

**Don't worry about anything; instead, pray about everything.**
(Philippians 4:6)

# "God Saves"

**Daniel 6: 25-27**
Then King Darius sent this message to the people of every race
and nation and language throughout the world: "Peace and prosperity to you!
I decree that everyone throughout my kingdom should tremble with fear
before the God of Daniel. For He is the Living God, and He will endure forever.
His kingdom will never be destroyed, and His rule will never end.
He rescues and saves His people;
He performs miraculous signs and wonders in the heavens and on earth.
He has rescued Daniel from the power of the lions." (NLT)

Throughout the ages of mankind God has been actively involved in the lives of people. He has directed the course of history to fulfill His redemptive plan for mankind and His creation. We know this because the inerrant Word of God tells us so. All words found in Scripture are God inspired words, and therefore, speak the absolute truth because God cannot be otherwise and be God. Just as it was in biblical times, our Gracious God is still working His miracles today, protecting and saving His people from the jaws of Satan, who is always on the prowl searching for some poor, unprotected soul to attack and trap in his web of lies and darkness. Dear souls, without the power of the Savior, all peoples of this fallen world are unprotected and easy game for the Destroyer, and every precious soul would suffer the sting of sin and the final wrath of God.

But when you know and believe the Truth, you will gain a healthy fear, because every child of the Living God knows the full story of mankind, and that should motivate anyone with common sense to turn away from the clever lies of the Enemy—lies that are sucking this evil world into the deepest depths of darkness unknown. Don't be sucked in with the world, my friends; instead, focus on the Truth of God, for it is the only way that you will escape the coming night that will be so dark and so deep and so hopeless that you will never find your way out no matter how sorry you are! Know the Truth and live according to His Way, for it will save you from being swallowed up in darkness, forever separated from the Light of the glory of God and all His goodness.

## A Whisper of Hope

**Walk with Me...**my child, for I Am your Great Protector. There is nothing I cannot do. The power I hold over creation is absolute. The authority of My inerrant Word is something that you can stake your eternal life on. It never changes and gives you the power to overcome this wicked world which thrives on the Devil's lies and your demise.

**James 1:21**
So get rid of all the filth and evil in your lives, and humbly accept the message
God has planted in your hearts, for it is strong enough to save your souls. (NLT)

**For You are God, O Sovereign LORD. Your Words are Truth.**
(2 Samuel 7:28)

# *"You Need Jesus"*

**John 17:1-3**

Jesus spoke these words, lifted up His eyes to heaven and said: "Father, the hour has come. Glorify Your Son, that Your Son also may glorify You, as You have given Him authority over all flesh, that He should give eternal life to as many as You have given Him. And this is eternal life, that they may know You, the only true God, and Jesus Christ whom You have sent. (NKJ)

Before the Lord Jesus Christ took His disciples into the garden of Gethsemane on the Mount of Olives where He allowed Himself to be arrested and later executed , He prayed to the Father in Heaven on behalf of Himself, His disciples, and for the believers who would go out into the world to spread the Good News and form His Church. Jesus is now our High Priest, the One who intercedes before God on our behalf. It is only the blood of the Perfect Lamb covering our sins that we can enter into the Holy Presence of God. There is no other Way to be saved from the fiery pits of Hell. Our good deeds won't get it done, nor will our good behavior. We cannot buy our salvation, nor can we fool God to get it.

The only Way to Heaven is through the death and resurrection of Jesus Christ, our Lord God and Savior. We must put to death our old life of sin and be born again in Spirit and Truth to a new life. And just as the power of God raised Christ from the grave, so, too, will all those who are born again into God's family. No one will get through the gates of Heaven stained with sin. No one will get past the final judgment without the blood of Jesus covering their sins. To get the crown of eternal life my friend, you need Jesus, because without Him, you belong to the Devil.

## A Whisper of Hope

**I Am your Hope and Salvation, dear child**...the only One who can bring you into the Glory of God's Holy Presence forever. All other ways are lies to deceive you. Don't be fooled by this fallen world, for I Am the Way, the Truth, and the only Savior for your eternal soul.

**1 Timothy 2:3-6**

This is good and pleases God our Savior, for He wants everyone to be saved and to understand the truth. For there is only one God and one Mediator who can reconcile God and people. He is the man Christ Jesus. He gave His life to purchase freedom for everyone. This is the message that God gave to the world at the proper time. (NLT)

> **Therefore, having been justified by faith,**
> **we have peace with God through our Lord Jesus Christ.**
> (Romans 5:1)

# *"Worthy Peace"*

**Psalm 86:15**
But You, O Lord, are a God of compassion and mercy,
slow to get angry and filled with unfailing love and faithfulness. (NLT)

Our Lord God is gracious and merciful to us because He knows how weak we are when it comes to fighting our temptations to sin. Because of our sinful condition, most people ignore the ways of God to indulge in the pleasures of sin, whether in ignorance or prideful defiance. Even though the hearts of mankind are dark and filled with evil, our gracious God provided the Way that would satisfy His anger and cover the sins that would eventually destroy us. But even though God's Son died for our sins, our rebellion against the Most High God is still the way of most people in this fallen world. God has been patient, gracious, and merciful to the people of this fallen world, but His patience is running thin, and one day He will put an end to all the rebellion and evil that has cost so many people the very lives of their souls.

God offers us the gift of salvation and it would behoove you to accept it while you can and seek His forgiveness, because with God's Truth and Spirit living in you, you will defeat many of the temptations to sin. Our weakness to sin is our fallen nature, but the blood of Jesus has covered our sins and given us the Way to defeat the power of sin and the fear of death. The fight against the forces of evil is futile and hopeless without the divine power of God, because there is no One mightier, more compassionate, or more forgiving than our Lord God and Savior, Jesus Christ. And when this truth is written on your heart you will be clean and free from the power of sin. And that my friend, is a peace worth having.

## A Whisper of Hope

**I Am your Redeemer...**My child, the only One you can trust with your life. There is no Power greater than Mine—it is your eternal life-line. I Am the only Way you can defeat sin and avoid Hell. This is the Truth, it's My Word, and this is My Promise to you.

**Romans 7:24, 25**
Oh, what a miserable person I am!
Who will free me from this life that is dominated by sin?
Thank God! The answer is in Jesus Christ our Lord. (NLT)

**God has purchased our freedom with His blood and has forgiven all our sins.**
(Colossians 1:14)

# *"No Bounds"*

**Daniel 9:18, 19**
O my God, listen to me and hear my request...We do not ask because
we deserve help, but because you are so merciful...O Lord, hear. O
Lord, forgive. O Lord, listen and act! O my God, do not delay... (NLT)

As Christians, our prayer life is an intricate part of building an everlasting relationship with God. It pleases the Lord when we earnestly pray to Him, it means that we believe in His sovereignty. The Lord God is our Creator and whether we choose to admit it or not, our lives depend on Him. Without God's Sovereign Word the universe would be nothing but a mass of disorder and chaos where nothing tangible could ever exist. I believe the reason many people pray to God as a last resort is because deep within they know He is their only Hope. Our God is who He says He is. He is the Creator and can do all things. Nothing is impossible for God. He is in charge of everything and there is nothing in either the physical or spiritual realm that is beyond His sovereign control.

When we humbly surrender our sin-filled lives in faith-filled prayer, we are telling the Lord that we are relying on His sovereignty, His wisdom, His unconditional love and compassion, His abundant mercy and abounding grace, His overwhelming goodness and His all consuming power. He creates everything we need to survive both physically and spiritually in this world, so we can experience the new world to come. The Lord knows that our lives depend on Him and when we come to Him in prayer, whether it is in desperation or thanksgiving, we can be sure that He hears our every word. Don't shut God out of your life my friend, for He is the only One you can fully trust and the only One who can give you exactly what you need. Our God's power and wisdom are boundless.

## A Whisper of Hope

**Pray in faith, dear one...** for I hear all that you think and say. And when you pray in faith, you can trust that I will answer in a way that is best for you. When your faith is centered on Me, you have a future that exceeds anything you can possibly imagine, because in Me everything is possible!

**Luke 11:11-13**
You fathers—if your children ask for a fish, do you give them a snake instead?
Or if they ask for an egg, do you give them a scorpion? Of course not! If you
sinful people know how to give good gifts to your children, how much more will
your heavenly Father give the Holy Spirit to those who ask Him. (NLT)

**And all things, whatever you ask in prayer, believing, you will receive.**
(Matthew 21:22)

# *"Our Great God"*

**Psalm 95:2-3**
Let us come to Him with thanksgiving. Let us sing psalms of praise
to Him. For the LORD is a great God, a great King above all gods. (NLT)

This psalm like many of the psalms in Scripture, are psalms of praise and thanksgiving to the God of creation—the Shepherd of our lost lives and the Savior for our condemned souls. The Bible is the story of God—His Mighty Power to create and sustain, His Incredible Love for mankind and His creation, and His Merciful Plan for our redemption and undeserved salvation. These are just a few of the incredible attributes that makes up our Living God—attributes that are praiseworthy no matter what our circumstances may be.

When the Lord first me rescued me from the deep darkness that had griped my life it was not easy to praise Him for anything, because the entire sum of my life had brought me to the brink of destruction. It was extremely difficult for me to praise the God who had allowed so much pain and tragedy and depression in my life, not to mention all the suffering of mankind since the dawn of time. Because of my limited knowledge of God, I had little desire to know Him. But that all changed when He finally opened my eyes to the Truth and I saw how He saved my life and soul time and time again. I learned why He came into this wicked world and voluntarily gave His life as the final sacrificial Lamb of God who saved the world from its sin.

As we grow to trust God's Word, we began to understand how everything in God's creation will in time, reflect and speak of His glory—that we ,His created human beings, were created in His image for the sole purpose of glorifying His greatness. When you know the Truth your eyes will be opened and in His glorious ways, you will be transformed from paganism to godliness, from pridefulness to humbleness, from hopelessness to joyfulness, and from fearfulness to peacefulness.

## A Whisper of Hope

**Be joy filled, My child…**even when this world brings you down. Lasting joy can only be found in Me, for the little joy you find in this world does not last and quickly fades away. When you bring glory and honor to Me with your life, I will honor you and bring glory to you as well.

**Revelation 4:11**
You are worthy, O lord our God, to receive glory and honor and power.
For you created everything and it is for your pleasure that they exist and were created. (NLT)

**But I will honor only those who honor Me.**
(1 Samuel 2:30)

# *"Unseen Belief"*

**John 20:29**
Then Jesus told him, "You believe because you have seen Me.
Blessed are those who haven't seen Me and believe anyway." (NLT)

The perfect world does not yet exist, and for the time being we must live in a fallen world that is dominated by the unseen powers of evil. Because of our fallen state most people only believe what they can see, disregarding the things they cannot and deeming the unseen realm as myth or foolishness. Probably the best example of this is the fact that we are living amidst a very real and a very dangerous spiritual battle for our hearts, souls, and minds, but most people could care less. Many people just live for the moment and simply ignore the spiritual battle of good and evil. I often wonder how many times the words "I'll have to see it to believe it" have been spoken throughout the ages. I believe there are even many Christians today who also struggle with the reality of the unseen world, wishing that Jesus would just show Himself and that would remove the doubt.

But I also believe there are many desperate people that are like I was, so lost and so hopeless and have so given up on life that they reach out in blind faith to grab hold of anything, visible or invisible that would offer them some hope, unsure of the only invisible Hope they have. And for many this is their last chance—the final option, for all other options have come and gone—all having the same disappointing, unfulfilling, failed results. Because everything from this fallen world is infected with sin and death, it can only offer us more of the same. The world with all its resources will never be able to fulfill the deepest desires of our hearts, because God designed us that way. My dear friend, until our Lord God and Savior physically returns in His glorified body you must believe in His Word and trust that He is working behind the scenes and directing the spiritual realm in your favor and that one day soon you will be able to see and touch and hear our Glorious God and Savior, Jesus Christ.

## A Whisper of Hope

**Believe, My child...**For I Am the only Hope you have in this world of hopelessness. One day your earthly life will end, but until that time you must trust in the path that I have paved for you; a righteous path that requires steadfast faith in Me, your Savior, and know that I am with you always!

**Ephesians 6:12**
For we are not fighting against people made of flesh and blood,
but against the evil rulers and authorities of the unseen world,
against those mighty powers of darkness who rule this world,
and against wicked spirits in the heavenly realms. (NLT)

**What is faith? It is evidence of things we cannot yet see.**
(Hebrews 11:1)

# "Eternal Promise"

**Psalm 119:49-50**
Remember Your promise to me, for it is my only hope.
Your promise revives me; it comforts me in all my troubles. (NLT)

There is no greater hope than the promise of a perfect eternal life--a gift from our Creator and God of our salvation, Christ Jesus. There is no promise under Heaven that is more encouraging for our world weary souls, because it gives us both the peace and the strength to persevere the troubles we all must suffer in this hard and unpredictable world dominated by evil. There is no better future than the eternal future provided by the Son of God who offered His perfect, sinless life as the final sacrifice that took away the sins of the world. Our gracious and merciful God did this because it was the only way for the complete atonement of sin that is needed to save us from the eternal condemnation we deserve. And when this selfless act of sacrificial love is written on your heart and embedded deep within your soul, your life will be changed forever. You will begin to depend on the Living God and He will help you transition from a life of sin and rebellion, to a life of righteousness and godly living—from a fallen world view to a Christ centered world view—from a decaying state of promised death to a joyful state of promised eternal life.

This new life in Christ will change from self-seeking pleasure, to seeking pleasure for others. You will focus on the eternal values of life, rather than the temporal pleasures of a dying world. You will learn the Absolutes of God's Truth that will expose the lies of this evil world so you can live as you have never lived before—with lasting joy, eternal hope, and the peace of God in all your circumstance. The Good News of eternal life through the death and resurrection of Christ Jesus is sadly rejected by most people who will life this live without knowing the joy of the Lord's Promise; who will then slip into their graves, never to see the light again. But for the children of the Living God there comes the sweet breath of a new and everlasting life, never knowing the darkness of the grave.

## A Whisper of Hope

**I Am your only Hope…**dear child, because the hope from this world is fading away into darkness. The hope of this fallen world is false hope that promises you nothing but disappointment—hope that never satisfies. Don't spend your life searching for something that this world cannot give you, for you will end up with the only thing it can promise you…death and darkness.

**Titus:2:11-13**
For the grace of God has been revealed, bringing salvation to all people. And we are instructed to turn from godless living and sinful pleasures. We should live in this evil world with self-control, right conduct, and devotion to God, while we look forward with hope to that wonderful day when the glory our great God and Savior, Jesus Christ, will be revealed. (NLT)

**But we are looking forward to the new heavens and new earth He has promised.**
(2 Peter 3:13)

# *"Hearts of Hope"*

**Psalm 119:81-82**
My soul faints for Your salvation,
But I hope in Your word. (NKJ)

As in the heart of the psalmist who penned these words, so, too, do our hearts and souls long for God to deliver us from this hard and difficult life. We long for that perfect peace and harmony that can only be found in our Great God and Savior, Jesus Christ. We long for a life without pain and sickness and even death—times of peace without wars and killing. We long to be set free from our doubts and fears that keep us bound in the chains of sin, which takes away the true joy of living. And just as God's people, Israel, cried out for God to save them, so, too, do many hopeless people cry out in desperation and fear to be saved from the decadence that surrounds them—crying out to be delivered from their days of darkness, pleading for help and hoping there is a just God.

Our Lord God and Savior, Jesus Christ saved us from the curse and the plunge into Hell. Jesus paid the full price for our forgiveness and salvation ushering in His redemptive plan for man. We now have the New Testament in our hands and the Holy Spirit in our hearts. And we know that the Great Day of the Lord is drawing near, when the King of the universe will put an end to evil and sin and create a new Heaven and earth where we will live in peace and in fellowship with the Living God. Unlike the days of old, we now have a new covenant and the clarity of God's Plan in writing. We know that our Savior will soon return and that my friend is our hope. The hour is rapidly approaching, and it's time to prepare and share the Good News of salvation, for the Lord wants no one left behind.

## A Whisper of Hope

**There is Hope, My child...**your salvation has been purchased with My blood. The price has been paid in full, for I Am the Perfect Sacrificial Lamb who gave His life to save your soul. Now sleep in peace! For I AM near.

**Romans 8:16**
For His Holy Spirit speaks to us deep in our hearts and tells us that
we are God's children. And since we are His children, we will share
His treasures—for everything God gives to His Son, Christ, is ours, too. (NLT)

**Your faith and hope can be placed confidently in God.**
(1 Peter 1:21)

# "Greatest of Gifts"

**Romans 8:3**
The Law of Moses could not save us, because of our sinful nature. But God put into effect a different plan to save us. He sent His own Son in a human body like ours, except that ours are sinful. God destroyed sin's control over us by giving His Son as a sacrifice for our sins. (NLT)

There is no greater gift than our undeserved salvation that our Lord God, Christ Jesus purchased for everyone. It is a glorious gift of complete forgiveness from our perfectly just and loving God. It's by receiving this wonderful gift that we are given a new life, for the old sinful life is nailed to the Cross to die and our new, redeemed life is graciously ushered in. Like so many people, I was trapped in the darkness of sin, cursing God for my existence, and wishing I was never born. And as my life was ebbing away, the Lord came searching and I unexpectedly fell into His saving arms. He forgave, He healed, and He set me free from the grip of sin and I was saved from the death I deserved and longed for. And with this undeserved gift and new life, I discovered life had a true purpose. I learned the Truth about our infinite God and why I was created. The Lord drew me into His Light and I was able to see the Truth for the very first time—Truth that set me free from the lies of this fallen world.

Without the hope of Jesus, we are unable to see beyond the darkness of our troubles, and the fear and uncertainty of the unknown can hold us in bondage to our sinful ways and lead us even deeper into the darkness. And because we look to the world for resolve instead of our sovereign God, we are usually let down and never rescued. It is because of God's mercy that any of us are spared the full consequence of our sin. It is because of God's love and justice that we have any chance of surviving in a world that is infected with sin and death. Even the most suffering soul can have Reason to hope, for God came to save the hopeless and downtrodden.

## A Whisper of Hope

**I came to free you, dear child...** from the chains of darkness that kills your soul. You no longer have to live in darkness, because you have the Light of Life that shines of Truth and gives you new life. And with this new life you are clothed in My righteousness and stand holy in the eyes of God.

**Romans 6:6-8**
Our old sinful selves were crucified with Christ so that sin might lose its power in our lives. We are no longer slaves to sin. For when we died with Christ we were set free from the power of sin. And since we died with Christ, we know we will also share His new life. (NLT)

**"Salvation is not a reward...it is a gift from God.**
(Ephesians 2:9, 8)

# *"Joy in Truth"*

**Nehemiah 8:10**
This is a sacred day before our Lord. Don't be dejected
and sad, for the joy of the LORD is your strength!" (NLT)

When we know the Truth about our awesome God and what He did to save us from our sins, everyday should be a sacred day lived in thanksgiving and joy. We should weep with joy because our rebellion against God and the eternal consequences that are justly due have been nullified by the blood of Jesus. And as I meditate on this passage from Scripture, I can recall those days when I lived apart from God, thinking that joy was just a word you heard at Christmas; a word I didn't really understand and something that was rarely attained. For most of my life the joy of Christmas was not joy at all, but rather depressing. It was just a brief moment in time to forget reality and mask the pain. I had no real understanding about the incredible message of hope that the birth of our Savior brought into this fallen world. But those days of no joy are gone forever, because I now know the Truth and where I'm headed when this life is over. Knowing the Truth, not only gives us the kind of joy that makes this difficult life worth living, but it also gives us the strength to be joyful in all our circumstances.

Knowing and believing that our Creator walked upon this earth, fully man, yet fully God, to save our wicked lives and give us hope for a glorious future without end, is enough to bring any sad and hopeless soul into great joy and peace. Jesus came to show us the Way, the Truth, and the Life, because it is God's nature to save that which is lost. There is no better reason for rejoicing my friend, than knowing our Lord God and Savior, Jesus Christ. Knowing the joy of the Lord brings hope to the hopeless, strength where there is none, and new life to the dead. And this amazing joy is yours for the asking.

## A Whisper of Hope

**Joy is My gift to you, dear child...**I came to forgive you, to save your eternal life and to comfort your weary soul with My peace. Rejoice in Me, the Truth, because one day soon we will be rejoicing together in Heaven forever!

**Psalm 126:5**
Those who sow in tears shall reap in joy. (NKJ)

**"For the Son of Man has come to seek and to save that which was lost."**
(Luke 19:10)

# *"Hope in Jesus"*

**Matthew 12:20-21**
He will not crush the weakest reed or put out a flickering
candle. Finally He will cause justice to be victorious.
And His Name will be the Hope of all the world. (NLT)

The Messiah did not arrive on earth with any kind of political agenda or military plan or did He draw a lot of attention to Himself as the King of Israel, which was unlike the Messiah that the Jewish leaders and people where looking for. God sent His Son into the world to rescue His people from the evil lies of the world—to save us from our sins and bring hope to the weak and downtrodden, not to save the pride filled Jewish leaders who thought they were already saved. Jesus came to fix that which is broken, to find those who were lost, and to rekindle a flame of hope to a world whose light is flickering out. The Messiah did not come to rescue His people from the Romans and become Israel's King. Instead, the world got the Messiah who gave it all for mankind—a Savior who suffered and died for the sins of the world. He was gracious, kind, and compassionate to the least of His people; those who were poor, diseased, handicapped and oppressed. He healed the sick, raised the dead, cast out demons, and gave us the Way to eternal life. Christ came and fulfilled the prophecy of God.

Christ Jesus came to battle the unseen evil forces, not the Roman government and to break the power of sin and its sting. The Son of God came to show His mercy and grace on the condemned who were lost in the darkness of this evil world and without hope of ever escaping. King Jesus set in motion God's plan for the redemption of mankind—a saving work that brings hope to the hopeless, peace to the anxious, and joy to the brokenhearted. Jesus ushered in the Age of the Church, revealed God's Truth, and shinned His saving Light into this very dark world. The Good News from Heaven is like a breath of fresh air or the arrival of spring after a long harsh winter. With the gift of redeeming salvation from Christ comes a new lease on life, a lease that never runs out and a life that just keeps on getting better!

## A Whisper of Hope

**I AM your Savior, dear child...**I came from Heaven to save all peoples from this wicked and dying world. I came to walk you through this difficult life-journey—to give you hope and a future; to be with you always. I came to bring Light and Life, for without Me there is no Light and no life.

**1 Peter 1:6**
So be truly glad! There is wonderful joy ahead, even though
it is necessary for you to endure many trials for a while. (NLT)

**For the grace of God has appeared, bringing salvation to all men.**
(Titus 2:11)

# "Living Words"

**1 Peter 1:23**
For you have been born again. Your new life did not come from your
earthly parents because the life they gave you will end in death. But this
new life will last forever because it comes from the eternal, Living Word of God. (NLT)

U nless you are born again in Christ Jesus you will die two deaths—the first, when your human body dies, and the second, when you stand before the Lord on Judgment Day. The first death is the death of your mortal body and the second death is eternal condemnation forever separated from God. Without the blood covering of Jesus you will be reunited with your physical body to be judged and thrown into the Lake of Fire that burns eternally. God created us as physical and spiritual beings and both will remain forever. When our physical body expires our spirit is either transported to the existing Heaven to be with the Lord for eternity, or it's put into the pits of Hell to await its eternal destination. And on the final day of judgment, our spirits and bodies will be reunited to be rewarded or condemned.

So what must a person do in order to escape the eternal condemnation of the second death which is Hell bound? And how can one receive this new life that will last forever? The answers are simple and true. You must first admit your need for a Savior and then surrender your life to the will and control of Christ, nailing your old life of sin and rebellion to the Cross, and be born again in Truth and Spirit. The Lord will then transform your godless life into a righteous life that is Christ like. The difference between an old life of sin and a new life in Christ is like night and day. Once you walked in the darkness of this evil world, following its wicked ways of pleasing the flesh. But now you walk in the Light of the Living God, knowing right from wrong, good from bad, and living and loving like Jesus. It would be wise my friend, to put your old life to death and choose the new life of living in the Light of God to escape the eternal darkness of the second death, that comes with keeping your old life of sin.

## A Whisper of Hope

**Come out of the darkness, child...**and into My Light and you will see the Truth that will save your eternal life. And once you see the difference, it will change your life forever. You will never again fear the darkness that would have swallowed you up forever. You will be free indeed!

**2 Corinthians 5:17**
What this means is that those who become Christians
become new persons. They are not the same anymore,
for the old life is gone. A new life has begun! (NLT)

**"Look, I am making all things new!"**
(Revelation 21:5)

# "Freely Given"

**Romans 4:4-5**
When people work, their wages are not a gift. Workers
earn what they receive. But people are declared righteous
because of their faith, not because of their work. (NLT)

We are sinless in the eyes of God because of our steadfast faith in Christ's redeeming death on the cross, not because of how good we think we are or the amount of good things we do. The only Way of complete forgiveness is by the blood of Christ Jesus, for we are all born sinners and we will die as sinners. We cannot keep from sinning no matter how hard we try, because it is the fallen condition of our human nature and this world. Without the blood of Jesus there can be no forgiveness and no justification. Without His death and resurrection, there is no eternal life. If our justification and salvation was based on our own good merits and hard work, then God would have to condemn us all because it is impossible for human beings to earn or achieve a sinless status on their own. Because of our human mortality and the pleasures we crave, we cannot refrain or justify our own sins because they are detestable and unjustifiable in the eyes of God. Our only hope of standing justified before the God Almighty, is dependent on the mercy and grace of our Lord God and Savior Jesus Christ, because the price for purity must be paid, and we cannot afford it nor can we achieve it.

A gift my friend, is something given freely—something of value that's given in love and appreciation, not because we deserve it, but because the one giving it wants you to have it. And our salvation is a gift, pure and simple, for God wants us to have it but we cannot be worthy of it. Those who receive the gift of salvation are undeserving of its value, and once received, we are humbly brought to our knees in thanksgiving and praise, because without the gift of forgiveness and redemption there is only deep darkness and death. There is no joy for those trapped in this dark world, only fleeting happiness that is short lived. But when we receive the greatest gift ever given, the weight of all the burdens and fears of this life are lifted from our shoulders and replaced with peace and eternal joy. The only way to victory over sin and death and condemnation is by accepting and putting your faith and hope in the undeserved gift of salvation that the Son of God paid for with His life.

## A Whisper of Hope

**Accepting My gift in faith...**dear child, brings joy to My heart. For the only way to survive the pounding this world gives you is by living in Me and I in you. For the beating you take from this wicked world will be well worth the struggle for the glorious gift in Heaven that awaits you. But in order to get there you must receive the gift of salvation in faith and I will show you the Way.

**Ephesians 2:8-9**
God saved you by His special favor when you believed.
And you can't take credit for this; it is a gift from God.
Salvation is not a reward for the good things we have done,
so none of us can boast about it. (NLT)

**For the wages of sin is death, but the free gift of God is eternal life
through Christ Jesus our Lord.**
(Ephesians 6:23)

# *"Let Freedom Reign"*

**Romans 6:6-7**
Our old sinful selves were crucified with Christ so that sin
might lose its power in our lives. We are no longer slaves to sin.
For when we died with Christ we were set free from the power of sin. (NLT)

The word "old" that the apostle Paul is alluding to does not mean something that is old in years, but rather something which is worn out, useless, and in need of being replaced. And since we are united with Christ by faith, His death and resurrection become ours as well. Our old ways of thinking and living die on the Cross when we accept Jesus as our Savior, and we are born again into a life that is new and washed clean of sin. We receive a new and better Way of living that was once hidden from our understanding and with our new understanding comes godly living with eternal value. But along with this new life we must stay connected to God and aware of your sinful nature, for although your old self has died and the power of sin has been broken, our nature to sin remains until that glorious day when we are fully sanctified in Christ Jesus. But we can remain confident that our record is clean and we have the resurrection power of God to keep us clean and forgiven.

This incredible gift of regeneration surpasses any gift this world has to offer, for when we die with Christ, He raises us above the shame and guilt and fear that once held us captive and addicted to sin. Jesus' death and resurrection removes these burdens that weight us down so we can focus on what is good and honorable and pleasing to God so we can enjoy life, rather than living in defeat and darkness. Our God is a saving God. He is the Savior who purchased your Way back into God's Holy Presence. Christ is your only Hope, for without the Savior this world will remain in the dark and so will you. You have been offered the Light my friend, accept it, relish it, and rejoice in it. Never be ashamed of it and share it with those who are still desperately searching for hope and finding none.

## A Whisper of Hope

**Rise up, dear one...**Don't allow this fallen world keep you down. Become a servant of righteousness, not of sin. For I will give you eternal purpose and free you from the power of sin and the fear of death. Although the journey up is much more difficult than the journey down, the up journey leads to eternal life and joy. The down journey ends in eternal darkness and pain.

**Ezekiel 36:26-27**
And I will give you a new heart with new and right desires, and I will put a new spirit in you. I will take out your stony heart of sin and give you a new, obedient heart. And I will put My Spirit in you so you will obey my laws and do whatever I command. (NLT)

**You are my refuge and my shield; Your Word is my only source of hope.**
(Psalm 119:114)

# *"Wise Wisdom"*

**Proverbs 1:7**
Fear of the LORD is beginning of knowledge.
Only fools despise wisdom and discipline. (NLT)

T he Book of Proverbs is a collection of wisdom from our LORD God to help people develop the skills they would need for godly living. It is a book of comparisons between common, yet solid images of life's most profound truths, and God's unchangeable Truth. Most people, especially those who have lived long lives upon the earth, know that having wise knowledge certainly helps us extend our lives and quality of living. All of us can make statements about life and truth based on what we have learned and personal experiences, but only those who live in the Truth of God's Word have the ultimate knowledge—knowledge that fills their hearts with peace and joy because they know what the future holds for God's children. This wisdom saves us from a lifestyle of sin that, if not corrected, eventually leads to Hell. Christians worldwide know how terrible and hopeless this world would be without the first coming of our Lord God and Savior Jesus Christ. Christians also know how hopeless and lost they were before Jesus rescued them from the darkness.

Christians learn the Truth by reading the Bible with the Holy Spirit giving them understanding. And what incredible, never before realized insight and joy we receive from God's Word—Truth that sets us free from following the lies of this wicked world. But sadly, most people will study and follow the ways of this wicked world, only to receive more of the same old hopeless lies that brings them even more doubt and anxiety, which causes even more frustration and hopelessness and defeat. The Son of God shines brightly in this dark and evil world, touching hearts and bring hope to those who are deceived and lost, and hopeless and afraid. The hope we have in Jesus is the deepest, most profound hope that the world has ever seen, for it has the power to transform any life and bless them with peace and joy that will ease their pain and comfort their souls until He comes to take them Home forever.

## A Whisper of Hope

**Live in Me, My child...**for only then will you find truth and life. Without Me leads to heartbreak, disappointment, and finally death, forever separated from God and never again seeing the light.

**Job 28:28**
And this is what He says to all humanity: The fear of the Lord
is true wisdom; to forsake evil is real understanding. (NLT)

**I am the Light of the world.**
(John 9:5)

# "New Beginnings"

**2 Corinthians 5:17**
Therefore if anyone is in Christ, he is a new creation; The old
things have passed away; behold, all things have become new. (NKJ)

W hat was found in this 2,000 year old message then is the same message that we find today, a life-changing transformation that occurs with receiving the redemptive gift of salvation from Christ Jesus, our Lord God and Savior. As believers in Christ we share in His promise of eternal life, the forgiveness of sins, and spared the eternal condemnation from God on the day of final judgment. As Christians, we are clothed in the righteousness of Christ and on the last day of this fallen world we will all be transformed into the likeness of Jesus and live with our Holy God forever. What the physical birth of our Lord God and Savior did was it brought Divine Hope into a world lost in a dark sea of evil. And with this divine Hope comes a new beginning that will continue to get better with no end in sight.

When you accept the death and resurrection of Jesus as your salvation, the old life dies on the Cross and you become a new creation. Your record cleared, your rebellion forgotten, and your new journey begins. The Holy Spirit opens your eyes to eternal truths you have never seen nor heard, truths that change the way you view life, death, and this world. Once you were blind but now you can see. You now discern what is real and what is not, what is right and what is wrong, what is true and what are lies. And as your life is being transformed into a life that is acceptable and pleasing to God, your world views, your values, your beliefs, and the temporal things you had staked your life on will change. You will gain new insight with a new perspective, for the old temporal things will no longer control the way you live. Instead, your new eternal perspective causes you to focus on the God of Glory—the One who created you. Jesus came to give us all a new beginning—one that is glorious—one that has no end!

## A Whisper of Hope

**The Father sent Me...**to shepherd His people; to gather up the lost and to bring them Home. The world seeks to blind and steal all that you have in Me and then destroy you completely. But I came to save you, dear child, and to give you a new life that is eternal. You must trust Me in this, for when you do—you are safe and secure.

**2 Corinthians 5:18, 21**
All this newness of life is from God, who brought
us back to Himself through what Christ did. (NLT)
For He made Him who knew no sin to be sin for us, that
we might become the righteousness of God in Him. (NKJ)

**For we are God's masterpiece. He has created us anew in Christ Jesus.**
(Ephesians 2:10)

# "Another Day"

**Romans 12:2**
And do not be conformed to this world, but be transformed
by the renewing of your mind, so that you may prove what the
will of God is, that which is good and acceptable and perfect. (NASB)

As children of the living God, we should strive to live each day according to the good and perfect will of our God in Heaven, especially if we desire true peace and lasting joy while traveling through this difficult leg of our life-journey. We must do this because the sinful ways of this fallen world with all its contemporary thinking and worldly system of values is being dominated and directed by the Prince of Darkness, the Devil. It is a self-seeking system of pleasing the sinful flesh that only focuses on the here and now of living for the moment and denying any consequences. And the only way to escape its grip and renew our minds and hearts is through the saving power of the God, who opens our eyes and softens our hearts so we can know the Truth and His will. Most of us, through no fault of our own, are taught the secular world views of this life and if it is the secular world view is all we know, then it is the world view that we are most inclined to follow—a system that slowly digs the grave of eternal darkness that separates us from the goodness and Light of God.

Sadly but true, it doesn't take long to discover that to survive in this harsh and unfair world is to harden our hearts and indulge in things that numb the pain of emptiness that comes with the fleeting pleasures of this fallen world. Even though God created within the fiber of our beings the moral difference between right and wrong, it is impossible for us to overcome our fallen nature to rebel against God's moral standards without His help, because all we know is our love of sin. Even though we may want to do the right thing, our sinful desires often trumps it—choices that often lead us down a path of self-destruction and eventually eternal judgment. The Truth my friend, is that we have all been fully acquitted of our sins by the sacrificial blood of Jesus, if you so desire. You have a powerful Helper that empowers you to live a new and better life, one that is not only pleasing to God and those around you, but you will gain a glorious new purpose that will fill your heart with the eternal peace and joy of the Lord; the kind of peace and joy that will give you the strength and wisdom to face another day with anticipation.

## A Whisper of Hope

**My will, dear child...** is to give you a hope and a future unlike anything the world can promise. The world leaves you empty, disappointed and hungering for more. Don't believe the lies the world embraces, because this life is short and next one has no end. Rise above the temporal and embrace the eternal, for in Me you will live, in the world you will die.

**2 Corinthians 4:4**
Satan, the god of this world, has blinded the minds of those
who don't believe, so they are unable to see the glorious Light
of the Good News that is shining upon them. They don't understand
the message we preach about the glory of Christ, who is the exact likeness of God. (NLT)

**Everyone who believes in Him is freed from all guilt and declared right with God.**
(Acts 13:39)

# May

# *"Power Gifts"*

**Acts 2:38**
Peter replied, "Each of you must turn from your sins
and turn to God, and be baptized in the name of Jesus Christ
for the forgiveness of your sins. Then you will receive the gift of the Holy Spirit. (NLT)

The glory of being born anew in Christ Jesus is that no repented sinner is excluded from receiving the gift of the Holy Spirit. When we humbly bring our broken lives to the foot of the Cross with sorrow-filled hearts, we also receive the gift of forgiveness and our sin-filled life that was once so vile and evil to our Holy God, is cleansed, forever forgotten, and is no longer held against us. And with these incredible gifts from God, we are able to start our new lives as a new creation, because our old life has died on the Cross and we are born again as the redeemed children of God. The moment you are forgiven, you will receive the Holy Spirit to help you submit to the ways of the Lord, and to help guide you in transitioning from ungodly living to living a life that is pleasing to God and brings Him glory. The Holy Spirit helps us understand God's Word, gives us the power to overcome our temptations, protects us when we need it, and teaches us to discern what is true from what is not. The Holy Spirit gives us everything we need for living a godly life in this ungodly world.

This transformation is not an easy one to make, because it goes against the very grain that this fallen world has taught you. But with the indwelling of the Holy Spirit you will gain the power and wisdom to learn and understand the Truth that the Lord has so graciously shared with mankind. Without the Holy Spirit as your Helper my friend, this transformation will not go so well, for the human will is weak and our nature is to sin. The Holy Spirit is not some invisible entity, but is fully God and He is hard at work in our world today, saving lives and changing hearts. You don't want to miss out on these life saving gifts that will change your life forever and bring great joy and glory to God. Without the power of the Holy Spirit you will remain a slave to sin, with no way to escape. The only Way to defeat sin and death is by accepting the death and resurrection of Christ Jesus as your own and with the power of the Holy Spirit, you will make it safely Home where you belong.

## A Whisper of Hope

**Only in Me, dear child...**will you find forgiveness, salvation, and the mightiest power in the universe dwelling within your heart and soul. With these gifts you will win the battles for your heart and mind and with My power living in you, you will prevail.

**Galatians 5:22-23**
But when the Holy Spirit controls our lives, He will produce
this kind of fruit in us: Love, joy, peace, patience, kindness, goodness,
faithfulness, gentleness, and self-control. Here there is no conflict with the law. (NLT)

**"And their sins and their lawless deeds I will remember no more."**
(Hebrews 10:17)

# "Saving Grace"

**Acts 4:12**
There is salvation in no one else! There is no other name
in all of Heaven for people to call on to save them. (NLT)

Because the LORD is both gracious and merciful to the people He so carefully creates, He sent His only Son to save mankind from the self-destruction of sin. Christ Jesus was the final Sacrificial Lamb of God who was slaughtered for the sins of the world. Our Lord God became fully human so He could live with His people, and heal the sick, feed the hungry and to bring hope to all peoples of this fallen world; a world that is cursed by sin, filled with suffering, sickness, heartbreak, and death. God knows that without His saving grace, mankind would perish forever. Jesus healed the sick, fed the hungry, raised the death and showed people who their God really is. The Lord came to us, because we would not come to Him. He lived on this earth as a man and suffered just as we suffer, was tempted just as we are tempted, and died just as we, too, will die.

The Creator of the Universe gave His own life and His own blood to cleanse us of our sin and to take our punishment. There are only two paths that we can choose to follow; there is a wide path that is well traveled for it is the path the world recommends—ways that are pleasure oriented, self-centered, prideful and self loving—ways that will ultimately lead to condemnation and eternal death. And there is a much narrower path that is God centered and takes you straight to the foot of the Cross of Christ, where you are cleansed by the blood of the Lamb and covered with the righteousness of Jesus. You will escape the final wrath of God and receive the gift of eternal life in the new Heaven on Earth. The sacrifice has been made and the price has been paid in full. You have been forgiven and your life has been saved! Believe it, accept it and let the Lord do the rest!

## A Whisper of Hope

**Take My Hand, dear child...**for I will lead you on a life-journey that is out of this world. There are many paths that lead nowhere but straight to Hell. Only one does not. Choose the path to salvation that I paid for with My blood and death because you cannot afford the price, nor can you be worthy to receive it. So I give it to you as a gift.

**Psalm 84:11-12**
For the LORD God is our Light and Protector. He gives us grace and glory.
No good thing will the LORD withhold, for those who do what is right.
O LORD Almighty, happy are those who trust in You. (NLT)

**For by grace you have been saved through faith...it is the gift of God.**
(Ephesians 2:8)

# "Know God"

**Psalm 19:14**
Let the words of my mouth and the meditation of my heart
be acceptable in Your sight, O LORD, my strength and my Redeemer. (NKJ)

We can gaze into the far reaches of the universe, we can marvel at the incredible beauty of the earth, and we can be awed by the complexity of life, and if these were all we had, we could certainly reason the case for a Creator who is far greater than our finite minds can imagine. But believing in a Creator is not enough for us to understand why we were created and why this life is so hard and confusing. Nor is believing in a Higher Power sufficient to give us any purpose that would make this difficult life worth the trouble it brings. There is only One Way my friend, to get the right answers that will bring you much needed clarity, peace of mind, and eternal hope, and that is by surrendering your lost life to the Lord our God and Savior. You must do this because God not only created you in His image, but He is your sole Provider who keeps you alive so you can accept the gift of eternal life.

We must rely on the protection that Jesus provides, because finite human beings would not survive against the incredible energy of the universe nor can we stand alone against the unseen evil powers of Satan. If you are living this life as I once did, just believing there is a God but knowing little else, it is both foolish and dangerously detrimental to the life of your eternal soul. Living in this ungodly world without knowing the Lord God will leave you empty, alone, and wondering why you were created. Sadly, most people will live this way until they die and then discover that their earthly life is only the beginning of a very long and dark existence—a hellish existence with no end in sight. Don't be like I was; indifferent to God, rather than knowing Him; disliking Him, rather than loving Him, and ignoring Him instead of knowing Him. Until you surrender to the Lord God who created you and saved you, you will never know what is to truly live in the Light of God's glory.

## A Whisper of Hope

**Come close, dear child...**and I will protect and teach you about this wonderful gift of life. I will bring you peace and understanding that will help you overcome this fallen world so you can live forever in the New World I will create for eternity.

**Matthew 11:28**
"Come to Me, all of you who are weary and
carry heavy burdens, and I will give you rest. (NLT)

**Be still and know that I am God.**
(Psalm 46:10)

# "In God We Trust"

**Jeremiah 17:7**
"Blessed is the man who trusts in the
LORD, and whose hope is in the LORD." (NKJ)

The truth of these words will not hit home until you realize the impact that the Lord has had on your life because of His conditional love and the forgiveness and salvation that He paid for with His life's blood by hanging naked on a piece of dead tree at the hands of the men He created and was dying for. These words are especially encouraging for us because we usually learn the hard way by trusting this fallen world and our own human efforts for the hope that only God can give. For those who don't trust in the Lord, it can be rather frustrating, often discouraging, and many times quite devastating, because they can see clearly the failed results in the world around them. God's blessings come in many different shapes and sizes and are all geared to bring His Plan for man into completion. But to whomever the blessings are given, we can be sure that they are all given according to the perfect will of God. And in like manner, the same can be said about the discipline of God, for He allows us the free will to choose the world's way or His Way and lets us suffer the consequences for good of His Kingdom.

Like most people, I learned that living apart from God, relying on my own abilities and strength, and trusting the world to satisfy the desires of my heart was not only a lie and a poor decision, but it also failed me miserably. And in my quest to satisfy the hungers of my soul, I discover that I could never work hard enough, say enough, do enough, or pay enough to fill the emptiness, that unbeknownst to me, only God could fill. And believe me, my friend, I suffered the dire consequences of my choices. When we travel through this difficult life-journey in the Light of God's Truth, the blessings we receive will always be more than enough to keep moving us forward in faith that our Savior will get us safely Home with the hope of God as our peace. God has put eternity in the hearts of all peoples and only the His gift of salvation can fulfill your desires and give you eternal hope.

## A Whisper of Hope

**My Words are True; child...**and so too are My promises. I Am your only Hope for eternal Life. You may not think that living forever is appealing because of this fallen world, but the eternity I give you is perfect. Trust not in yourself or this world, for both are broken.

**Ecclesiastes 3:11**
God has made everything beautiful for its own time. He has
planted eternity in the human heart, but even so, people cannot
see the whole scope of God's work from beginning to end. (NLT)

**It is better to trust in the LORD than to put confidence in man.**
(Psalm 118:8)

# "Path to Life"

**Psalm 25:4, 5**
Show me Your ways, O LORD; teach me Your paths. Lead me
in Your truth and teach me, for You are the God of my salvation. (NKJ)

This psalm from thousands of years ago is a plea for deliverance—a plea that should be on every lip and in every heart of every person—a plea that has been answered, because our God and Savior left the glory of heaven and delivered us from the fate of this fallen world. The Living God came to show us the path of Truth that leads to life—the only path that gives us eternal hope and encouragement while living in a world that hates the Word of God. Within the written pages of the Bible are God inspired words that are absolute in their truth, without error, and never changing revelations that our infinite God has so graciously shared with us. We learn why the world hates its Creator who came to us in a human body so He could give His life and shed His perfect blood as the final sacrificial Lamb of God. When we know and believe the Truth, we can make the right decisions that will not only save us from the final wrath of God, but will give our lives moral purpose and eternal value. In other words, the Lord has given us the Map that will lead us back to God and eternal life.

When you humbly surrender your life to the Lord and accept the blood of Christ as the atonement for all your sins, you will receive the Holy Spirit as your guide, paving the path that will take you on an amazing life-journey unlike anything this hate-filled world could ever offer. When you began to learn who this amazing God is and all the glorious plans He has for His people, it will became quite apparent that it is far better to trust in God's Way rather than the world's way, for I, like many others, had chosen the ways of the world that left me empty and depressed. The only real promise that this world can deliver is trouble and death. There is absolutely no One more qualified to lead you in the Truth than the omnipotent Creator who is the Truth. And there is no One that cares more about your future than the One who created you. Don't follow the world and its empty promises; follow the Living God who paved the path to life for you.

## A Whisper of Hope

**I came to light the path, dear child…**that leads to life. You no longer need to live in darkness nor follow the paths that lead nowhere. Life on this earth will never be without struggle or pain or void of uncertainty and disappointment, but if you step into the Light, you will find the path to life.

**Psalm 16:11**
You will show me the path of life; in Your presence is
fullness of joy; at Your right hand are pleasures forevermore. (NKJ)

**Your word is a lamp to my feet and a light to my path.**
(Psalm 119:105)

# "Race of Grace"

**Acts 20:24**
But my life is worth nothing to me unless I use it for finishing
the work assigned me by the Lord Jesus—the work of telling
others the Good News about the wonderful grace of God. (NLT)

Many people spend much of their lives, as I did, consumed with worldliness and running to finish the race with little rest, but uncertain about its outcome. Most of us run desperately through this difficult life-journey searching for something that will make us happy and content but unfortunately, the happiness never lasts and we are never content. And many times we get so focused on our failures in the search of that which we cannot find, that in time, the hopelessness and discouragement sets in and we assume that lasting happiness is beyond our grasp. Many people live only for the worldly pleasures of this life and most of us end up so defeated and discouraged that numbing the mind will ease the pain. And then, like I did, we begin to look forward to the end of our lives so we won't have to deal with it anymore. When my life became nothing more than surviving and easing the pain, I became easy prey for the Enemy and Satan had his way with me.

Without the love, strength and wisdom of God and without the mercy of His saving grace, this life with all its empty promises becomes a rather futile and dangerous race that will take you over the cliff and down into the pits of Hell. But God has intervened and given us the Way we can redirect the race of self-destruction and run straight into the arms of our Savior Jesus Christ, the ultimate Coach who gives us the strength to finish our race with a glorious win. When you look for the Source of all happiness, He is there waiting. With Coach Jesus, you know how the race will end, and the peace you receive is priceless. You will discover that this amazing race of grace is not just about winning, but it's about the glory of our God, the Most Holy and Righteous One who stands at the finish line waiting to welcome you into His Kingdom.

## A Whisper of Hope

**Let Me train you for the race, My child...**for I will coach you safely across the finish line. Without My help you will get lost and run to death. But with My training, your race will not only be won, but you will celebrate with Me and all those who finished before you!

**Titus 2:11-14**
For the grace of God has been revealed, bringing salvation to all people. And we are instructed to turn from godless living and sinful pleasures. We should live in this evil world with self-control, right conduct, and devotion to God, while we look forward to that wonderful event when the glory our great God and Savior, Jesus Christ, will be revealed. (NLT)

**Let us run with endurance the race that is set before us.**
(Hebrew 12:1)

# "Joy in Living"

**Psalm 32:1, 2**
Oh, what joy for those whose disobedience is
forgiven, whose sin is put out of sight! Yes, what
joy for those whose record the LORD has cleared of guilt. (NLT)

We are fallen human beings living in a fallen world that continues to drift further away from the will of God. We are sinners and will remain that way until King Jesus makes all things new. Throughout the history of mankind, people become so consumed with the world that they are oblivious to the fact that their lifestyles are detestable to God even when they believe He exists. It is not until we surrender our lives to the Living God that we began to learn who He is and what He expects from us. It wasn't until my eyes were opened to the Truth of God's Word that I discovered just how repulsive and detestable my life was and I realized how undeserving I was for the gift of salvation that He dearly paid for. And I was awakened to the fact of how desperately we all need Jesus who freed us from our bondage to sin and death. What an incredibly loving and forgiving God we have in Christ Jesus, for He took all of mankind's sins upon Himself and paid the price for our sins with His blood, and died the death which belonged to us.

My life of total disregard for God's Way was more than enough reason for Him to let me die in my sin and be justly condemned for all eternity. But when you are forgiven and living in Christ Jesus, you are made a new person and no longer live in darkness. You are no longer enslaved by the power of sin. Neither fear nor death has its grip on you, and you will be able to move forward with astounding hope and incredible peace, because you not only know the King of all creation personally, but you can trust Him to direct your every step. When sin no longer controls the way you live, and you know you have been forgiven, this life, although remains a difficult journey for most, becomes a joy.

## A Whisper of Hope

**Come humbly, dear child...**with a sorrowful heart and I will forgive your sins and wipe your stained record clean. I will breathe a spirit of new life into your soul; an eternal life that brings glory to Me and honor to you. For when you live in Me, I will bring you hope for today, peace about yesterday , and joy for the future I have made for you.

**2 Peter 1:3-4**
As we know Jesus better, His divine power gives us everything we need for living a godly life. He has called us to receive His own glory and goodness. And by that same mighty power, He has given us all of His rich and wonderful promises. He has promised that you will escape the decadence all around you caused by evil desires and that you will share in His divine nature. (NLT)

**But if we confess our sins to Him, He is faithful and just to forgive us
and to cleanse us from every wrong.**
(1 John 1:9)

# "Life Healing"

**Mark 2:16-17**
And when the scribes and Pharisees saw Him eating with the tax collectors and sinners,
they said to His disciples, "How is it that He eats and drinks with tax collectors and sinners?"
When Jesus heard it, He said to them, "Those who are well have no need of a physician,
but those who are sick. I did not come to call the righteous, but sinners, to repentance." (NKJ)

There are those who recognize their sin infected condition and turn to the only One who can heal their wounds and stop the infection that leads to death. And there are others who think they are either immune to the infection, are too proud to admit they are infected, or they simply deny the reality of their sickness. And there are still others who believe they can heal themselves. But the Truth is my friends, without the cleansing blood of Jesus Christ, there is no hope of stopping the infection that decays the spirit and kills the soul. Jesus was the spotless Lamb of God, whose sacrifice cleansed our infection and saved us from eternal death. And it is the poor in spirit that are first on His list to be healed and saved—the people who are desperately searching for hope that would give them some peace about the array of discouraging circumstances that living in this fallen world brings them.

Jesus came to heal the sick and to save the downtrodden, not to make the healthy or the proud feel good about themselves. He came to rescue those who are wandering like lost sheep, afraid, alone, wounded and dying, with no hope and no future. Our Savior came, He saw, and He healed the sin condition of man, and in the process defeated the power of Satan. He paid the price for our sins and brought us back into the Presence of our Holy God. Since the dawn of time we have been infected with sin and death and the only cure is found in our Great God and Savior Jesus Christ. Without Jesus there is only death and darkness. You cannot deny the Truth and live.

## A Whisper of Hope

**I AM your only Hope, child…**that can save you from the darkness of death that sin has infected you with. The power of sin is puny when compared to My Power. When you live in Me, you have nothing to fear, for My Power is greater than your weakness.

**1 Chronicles 29:11**
Yours, O LORD, is the greatness, the power and the glory,
the victory and the majesty; for all that is in Heaven and in Earth
is Yours; Yours is the Kingdom, O LORD, and you are exalted as Head over all. (NKJ)

**If we say we have no sin, we are only fooling ourselves
and refusing to accept the truth..**
(1 John 1:9)

# "Life Anew"

**Ezekiel 11:19-20**
"Then I will give them one heart, and I will put a new spirit within them, and take the stony heart out of their flesh and give them a heart of flesh, that they may walk in My statutes and keep My judgments and do them; and they shall be My people, and I will be their God." (NKJ)

Because of our sinful nature we come into this fallen world with a heart that is also sinful and in time becomes hardened with self preservation and pride—conditions that causes us to drift away from our Creator without knowing how dangerous it is without Him. This world and everything in it is cursed because of the evil one, who poisons our minds, hardens our hearts, and kills our souls, and he will continue doing so until the Lord locks him away for good. We must live and deal with our sinful nature as long as we are alive or until Jesus takes us Home. And for the living, our Lord God has provided the Way that we can escape the grasp of evil that holds us captive to the self-destructive sins that leads to eternal separation from the Light of God.

Our world has been so deceived by the lies of Satan that it's really hard for people to know and understand what is truly true and what is not. God's Truth frees us from the power of sin and death and promises us new life, while Satan's false truth draws us deeper into our sin and promises only death. God's Truth teaches us to know, love, and respect the One who created us, while the dark truth inspires us to ignore and hate God, and blame him for the woes of the world. God's Truth helps us accept our circumstances, and tells us to live in thanksgiving to God for the good things we have. But the false truth causes us to despise our circumstances and blame others. Knowing the Way and the Truth that comes from above will bring Light and Hope into your life. Our Lord God and Savior came, He taught, and He sacrificed His life to bring us a new eternal life.

## A Whisper of Hope

**I rescued you, dear child...**to give you hope and a future, to earn your trust, and to give you a new heart. I did not create you to live apart from Me, for you cannot survive on your own. And I can give you what you need for a new and glorious life that will never end.

**Jeremiah 17:9**
"The heart is deceitful above all things, and
desperately wicked; who can know it? (NKJ)

> **Therefore if anyone is in Christ, he is a new creation;**
> **old things have passed away; behold, all things have become new.**
> (2 Corinthians 5:17)

# *"Praise and Worship"*

**Psalm 52:9**
I will praise You forever, O God,
for what You have done. (NLT)

It is only right that we worship our Almighty God with as much praise and thanksgiving as possible, because without His sovereign power, His unconditional love, His abundant mercy, and amazing grace we would not exist. Without the love of God there would be nothing good in this life. Without the wise council of God our lives would be lived in vain and unhappiness. But we have an incredibly wonderful Creator who created the universe and the earth for us to enjoy with His help—He didn't just leave us to chance. Instead, He has kept a protective eye on His creation and has been actively involved in mankind's history and future. The Lord is our Heavenly Father and He takes care of us, whether we like it or not. He loves us, and it's His job to protect us from the enemies that want to destroy us. God created us to live in His Presence; to have a loving, trusting, and an eternal, life-bonding relationship with Him. He created us and we depend on Him for everything. He is not an absentee Father or promise breaker. What I find so incredible about God is His unchanging, unconditional love for all peoples, for even though we rebel against His laws, oppose His ways, and mock His eternal justice, God has chosen to forgive and forget and give us chance after chance.

Our Savior has paved the Way to eternal life for those who humbly repent and live in obedience. Christ Jesus voluntarily left the glory of Heaven to live in this fallen world that hated Him so much, He would have to suffer and die a criminal's death. Our Lord God my friend, is the One that loves you so unconditionally, that He allowed Himself to be unjustly condemned and nailed to a piece of dead tree where He would hang shamefully naked, despised, and abandoned by God the Father so you could escape the horrors of Hell. Our sinless Savior paid your sin debt because He knows how helpless you are with fighting sin and how hard it is to change. You and everyone else are headed straight into the pits of Hell without the saving grace of our Lord God Jesus Christ. He gave His life so you could keep yours. He paid the price you could not, and gave you a gift you do not deserve.

## A Whisper of Hope

**Honor Me, dear child…**with your praise and thanksgiving. For when you live in thanksgiving, I am faithful to watch over you and guide you in ways that are good for you and glorify Me. This is My Way and this is your life. Let us walk together in this troubled world and I will give you My peace—a peace unlike any you have ever known.

**Ephesians 1:14**
The Spirit is God's guarantee that He will give us everything
He promised and that He has purchased us to be His own people.
This is just one more reason for us to praise our glorious God. (NLT)

**Stand up and praise the LORD your God, for He lives from everlasting to everlasting!**
(Nehemiah 9:5)

# "Eternal Choice"

**Philippians 3:18-19**
For I have told you often before, and I say it again with tears in my eyes, that there are many whose conduct shows they are really enemies of the cross of Christ. Their future is eternal destruction. Their god is their appetite, they brag about shameful things, and all they think about is this life here on earth. (NLT)

These words from the apostle Paul, reinforces the urgency I feel for all those who are lost and don't know what to believe about life and death; those who believe there is no accountability after this life and others who are oblivious to the evil forces that are leading them into the darkness of their eternal graves. There are so many people who have no clue to the eternal state of their God given life. I believe the greatest concern that everyone should have about this life, is not where your next meal is coming from or if you will have enough set aside to retire on, but that very moment when the flame of life flickers out, because this life is the only chance we have to be reconciled with God through Christ Jesus. When you breathe your final breath on this earth, the state of your eternal soul will have already been determined—you will have either made your choice or face the judgment of God—you have either accepted God's gift of salvation or not. Our gracious and merciful God wants no one to suffer eternal death and damnation. But we should know and understand that the Lord our God is not only perfectly holy, but He is also the final perfectly just Judge.

There is an ultimate choice that is put before every person living on this earth—a decision that will determine where you spend your eternal life. You can choose to follow Christ or this world. You can choose the gift of salvation or take your chances. You can choose Heaven or Hell. God has given us the freedom to choose how we live this life. But because God loves the people He creates, He saved us from certain eternal death. He loves us so much that He shared the Truth so we could make a wise decision before we die. Knowing the Truth should bring you to your knees in thanksgiving, because without Jesus, there is only eternal darkness and pain. If you are living apart from God and taking your chances, you need to seriously reconsider your choices before it is too late.

## A Whisper of Hope

**My beloved child...**do not allow the deception of this dark world to cloud your mind. Live with eternity on your heart, because this life is only the beginning of a very long time. Don't be caught off guard by your death, for the choice will have already been made.

**John 6:27**
Spend your energy seeking the eternal life that I, the Son of Man,
can give you. For God the Father has sent Me for that very purpose." (NLT)

**"This is what God wants you to do: Believe in the One He has sent."**
(John 6:29)

# *"God Works"*

**Philippians 1:6**
For I am confident of this very thing,
that He who began a good work in you
will perfect it until the day of Christ Jesus. (NASB)

No matter what kind of struggles Christian people are faced with, or how hard their lives become, or how frustrated they may be in their faith walk, the Holy Spirit who dwells in our hearts will continue to grow and transform us into the person that God calls us to be. And this transformation will continue in its perfection until we are taken up to be with the Lord in Heaven. But even with the Holy Spirit to guide and reveal God's Truth to us, there are some things that the Christian must do in order for God's good work to move forward in this life-changing process. You must accept the total forgiveness for all your sins through the sacrificial death of Jesus Christ on the cross at Calvary. You must seek a loving and personal relationship with the Lord and stay connected to the Church. You must seek God through prayer, reading His Word, and live in repentance. When you are steadfast and faithful in these things the Lord will work miraculously in your life, giving you godly wisdom, fearless confidence, and the power to break away from your sinful lifestyle one step at a time.

God does not normally change a person overnight even though He has the sovereign power to do so, nor does He expect us to. The Lord knows we are weak and the old sinful habits are hard to break and slow to change. But He knows exactly what we need when we need it and by surrendering our fallen will to Him our transformation is in His hands. And as you draw closer to God, the more you learn to trust Him. And the more you trust Him, the more you rely on His help. And the more you trust and rely on His help, the more at peace you are with this world and the part you are given in it. But with that said my friend, this life is never easy with or without the power of God backing us up, and many times our transformation can get quite difficult and frustrating as we face the Enemy of our soul. But as your faith grows, so too, does your confidence, because the more time you spend with God, the more time He spends with you.

## A Whisper of Hope

**My Spirit will guide you, child**...I will never lead you astray, for I only want what is best for you. I have given you My Word, My Truth, and My Life. You are safe and secure when you travel this life-journey with the One who created you.

**Titus 2:11-13**
For the grace of God has been revealed, bring salvation to all people. And we are instructed to turn from godless living and sinful pleasures. We should live in this evil world with self-control, right conduct, and devotion to God, while we look forward to that wonderful event when the glory of our great God and Savior, Jesus Christ, will be revealed. (NLT)

**And the LORD will rescue me from every evil deed
and bring me safely to His heavenly Kingdom.**
(2 Timothy 4:18)

# "Find it In God"

**Colossians 2:8**
Don't let anyone lead you astray with empty philosophy
and high-sounding nonsense that come from human thinking
and from the evil powers of this world, and not from Christ. (NLT)

Since the dawn of Christianity in the first century AD until the present day we are still bombarded with the shallow, self-centered ,humanistic speculations, ideologies, philosophies, and religions that teach the ways of Satan rather than the ways of God—worldly ways that diminish God's sovereignty and deny the deity of our Lord God, Jesus Christ. This fallen world sees the Bible as allegorical or fiction and Christianity as foolishness. It deems God highly irrelevant in today's modern age. The world tells us that God is what you want Him to be, that Jesus was just a good man who died a martyrs death, that there are no absolutes, that this life is all there is, and that all wisdom is man's intellect. These lies are designed to draw us away from God and the truth about creation, life and death. The wisdom of man is utter foolishness to God, for God's wisdom is eternal and it leads those who embrace the Wisdom of the Living God into eternal life.

The false teachers have been many throughout the ages of mankind. These clever lies of Satan have infiltrated every area of our human lives. They are being taught at every level of education and in our Christian Churches. This humanistic world is spreading man-made lies inspired by Satan—evil ideologies that are causing children and adults to embrace a godless life-style of darkness. Don't take this deadly journey, my dear friend. Instead, follow the Truth that leads straight into the arms of God where you will find true peace in knowing the Infinite One who hung bloody and naked on a cross to die your death. There is only One Way and One Truth. You must believe that Jesus Christ is the resurrection and the life—the God of gods, Lord of lords, and the King of kings—the One who has always been, and always will be. Embrace this Truth and live!

## A Whisper of Hope

**Embrace My Truth...**dear child, for all others end in death. My Truth brings you life to the fullest, just as I created it to be. Love Me and not the world, because the world can neither save you nor give you your heart's desire. Only I can!

**2 Peter 2:1, 2, 17, 19**
But there were also false prophets in Israel, just as there will be false teachers among you.
They will cleverly teach their destructive heresies about God. Many will follow their evil
teaching and shameful immorality. These people are as useless as dried-up springs of water
or as clouds blown away by the wind—promising much and delivering nothing. They promise
freedom, but they themselves are slaves to sin and corruption. (NLT)

**You must stay away from people like that.**
(2 Timothy 3:5)

# *"Heavenly Minds"*

**Colossians 3:1-2**
Since you have been raised to new life with Christ, set your sights on the realities
of Heaven, where Christ sits at God's right hand in the place of honor and power.
Let Heaven fill your thoughts. Do not think only about things down here on earth. (NLT)

The secular world tells us that Christians are so heavenly minded they are no earthly good. But in reality this is a lie straight from the mouth of Satan. It is the heavenly minds of Christ Jesus that have changed the world for the better, giving people a true reason for living and the hope of better things to come. The Lord has transformed many worldly minds into heavenly ones filled with truth and hope, and a peek into the future so we can be prepared for the inevitable. Heavenly insight is eternally glorifying, while the world's insight is eternally damning. Being heavenly minded is not living in a dream state. in order to escape the hard reality of this life, but is learning God's Wisdom and preparing for the eternal life to come. People who are heavenly minded focus on the eternal things of God and accomplish more good works that benefit this world than those who are not—the ones who are so worldly minded that they are of no heavenly value whatsoever. The Devil has duped the world's minds into believing his many lies and they shoot for the moon, but land in Hell.

Our God in Heaven wants us to focus on eternity, believing His Truth, and living like He designed us to live. Our brief time in this world is but a blink of an eye, but eternity is void of time. So why chance it? For the only risk in doing life God's way is forfeiting a few moments of earthly pleasure now for the heavenly pleasures of eternity later. We can choose to ignore our Creator and do whatever we want with our lives by enjoying the moment, but the end results are devastating, because when you are worldly minded, you are an enemy of God. Refuse the Devil's bait and focus on your Savior and Heaven because it's far better for you and those around you!

## A Whisper of Hope

**To be heavenly minded, My child…**is eternally good. The world promises you much, but delivers only death. Being heavenly minded is not a dream state, but a condition that takes strength and courage to maintain. Focus on what will be, dear one, not the present moment.

**Romans 8:6**
For to be carnally mind is death,
but to be spiritually minded is life and peace. (NKJ)

**If your aim is to enjoy this world, you can't be a friend of God.**
(James 4:4)

# "God Safe"

**Psalm 73:26-27**
My health may fail, and my spirit may grow weak, But God remains the strength of my heart; He is mine forever. But those who desert Him will perish, for You destroy those who abandon You. (NLT)

Our wise God created the universe in such a way that it and everything in it would always need Him to exist. By the power of His Word, He keeps it in a well defined order instead of a great big, gigantic mass of absolute chaos without purpose. So we can reason that mankind must also depend on God to provide all our needs and protect us in order to sustain our lives. He also teaches us how to live in ways that are good for us and glorifies Him; ways that are righteous, eternal, and God directed. But what we need the most is His forgiveness, the gift of salvation, and the power to help us live godly lives in an ungodly world. Sadly, most people choose to ignore God to follow their own ways that are flawed by sin and reeks with the wickedness that leads to a life filled with a lot of chaos, doubt, and fear—lives that are filled with pain, heartache, and feeling hopelessly lost in the dark with nowhere to go. Since the falling away of mankind from God we foolishly created our own gods (with the help of Satan) that we could turn to for justifying our sin and to appease our carnal flesh, instead of relying on the living God who can forgive us and holds our eternal destiny in His hands.

There have been many worldly driven people who have prospered greatly in this life, but missed out on the joy of knowing the Lord. There will always be those who deny God and don't look beyond this life. They spend this short life grabbing all they can while they can, having no concern for the consequences that they deny exists. But the Lord tells us that no matter how powerful or rich or successful a person becomes in this life they will lose it all on that inevitable day when they breathe their last and final breath. And when they regain conscienceless, will find themselves trapped in a dark pit in Hell awaiting their final judgment, only to be thrown into the Lake of Fire that burns forever. But for those who honor their Creator and Savior and accept His saving grace, they too, will lose their earthly stuff, but will gain an eternal life in the glory of Heaven with not only riches beyond our imagination, but the awesome reward of living with our Great God and Savior, Jesus Christ.

## A Whisper of Hope

**Depend on Me, dear child…**not on the manmade gods of this immoral world, because they cannot promise you anything but temporary pleasures and eternal darkness. These manmade gods will expose you to the harsh realities that come with living apart from your Provider. Don't be duped by the likes of the Enemy, for if your do I will also abandon you!

**Colossians 1:16-17**
Christ is the One through whom God created everything in heaven and earth.
He made the things we can see and the things we can't see—kings, kingdoms, rulers, and authorities. Everything has been created through Him and for Him.
He existed before everything else began, and He holds all creation together. (NLT)

**There is a way which seems right to a man, but its end is the way of death.**
(Proverbs 14:12)

# "The Road Home"

**Ephesians 2:4**
But God is so rich in mercy, and He loved us so very much,
that even while we were dead because of our sins,
He gave us life when He raised Christ from the dead. (NLT)

When people take God out of the equation of life they are embracing Satan, the mighty prince of this wicked world. And his evil forces are hard at work deceiving people who then refuse the love, holiness, and authority of our Holy God and Creator. The Lord did not create us to die, but to live. God did not save us from death because He had to. God saved us because He is a gracious and merciful God who knew we could never save ourselves from the just punishment that sin brings. The Lord knows and sees all things and He is perfect in everything He does. God's love is something we cannot fully understand this side of Heaven, but we know that God is Love in the purest form because He tells us so, and He cannot lie. Mercy and grace and love are His very nature and He watches over His entire creation like a hawk, directing our paths so that we might find our way Home.

There are many worldly paths to choose from, but they all lead to eternal death, because we were not made to travel through this life-journey apart from God. Our Lord God and Savior came to this earth because we could not come to Him. He came to be the Final Sacrificial Lamb of God. Jesus sacrificed His life for the sins of the world and received the punishment that was due. You have been cleansed by the blood of Jesus, your sins have been forgiven and forgotten, and you are now righteous and holy in the eyes of God if you so desire. It doesn't matter who you are or what you have done, Jesus can give you a new life now and raise you to an eternal life when this one ends, for He is after all, the God of creation.

## A Whisper of Hope

**The paths of this world...**lead into the darkness of the abyss. But the path I paved for you will take you Home where I made you to live forever. Many paths of this world seem pleasing and right, but they will deceive you into a slumber that is both dangerous and difficult to wake up from.

**2 Corinthians 4:6**
For God, who said, "Let there be light in the darkness,
has made us understand that this Light is the brightness
of the glory of God that is seen in the face of Jesus Christ. (NLT)

**Awake, O sleeper, rise up from the dead, and Christ will give you light.**
(Ephesians 5:14)

# *"A Right Life"*

**Ephesians 5:3, 5, 6**
Let there be no sexual immorality, impurity, or greed among you.
Such sins have no place among God's people. You can be sure that
no immoral, impure, or greedy person will inherit the Kingdom of
Christ and of God. Don't be fooled by those who try to excuse these sins,
for the terrible anger of God comes upon all those who disobey Him. (NLT)

Our Father in Heaven has made it quite clear that we are to live right. We are expected to obey His Laws—holy and just laws that are of great value in this life and eternal value in the next. Being the natural born sinners that we are, obeying God is not any easy task for anyone, especially for those of us who have lived many lawless years without knowing it. I lived many years obeying mans laws and ignoring God's, because I saw God as an angry God who purposely made this life difficult so He could send us into eternal Hell and not have to deal with us again. I saw a God who consciously made it impossible for us to live right. And with this misguided view, I went out into the world trying to live a good life, but knowing I would never be good enough, which left me feeling depressed, empty, and filled with a hopelessness that was, indeed, very dark. But by the mercy and grace of God, the Lord opened my eyes to the Truth and I began to see this difficult life as it truly is. And with my new found revelation I saw the world, this difficult life, and my own personal life, in the Light of God's Truth and my existence took on a whole new meaning with an everlasting purpose.

This fallen world and its people are under the curse of sin because of the deceitful, wicked ways of the Devil, and neither Satan nor this fallen world wants us to know the goodness of God and His plan for man. The Devil has a plan, but God has a better one. The Devil's plan is death and destruction, God's plan is eternal life. And the moment you know God's Plan, you will change course and move away from the things that make you an enemy of God—things that are wicked and immoral. Befriending a world that hates God and could care less about you is not only foolish, but this world will eventually turn against you, leaving you empty handed and alone. But know this my friend, as long as you have the breath of life in your lungs and your wits about you, you have the opportunity to choose God's Plan and escape the plan of Satan that is sucking this world into darkness. And with the power of God in your hands, you will be able to overcome this sin cursed world, and share in the goodness and glory of God's Plan, which is the greatest Plan ever this side of Heaven!

## A Whisper of Hope

**When you live in Me, dear child...**I will live in you, and no matter what this fallen world does, I will give you the power to fight it and the peace to accept it. Do not believe the lies of the Enemy and his world, for they only seek to destroy you. I, on the other hand, will bring you everlasting life.

**1 John 5:20**
And we know that the Son of God has come, and He has given us understanding so that we can know the true God. And now we are in God because we are in His Son, Jesus Christ. He is the only true God, and He is eternal life. (NLT)

**And anyone whose name was not found recorded in the Book of Life
was thrown into the Lake of Fire.**
(Revelation 20:15)

# "Simple Wisdom"

**1 Corinthians 1:18**
I know very well how foolish the message of the cross sounds
to those who are on the road to destruction. But we who are
being saved recognize this message as the very power of God. (NLT)

Even the simplest mind can reason why it's impossible for someone to come back to life after being dead and buried for days. This is why it is so hard for the most brilliant minds of the world to believe in the Resurrection Power of the Living God. It is also too simple to believe in a Sovereign God who created the universe and life with a spoken word. The greatest minds of the world have rallied around each other for thousands of years to debate the origin of the universe and life, but what they always come up with is by far more difficult to believe than the simple Truth. The Lord tells us that human wisdom is foolishness and the most brilliant people lack real understanding. The simple and easy to understand plan that God created for mankind makes the most brilliant plans of a man look utterly foolish when the Truth is known. Although God uses brilliant people to advance His Kingdom, He also uses many average, everyday people as well. Our wise God uses brilliant minds to discover new things about the universe, this world, and the bodies we live in, but sadly, many gifted and brilliant people never discover the real truth for which they seek; truth that opens the mind and softens the heart to God's incredible eternal Plan for those who would simply believe.

Mankind's brilliant reason for creation is foolish, hard to grasp, has no purpose, and if you believe and embraced it, this life will end badly for you. God's sovereign plan, on the other hand, is beyond brilliant, easy to understand, has a truly divine purpose, and if embraced, this life will end gloriously. The knowledge and capability of God compared to that of the most brilliant human mind is much like comparing the size of the universe to a single atom. God is so far above mans understanding that a rational comparison cannot be made, for with God there are simply no bounds or restrictions. No amount of human wisdom can save anyone from dying, but God can with just a word. The best of man's plans cannot stand the test of time, but the Master Planner's does. Simply put; without God and His Divine Plan, all of your plans will crumbled and disappear into the abyss forever. But if all you have my friend, is the basic knowledge of God and His glorious Plan in the bag, you have more of everything than the most brilliant of worldly minds, including wisdom and insight.

## A Whisper of Hope

**I AM the Creator, My child…**And the One who creates is always greater than that which He creates. Never forget where you came from and always seek the Truth. The world will deem you foolish and weak for believing in the Resurrection and the Life. But let not your heart be troubled, for you will overcome this foolish world and experience the brilliance to come.

**Jeremiah 10:12**
He has made the earth by His power, He has established the world by His wisdom;
And has stretched out the heavens at His discretion. (NKJ)

**Turn to Me and be saved, all the ends of the earth; for I am God, and there is no other.**
(Isaiah 45:22)

# "In Coming"

**1 Corinthians 5:7-8**
Christ, our Passover Lamb, has been sacrificed for us.
So let us celebrate the festival, not by eating the old bread
of wickedness and evil, but by eating the new bread of purity and truth. (NLT)

When a person accepts the undeserved gift of forgiveness and salvation from our Lord God and Savior, there is great reason for all Christians to rejoice and celebrate this new life, as they do in Heaven. But with the celebration of your new life of freedom from the power of sin and death, the Lord also calls you to live the remainder of your life in repentance, discarding the old sinful life that loves to sin, and put on the robe of righteousness that loves to please God. What a marvelous second chance this is my friend; to be born again in spirit and truth that changes your eternal destiny no matter how stained with sin you are; to have a new beginning—a brand new start. You have been cleansed from a life of sin that kept you separated from God and chained to death row.

The Son of God died to set you free from the power of sin that this wicked world embraces. You no longer have to fear what tomorrow my bring or even your death.. And what joy it brings when you know that all of our sins have been forever forgiven and forgotten by the Living God. What calm it brings during the storms of life when you know that your name is written in God's Book of Life. When you accept and embrace the death and resurrection of Jesus Christ as your own, you should honor the One who saved you from the pits of Hell by not hiding in the safety of your salvation. Instead, hold the Light of Life as high as you can so other fellow travelers of this difficult life-journey can see the Truth and be born again into the Kingdom of our Lord God and Savior, Jesus Christ. If you have not surrendered your old life of sin to the Lord, it would be wise to do it soon. But if you have already become a new creation, then rejoice so the whole world can see!

## A Whisper of Hope

**Rejoice and celebrate, My child...**for I have given My all so you could have it all. This new life I offer is a life of honor and glory; one of truth and righteousness. This new life in Me is truly worth living—a life that is filled with hope and joy that no one can take from you. It is yours to keep!

**Colossians 2:13-14**
You were dead because of your sins and because your sinful nature was not yet cut away. Then God made you alive with Christ. He forgave all our sins. He canceled the record that contained the charges against us. He took it and destroyed it by nailing it to Christ's cross. (NLT)

**Therefore if anyone is in Christ, he is a new creation; old things have
passed away; behold, all things have become new.**
(2 Corinthians 5:17)

# "For the Love of God"

**Psalm 91:14-15**
The LORD says, "I will rescue those who love Me. I will protect those who trust in My Name. When they call on Me, I will answer; I will be with them in trouble. I will rescue them and honor them." (NLT)

Even though the Almighty God commands us to love Him above all else and to obey His Law, He does not force us to. But because He created man with a free will, we do not always love and obey Him as we should, instead, we tend to love ourselves more and do whatever we feel like doing. It is only by knowing who God is and who we are not, that we grow to love, honor and obey Him. It is crucial that we personally know the Lord God if we are to learn what He expects and why we need to obey and follow His Way. I have learned (often the hard way) that whether we love and obey God or not, He loves us. God's love is not dependent on what we do or don't do, say or don't say, and even when we are unfaithful to Him time and time again, He remains faithful to us. God's Holy character never changes. Though we make Him unhappy and angry at times, He knows and understands our fallen nature, yet He loves us in spite of that dilemma. We can cause Him great joy, but that doesn't make Him love us any more than He already does. We can mess up big time and sadden His heart deeply, but that doesn't cause Him to love us any less.

The Almighty God loves you my friend, just has you are, broken, sinful, and hard headed. Most people don't want to know God or His Way, because it would ruin their fun. But the children of God want to know their Creator and choose to follow Him rather than this wicked world, and so He gives them the power and wisdom to overcome the ways of this fallen world that are forged in darkness. The Devil wants you to believe that God is too high up to care, too angry to love, and too strict to obey. But the Living God is love and proved it by coming to us so He could shed His blood upon the earth to cleanse our sins. Jesus Christ is our Saving God, Protector, and Sovereign King. His love never ceases no matter how far you may have strayed from Him. God knows you are sin flawed and in need of His mercy and grace, so He has provided a second chance for you to slip on His robe of righteousness that hides your sin condition. Embrace His love. Embrace your Savior!

## A Whisper of Hope

**My love for you, dear child…**does not depend on you. Your life will always be filled with mistakes and regrets, with doubts and fear, and with failure after failure, but I will always love you perfectly.

**Romans 8:38-39**
And I am convinced that nothing can ever separate us
from His love. Death can't, and life can't. The angels can't,
and the demons can't. Our fears for today, our worries about
tomorrow, and even the powers of Hell can't keep God's love away. (NLT)

**As we live in God, our love grows more perfect.**
(Romans 4:17)

# "Father and Son"

**1 Corinthians 8:6, 7**
But we know that there is only one God, the Father, who created everything,
and we exist for Him. And there is only one Lord, Jesus Christ, through whom
God made everything and through whom we have been given life. (NLT)

What a powerful and clear affirmation of the essential equality of God the Father and God the Son and where we perfectly fit into the equation. Unfortunately, most of the people living in this fallen world do not receive this truth with an open mind nor the desire to know more. They stumble blindly through this difficult life never hearing the truth, because they are too busy trying to satisfy their lusts for life from a world that doesn't want the Truth known—a world that hates Jesus and wants to keep its people enslaved to the lies of the evil Enemy of their souls. There are many lost souls that have ignored the Truth and remain trapped in the darkness of this world that promise them much, but delivers only death. But there are also many lost souls who have been found and set free by the Truth, who struggle courageously every day to remain free from the darkness that had once held them enslaved to their sinful appetites . Although our Lord God, Christ Jesus has paid the price that set us free from the power of sin, walking away from the sinful things that we love to indulge in is never easy, for the chains have been broken, but the sinful nature remains.

Freedom from this wicked world is not easy my friends, especially when you have been enslaved by its lusts for most of your life. We need a powerful Savior, a Strong Tower, and a safe Place where we can go for protection and regeneration. God paid a very hefty price to break us free from the power of sin and death, and personally purchased our tickets to Hell. It is far better to be bought by God than to be caught in the snares of Satan. It is better to be a friend of God than it is to be His enemy. It is both an honor and a privilege to serve our Lord God Jesus Christ, much more rewarding than hording the meaningless things of this world that will be lost. If you long for the Truth, you can find it by raising your hands high, looking up, and cry out for God's forgiveness and Amazing Grace. When you sincerely searched for the Truth, He will find you and set you free to live in this fallen world with the joy of the Lord in your heart, the gift of Salvation as your ticket to Heaven, and the Peace of God that will get you there safely.

## A Whisper of Hope

**I Am the only God...**dear child. There is no Other. Do not let the many false gods of this fallen world tempt you otherwise, for they do not have your best interest in mind. It is difficult to discern right from wrong in this darkened world that thrives on deceit, but when you know Me, I will set you free from the lies.

**1 John 5:20**
And we know that the Son of God has come, and He has given us understanding so that we can know the true God. And now we are in God because we are in His Son, Jesus Christ, He is the only true God, and He is eternal life. (NLT)

**God purchased you at a high price. Don't be enslaved by the world.**
(1 Corinthians 7:23)

# *"Pure Love"*

**1 Corinthians 13:4-7**
Love is patient and kind. Love is not jealous or boastful or proud or rude. Love does not demand its own way. Love is not irritable, and it keeps no record of when it has been wronged. It is never glad about injustice but rejoices whenever the truth wins out. Love never gives up, never loses faith, is always hopeful, and endures through every circumstance. (NLT)

Love is everything that our sinful nature is not. Although our mouths can speak the words, "I love you, and our minds can reason with love, and our hearts can long for it, but do we really know what true love is? The people of this world know nothing about God's love, nor will they ever experience the true and lasting love that God designed for us. Instead, the world substitute's lust, pleasure and self-importance as love, and the people who live in this kind of love are enemies of God. Our Creator commands all people to love Him above all else, but this is not an easy command for sinners to follow, because we are lovers of self and the world of pleasure. Most of us have been betrayed or hurt by worldly love and we become afraid of it. It's hard for people to know or even recognize what true love is when all they know is what this loveless world has taught them. They don't know from where it comes, why it's needed, or how to find it—all they know is the emptiness of not having it.

What the world knows of love is shallow at best. We all have our own views on what love should look like, but we search for it in all the wrong places and in all the wrong ways. It is only by seeking the Truth that you find love, and when you belong to God, He will fill your life with His never ending love. When you know your Creator, He opens the eyes of your heart to receive His love and how to return it. When you know your Savior and what He has done to prove His unconditional love, you will then discover what real love means. Although you can never fully understand God's love this side of Heaven, you can accept it and then live in it. No one will ever perfect the art of loving the way God loves, but you can begin your journey of love by exalting and loving the Living God who created you and then He will teach you how to live and love like Christ Jesus.

## A Whisper of Hope

**Loving others, dear child...**is not an easy thing to do. But as you spend time with Me, the Lover of your soul, I will teach you to love as I have loved you. When you are in love with this world, you will never know Me or My love. Instead, be in love with Me and I will fill you with an everlasting love.

**Matthew 22:37-38**
Jesus replied, "'You must love the Lord your God with all your heart,
all your soul, and all your mind. This is the first and greatest commandment.
A second is equally important: 'Love you neighbor as yourself.'" (NLT)

**The one who does not love does not know God, for God is love.**
(1 John 4:8)

# *"Soul Shepherd"*

**Psalm 100:3**
Acknowledge that the LORD is God! He made us,
And we are His. We are His people, the sheep of His pasture. (NLT)

When I think of Jesus I think of the Living God, our Almighty Creator, the King of the Universe, the Savior of the world, and the Good Shepherd of our souls. The Good Shepherd laid down His life for the souls of His flock, for they are in His care to protect, heal, comfort, and lead safely Home. In many ways we are like sheep in the great pasture of God, for our lives depend on Him, and like it or not, we belong to God. He not only created us, but He paid the ransom that set us free from the power of sin the eternal death we deserve. Our Good Shepherd could have thrown in the towel and given up, leaving us unprotected and easy prey for the Enemy. But the Lord chose to became a man in order to shepherd His people who were hopelessly lost and without direction. Much like sheep, we, too, tend to wander aimlessly with our heads to the ground, oblivious to the real dangers around us because we are too busy feeding our sinful appetites. And when we get so focused on our own hungers, we get attacked by soul eating beasts and become soul food for the Devil.

We are a prideful and rebellious people, always going our own ways, believing we are self-made, self-sustaining, and self-sufficient, but we are not. We need God the Father, Son, and Holy Spirit if we are to survive this leg of our dark journey through a world that hates God and everything that belongs to Him. The Father sent His Son to save the flock from wandering too far into the darkness where we become easy prey for the soul hungry jaws of Satan. The Good Shepherd knows how vulnerable and helpless we are without Him. The Good Shepherd never sleeps, is never surprised, or caught off guard. He searches, finds, heals our wounds, and saves. It's a soul saving miracle my friend, to be found by the Good Shepherd, who carries you out of the darkness and into His marvelous Light. How glorious it is to be in the arms of God, the Good Shepherd of your soul!

## A Whisper of Hope

**Remain close to Me, child...** because apart from Me you are easy prey for the hungry jaws of soul eating beasts. Without the Good Shepherd of your soul, you wander without direction being deceived by the Evil One and forfeiting the life of your soul.

**John 10:27-30**
Jesus replied, "My sheep hear My voice, and I know them, and they follow Me; and I give eternal life to them, and they will never perish; My Father, who has given them to Me, is greater than all; and no one is able to snatch them out of the Father's hand. I and the Father are One." (NASB)

**Once you were wandering like sheep,
but now you have turned to your Shepherd, the Guardian of your souls.**
(1 Peter 2:25)

# *"Break Out"*

**Psalm 107:13-14**
Then they cried out to the LORD in their trouble, and He saved
them out of their distresses. He brought them out of darkness
and the shadow of death, and broke their chains in pieces. (NKJ)

Even today people are still crying out to God, but sadly as a last resort—a desperate cry to
be rescued by a God they hope exits. Most people in this fallen world do not believe in
the Living God of creation, yet when their troubles are dire they cry out anyway, hoping He is
real and that He hears their cry. There are many Christians in our world who claim they believe,
but they, too, only cry out to God when the chips are down. But the number of true believer's
is growing in our world and they not only cry out to God when things are not going so well,
but they also cry out to God when things are good; when all they need is to praise and worship
the Living God for the greatness and glory that is His alone. Our God is gracious and merciful
to all people, even those who deny His existence. I know that when it is in God's good will to
do so, He helps many skeptics who cry out to Him when all else fails; when they can no longer
depend on their own strength and wisdom. I also know from my own life, that our God saves
people who are lost in utter hopelessness not wanting any help, just death.

God is love and He takes pity upon the lost and hopeless; even those who have turned away
from His love and are trapped in the deepest depths of darkness and defeat. Our Lord God and
Savior, Jesus Christ, faithfully rescues all those who humbly fall on their knees in complete surrender. The same God who saved His people Israel from their bondage in Egypt is our Almighty
Savior who is not hindered by anything. Only God can save you from the prison of darkness
that holds you chained to your sin. Only the Savior can free you from the pain and shame of
that sin. Only the Creator can give you a new heart. Only the Redeemer can give you the fresh
air of victory and a brand new start. Only Jesus can bring you back from the dead!

## A Whisper of Hope

**I hear every cry, dear child**...even those in the deepest and darkest dungeons of sin. I hear
every plea for mercy and grace. And for all those who humble themselves in My Presence, I
will part those iron bars and shatter the chains of sin that hold them down. Their rescue will
be complete and final.

**Deuteronomy 31:6**
"Be strong and of good courage, do not fear nor be afraid of them;
for the LORD your God, He is the One who goes with you.
He will not leave you nor forsake you." (NKJ)

**For every child of God defeats this evil world by trusting Christ to give the victory.**
(1 John 5:4)

# *"Renewed"*

**2 Corinthians 4:16-17**
That is why we never give up. Though our bodies are dying, our spirits are
Being renewed every day. For our present troubles are quite small and won't last
Very long. Yet they produce for us an immeasurable great glory that will last forever! (NLT)

W hen people turn their lives over to the care and control of the Lord Jesus Christ, there are two things going on in unison that are important to understand. On the one hand; our physical life will continue to age with time, wear out, and will eventually die. And while this natural aging process is taking place, the stress of living in a broken world will often quicken that process. Most people who still have their youth don't spend a lot of time thinking about growing old because life is new, filled with excitement, and they are energized by it. But as their bodies begin to break down and aging becomes more of a reality, the final countdown begins to weigh a bit heavier on their hearts. And on the other hand; as this aging process is moving forward, the people who are Christians, continually draw inner strength from the power of the Living God that gives us new life by the renewing of our spirits, the heart and soul of our eternal life in Christ Jesus.

As Christians, we must live in a fallen world that hates the very name of Jesus and we are attacked for our faith no matter whom we are or where we live. Some Christians are physically assaulted, imprisoned, and even killed. We are sometimes denied an opportunity to better our lives or fired from our jobs. We are slandered verbally by hate speech through TV, radio, and the Internet. We are sued, taken to court and deemed as bigots, because when you belong to Christ, you become an enemy of a world that is ruled by the Prince of Darkness. People who are not living in the Light of Christ Jesus are living in the darkness of the evil one and they deny God, eternal damnation, and Hell. But those who belong to God are living in the Light of His glory and can be renewed every day to persevere this godless world that hates God, righteousness, and moral behavior.

## A Whisper of Hope

**Life in Me, dear child…**has no end. This world has never been kind, nor will it ever be a friendly place to live. But the short time of hardship that you suffer now does not compare to the blessings that are yours later. Be glad, for the hardship and pain are not in vain when you live in Me.

**John 11:25**
Jesus told her, "I am the Resurrection and the Life.
Those who believe in me, even though they die like everyone else,
will live again. They are given eternal life for believing in Me and will never perish. (NLT)

**Create in me a new heart, O God. Renew a right spirit within me.**
(Psalm 51:10)

# "Mercy and Goodness"

**Psalm 118:1**
Oh, give thanks to the LORD, for He is good!
Because His mercy endures forever. (NKJ)

The Author and Finisher of Life deserves every ounce of thanks and praise that we can possibly muster, because without God, the merciful Giver of all good things, we would have no Hope and nothing good to enjoy. Mercy and goodness are His nature; the very essence of who He is and what He does. God is God. He always has been and always will be, for He can never cease being God. Everything that is good and righteous comes from above in Heaven; everything else comes from the darkness below. If you are the kind of person that can only praise God when life is good, you must rise to a higher level and praise God no matter what your circumstances are. Although there are things about this fallen world that can certainly question God's mercy and goodness, there remains one absolute truth that we should never question: God's desire to save all the people He creates from certain death and destruction. The Father's disposition concerning mankind may vary from time to time, but the mercy and goodness of His steadfast faithfulness to save remains the same.

The Living God is still pouring out His amazing grace on a world that is filled with people who have embraced the darkness of Satan—a world filled with people who love their sin and themselves more than God, and are rebellious against anything that is godly or righteous. The steadfast patience of our Lord God and Savior is beyond our understanding, because the stench of evil in this world is out of control. Even though we are all deeply guilty of sin and deserve condemnation, God has (in His mercy and goodness) graciously chosen to forgive all of our sins through the sacrificial death of His Son, Jesus Christ. If you have accepted this undeserved gift from God, you should thank Him every day of your life. But if you have not accepted His offer, you should thank Him anyways; because He is giving you time to repent. There are many reasons to praise our God in Heaven with joy and thanksgiving, especially when you know Him!

## A Whisper of Hope

**My goodness, dear child...**is found in the mercy that I pour out on you every day of your life. It is my nature; the essence of who I AM. I AM Love, Kindness, Gracious, Merciful, and Goodness. But I AM also perfectly Holy and Just in everything.

**James 1:17**
Whatever is good and perfect comes to us from
God above, who created all heaven's lights. (NLT)

**If we confess our sins to Him, He is faithful and just to forgive us.**
(1 John 1:9)

# *"The God Equation"*

**Jeremiah 9:24**
But let him who boasts boast of this, that he understands and knows Me,
that I am the LORD who exercises lovingkindness, justice and righteousness
on earth; for I delight in these things, declares the LORD. (NASB)

As sinful people living in a sinful world, we have little or nothing to boast about other than the mercy and grace of our Lord God and Savior. This fallen world has no shortage of prideful people who hold themselves in the highest esteem, whether they are successful or not. Those that have succeeded often pat themselves on the back, giving little credit to anyone or anything for their success. But in reality, these kinds of people are denying the sovereignty of God and putting themselves above the Creator who sustains all life. Throughout the history of mankind, people have been blind sighted by the lies of Satan who wants everyone to believe that they are the captain of their souls and in control of their destiny. This godless world view of self-importance and self-love is taught to us from the time we are born. Human beings have never been and never will be in control of anything even though we are brain washed into believing we are. Without the Creator there is only chaos, because it is the power of God's Word that keeps the universe in tune so we can breathe and live. Our Lord God is the One who is in total control—we on the other hand, are out of control.

There are only two major choices to make that will shape our lives and determine our eternal destiny. We can surrender to the Lord and let Him lead the charge, or we can go our own way to walk with the Devil and let him satisfy our sinful lusts. The first choice leads to Heaven; the second choice leads to Hell. The first choice teaches us the absolute truth and we experience peace and the joy of knowing the Lord, while the second choice leads to deceit, confusion, uncertainty, and the fear of death. When you ride with the Lord and let Him do the driving, your journey through this life will not end in vain, but will be the start of a glorious journey without end. You can choose to live on our own and hope for the best results, or you can choose God and get the best.

## A Whisper of Hope

**Be humble and contrite, dear child…**and follow the One who gives and sustains your life. You can be pleased with your accomplishments, but remember from whom all things come. When you journey with Me in charge, you will find true purpose in this life and vast riches in the next.

**Job 34:14-15**
If God were to take back His Spirit and withdraw His breath,
all life would cease, and humanity would turn again to dust. (NLT)

**Boast only of what the Lord has done.**
(2 Corinthians 10:17)

# "Cross Message"

**Galatians 2:20**
I have been crucified with Christ; and it is no longer I who live, but
Christ lives in me; and the life which I now live in the flesh I live by
faith in the Son of God, who loved me and gave Himself up for me. (NKJ)

What an incredibly freeing truth this is for anyone who can grasp its true meaning and then embrace its significance. We live in an extremely evil world that is only getting more evil, and those who have chosen the world rather than Christ Jesus should be thankful that they are not dead and still have time to change their minds. The Lord gives us the freedom to choose how we live our lives; He does not force His will on us. When you believe in God, you can trust His every Word or you can pick and choose what fits your agenda. You can trust in the sacrificial death of the Lamb of God Jesus Christ, or you can deny the gift of salvation and trust in your own goodness and hope you are good enough. You can surrender your life to God and know that your eternal life is safely in His hands, or you can continue down your own path that leads into the jaws of Satan. You can choose the Lord to satisfy your every need, or you can choose the world to satisfy the sinful lusts of your flesh.

There are many choices put before you that seem good but are detrimental to your spiritual health but when you surrender your life to God there is peace, comfort, joy, and the eternal promise of Heaven. But if you remain hard headed and filled with pride, relying on the world and yourself, there is no peace, little comfort, sporadic happiness, and the fear of death. You can trust the Way of God and stand blameless before the Lord on the Day of Judgment, or you can trust the ways of the world and live in fear of that day. When you understand who God is and what He did for you my friend, you will feel so liberated and thankful that you will dedicate your life to God for the rest of your days. You can embrace the message of the Cross or not, but either way the consequences of your choice will have no end.

## A Whisper of Hope

**Never forget, dear child…**that I died for you on the Cross. Bring all your sins and failed attempts at being good enough and nail them to My Cross. I canceled your debt and took the punishment that you deserved. Embrace the Cross and the message is yours!

**1 Timothy 2:4, 5-6**
He wants everyone to be saved and to understand the truth.
For there is only one God and one Mediator who can reconcile God and people.
He is the man Christ Jesus. He gave His life to purchase freedom for everyone.
This is the message that God gave to the world at the proper time. (NLT)

**We trust in the Living God, who is the Savior of all men.**
(1 Timothy 4:10)

# *"Vainly Living"*

**Psalm 127:1**
Unless the LORD builds the house, they labor in vain who builds it;
Unless the LORD guards the city, the watchman stays awake in vain. (NKJ)

Unless you know, love, and live for the Lord our God, your life is lived in vain, because apart from our Creator we gain nothing worth dying for. Without knowing the Truth of God's written Word there is no purpose for anything. Without a God driven life we run around in circles, making the same foolish mistakes hoping for better results. When you merely live for the sole purpose of existing, you end up living for the moment and hoping it is not your last. Without the absolute Truth anything and everything is game. Without knowing how you came to be and who you were created to be and for what purpose you are here and where it all leads, there is only confusion, disappointment, doubt and death. People who live apart from God and do whatever they feel like doing are living on the edge of the abyss. When your life becomes all about yourself, it leaves you empty and living in vain. When you live by our own rules and for your own sinful passions you are of no value in the Kingdom of God's Garden and the Gardener will cut you off and throw you into a heap to be burned.

The life that God has graciously given you is not an accident my friend, but a careful, well thought out plan by the Creator and Master Gardener. Without the Gardener the garden would have never been planted. Without God's gardening precision, the universe that supports garden Earth would be spinning wildly out of control with no purpose, much like a garden without a gardener would turn wild with very little produce. Without God's direction and intervention, people would feed on anything in the garden that would satisfy their appetites regardless of the consequences, much like eating from a garden without knowing what is good or what is poison. People who deny the existence of the Master Gardener have emptiness so deep that it will never be filled. People who live apart from their Savior are left unprotected, unaware, and helpless prey for the jaws of Satan.

## A Whisper of Hope

**Without Me as your** Foundation...life's storms will bring you down. Without My sustaining power your life will spin out of control. But a life build on the Foundation of Truth will stand strong through the many storms of this fallen world. Build wisely, child and I will bring eternal purpose to your life.

**John 15:5-6**
"Yes, I am the Vine; you are the branches. Those who remain in Me,
and I in them will produce much fruit. For apart from Me you are nothing.
Anyone who parts from Me is thrown away like a useless branch and withers.
Such branches are gathered into a pile to be burned." (NLT)

**But on the judgment day, fire will reveal what kind of work each builder has done.
The fire will show if a person's work has any value.**
(1 Corinthians 3:13)

# "Battle Wise"

**Galatians 5:17**
The old sinful nature loves to do evil, which is just opposite from what
the Holy Spirit wants. And the Spirit gives us desires that are opposite
from what the sinful nature desires. These two forces are constantly
fighting each other and your choices are never free from the conflict. (NLT)

The battles for your physical life and that of your eternal soul begin the very moment you are conceived. Our world and everything in it has been infected with sin, decadence, and death because of our rebellion against God. The battles that we face are indeed difficult and unpredictable, but the real battles for our hearts minds and souls are against the evil powers of Satan, who wants to keep people from knowing the Living God and to destroy everything that belongs to Him. Satan was once God's most beautiful and powerful angel who, in his quest to take over God's Kingdom, persuaded a third of all the angels to follow him in an uprising against God, but of course they failed. Satan was kicked out of Heaven and has been wreaking havoc upon the people of earth for thousands of years. Satan is the dark force of evil that drives this world; a force that every man, woman, and child must face every waking moment of their earthly lives. The unseen evil forces are very dangerous, because they not only threaten our very existence in this life, but the life of our eternal souls. The Devil is alive and working overtime in our world, and to make matters worse, our human hearts are born with a wicked and deceitful nature that loves to sin.

The evil we face is powerful and its darkness is overwhelming and it will get even more so until that glorious day when our Lord God and Savior Jesus Christ, returns to set up His Kingdom on earth. And at that time one of God's angels will bind Satan in chains and lock him in the bottomless pit for a thousand years, where he can no longer deceive the world. But until that great and awesome day, the battles rage on—battles you will fight until you breathe your very last breath—battles that you cannot win apart from God. The only hope you have in overcoming our Satan induced, evil nature to sin is found in the Power of the Holy Spirit, which you receive when you are born again in Christ Jesus. When you turn your life over to the care and control of the Lord, He will help you win the everyday battles of good and evil. With the renewing of your heart, you will gain the strength and wisdom to fend off the attacks of the Devil. Never doubt the powerful hold that sin has over you my friend, and never doubt the inherent weaknesses you possess in fighting that power. For without the power of God, you will lose.

## A Whisper of Hope

**Awaken; dear child...**for your very life depends on it. You can love this evil world or you can love Me. You can love to sin and follow Satan into Hell, or you can love Me and journey Home. You can hide in the darkness and loose, or live in the Light and win. It is a choice of death or life.

**2 Peter 1:3, 4**
As we know Jesus better, His divine power gives us everything we need for
living a godly life. He has promised that you will escape the decadence all
around you caused by evil desires and that you will share in His divine nature. (NLT)

**Fight the good fight of faith**
(1 Timothy 6:12)

# Down and Out

**Psalm 119:144**
Your decrees are always fair; help me to understand them that I may live.
I pray with all my heart; answer me LORD! I will obey Your principles. (NLT)

I t is not wise to disobey the Lord our God and Creator, because the consequence of unrepentant disobedience is eternal death, forever separated from God and His goodness. For most of us this fallen world shapes our views about right and wrong and we have a difficult time understanding God's holy ways and the standards that He commands us to live by. But once we begin to know who our God is, why He created us, and why we should live the way He designed us to live, everything about this life becomes a bit clearer. Many of us come to the Lord desperate for the Truth, because the world's truth leaves us empty and with many questions that cannot be answered. For those who are living the world's way, they have been deceived by the false god of this fallen world; the Prince of Darkness. The world is an evil place because it is ruled by the Devil who has twisted and reshaped God's truth to fit his own agenda, which is to destroy God's creation.

If you think that God's Way is old fashion, my friend; that it is too righteous and a fun destroyer, then your future is rather bleak and very dark. For you have been fooled by the Devil and his false ways and you are a slave to sin and darkness. But you are not alone, for most people lose their way and never recover, because one day they wake up in a pit of Hell and wonder what happened. Don't follow the world and lose your eternal soul. Instead, discard your old sinful life and let Christ Jesus put His robe of righteousness on you so you can live forever. It is easier to take the path of least resistance—the one that looks to be good, but in reality it is a well disguised path that leads you nowhere but down and out.

## A Whisper of Hope

**With Me in your corner, dear child...**you may go down, but not for the full count. For only I have the power to get you back on your feet and on solid ground, so you can win the prize of eternal life with Me. Although the Devil is clever, He is no match for my infinite knowledge and sovereignty.

**Isaiah 41:10**
Don't be afraid, for I am with you.
Don't be discouraged, for I am your God.
I will strengthen you and help you. I will
hold you up with my victorious right hand. (NLT)

**Have mercy on me, O God...Purify me from my sin...For I was born a sinner.**
(Psalm 51:1, 2, 3)

## June

# *"Nail and Cross"*

**Galatians 5:24**
Those who belong to Christ Jesus have nailed
The passions and desires of their sinful nature
To His cross and crucified them there. (NLT)

O ur Lord God and Savior became the perfect sacrificial Lamb of God and His blood was shed upon the earth to cleanse the world of its sin. This undeserved gift of forgiveness and salvation should never be taken for granted, nor should it be refused, because it guarantees the life of your eternal soul. When your sins are covered by the blood of Christ, you are not only clothed in the righteousness of the Son of God, but you are a new creation with a new heart, and you will begin an everlasting journey with the One True God who saved you from darkness and certain death. And with this new life, you will receive the Holy Spirit to keep you free from the power of sin and death—an evil power that has ruled mankind since the dawn of time.

This does not mean that your sinful nature suddenly disappears and you will never succumb to its temptations again, but when you sorrowfully recognize the sin you commit, it is forgiven and not held against you. The old sinful nature that loves to sin is being transformed into a new nature that hates sin and loves God. What an amazing peace that God's forgiveness brings to our hearts. I have found no greater joy in living than knowing my Creator and Savior, Jesus Christ. We have an amazing God, my friends, the One you should know and love. Accept God's amazing gifts of love and forgiveness, nail your sins to the Cross of Christ, and be resurrected anew, for only then will you know Peace!

## A Whisper of Hope

**I AM your Savior, dear child…**the One who sets you free from the dark and evil forces that keep you enslaved to your sin. It is My Sovereign Power that saves you from Hell and Satan, the evil enemy and killer of your soul. Walk safely with Me as your redeemer and you shall remain safe!

**Ephesians 1:13-14**
And when you believed in Christ, He identified you as His own by giving you
the Holy Spirit whom He promised long ago. The Spirit is God's guarantee that
He will give us everything He promised and that He has purchased us to be His
own people. This is just one more reason for us to praise our glorious God. (NLT)

**He has delivered us from the power of darkness.**
(Colossians 1:13)

# "Saving Nature"

**Psalm 145:14**
The LORD upholds all who fall,
And rises up all those who are bowed down. (NKJ)

As I draw closer to the Lord, the greater my desire is to honor Him for being the saving God that He is. And as I learn about God's unconditional love, and His mercy and grace, the more I want to fill my life with Him. We are blessed by the faithful patience He has for such a rebellious people, because He keeps many of us from dying in our sins that would have otherwise put us away forever. I, like many before me, experienced the saving grace of our sin-less Savior Christ Jesus, who saved us by dying in our sin. Jesus rescues us before wandering so far away that we can never get Home. He never stops pursuing the lost and downtrodden, for He is, by nature, a Holy and Saving God. How blessed I feel for having the God of Creation transforming my once lost and hopeless existence into a God driven life that has been cleansed, renewed, and filled with the joy of the Lord. And no matter what transpires in this fallen world, I have the Promise of Salvation, and the guarantee that nothing will ever separate me from Jesus' love or protection.

Our awesome God loves completely. Both His love and commitment are unconditional, because He knows we are all sin flawed and can never be good enough. The Lord takes pity upon the lowly; those dejected souls who are suffering and discouraged, laden with the heavy loads of this hard and unfair world. It is the Lord's hand that is holding everything up, giving people time to chose and His children the strength and courage to live faithfully through the many storms that are raging in our world and getting more dangerous with time. The Lord hears every cry of those who are lost in the hopelessness of this dark world and desperately reaching out for a miracle. God is our only Hope. He is our Heavenly Father, our Mighty Savior, and our Sovereign Helper; a God filled with lovingkindness and amazing grace. Whether you are strutting on high ground or low crawling in shame, God receives everyone just as they are, for none are too high, nor is anyone so low that they are beyond His incredible saving grace. God's plan is redemption, His goal is perfection, and there is nothing greater than He who saves!

## A Whisper of Hope

**Be not afraid or discouraged, My child...**for I Am with you always. I will pick you up when you fall and remove the burdens you were not created to bear. I lighten your loads and help you stand strong. I dust you off when you fall, and put you on a good path; it is who I AM; it is what I do!

**Mathew 11:28-29**
"Come to Me, all you who labor and are heavy laden,
and I will give you rest. Take My yoke upon you and learn from Me,
for I am gentle and lowly in heart, and you will find rest for your souls." (NKJ)

**For He wants everyone to be saved and to understand the Truth.**
(1 Timothy 2:4)

# "Safe Bedfellow"

**Psalm 4:8**
I will lie down in peace and sleep, for
You alone, O LORD, will keep me safe. (NLT)

K ing David was a man after God's own heart; a man who was able to lie down and sleep in peace even though his bed was that of hard barren ground and his enemies were in hot pursuit and quickly closing in. David was able to sleep, because he knew God would protect him, even while he slept. And much like David, we too, are being hunted down and pursued by a relentless Enemy who wants to destroy everything that belongs to God. Satan and this fallen world will never grow weary in their quest to destroy the human race, especially the Church of our Lord God and Savior, Jesus Christ. God's most powerful enemy will indeed succeed in destroying you without the armor of God as your protection. Once we are born again, the battles for our hearts, souls, and minds intensifies, because while we lived apart from God, we were already dead in our sin. But as a Christian with the power of God in you, you are a threat to Satan's plan, and for the reminder of your earthly life you will be fighting the ungodly and evil forces of darkness that have enslaved our world.

Our Christian lives become a battle field when we stand for the Truth, and the enemy will try to discourage you, deceive you and draw you away from God's protection. But as a Christian you will learn how to fight and win the battles that come with every new day. The Lord does not call us to Himself so we can become complacent and comfortable in our salvation, but to put on the full armor of God and defend our faith. God calls each of us to fight for the privilege of being called by His Name, and to help those who are trapped in the darkness of sin--those unaware of the spiritual battle for their souls. Never doubt the spiritual warfare that is raging, my friends, for the battles are increasing as the Devil's demise grows closer. And the only way we can lay down and sleep in peace, is by knowing that whether we wake up in this world or not, we will be in the arms of the Savior, the most powerful and faithful Bedfellow ever!

## A Whisper of Hope

**Let Me cover you, dear child...**with My love and protection. There is no better place to lay your head than on My promise of safe-keeping. And whether you awaken from your earthly slumber or not, you are safe with Me. You need not fear the darkness that is closing in, for I am with you always.

**1 Peter 5:8, 9**
Be careful! Watch out for attacks from the Devil, your great
enemy. He prowls around like a roaring lion, looking for some
victim to devour. Take a firm stand against him, and be strong in your faith. (NLT)

**Every word of God proves true. He defends all who come to Him for protection.**
(Proverbs 30:5)

# "Above Meditation"

**Philippians 4:8**
Finally, brethren, whatever things are true, whatever things are noble, whatever things are just, whatever things are pure, whatever things are lovely, whatever things are of good report, if there is any virtue and if there is anything praiseworthy—meditate on these things. (NKJ)

Even born again Christians can find themselves trapped in all the business that this fast paced world demands of us, and are often distracted from the good will of God. As imperfect people, we are basically self-focused and easily tempted, and we are bombarded everyday with temptations that are created by the Devil and implemented by this wicked world. Without the power of God it's impossible for anyone to resist the power of sin, so most people fall prey to sinful pleasures that seem good, but are really our death sentence. People tend to believe the lies that this fallen world embraces as the truth, because this world is further away from God than it ever has been. Instead of trusting in the Absolute Truth from our Creator, which we need, most people simply go with the flow, unaware of the danger it imposes. Everything that is true and noble and just and pure and lovely and good and perfect comes from God, because they are the very characteristics that radiate the glory of who He is. His perfect and infinite truths never change nor will they ever cease to exist.

It's the Lord's godly characteristics and truths that He wants all people to know and develop, not only for their own well being, but also for the world to see. This sinful world is filled with ungodly people who follow their own lustful desires, who are led by Satan and they thrive on deceit and trickery, dirt and scandal, sexual immorality and perversion, murder and theft, shamelessness and boasting, violence and murder, and greed and self-seeking gain. And because these things surround us on all sides, it never has been nor will it ever be easy to block out the world and meditate on the admirable things of God that are truly worthy. Satan and his wicked world will do everything in their power to keep you away from God so they can devour your soul. Only by the power of the Holy Spirit can you live in ways that honor God and glorify His Name. God will give you the desire and wisdom to live and love like a child of the Living God when your meditation is above.

## A Whisper of Hope

**It is good, My child…**that you focus on the Me, the Creator of life and all that is good. If you are to live in peace with this world you must meditate on things from above, for when you do you will escape the decadence around you.

**James 3:17**
But the wisdom that comes from Heaven is first of all pure.
It is also peace loving, gentle at all times, and willing to yield to others.
It is full of mercy and good deeds. It shows no partiality and is always sincere. (NLT)

**Every word of God proves true.**
**He defends all who come to Him for protection.**
(Proverbs 30:5)

# "Secret Treasure"

**Colossians 2:2-3**

My goal is that they will be encouraged and knit together by strong ties of love. I want them to have full confidence because they have complete understanding of God's secret plan, which is Christ Himself. In Him lie hidden all the treasures of wisdom and knowledge. (NLT)

E ven though this first century letter from the apostle Paul was written to encourage the believers in Colossi, it is also a message that every Christian today should pay close attention to. God is giving us some good pointers on how to avoid being deceived by the many false teachers who are still busy spreading their false doctrine to the Church of our Lord Jesus Christ in order to confuse and mislead us. Because the satanic power of the Devil is driving this fallen world, it has infiltrated the Church from its very beginning. So just as it was in the first century AD, the message of our Lord God is being twisted and rewritten to justify the endless array of sinful pleasures that we love to indulge in. Many churches claim they are teaching sound biblical doctrine, but they are really compromising God's sovereign authority, misinterpreting His holy Word, and spreading the lies of Satan—that this life is all about you and what you can get while the gettin' is good—that we are the captains of our souls and God is whomever we want Him to be—that He is just too loving and too kind to send people to Hell so they can suffer in the fire that never goes out.

The world is bursting at the seams with false teachings and it is spreading rapidly throughout the entire world via the Internet. World wise scholars are teaching us smooth sounding philosophy that is utterly foolish, and it leads us down paths that are both futile and eternally dangerous. The world says that true wisdom and knowledge are hidden away from most of us and are only found in a mystical experience from a higher knowledge. Many of these false teachers claim that this "secret knowledge" is only available to a few select elites with the highest IQ and a special calling. But that is not true, for God's secret plan is not hidden from you my friend, it is for everyone to know. It is easily found in the pages of God's Book, clear and concise words that are simple to understand and clear enough to follow. All the wisdom and knowledge you will ever need comes from the Author of Life.

## A Whisper of Hope

**Come close, dear child…**and listen carefully, for it is by hearing and believing My Word that the treasures of life are revealed. Do not be duped by the world's nonsense, because its treasures last only a moment!

**Romans 16:17-18**

Watch out for people who cause divisions and upset people's faith by teaching things that are contrary to what you have been taught. Stay away from them. Such people are not serving Christ our Lord; they are serving their own personal interests. By smooth talk and glowing words they deceive innocent people. (NLT)

**Wherever your treasure is, there your heart and thoughts will also be.**
(Matthew 6:21)

# "He Watches"

**Psalm 16:1**
Preserve me, O God,
for in You I put my trust. (NKJ)

Even though Jesus Christ was fully God clothed in human flesh, He did not rely on His sovereign power while He lived on the earth. Instead, He prayed to the Father in Heaven and followed the Father's will. God has been called "the Watcher of Men" because He sees all things at all times and He pays special attention to His children, which He preserves in Christ Jesus—He protects and provides everything we need to live a godly life. Even though our Lord Jesus left the glory of Heaven to save the world, He kept His focus on God's will, as we should all do. And just as Jesus cried out to the Father in His time of need, so too, should we cry out to our Redeemer, the Holy One of Israel, to safely watch over us until it's time for us to go Home. If Jesus, who was fully divine, looked outside of Himself, how much more should we do the same as flawed, sinful people who cannot even begin to protect or save ourselves from the powers of darkness that rule this world?

Oh, how we should fully trust in our Omnipotent Protector with an unwavering faith and a heart filled with thanksgiving. Our Father in Heaven is indeed, graciously watching over all those in need of His divine intervention. And when anyone, sincerely declares Jesus Christ as their Lord and Savior and cry out for His mercy and grace and forgiveness, they can be sure, with the utmost confidence, that their cry will be heard and their needs will be met in God's perfect timing. And as our Savior prayed to the Father which art in Heaven, we should follow suit and pray to Him as well. And just as Jesus conquered sin and death, we too, will become conquerors through Him. When you are being ravaged by the storms of life, dear friends, cry out to the Lord God for resolve and say: "I put my trust in You alone, O Great and Mighty God," and you will gain an indescribable heavenly peace as you wait quietly and confidently for His perfect help to come. And when it comes, it may or may not be the kind of help you think you need, but whatever God does, it will be perfect for you!

## A Whisper of Hope

**Trust in the Father, dear child...**for when you do, He will gladly help you. Whenever you put your confidence in the Me, the Living God, you will find peace and resolve, for I am always watching over you.

**Jeremiah 23:23**
"Am I a God who is only in one place?" asks the LORD.
"Do they think I cannot see what they are doing? Can anyone hide from Me?
Am I not everywhere in all the heavens and earth?" asks the LORD. (NLT)

### For the LORD hears the cries of His needy ones.
(Psalm 69:33)

# *"Close Quarters"*

**Hebrews 4:16**
So let us come boldly to the throne of our gracious God.
There we will receive His mercy, and we will find grace
To help us when we need it the most. (NLT)

Because our Lord God and Savior, Jesus Christ, shed His blood and died as the finial sacrificial Lamb of God, we who believe that no other sacrifice is needed for our salvation are now able to come boldly into God's Holy Presence, to ask for His forgiveness and His help—help that is needed every day of our lives if we want to survive the onslaught of evil that has gripped this godless world. And now that Jesus has set us free from our bondage to sin and death, we not only have the ultimate High Priest in Heaven as our Advocate, but we also have the Good Shepherd providing us with everything we need to live a righteous and holy life. And with our sovereign Advocate and Good Shepherd, there comes peace and protection while we live in a world that is anything but peaceful or safe. We live in a deceitful world filled with soul hungry beasts that are preying on the weak and destroying their lives. But Christians live in the safety of the Shepherd's flock and we do not live in fear, but in Truth. And we are protected from the jaws of eternal death by the blood of Christ.

If you want to survive in this Jesus hating world, you would be wise to remain close to the One who died to save you from the pits of Hell, and let Him lead you to greener pastures where you will drink the living water of eternal life. People are weary with thirsty souls that long to be refreshed and strengthen for the difficult life-journey that we didn't volunteer for. There is no One greater than the Good Shepherd of our souls, because Jesus is the Sovereign Living God who knows all things and nothing slips by Him. You should listen when He calls, my friend and do what He says. For when you do, it will not only save you from an eternity of darkness and regret, but Jesus will heal your wounds, comfort your soul, and make all things new, which will give you a peace so incredible that you can't keep it to yourself.

## A Whisper of Hope

**I AM the Good Shepherd...**you are Mine. I will never abandon you in darkness, nor leave you unprotected and alone. My Light will keep the enemies of your soul at bay and save you from the Devil, who lurks in the darkness ready to pounce and rip your life to shreds. Come into My flock, dear one and you will find rest and safety for your battle weary soul.

**John 10:14-15**
"I am the Good Shepherd; I know My own sheep,
And they know Me, just as My Father knows Me and
I know the Father. And I lay down My life for the sheep.

**The LORD is my shepherd; I have everything I need.**
(Psalm 23:1)

# *"God and Friends"*

**Psalm 25:14**
Friendship with the LORD is reserved for those who fear Him.
With them He shares the secrets of His covenant. (NLT)

Much like it is with good friends who walk together sharing their secrets, so it is with Christ Jesus and those who call Him Lord. Because our Lord God and Savior sacrificed His life on the cross we can now be in the Holy Presence of God, sharing our deepest secrets and learning His. When you humbly go to the foot of the cross and fully accept the gift of forgiveness and salvation, the Holy Spirit begins to reveal the secrets of God concerning life and death and everything in between. In the old covenant between God and His people Israel, the dwelling place of God was in a tent and was called the Most Holy Place, which was hidden from His people by a sacred curtain. Only the high priest, and only once a year, was he allowed to enter through the sacred curtain with the sacrificial blood of animals as an offering for all the sins of Israel. But now we are under the new covenant of grace that was fully paid for with the blood of Jesus. The moment our Savior gave up His Spirit in death, the sacred curtain that separated sinful man from the Most Holy God was ripped in two, making it possible for all men and women to personally be in the Presence of God no matter where they are. And with this new covenant comes a new friendship with God, for He shares His Spirit, giving us the power to understand His secrets as we read and study the Book of God's Story from Creation to Revelation. When you have true fellowship with the Author of Life, my friends, He listens closely to the secrets that trouble your soul and offers you comfort and peace while sharing His secrets of salvation and redemption. Never take for granted the sacrifice God made to save your eternal life from Hell, and don't ever pass up the chance to be called His friend, because without His friendship, this dark world will hunt you down and draw you into its darkness until there is no way out!

## A Whisper of Hope

**I invite you, My child...**to come into My Presence where we can share our secrets. For it is through our relationship that you find the truth about life and death. To be a friend of God you must fear and respect My sovereignty and never doubt My faithfulness, for I Am called Faithful and True. To be a friend of the King is a glorious blessing; one that will last forever.

**John 15:15**
"No longer do I call you servants, for the servant does not
know what his master is doing; but I have called you friends,
for all things that I have heard from My Father I have made known to you. (NKJ)

**But there is a God in heaven who reveals secrets.**
(Daniel 2:28)

# *"Mourning to Morning"*

**Psalm 30:5**
For His anger is but for a moment, His favor is for life;
Weeping may endure for a night, but joy comes in the morning. (NKJ)

People who believe in and follow Jesus Christ (especially those of us who have been so graciously rescued from the deep darkness of unending pain and shame) will never be able to thank God enough for His incredible mercy and amazing grace. He has shown us who He is through the wonders of creation, through the shedding of His blood, and through the transforming power that gives us new life. It is because of God's great love and compassion for people that everyone should live in thanksgiving, because without God's provision, protection, and His glorious Plan of Redemption, His wrath would have completely destroyed every man, woman, and child in this evil world a long time ago. Instead, God choose to give this world another chance by saving Noah and his family from the flood that destroyed the rest of mankind. The Lord gave mankind a new start on an earth that was reshaped for our good pleasure. Now we have the blood of Jesus covering our sins so we can live this life-journey in the Presence of the Living God, because when we accept the undeserved gift of salvation we become God's very own children. We are blood bought, personally called, and divinely set apart for God and His eternal purpose.

But because we are not yet made perfect, we still fall short of God's glorious standard and suffer the consequences of our sins. There will be times when we are personally disciplined by God because He wants us to learn from our weaknesses to grow strong in His righteousness. But even though the Lord's discipline is justly deserved and can seem rather harsh at times, we soon discover the peace in knowing that His anger lasts but a moment. When the Lord's frown is upon us, we are like a flower in darkness, but when the darkness is lifted and His favor shines again, our lives will once again reflect the glory of who God is and all that He has done. When you belong to the Son of Righteousness, He will rise up and shine His Face upon your life and you can be sure that your mourning will fade in the morning because the Son's Light can never be snuffed out!

## A Whisper of Hope

**In this fallen world...**dear child, there will always be sorrow, pain, disappointment, failure, shame, and guilt. And when your night is dark and your grief is great, know that the Light of the Son is greater. For the darkness cannot exist in God's glorious Light.

**Jeremiah 31:13**
I will turn their mourning into joy.
I will comfort them and exchange their sorrow for rejoicing. (NLT)

> **"I am the Light of the world; he who follows Me
> will not walk in the darkness, but will have the Light of life."**
> (John 8:12)

# "Be Still"

**James 1:19-22**
Be quick to listen, slow to speak, and slow to get angry. Your anger can never
make things right in God's sight. So get rid of all the filth and evil in your lives,
and humbly accept the message God has planted in your hearts, for it is strong enough
to save your souls. And remember, it is a message to obey, not just to listen to. (NLT)

Because the world we live in is infected with sin, we tend to focus on ourselves and what we want. This "all about me" way of living does not come from our Creator, but from the Destroyer. We live under the domain of the Prince of Darkness, making us prideful, hard headed and very difficult to hold our tongues and listen, especially when it comes to the absolute Truth of who God is, who we are, and for what purpose we were created. It is our nature to want to believe we are in charge. But in reality we know that we are in control of very little. It is the Creator, our Lord God and Savior who is in control and our lives rest solely in His mercy and grace. It is only by the blood of Jesus and the resurrection power of God that saves us from this wicked world that is decaying rapidly. When we don't know the Truth, we are allowing the evil in this world to control the way we think and speak and act, and the results are anything but good and the consequences are even worse. Following the world's ungodly ways will take you into the darkness of evil where Satan reigns, and the deeper you go, the more enslaved to it you become. You cannot escape on our own. Without the saving grace of our Savior, we are all Hell bound and in very deep trouble, because we are born as children of wrath. Without Jesus my friend, you are headed for Hell because the lust for living in sin is great and you get too busy with this world to hear the Voice of God. And when you cannot hear the Voice of God, the only voice you hear is that of the Destroyer.

But Christ Jesus defeated the power of sin and death and we are now free to follow the Way that leads to better living in this world and eternal life in the next. We can escape the prison of darkness that holds us captive to our sin and lusts if we so desire, because our Savior has been here and paid the price for our freedom, making it possible for anyone to find their way out of the darkness and into the Light. So live quietly and be still my friends, listening for the saving voice of Jesus. Living in this dark world without God becomes miserably empty, extremely unsatisfying, and will eventually end badly. When you listen for God's voice you will hear it and you will find everlasting peace and joy. The only hope you have of escaping the death grip of the Destroyer is found only in the arms of God, the Creator and Savior of your Life. Be still and listen for that still small voice whispering your name and calling you Home.

## A Whisper of Hope

**Listen to Me...**and I will lead you to victory, so you can wear the crown of eternal life. For by hearing and believing the Truth will set you free from the darkness that enslaves our world. Listen and escape! Listen and live!

**Isaiah 53:3**
Come to me with your ears wide open. Listen, for the life of your souls is at stake. (NLT)

**Be still and know that I am God.**
(Psalm 46:10)

# *"The Cure"*

**James 4:7, 8, 9, 10**
So humble yourselves before God. Resist the Devil, and he will flee
From you. Draw close to God and He will draw close to you. Let there
Be tears for the wrong things you have done. When you bow down before
The Lord and admit your dependence on Him, He will lift you up and give you honor. (NLT)

To find any lasting peace in this life or avoid the darkness of decadence that blinds us from the Truth and if we are to escape the deadly and final wrath of God's judgment, we must first and foremost believe and accept that Jesus Christ is the Lord over all creation and humbly accept His gift of forgiveness and salvation. We must believe that Jesus is the Son of God—that He was fully man and fully God—One with the Father and One with the Holy Spirit, who created the universe and everything else that exists. We must know about and believe in God's ultimate plan for man and creation. And if you want to participate in His glorious redemptive plan, you must live in Christ Jesus and follow the Way that leads to righteous living and everlasting life. But if you decide to follow your own way, just as this fallen world teaches us to do, you will become a recipient of the unfortunate part of God's Great Plan for man.

All of us come into this world as sinners who love to do whatever we want. Most of us are shaped by the world's view on life and death, and most of us spend much of our allotted time on this earth living the lie with a false sense of security. And because of this, many of us have experienced the hope and joy of life sucked right out of our very being, leaving us miserable, hopeless, and wondering why we even try hanging on. Without the hope we have in Jesus, we have nothing, but more broken promises and more fear of the unknown until the light of our life is snuffed out. Everything this world has to offer is at best temporary and the only real promise it can keep is death. God has been more than gracious since the day the world fell into the darkness of sin, because He had the plan for man before the world was created. Are you tired of being betrayed and lied to by this world? Are you sick of always being disappointment and craving more from a world that cannot deliver enough? Well, my friends, there is a cure for the emptiness and hopelessness that ravages our world, and that cure is found in Jesus, for in Him there is forgiveness and a glorious new life that lasts forever.

## A Whisper of Hope

**Be cured, My child…**of the disease that leads to eternal death. Let Me save your life, because living in the pleasures of this sin-filled world is a death sentence. Living in Me is your life sentence. You have the freedom to choose, but choose wisely while you have the breath of life.

**Revelation 7:17**
"For the Lamb who stands in front of the throne will be their Shepherd. He will lead them to the springs of life-giving water. And God will wipe away all their tears." (NLT)

**Thank God for His Son—a gift too wonderful for words.**
(2 Corinthians 9:15)

# "Thirsty Souls"

**Psalm 42:1, 2**
As the deer pants for the water brooks, so pants my soul
for You, O God. My soul thirsts for God, for the living God. (NKJ)

Amid every human life there are always seasons of drought; times when it feels as if you are being scorched by hell itself and it seems like your life is burning out of control and you are desperately searching for even one drop of water that would ease the thirst and put the fire out. We all have times when our efforts are never good enough and the options seem to run out. No living soul is exempt from the fire storms that this hellish world brings. And all it takes is one lone spark, one unexpected strike and your life is ablaze with fire storms that can take your life and burn it to the ground. Even seasoned Christians who faithfully live in the Lord experience times of drought, sometimes feeling defeated or discouraged or abandoned by God. Whether you choose to follow God or the world, we are all destined to experience times of sadness, hopelessness, fear, helpless, and a longing to be refreshed and given a speck of hope.

This thirst we have for something or someone greater than ourselves is really a longing for the Living God. And the desire we have to hang on to this life as long as we can is because we do not want to die, for God has put eternity on every human heart He creates. We all have it, we all experience it, and it is only the Living Water from Heaven that can quench the thirst you have for the Creator who gives you life—the Savior who saved your life—the Sovereign God who protects your life and provides everything you need for life. When you drink the Living Water from the cup of God's amazing grace you will find yourself refreshed, strengthened, and ready to put out the fire storms that are hot on your heals. You are never alone my friend. The Lord is always there to offer you His cup of Living Water. Take it, put it to your lips, drink deeply from it, and it will give you eternal life!

## A Whisper of Hope

**Come to Me, child...** for only I can quench the thirst you have for life. This life can often become one drought after another, but when you come to Me I will put My Spirit in your life and bring you hope. This world cannot quench your thirsty soul with what it does not have. But I can! And I will!

**John 4:13-14**
Jesus answered and said to her, "Whoever drinks of this water will
thirst again, but whoever drinks of the water that I shall give him
will become in him a fountain of water springing up into everlasting life." (NKJ)

**To all who are thirsty I will give the springs of the water of life without charge.**
(Revelation 21:6)

# "Wanted Alive"

**Psalm 49:15**
But as for me, God will redeem my life.
He will snatch me from the power of death. (NLT)

D eath is not a subject that most people like talking about, especially when it comes to their own death or the death of those they love. But death is a reality and at some point it does require our attention, especially for those we leave behind. But our earthly death is not the end, but the beginning of a very long eternal life. Sadly, the vast majority of people in the world do not know the Truth about death or life, because the Devil has poisoned their minds with his lies. The only Truth there is comes from our Creator and He has graciously shared it with those who desire to know it. Unfortunately, God's Truth never has been nor will it ever be accepted by this evil world driven by secular humanism and many false gods created by the powers of darkness. Man made truth and wisdom is not only utter foolishness to God and those who know Him, but it is always changing with the times and is therefore, not always true. In order to know and understand the real Truth that never changes, you must first believe that it is our Lord God Jesus Christ who created all things, and it is He who sets the true standards that we must live by and believe in.

Creation is a well thought out plan that has order and purpose with rules and consequences. It is easy to do whatever you feel like doing when you believe that this life is all there is. But when you know the Truth and believe there are eternal consequences for your thoughts and actions, it is not so easy to rebel against the holiness of the One who sets the standards. It is much harder to live in righteousness than it is live in sin, because the world hates the Lord and all those who follow Him. When you see yourself as a product of chance and evolution, living becomes nothing more than raw survival, grabbing what you can while you can and you become nothing more than a thoughtless animal with instincts only for survival. When you live apart from our Lord God Jesus Christ, you become self-centered, closed minded, hard headed, and dead, because without the Savior, the darkness of the grave will swallow you alive forever.

## A Whisper of Hope

**Do not believe, dear child...**the foolish mindset of this fallen world's view on life and death. Instead, know and believe the only Truth that is found in the inerrant Word of God, for your eternal life is at stake.

**Romans 14:7-8**
For we are not our own masters when we live or when we die.
While we live, we live to please the Lord. And when we die, we go
to be with the Lord. So in life and in death, we belong to the Lord. (NLT)

**For to be carnally minded is death, but to be spiritually minded is life and peace.**
(Romans 8:6)

# *"Heart in Hand"*

**Psalm 51:10, 12**
Created in me a clean heart, O God, and renew a steadfast spirit within me.
Restore to me the joy of Your salvation, and uphold me by Your generous Spirit. (NKJ)

It is from the fallen human heart that sin and evil begins. And from the heart it goes into the mind where it grows to take action, and although the forbidden fruit seems pleasing enough to the eye, it is poison to the soul. Everyone is born with the nature to sin first and enjoy it. Since sin is our nature, we love our sin more than we love our God, causing us to rebel against the holiness of God. The evil powers of Satan are responsible for the curse, and it's futile to combat on our own, because it's a power much greater than our sin corrupt wills can restrain. No matter how hard we try, we tend to succumb to its power even though we are aware of the possible consequences. And what is even more unfortunate, is that most people go about their lives happily sinning away without a clue to what is at stake—that they are wasting their short precious lives on the very things that are pulling them away from God's saving grace and the eternal glory that is theirs in Christ Jesus.

It is for this very reason that the Lord took matters into His own hands and physically came into our broken world to break the chains that held His people in bondage to sin and death. And when His mission was completed, He sent the Holy Spirit to show us the Way to remain free from the powers of Hell. The Lord came, the Lord saved, and the Lord provided, but He left the decision to us: We can choose to remain living in our sin and suffer the consequences later, or we can choose a life in Christ so we can enjoy the glorious rewards later. But no matter how strong or how good you may think you are, the Enemy will find a way to sneak in and plant the seeds of sin into your mind, where it will either take root and grow, or be discarded and thrown out by the Power of God. The heart is the rudder for your life-journey and unless the Lord has it in His hands you can be sure that the sin in your heart will steer you on a long, dark journey that is far removed from the wonderful life-journey the Lord is calling you on.

## A Whisper of Hope

**My Power in you...**is sufficient, dear child. You are born with sin in your heart and if gone unchecked will lead you on a journey of unending darkness. Come to Me and I will give you a new heart and restore what is broken. Come to Me, for I AM the Restorer of hearts and the Giver of Life.

**Psalm 34:18**
The LORD is close to the brokenhearted;
He rescues those who are crushed in spirit. (NLT)

**"I will give them hearts that will recognize Me as the LORD."**
(Jeremiah 24:7)

# *"Live in Light"*

**1 John 1:5-6**
God is Light and there is no darkness in Him at all.
So we are lying if we say we have fellowship with God but go on
living in spiritual darkness. We are not living in the Truth. (NLT)

When you surrender your sinful life to the Lord, the first thing you do is nail it to His Cross and be resurrected anew, because from that moment on you are a child of the Living God—you no longer live just to satisfy the desires that once controlled how you lived—you are no longer a slave to the sins that this dark world embraces. With God's Light shinning upon the darkness around you, you will see the deceit and better understand the utter hopelessness it offers. Just as light and dark cannot co-exist at the same moment in time, neither can we live in God's Light while embracing the darkness of the world. The apostle John goes on to tell us: "Stop loving this evil world and all that it offers you, for when you love the world, you show that you do not have the love of the Father in you. For the world offers only the lust for physical pleasure, the lust for everything we see, and pride in our possessions. These are not from the Father. They are from this evil world. And this world is fading away, along with everything it craves. But if you do the will of God, you will live forever" (1 John 2:15-17) .

It is certainly not a sin to enjoy the good things that God has given us to enjoy, but where we go wrong is when we make them our gods. Our sinful natures crave the pleasures of the flesh that will pull us into darkness where we are fair game for the jaws of Satan. Without the Light that the Lord has so graciously provided, you will journey into a darkness that will not only wreak havoc upon your present life, but will have horrific eternal consequences that never go away. But living in the Light of God's Truth is everlasting and God centered. You cannot fool God my friend, nor can you hide in your sin, for it is either God's Way or the highway to Hell. You are either with God or without Him. There is no gray area, just light and dark. You are either in or you are not!

## A Whisper of Hope

**Wake up, My child...**and walk into the Light. Avoid the evil traps found in the darkness by living in My Light of My Truth. Although you are safe in the Light, you must be aware and look for the traps that come cleverly disguised as gray.

**Romans 8:7-8**
For the sinful nature is always hostile to God.
It never did obey God's laws, and it never will.
That is why those who are still under the control
of their sinful nature can never please God. (NLT)

**I have come as a light to shine in this dark world,
so that all who put their trust in Me will no longer remain in the darkness.**
(John 12:46)

# "Live In Truth"

**Jude 3-4**
Dearly loved friends, I had been eagerly planning to write to you about the salvation we all share. But now I find that I must write about something else, urging you to defend the truth of the Good News. I say this because some godless people have wormed their way in among you, saying that God's forgiveness allows us to live immoral lives. The fate of such people was determined long ago, for they have turned against our only Master and Lord, Jesus Christ. (NLT)

Although Jude wrote this letter to warn the first century Church of the apostasy that was taking place, it is also meant for the Church today, because the Good News is still being compromised. This only message of Hope we have is being mixed with many different world views and false religions to be carefully twisted out of context in order to accommodate the carefree life-styles of the modern age that justify mans love of sin. We are being bombarded with many false prophets who are successfully drawing crowds of new Christians into a false Church under false pretense while drawing many other Christians away from the unchanging, inerrant Truth of God's Word. These clever lies are taking many churches into some gray areas that are very dangerous, for they cause division and strife that sometimes lead to the church's demise. The Truth of God cannot be changed for any reason nor can it be compromised to fit our agenda. Since the beginning of the Church there have been false teachers spreading their deadly lies, but they are now better equipped and more refined than ever before.

It is not wise to twist the message of salvation from our Lord God and Savior to justify your sinful passions, because God will not be mocked. As this fallen world changes, so too, do human lifestyles, but do not allow the clever lies of this ever-changing world draw you away from the Absolute Truth, because if you do, you will be led into a grayness that leads to utter darkness. The world wants you to believe in many gods and many ways to Heaven and that God is too loving to allow people to go to Hell. We must always be careful and remain steadfast in our Christian faith as found in God's Word. The amazing grace of God is running quite thin my friend, and when our Lord God and Savior Jesus Christ comes again, it will be to judge not to save.

## A Whisper of Hope

**My dear child…**walk carefully and live in Truth and Spirit as your Guide. The evil forces in this world are so powerful and so deceitfully convincing that you must stay focused on the Truth of My Word if you want to survive the Day of the Lord.

**2 Peter 2:2**
Many will follow their evil teaching and shameful immorality.
And because of them, Christ and His True Way will be slandered. (NLT)

**If you wander from the teaching of Christ, you will not have fellowship with God.**
(2 John 9)

# *"Fountain of Life"*

**Psalm 62:1**
I wait quietly before God,
for my salvation comes from Him. (NLT)

It is in the Presence of our gracious God and Savior that awes our hearts into quiet submission, for it is here that we always find the peace that comforts our weary souls, and the Lord delights in the quiet times we spend with Him. Charles Spurgeon, explained it this way: "It is an eminent work of grace to bring down the will and subdue the affections, so that the mind lies before the Lord like the sea beneath the wind, ready to be moved by every breath of His mouth." It is when we quiet our hearts and wait patiently for His reply that we hear God's Still Small Voice drawing us gently into His Presence where He can touch our lives in just the right way. There is neither a man nor a plan from this world that is able to offer us a perfect life that never ends—a life that so many of us long for—an eternal longing that God has put deep into the very fibers of our being. Only the Plan of Salvation can deliver the promised gift of everlasting life, where every child of God will live perfect lives and be able to walk and talk with the Creator at any time.

Whenever you wait quietly in the Presence of the Lord, you are silently telling God that you are faithfully trusting Him to do what is best for you; that you are confident He is who He says He is and will do what He promises He will do. When you know that your salvation is secured safely in the nail scared hands of our God and Savior Jesus Christ, there is absolutely nothing that can take your life out of His hands. Because the great minds of mankind tell us this life is an accident and it is all we have, people have always been searching for that fountain of youth that could keep them from getting old and dying. And since these same great minds think this earth is our home, they are always coming up with new ways to save the planet from self-destruction. But the reality, my friends, is we cannot save ourselves from death nor can we save this earth, because this earth and all those who belong to it will one day perish and be replaced for those who belong to God. Jesus is our Fountain for life!

## A Whisper of Hope

**Quiet your heart, dear child...**and listen closely for My voice to be calling you into salvation. When you are quiet and patiently waiting, you can be sure that I Am not doing the same, for My Plan is always working, and My Fountain is always flowing!

**Zechariah 2:13**
Be silent before the LORD, all humanity,
for He is springing into action from His holy dwelling. (NLT)

**But those who wait on the LORD will find new strength.**
(Isaiah 40:31)

# "The Reason"

**Revelation 1:8**
"I am the Alpha and the Omega—the Beginning and the End," says the Lord God.
"I am the One who is, who always was, and who is still to come, the Almighty One." (NLT)

The Lord God Jesus Christ, is both the Creator and Finisher of life; the Almighty One. And it is from this one verse that we learn exactly who Jesus is. With that said, you need to ask yourself why it matters that we, mere mortal humans beings, should know and develop a relationship with the only infinite Being—the Living God of creation? Because I spent most of my life not knowing it was possible to have a personal relationship with the Lord God Almighty, I never knew or understood who God is nor did I know or understand the purpose of life, especially my own miserable life. But that has all changed since I surrendered to the Lord and put my life into His hands. He has removed the blinders so I can see more clearly the decadence around me so I can be better prepared for the plan He has for me and what is yet to come.

For those who believe in a universe and life that is nothing more than an accident of random chance, no explanation for living is needed, because it is survival of the fittest. But for those of us who believe in the Lord God as the Creator, it is vital that we know and understand the Truth about why He created what He did and where it's all going. These are essential things you must know and understand if you are to have any real sense of true purpose while living this very short life, because on the surface this life makes little to no sense. We are now able to watch the whole world as it spins wildly out of control and it's not hard to wonder how much time is left before we annihilate ourselves. This is the reason you must know the One who created you, why you were created, and where it's all headed. God has a good reason for creating you my friend, and a good Plan designed just for you. Find out what it is. Embrace it. And then live by it!

## A Whisper of Hope

**You belong to Me, My child...**and I created you for My good purpose. The reason you are who you are is because I designed it that way. I have a plan, but I will not force it upon you. You must choose My Plan or the world's plan. But choose soon, because your time is limited!

**Ephesians 1:13, 14**
And now you also have heard the Truth, the Good News
that God saves you. He has purchased us to be His own people. (NLT)

**He created everything there is. Nothing exists that He did not make.**
(John 1:3)

# *"One Savior"*

**Psalm 68:19-20**
Praise the Lord; praise God our Savior! For each day He carries us in His arms.
Our God is a God who saves! The Sovereign LORD rescues us from death. (NLT)

I t is impossible for born again Christians to praise and thank the Lord enough for rescuing us from our bondage to sin and the eternal darkness it brings. If you feel as undeserving of the gracious gift of salvation as I do, it's because you are. The Lord our God is sovereign and perfectly holy and just in everything that He does and only He can save us from the eternal punishment that is justly due. The Lord rescued us from the clutches of damnation, opens our eyes to the Truth, and embraces us in His mighty arms where we find protection from our enemies who want only to drag us back into captivity and devour our souls. We cannot stand alone against the evil powers of darkness because our will power is weak, but our nature to sin is not. The Lord knows our needs and does not leaves us on our own, but supplies us with everything we need to keep our freedom and fight the enemies of God.

The Lord is always faithful, even when we are not. We can trust Lord Jesus with every area of our lives, whether they are large or small, because He is our God and He watches the lives of His children very closely. There is no defense against the Power of God, because He is the Almighty. Jesus is also our High Priest who cleansed our sins once and for all. He clothes us in His Righteousness, so when we stand before Him in judgment, we will receive the Crown of Life. As finite human beings we are unable to comprehend the magnitude of God's amazing grace this side of Heaven, but as we walk with the Lord in this brief journey Home, we can be sure that He will give us as much clarity as we need to know and can handle. Even in our darkest hours, we should always praise and honor the Living God of our salvation, because without the blood of Jesus we would all be trapped in the eternal darkness without hope of ever seeing the Light again.

## A Whisper of Hope

**I Am the only One, dear child...** that can lead you out of the darkness and bring you Home where you belong. In Me you have everything you will ever need. Without Me you have nothing but the eternal darkness of the grave. It is as simple as that, like night and day.

**Ephesians 1:4-5**
Long ago, even before He made the world, God loved us and chose us in Christ
to be holy and without fault in His eyes. His unchanging plan has always been
to adopt us into His own family by bringing us to Himself through Jesus Christ. (NLT)

**For He has rescued us from the one who rules in the kingdom of darkness,
and He has brought us into the Kingdom of His dear Son.**
(Colossians 1:13)

# *"Chance"*

**Galatians 1:4-5**
He died for our sins, just as God our Father planned, in order
to rescue us from this evil world in which we live. That is why
all glory belongs to God through all the ages of eternity. Amen. (NLT)

For every breath we take in, we should breathe out in praise and thanksgiving, because without the Lord; our God, our Provider, and our Savior, there would be no hope for anything, least another chance. Without the sacrificial death and resurrection of Christ Jesus, we would be hopelessly lost in the darkness, deemed as unforgivable, and condemned for eternity. Without the sacrificial blood of Jesus there would be no atonement for our sins and we would all be hell bound. God created both the angels and mankind with free wills and the intelligence to make choices. God did this because He didn't want the heavens and earth filled with mindless beings that He had to control and manipulate in order to have them love and obey Him. And much like the angels who chose to disobey God and follow Satan, man too, made the same fatal error. But unlike the rebellious angels, God has offered us complete forgiveness, and given us another chance to change our rebellious ways so we can escape the eternal condemnation that was created for Satan and his fallen angels.

Because God loves man above all His creation and because He is an honorable and just God, He has provided the Way for us to regain our right standing before Him. But once again, God does not force us to accept His gift of forgiveness and salvation; instead, He gives us the freedom to choose His Way or not—to receive the Crown of Life or eternal condemnation. You can choose living with the Lord God Jesus Christ in the new Heavens and Earth or you can choose to be thrown into the Lake of Fire with Satan. Either way, the choice is yours to make my friend, because God will not choose for you while you are alive. Time on this Earth is short and should not be wasted, because you never know what tomorrow will bring, or if there will even be a tomorrow.

## A Whisper of Hope

**Take My hand, dear child...**because there is no other way to escape the coming night. When you choose to live in My Light, you will not only be saved, but you will find the peace to comfort your soul in any circumstance. Remember child, this earthly life is but a moment.

**Genesis 2:15-17**
The LORD God placed the man in the Garden of Eden to tend
and care for it. But the LORD God gave him this warning: "You
may freely eat any fruit in the garden except fruit from the tree of
the knowledge of good and evil. If you eat of its fruit, you will surely die." (NLT)

**But I will call on God, and the LORD will rescue me.**
(Psalm 55:16)

# *"Heavenly Bound"*

**Psalm 71:19-21**
Your righteousness, O God, reaches to the highest heavens. You have done such wonderful things. Who can compare with You, O God? You have allowed me to suffer much hardship, but you will restore me to life again and lift me up from the depths of the earth. You will restore me to even greater honor and comfort me once again. (NLT)

There is nothing in all of creation that can compare to the flawless and holy character of our Almighty God. For His Perfect Plan to bring us back into His Glorious Presence has literally snatched us from the eternal grave of darkness, to put us in the Everlasting Light of the Son that leads to Heaven's gate. The greatest achievements of mankind are utterly puny compared to the Lord's incredible creativity that we are just now beginning to discover, or to His ability to breathe life into the lifeless, or in His persistence to find and rescue the lost so He can heal and give them a new life that has no end. In Light of God's sovereign power, righteousness, and perfect love, it is often difficult for us to understand why God allows so much pain and suffering that comes with living in a world that holds us hostage to our fallen nature that loves to rebel against the holiness of God. I spent most of my life disliking God because I could not understand why this life was so cruel, or why so many people were born only to suffer and then die, or why it was so futile to even try to find the true happiness that our hearts so long to find.

But there was one thing that I did learn to understand, and that was why so many of us turned to things that would numb the pain of living—so you could forget the seemingly senseless existence that always ended in death. We don't choose this life, nor do we choose our parents or where we are born. It is as if all of a sudden we are magically here and dealing with whatever we are given. Because we are finitely born into a broken world with a sinful nature, we are weak and vulnerable to the things that always lead us away from God where we are easily preyed upon by the dark forces that rule this fallen world. But our gracious and merciful God created the Perfect Plan—a Plan that works for everyone. Because we are powerless against our sinful natures and cannot save ourselves from destruction, the Lord did it for us. The Savior can pull anyone from the muck of this wicked world, cleanse their sins, and then clothe them in His robe of righteousness!

## A Whisper of Hope

**Fear not, My child...**for the Hope you find in Me is Heavenly bound. It is the only way to survive this cruel and evil world that will drag you down and eat you alive. Nothing compares to the saving Power of the Living God—the only Hope you have.

**2 Corinthians 7:10**
For God can use sorrow in our lives to help us turn away
from sin and seek salvation. We will never regret that kind of sorrow. (NLT)

**This "foolish" plan of God is far wiser than the wisest of human plans.**
(1 Corinthians 1:25)

# *"Guiding Light"*

**Psalm 73:22-24**

I was so foolish and ignorant—I must have seemed like a senseless animal to You. Yet I still belong to You; You are holding my right hand. You will keep on guiding me with Your counsel, leading me to a glorious destiny. (NLT)

Prior to my new life in Christ Jesus I lived much like the animals do—driven by lust and survival, but trying desperately to do what I thought was right. Even though I had the God given sense of right and wrong, of good and evil, the difference was still confusing, because much of what the world saw as right and good was in fact wrong and evil. And the longer I lived abiding to the ways of this world, the more I felt there was something terribly wrong, and unbeknownst to me, I was getting further away from the Truth that I so desired. Finally, after many years of living the world's way, I came to the depressing conclusion that nothing of this world made any sense. So in the defeat of my quest for truth, I simply gave up trying to find purpose in this pointless life that seemed to always end in disappointment and death. And in my defeat, I began to set my sights on the foolish folly of this world that would bring about my death and hopefully an end to my pain. And what still boggles my mind to this very day is the fact that God would not allow me die in my sin, because if He had, I would be, at this very moment, chained in the pits of Hell awaiting the final judgment. But because of God's incomprehensible love, mercy and grace for me, He never stopped calling into the darkness so He could rescue me from the rancid mire that this evil world had sucked me into.

Sometimes the Lord lets us sink deep into our darkness before He is able to get our full attention. And when He finally woke me up, I wasted no time surrendering to Him, confessing my sins, accepting His forgiveness, and receiving the gift of salvation—I finally found the peace and hope I had always longed for. When you surrender your life to God, He will pull you out of the dark and into His Light, where you will find the only Truth that can lead you Home. Whether it is fear or doubt or whatever it is that is keeping you from the Lord's calling, let it go my friend. Only Jesus can pull you out of the muck. Only Jesus can save you from the just punishment that you deserve. Do not be duped into believing the lies of the world. Instead, Discover the Truth.

## A Whisper of Hope

**Being born again, My child...** is to know the Truth. I Am the Way, the Truth, and the Life. The world will tell you different, but the world hates the Truth. The false truth of this world will leave you unsatisfied, confused, and headed down the many paths that leads to darkness and death. Know the only Truth and I will set you free!

**1 Peter 1:22**

For you have been born again. Your new life did not come from your earthly parents because the life they gave you will end in death. But this new life will last forever because it comes from the eternal, living Word of God. (NLT)

**He is our God forever and ever. And He will be our guide until we die.**

(Psalm 48:14)

# *"Saving Face"*

**Psalm 80:3**
Restore us, O God; Cause Your face
to shine, and we shall be saved! (NKJ)

Only the Savior can save us from the sinful condition that leads to eternal damnation. Only the Redeemer can transform our sin-filled lives into God-filled lives that only get better and better—as in an eternity of living in the Presence of God, learning the mysteries of life and creation. Because of the blood of Christ Jesus, we are blameless in the eyes of God, but we must live righteously before the Lord. One of the most important areas in God's restoration process is our sanctification, not so much our personal circumstances, because when the Lord restores the person their circumstances will almost always follow suit. The divine restoration that we are blessed with upon receiving salvation comes from only One Source my friends, the Holy Spirit sent by our Savior, Jesus Christ. And throughout our restoration, God's face shines favorably upon our everyday lives, blessing us in ways that brings hope for the future, comfort in the present, and peace about our past and this dark world we must live in before we go Home.

It is actually the Lord's favor that brings all people into salvation, because His love is unconditional and His mercies are limitless. No matter how far away from the Lord you may be, His Light will shine favorably upon all who ask, ensuring both victory and liberty from the chains of darkness that hold you captive to this evil world that is head for destruction. Only the Lord can save us from dying in our sin. Our conversion from a godless life-style is as divine a work as creation itself. And with the Holy Spirit as your Helper and God's Word as your sword of defense against the evil powers of darkness, you will be redeemed; becoming a new creation and a child of the Living God. When you have the Lord's face shinning favor upon your life, you will be saved no matter how deep in the darkness you have been, because nothing can trump God's favor.

## A Whisper of Hope

**My Face shines favor...** on those who come to Me broken and ashamed. Search diligently in the Word I have written, for within its holy pages you will find the Truth about who I Am, who you are, and the deception this fallen world wants you to believe. Without the Truth, your life will be wasted and it will end in tragedy.

**John 8:44**
Let all the world look to Me for salvation!
For I am God; there is no other. (NLT)

**May the LORD show you His favor and give you His peace.**
(Numbers 6:26)

# "Justice Reigns"

**Psalm 89:14**
Righteousness and justice are the foundation of
Your throne. Mercy and truth go before Your face. (NKJ)

Since the Lord God is the One who created us and then personally paid for our salvation, it is only right that we are His, because without our Creator and Savior we would be nothing and we would have nothing to celebrate. We should celebrate that God is love, righteous, just, merciful and filled with amazing grace. Our God refused to leave us to our own demise. Instead, He gave us the wisdom that would give us a clear picture of how to live in this life so we could live in the glory of the eternal life to follow. Our God is also perfectly holy and just in all His ways, sovereign in all He does, and fully knows all things. We can always trust in God's divine governance, because He is too right to be wrong, too powerful to be stopped, and far too wise to make mistakes. The Lord Jesus Christ foreshadows who God is and how He will deal with mankind in the last days.

Sadly, there are many people who believe there are no afterlife consequences for what they do in this life. But Scripture tells a different story, my friends. Jesus has personally told us about the dark consequences awaiting those who die hanging on to their sin, and the glorious rewards in Heaven for those who seek forgiveness and salvation from the Lord. No one can survive in the Presence of God without the blood of Jesus covering our sins. Because we are unable to refrain from sinning, the Lord became our sin and died our death. We have a just God who judges fairly, and we have a merciful God who gives us the chance for salvation. But for those who refuse the blood of Jesus to go their own way, they will justly end up where they belong.

## A Whisper of Hope

**Do not believe...**in the foolishness of manmade doctrine and the world's philosophy on life. Instead, believe in Me, your Creator and Savior. You live in a world that hates Me and all that I Am. Therefore, the world hates anyone who belongs to Me. Rejoice, for My justice reigns.

**Deuteronomy 32:4**
He is the Rock, His work is perfect; for all His ways are justice, a
God of truth and without injustice; righteous and upright is He. (NKJ)

**And there is no other God besides Me,
A just God and a Savior, there is none besides Me.**
(Isaiah 45:21)

# "Living Wisdom"

**Psalm 90:12**
So teach us to number our days,
that we may gain a heart of wisdom. (NKJ)

As finite human beings with a self-centered, sinful nature, we are more inclined to put our energies into finding ways to enjoy this life while we can, rather than dwelling on the reality of our days end and the possibilities thereafter. Because of our limited ability to look beyond the moment, we need God to teach us the true value of the short time we have on this earth. We need the Lord's infinite wisdom to teach us who He is and who we are in relation to who He is, because it is only when we understand God's purpose for us that we can wisely make the best use of our time. If you are searching for the truth about the life you didn't ask for, and if you want to know what lies beyond this difficult life-journey you are on, you must come boldly and unafraid to the Creator, our God and Savior Jesus Christ, and He will teach you the Truth . God calls all people to reflect more deeply on the brevity of time, for by doing so we are more apt to pay a little bit closer attention to the eternal consequences of how we live this life.

It's a humbling experience to look into the grave that will one day hold your dead decaying body, because the temporary earthly pleasures that we crave for tend to lose their grip in the presence of our mortality. So be wise dear friend, and ask the Spirit of God to fill your now beating heart with the love of God and the wisdom of Heaven. Every moment of this short life should be wisely spent discerning the eternal from the temporal, the good from the bad, and the right from the wrong, for we know not the hour of our earthly death. There is neither time to waste nor is there time to justify our misuse of it, and it's downright foolish to think there will always be a tomorrow. Living in the wisdom that God has so graciously shared with us is much more satisfying and a lot longer lasting than the here today, gone tomorrow foolishness that comes from the wisdom of man.

## A Whisper of Hope

**The wisdom of this world...**is foolishness. It is I, your Creator and Savior, who holds the key that unlocks the door of wisdom that brings life to the fullest. Do not believe the lies of this world ruled by Satan, for this foolish wisdom will bring only death, decay, and darkness.

**James 1:5-6**
If you need wisdom—if you want to know what God wants you to do—ask Him, and He will gladly tell you. He will not resent your asking. But when you ask Him, be sure that you really expect Him to answer, for a doubtful mind is as unsettled as a wave of the sea that is driven and tossed by the wind. (NLT)

**Our days on earth are like grass; like wildflowers, we bloom and die.**
**The wind blows, and we are gone—as though we had never been here.**
(Psalm 103:15-16)

# "Joy In the Lord"

**Psalm 119:7-8**
When I learn Your righteous laws, I will thank You by living as I should.
I will obey Your principles. Please don't give up on me. (NLT)

A lot of people think it is more difficult to obey God's ten simple, yet life saving laws than it is to comply with the thousands of complex, man-made laws that people cannot even understand, little less obey. This is not because God's laws are more complex or harder to understand, but it is because we are all born with a sinful nature that loves to rebel against God's timeless and perfect laws. And even though our conscience tells us that our sinful behavior will cause us shame and guilt and possibly death, we go ahead and do it anyways. One of the best lies by the Enemy is that obeying the laws that God wrote in stone takes the fun out of life—that it is impossible to enjoy life when we are bogged down with a bunch of righteous rules that we cannot bend to fit our desires. This cannot be further from the truth my friends, because our obedience to God leads to amazing peace and an amazing joy that the world cannot take away nor compete with. It is not easy living against the swift currents of this fallen world that threatens to pull you down into its utterly cold darkness, but with the life-vest of salvation, you are held safely above the darkness. When obeying God and submitting to His will becomes your first priority, you begin to discover what the joy of the Lord is all about.

The righteous ways of the Lord are always perfect and true and when followed, they will in return, give you the desire to please the Living God who created you to live and reign with Him forever. The Lord has given us many things to enjoy while living on this earth, but in our fallen state we often take the very things God gave us to enjoy and turn them into our only reason for living, and many people end up doing almost anything to get them, often ignoring what is right and what is not. The first command that God gave Adam and Eve was to be obedient (which they weren't), least they die, (which they did). The first law that God wrote down in stone was to love Him above all else, but we quickly become lovers of self and the world instead. But for the children of God who have learned and accepted His Truth, they not only find it easy to love the God who saved them, but they also develop a burning desire to follow His Way, which pleases Him and gives us pleasure as well. God not only teaches us the right way to live and die, but He also points the way to Heaven as well.

## A Whisper of Hope

**Unlike this world, dear child...**I do not enforce My Way upon you, nor do I force you to obey. But know this, child, when you blatantly disobey Me with glee and without remorse you will receive the death penalty. Ignoring My Ways to embrace the ways of this evil world is both foolish and short-sighted. For when you live in the world, life is short, but when you live in Me, life is never ending.

**Jeremiah 7: 21, 23**
This is what the LORD Almighty, the God of Israel says;
"Obey Me, and I will be your God, and you will be My people.
Only do as I say, and all will be well." (NLT)

**If the righteous are barely saved, what chance will the godless and sinners have?**
(1 Peter 4:18)

# *"Simple but True"*

**Psalm 119:130**
As Your words are taught, they give light;
even the simple can understand them. (NLT)

Immediately after God's words pierced the outer toughness of my hardened heart, the Light of His Truth began to brighten up the darkness that I had been trapped in all of my life, and it began to fill that empty space with love, understanding and blessed hope. For it was out of my deepest darkness and the hopeless desperation of my soul that my depraved heart and soul received the Lord and He healed my wounds, took the burdens that I bore, and gave me some believable understanding about this life and what it all means—Truth that would comfort my weary soul and give me a life that was really worth living. Anyone can read God's Word, but if we fail to read it through the eyes of the Holy Spirit and let those God breathed words seep deep into our hearts, the light may flicker on for a while, but the power of darkness will raise its ugly head and blow it out cold.

When the Holy Spirit reveals the Truth to us, it penetrates our hardened hearts and softens it with His love and grace. You cannot merely see or hear the Word of God in order to experience the transforming power that it offers. We need the Light of Truth shining brightly on the pages of our lives, for without the Light, God's words will either fall on deaf ears or remain foreign and impossible to understand. Mankind has proven over and over throughout the ages, that when we are disconnected from our Creator we are oblivious to the Truth, leaving us unprotected from the schemes of Satan that have deceived the world and killed many a soul. Without the Word of God and His Everlasting Light, the world is a very lonely and hopeless place my friend, for it was there from which I personally came. Respond to the Word of Life and feel the power of His Truth and forgiveness. Let the Light of God subdue the darkness, because it brings life to the fullest!

## A Whisper of Hope

**I Am the True Source...**for Light and Life, dear child. I Am the Word of Life for any and all. I have given the world My Light so you could see through the darkness of this difficult life-journey. My Light brings you hope and peace; the darkness brings you death and condemnation.

**1 John 1:1-2**
The One who existed from the beginning is the One we have heard and seen.
We saw Him with our own eyes and touched Him with our own hands. He is
Jesus Christ, the Word of Life. This One who is life from God was shown to us,
and we have seen Him. And now we testify and announce to you that He is the
One who is eternal life. He was with the Father, and then He was shown to us. (NLT)

**Your Word is a lamp for my feet and a light for my path.**
(Psalm 119:105)

# "Seeing Eyes"

**Psalm 123:1**
Unto You I lift up my eyes,
O You who dwell in the heavens. (NKJ)

Because we are God created, finite human beings, we tend to look beyond ourselves for something or someone that we can look up to—someone greater with whom we can rely on to inspire or encourage us while we live in this difficult world that is getting even more difficult as the days go by. For those of us who have our Lord God and Savior Christ Jesus as that Someone we can look up to and rely on to inspire, encourage and give us hope, we are blessed with spiritual eyes—eyes that see through the darkness that this fallen world wants you to be trapped in—a darkness of lies that is created by the leader of Hell's fallen angels. Christians are utterly filled with thanksgiving and praise to the Lord our God, because there are billions of spiritually blind people in this world that cannot see beyond this world that they are trapped in and trying to make sense of. There are so many lost souls who, because of ignorance or pride, are more inclined to look inward for some hidden inner strength. There are still other discouraged souls who look downward at the futility of it all and simply give up. And what's left are people who will look everywhere they can, rather than looking upward to the Living God who knows and sees all things visible and invisible.

If God is your last option, you may not see Him at first glance, but with persistent gazing upwards into the heavenly realms in search of Him, God will, in His own time and His own way, open the spiritual eyes of your heart and you will find the absolute Truth in the Living God—the only One who can rescue you from the hopelessness that we all face without God in our lives. Our God is very real, my friends, and He resides in the hearts of all His believing people. How blessed we are that our God is always Home, always watching, and always waiting for you to walk through His door. He is always there where you are, because He is your Sovereign Keeper; the One who never sleeps and is always alert. The Almighty, Sovereign God is the infinite Watchful One who has eyes that see it all and the powers to fix it all.

## A Whisper of Hope

**I see it all, My child...**nothing is hidden from Me. When you look up to Me for truth and resolve, you are looking in the right place, for I Am your Creator and the Keeper of your soul. You need only look up into the heavens to find the help and hope you need. I Am always Home and ready to help.

**Isaiah 55:6-7**
Seek the LORD while you can find Him. Call on Him now while His is near.
Let the people turn from their wicked deeds. Let them banish from their minds
the very thought of doing wrong! Let them turn to the LORD that He may have
mercy on them. Yes, turn to our God, for He will abundantly pardon. (NLT)

**The LORD is watching everywhere, keeping His eye on both the evil and the good.**
(Proverbs 15:3)

# "A Choice"

**Deuteronomy 30:20**
Choose to love the LORD your God and to obey Him
and commit yourself to Him, for He is your life. (NLT)

Although this message from God was spoken through Moses to the people of Israel, it remains today a most powerful message for every living person on Earth. Every day we are faced with many different kinds of choices that must be made, but choosing God is by far the most important choice you will ever be face with to make, because without the blood of our Lord God Christ Jesus, you will surely die the sinner's death, which leads to everlasting condemnation. This one choice that stands before us today is much different from the days of Moses, for it now involves our God in the flesh, who provided the life-giving gift of salvation that was bought and paid for with the blood of our Savior Christ Jesus, the Lord and Creator of Life. We can either choose the gift of salvation that God offers us or we can turn it down and hope for the best. We can accept the robe of righteousness from Christ and stand on His merit or put on the robe of death and follow Satan into the Lake of Fire. We can choose to put our hope in the blood of Jesus or we can put our hope in a fallen world that is destine for destruction. These choices are not so easily made, because people today are as they have always been since the Fall; selfish, greedy, corrupt, evil, sinful and prone to making the wrong choices.

Because of our sinful natures people tend to choose the paths that are easy and the ones most traveled, because they want an easy fix to satisfy the hungers of their flesh, driving them to do what is wrong rather than right. In general, we are a rebellious people, especially when it comes to obeying our Lord God who knows what is best for us. And for many people it is only when the world crashes down upon them that they call out to God as a last resort; even those who say they don't believe in God. People do this because God created us (whether we believe it or not) to depend on Him. Everything that keeps us alive is provided by God; not by man, not by our own accord, and certainly not by chance or luck of the draw. Most of us discover sooner or later that nothing from this world can fully satisfy our deepest needs. The two things that this world can definitely promise and deliver are disappointment and death. But our gracious Lord God promises us peace, joy, and the gift of eternal life. You can choose it or lose it, but the choice is yours!

## A Whisper of Hope

**Choose carefully, My child...**for the choices you make all lead to either life or death, light or darkness, God or Satan, and Heaven or Hell. And they are all eternal by nature. Satan and his world will try to tempt you into its darkness and discredit My Name. Don't focus on the world of the here and now. Instead, focus on Me and the world to come, and then be grateful for all I have given you.

**Daniel 12:1, 2**
Then there will be a time of anguish greater than any since nations first came into existence. But at that time every one of your people whose name is written in the book will be rescued. Many of those whose bodies lie dead and buried will rise up, some to everlasting life and some to shame and everlasting contempt. (NLT)

**Jesus is the Messiah, the Son of God, and that by believing in Him you will have life.**
(John 20:31)

# "God and You"

**Psalm 139:1**
O LORD, You have examined my heart
And know everything about me. (NLT)

Our Creator is not only an all knowing God, but He is also an omnipresent God whose whole being is everywhere at every moment in time and space. It is simply His sovereign nature. And God knows each and every person He creates completely, just as if He probed into the deepest depth of our very being. God sees everything at all times because He is the sole proprietor of creation. We should never doubt who the LORD is, for His knowledge and power are perfectly thorough and complete and His plans are well thought through and final, for anything less and He would not be God. Even though our God is bigger and greater than we can ever comprehend, His door is always open for those who want to know Him personally or for those who are desperately needing His divine intervention. He is a caring God who continually watches over His creation and is deeply involved in the most minute areas of our existence. When we come to understand and believe these incredible attributes of our Creator, it only makes sense that we would want an up-close and personal relationship with Him, rather than trying to alienate ourselves from Him as if He doesn't even exist .

For those who learn and believe who our God is, know that it is impossible to hide anything from the Lord and it's quite frivolous to even try. By knowing God is always there and watching over us not only holds our thoughts and actions accountable, but it gives us an opportunity to confide in Him, because we know He understands us completely. And you need not feel uneasy about sharing your darkest sins, your deepest thoughts, or your greatest sorrows with Him, because He already knows. We have no reason to fear how God feels or reacts when we humbly come to Him, because His love and compassion for you is perfectly righteous, unchangeable, and completely unconditional. God is always with you my friend, to be your everything for all eternity. He is a complete Provider and a personal Savior; the only One who will never ever let you down or leave you high and dry to die.

## A Whisper of Hope

**I Am the God of everything, dear child...**I can be nothing less. I Am perfect in every way. I loved you first and long before you ever loved Me. Draw close to Me and I will draw close to you. I made you to depend on Me and to have a personal relationship with. It is Me and you against the world—a world that could care less about you and one I have overcome for just that reason!

**Jeremiah 23:23-24**
"Am I a God who is only in one place?" asks the LORD. "Do they think I cannot see what they are doing? Can anyone hide from Me? Am I not everywhere in all the heavens and earth?" asks the LORD. (NLT)

**Nothing in all creation can hide from Him.
Everything is naked and exposed before His eyes.**
(Hebrews 4:13)

# July

# *"Facts of Life"*

**Psalm 143:7**
Answer me speedily, O LORD; my spirit fails! Do not hide
Your face from me, lest I be like those who go down into the pit. (NKJ)

People who live their lives knowing and believing that they truly belong to the Living God of the Bible, humbly and prayerfully cry out for God's help when they need it. They are not exempt from the hardships that come with living in this fallen world, for there will always be times in this life when our circumstances are far beyond our control—when we feel as if our life is simply ebbing away, where each moment is critical and we feel as if we may soon succumb to the pressure. And it is when we come to the end of ourselves that our spirits can soon follow suit and we become dangerously distraught. It is during these kinds of moments that our dependence on God is not only of the utmost importance for our very survival, but the personal relationship it creates with the Lord becomes critical to our spiritual health.

Whenever we back peddle from our dependence on God this life not only brings us despair, but it can also zap our strength and our desire for living. When God is absent from our lives, His absence enables the enemies of God to gain easy access into our hearts and reek even more havoc at a time when we are the most vulnerable. It is for this very reason that we must remain steadfast in both our faith and in His Presence, so He can win the battles for us. When we have God's countenance, we have victory! Without it, we lose! Although God may not always help you exactly how you want Him to or when you want Him to, you can be sure that when you belong to God and remain faithful, He will pull you through your troubles and shine His favor upon your life. God's children can always be sure that His mercy has wings when our troubles are extreme!

## A Whisper of Hope

**Without Me, dear child...** you will surely succumb to the hard realities of this lost and decaying world. Without Me you will blindly stumble through this dark world in vain. Without My Guiding Light for your life-journey you will surely fall into a pit of darkness and despair with the possibility of being forever separated from My Presence. This is the Truth—it is a fact of Life!

**Daniel 6:26-27**
For He is the living God and He will endure forever.
His kingdom will never be destroyed, and His rule will
never end. He rescues and saves His people; He performs
miraculous signs and wonders in the heavens and on earth. (NLT)

**The LORD is faithful in all He says; He is gracious in all He does.**
(Psalm 145:13)

# *"In God We Hope"*

**Psalm 146:5**
Happy are those who have the God of Israel for their
Helper, whose hope is in the LORD their God. (NLT)

By not trusting the Lord and putting our hope in Christ Jesus for this life and the one to follow is not only foolish, but dangerous as well. When we trust other flawed human beings, there is a false sense of security that usually leads to disappointment, discouragement, and a broken heart, which weakens our spirits and leaves us vulnerable to the Enemy of our souls. And when we put our trust and hope in the ways of this fallen world, we are putting our hope in a dying world that is not only unstable and unpredictable, but has the Devil as its god; the destroyer and hater of anything and everything that is God's. Your best hope my friend, is your only Hope—the living God and Savior, Christ Jesus. When we trust and put our hope in the infinite living God, we find the rest that our weary souls so desperately need because of this fallen world and its evil ruler.

Our loving and compassionate God has graciously given us the Word of Life so we would know what lies ahead in the future as both a warning and for encouragement. When you have the Helper, Healer, Provider, Prophet, Redeemer and Savior, you basically have everything you will ever need and so much more. When you are living for the Lord and believing in His plan for man, you want to share this phenomenal Good News with those who either rely on the false hope of this dying world, or have absolutely no hope at all. When the Savior who defeated sin and death for you is your only God, the hope of Jesus will give you a peace unlike anything the world can offer or deliver. When you have the peace of God, you can fearlessly live each day with the King of the universe, Jesus Christ, for He has great plans for all those who belong to Him and confess Him as LORD over all.

## A Whisper of Hope

**Call on Me, dear child…**for there is nothing I cannot do. I have all the knowledge you need to live a good life that honors Me. When I AM your Helper, you need never fear what tomorrow may bring, for I AM God and I AM with you always. There is none greater than I AM.

**Revelation 1:8**
"I am the Alpha and the Omega, the Beginning and the End,"
says the Lord God. "I am the One who is, who always was, and
who is still to come, the Almighty One." (NLT)

**Happy indeed are those whose God is the LORD.**
(Psalm 144:15)

# *"Living Wisdom"*

**Psalm 1:1-2**
Blessed is the man who walks not in the counsel of the ungodly, nor stands
in the path of sinners, nor sits in the seat of the scornful; But his delight is in
the Law of the LORD, and in His Law he meditates day and night. (NKJ)

There is no doubt that God blesses those who walk with Him in faith. There is also no
doubt that all who continue to follow the sinful ways of this wicked world and die in their
sin will regret the unwise choices they made. When your life-journey is under the direction and
protection of God's gracious favor—when you choose to follow His will for your life, you will
receive many blessings from the Lord that brings peace amidst the chaos and a preserving joy
for the difficult days that lay ahead. When you live in obedience to the Word of God, you learn
to avoid the crafty and sin-filled devices of this wicked world, which if unabated, will trap you
in the darkness of evil that it so boldly embraces. God's Word teaches us and the Holy Spirit
empowers us to not only be gracious with those who have chosen to follow the world's ungodly
ways, but to also be a witness to the goodness and healing touch of the Savior Jesus Christ, rather
than conforming to the ways of the world in order to be a part of the crowd.

Even though we Christians, too, are sinners by nature and continue to sin, we have been set
apart from the wicked by the blood of our Savior. And by the power of the Holy Spirit we are
able to discern the company we keep so that we can remain justified by God's grace and continue
growing in our quest to live and love like Jesus. Christians find no pleasure in the company of
atheists and their scornful mocking of God and Christianity, because we know the Truth and
have a much better way to live and a glorious way to die. Be ever so careful my friends, because
the seat of the scoffer is dangerously close to the pits of Hell. You must stay clear and flee from
its grip, because the seat of evil may seem pleasingly comfortable in the moment, but its cushion
will eventually sink and swallow you up forever.

## A Whisper of Hope

**Listen not, My child...**to the tempting voice of the wicked, or to those who embrace the
darkness of this world. I know the pull is strong because of your sinful nature, but embrace Me
instead, and I will give you strength when you are weak and wisdom when you are confused.
And in the meantime, stay clear of those who would steal you away from the Light and into
the darkness that consumes.

**2 Peter 1:3**
As we know Jesus better, His divine power gives
us everything we need for living a godly life. (NLT)

**He who trusts in his own heart is a fool, but whoever walks wisely will be delivered.**
(Proverbs 28:28)

# "Mercy and Grace"

**Psalm 6:1, 2**
O LORD, do not rebuke me in Your anger, or discipline me
in Your rage. Have compassion on me, LORD, for I am weak. (NLT)

It is never easy to break the old habits of sin; it is simply our nature to oppose the righteous ways of God to go our own way. Because of our stubborn pride it is never easy admitting our fallen human weaknesses to resist the sin that we so love to indulge in. But I find the closer I am to God and His will for my life, the better equipped I become in fighting the sin that I so easily fall prey to without the protection and wisdom of the Lord. And when I find myself being tempted by this evil world, I am reminded of just how in need we are of God's mercy and grace. No matter how good or strong we think we are, we would all justly receive what we deserve; the condemnation of God and the eternal punishment that is rightly due. What a blessed gift we have in knowing that whenever we fall short of God's holy standards we can immediately seek God's forgiveness and gain yet, another chance to get it right. It is never easy living a godly life in this ungodly world.

It is impossible to fully escape the God opposing, worldly temptations that promise incredible pleasure and happiness, because they surround us on every side trying to gain entrance into our hearts and get a foothold on our lives. If you are to win the never ending battles between good and evil; those evil temptations that want to destroy your hope and entrap your soul, you must put on the armor of God, because without it you are no match for the powers of darkness that rule this world. No matter how strong or godly we aspire to be, we will always fall prey to the sin that is deserving of God's rebuke. When you are humble before God, sincerely seeking His incredible transforming Power, you can be sure that His amazing grace will always be sufficient in your times of struggle. For when your heart is right with God my friend, so too, is your life.

## A Whisper of Hope

**I came into this world…**to give you life—one that would give you hope and peace and joy in spite of the corrupt world you live in. By living in Me you will find the mercy and grace and forgiveness you need until I return to make all things right and dispose of what is not. Be faithful and true, My child, and know that the gift I offer does not depend on you—but on Me!

**Titus 3:4-6**
But then God our Savior showed us His kindness and love. He saved us,
not because of the good things we did, but because of His mercy. He washed
away our sins and gave us a new life through the Holy Spirit. He generously
poured out the Spirit upon us because of what Jesus Christ our Savior did. (NLT)

**So correct me, LORD, but please be gentle.
Do not correct me in anger, for I would die.**
(Jeremiah 10:24)

# Simple Truth

**Proverbs 1:32-33**
For the turning away of the simple will slay them, and the
complacency of fools will destroy them; But whoever listens
to Me will dwell safely, and will be secure, without fear of evil. (NKJ)

The Book of Proverbs is the God given wisdom of King Solomon that is timeless in its truth. They give us a clear picture of sound, reliable wisdom from the Creator of all wisdom and truth. If the wisdom from God is used wisely, it brings our lives a true and lasting purpose that is not only highly valuable for us now, but has eternal value as well. Knowing and living in God's wisdom is critical for living this life, because we must have the ability to discern the foolishness of manmade wisdom (which brings temporary pleasure and eternal darkness) from the godly wisdom, that brings us hope in the Light of true living. The wisdom of God is not only concise and to the point, but was made simple so that everyone could understand. When you build the foundation of your life on God's Word and are guided by His wisdom, you experience the kind of pleasure and joy in living that is unknown to those who pursue the ways of the world.

When you are a child of the Living God you know where the Lord is leading you and why you are being led there. By following God's ways and His infinite wisdom we are able to learn the truth about life and death, which is something that people desperately need, for they are being led away from God's Truth and down the paths of Satan. When people simply reject God, they live only to pursue their own selfish needs that satisfy their lustful desires, and if this misdirection is not diverted, it will lead into the hellish darkness of the abyss. When you walk wisely alongside the Lord, listening, meditating, and following His wisdom for life, you will travel this life-journey in peace, knowing that God will never lead you astray. God's wisdom has the power to defeat the evil that consumes this foolish and wayward world—and it's available for all who seek it.

## A Whisper of Hope

**I Am the Voice of Wisdom, dear child...**Do not listen to the call of manmade wisdom that threatens your very soul by leading you into the darkness of this evil world. The foolish and sin filled wisdom of this fallen world pursues you with a vengeance to be against My Infinite Wisdom, and when ignored, you will be filled with lingering sorrow and regret that never goes away!

**1 Kings 4:29-30**
And God gave Solomon wisdom and exceedingly great understanding,
and largeness of heart like the sand on the seashore. Thus Solomon's wisdom
excelled the wisdom of all the men of the East and all the wisdom of Egypt. (NKJ)

**You will keep on guiding me with Your council, leading me to a glorious destiny.**
(Psalm 73:24)

# "Lips for God"

**Colossians 1:13-14**
For He has rescued us from the one who rules in the kingdom of
darkness, and He has brought us into the Kingdom of His dear Son.
God has purchased our freedom with His blood and has forgiven all our sins. (NLT)

N o one who has sincerely accepted God's gift of salvation should ever let this incredible, life saving truth be silenced from their lips. Without the mercy and grace of our Lord God, where would we look for the everlasting peace and joy that comes from knowing the eternal plans that God has for His children? For the many people living in this dying world without the Wisdom and Hope of God directing their lives, there is a lot of uncertainty, confusion, and often times great fear about the future. People who do not know the Truth are often scared to death of dying because they are not sure of what lies beyond the grave, if anything. Sadly, there are many deceived people who put most of their hope in denying the realities of Hell, believing that an all loving God could not hold anyone accountable for just enjoying life and ignoring His Son and the Way—that everyone goes to Heaven except mass murderers. There are also those who believe that we simply cease to exist.

This is why every true Christian must be steadfast in their faith that the living God of the Bible is who He says He is and will do what He says He will do. Without a firm hold on the hope we have in Christ Jesus, our faith will waver up and down, causing us to look weak and uncertain in the eyes of the unbeliever who is desperately searching for truth and finding none. Weak Christians are a weak Church, which Satan uses to deceive a world that is chaotic and already confused. If you are a true Christian, you will stay grounded in God's Word learning how to live and love like Jesus, and you will be spreading the Good News that Jesus can save anyone from the fate of this fallen world. Don't let this evil world convince you otherwise my friend, because God wants us to be a shining light on a hill for the world to see. We are to be a voice for God and He calls us to give Him our best lip service and never forget that our words can bring life through Christ, or they can bring death through weakness and doubt.

## A Whisper of Hope

**I have given you much, My child...**I have given you Hope in a world gone bad. I have given you My life and the Way to escape the darkness that is coming. I have given you My blood. I have given you My forgiveness. I have given you the Gift of Eternal Life. Now go out and share this Good News with others, for it is with your lips that My message is known.

**Psalm 30:11, 12**
You have turned my mourning into joyful dancing.
You have taken away my clothes of mourning and clothed
me with joy, that I might sing praises to You and not be silent. (NLT)

**It is I, the LORD, who is mighty to save!**
(Isaiah 63:1)

# *"Never Ending"*

**Colossians 3:3, 5**
For you died when Christ died, and your real life is hidden with Christ
in God. So put to death the sinful, earthly things lurking within you. (NLT)

O ur merciful Lord God left the glory of Heaven to be born into this sin-filled world as a
man of flesh and blood so He could do for us what we could not do for yourselves—to
save us from eternal Hell. Jesus shed His perfect blood as the final sacrificial Lamb of God,
which cleansed the world of its rebellion against our holy God. When you accept the death of
Jesus as your own death to sin, you are born again into a new life wearing Jesus' robe of righteousness. So when the Father sees you now, He sees the righteousness of His Son and you will
remain holy in God's sight until your sanctification is complete. Jesus died for the sins of mankind so we would have the Way to escape God's final wrath and condemnation. But the most
amazing part of this undeserved gift of salvation is that Jesus defeated sin and death for us and
just as He was resurrected from the grave into a new eternal body and was taken up into the
glory of Heaven, so, too, will all believing Christians.

God had the plan for man's redemption before the foundation of the world was made.
God wants no one to miss out on the glory of Heaven—He wants no one to suffer the eternal
agony of Hell. God is holy and perfect and we must also be holy and perfect if we want to live
in His Presence forever. And the only way we can come into God's Holy Presence my friends,
is through Jesus Christ our risen Lord God. Our holy God cannot be in the presence of sin,
much like light and darkness cannot share the same time and space. This is why we all need the
covering of the Son, for it is through His sacrificial death that we have been reconciled with the
Father. There is no better offer than the gift of salvation, and there is no other Way to escape the
wrath of God's final judgment. And there is no better way to glorify the One who created you
and then came to earth and saved you, than by trading your old life of sin for a new life in Him.

## A Whisper of Hope

**Die with Me, dear child…**and live your new life close to Me, for I give graciously and generously. Don't let this evil world tempt you away from Me, for I know you are weak and unable
to stand on your own. I have made it so you could walk in My Presence anytime and anywhere,
so put on My robe of righteousness and truly live!

**Ephesians 1:4**
Long ago, even before He made the world, God loved us and chose us in Christ
to be holy and without fault in His eyes. His unchanging plan has always been
to adopt us into His own family by bringing us to Himself through Jesus Christ.
And this gave Him great pleasure. (NLT)

**So now we can rejoice in our wonderful new relationship with God.**
(Romans 5:11)

# "The Light Way"

**1 Thessalonians 5:14, 16**
Brothers and sisters, we urge you to warn those who are lazy. Encourage those who are timid. Take tender care of those who are weak. Be patient with everyone. No matter what happens always be thankful, for this is God's will for you who belong to Christ Jesus. (NLT)

As disciples of the Lord Jesus Christ, Christians must live in the Light of God's Truth. The Lord has commissioned us to shine His Light of eternal life on those who live in darkness. The life-saving Truth that we carry in our hearts is not just for a select few, but for everyone to hear and accept. Without the Truth we will not find much peace or lasting joy in this dark world that is crying out for some blessed light that would give them real hope. Sadly, the lost souls of this struggling world are dependent upon their governments, other people, or on themselves to meet their needs, rather than depending on their Creator and Provider. Many people will discover, as I did, just how hopeless this difficult life becomes without God's direction and provision, because when you trust and rely on the world's array of empty promises you will inevitably find yourself dissatisfied, discouraged, bitter and resentful, and angry at the world or God or both for your seemingly hopeless circumstances.

This is why believing Christians must not hide in the Truth they have and then sit back looking forward to that great and awesome Day when Jesus Christ removes His Church. For when this day suddenly arrives, all hell will break loose and many lost and hopeless souls will lose their lives violently and forever—including people you know and love who have rejected Christ Jesus. Even though we are limited in our individual abilities to touch the masses, our God is not, for He is Light. As Jesus' disciples we are called to shed God's much needed Light in this dark and damned world wherever we are, because there are many lost souls who are longing for what we know and have, because they are not finding it in the world. Shine God's Light dear brothers and sisters, on the people trapped in their darkness, so they, too, can avoid that terrible day when God's just wrath is poured out from the heavens to destroy all those who love themselves and the world rather than loving the Lord God Almighty.

## A Whisper of Truth

**Carry My Message, dear child...**Do not bury this treasure or hide in it, but shine the Light, so the lost can see where they are headed and avoid condemnation. Invest in the many lives that are desperate for hope and help them escape the darkness of the grave. I AM that Blessed Hope.

**Matthew 28:18-20**
Jesus came and told His disciples, "I have been given complete authority in heaven and on earth. Therefore, go and make disciples of all the nations, baptizing them in the name of the Father and the Son and the Holy Spirit. Teach these new disciples to obey all the commands I have given you. And be sure of this: I am with you always, even to the end of the age." (NLT)

**God is Light and there is no darkness in Him at all.**
(1 John 1:5)

# "High and Lifted Up"

**Psalm 25:1, 2**
To You, O LORD, I lift up my soul,
O my God, I trust in You. (NKJ)

Whether we are on our knees pleading for God's mercy and grace, or our hands are lifted high into the heavens, praising and glorifying God's awesome Presence in our lives, it is our precious souls that cry out for a life of dependence and fellowship with God. There is no One, or anything in all existence that can satisfy the longings of our hearts but the One who was and is and always will be; the Creator, our Lord God and Savior, Jesus Christ. The Lord God is our omnipresent Father who provides everything we will ever need in our life-journey's. He is our omnipotent Savior who has saved us from our own destructive, sinful behavior that would have otherwise led us into the pits of Hell. And He is your omniscient Spirit who guides us in all truth and leads us through Heaven's gate. He is your Creator, your Provider, and your trusted Redeemer.

If it were not for the outpouring of the Lord's gracious favor, we would either cease to exist, or wished we didn't. If it were not for His mercy and grace we would be left to our own demise, which would fail us miserably. You have in Jehovah the only Living God, who is everything you could possibly dream of and so much more. And when you pray to the One who has gifted you with the breath of life and the hope of Heaven, let your soul be lifted high into His mighty arms, for it is there you will find the peace and comfort that exceeds anything you can explain. It is by lifting your soul as high as you can that you are able to leave your troubles and fears behind to meet the God who gave it all for you. Our Sovereign God in Heaven will meet you wherever you are dear friend, but the higher you lift your soul, the closer you are to God, and it's in His Presence that you can be sure of His provision and protection forevermore!

## A Whisper of Hope

**Ask in faith, my child...**and it will be given unto you. When you honor Me with your life, I will honor you in return. When you give Me your life, I will give you new life beyond your limited understanding—an everlasting life that exceeds anything you can possibly imagine. Lift up My Name before the world, and I will lift you up into the heavens high above, where I will meet you in all My Glory and take you Home!

**1 Corinthians 9:6**
But we know that there is only one God, the Father, who created everything, and we exist for Him. And there is only one Lord, Jesus Christ, through whom God made everything and through whom we have been given life. (NLT)

**For He satisfies the longing soul, and fills the hungry soul with goodness.**
(Psalm 107:9)

# *"Faithful and True"*

**Romans 1:17**
This Good News tells us how God makes us right in His sight. This is
Accomplished from start to finish by faith. As the Scriptures say, "It is
through faith that a righteous person has life." (NLT)

No matter how good we think we may be, we can never be good enough to get into Heaven without the blood of Jesus covering our sins. Everyone must have faith in the Cross of Christ in order to stand justified on Judgment Day. But our faith must begin somewhere, and that beginning is believing that God is real; that He is infinite; that He is perfect in every way and He is sovereign over all creation; that He is a living God who deeply loves the people He so carefully creates in His image. It takes faith to believe that our infinite God has a plan for every person He creates, and it is by His gracious favor alone that we are able to carry out His will. It takes faith to believe that the universe would cease to exist without the power of God's Word holding it in perfect order so we can live to breathe another day. But we are a people who take far too many things for granted—who foolishly put our faith in things that have a very short longevity, because everything of this world is temporary at best.

Because of our sinful natures, we are a stubborn and self-centered people, who are filled with self-gratifying lusts of our carnal flesh even though they carry the death penalty. We are a flawed people who want things now, rather than waiting on the Lord and trusting Him. We live in an evil world that is being used by the Devil to create man-made philosophy that deems God's redemptive plan for man as foolishness. Satan is the god of this world and many lost souls have been deceived into believing his convincing lies that draws them away from the Truth of God. And to be away from the One who sustains and protects your life is utterly foolish my friend. The greatest and most reliable hope you have, is in the Living God. Having faith in anything other than the eternal Word of Life is not only short sighted and unwise, but it also saddens the One who created you.

## A Whisper of Hope

**Choose wisely, My child...**where you put your faith and hope. For one leads to a life of eternal joy while the other leads to eternal misery and darkness. There are two life or death options that we are all faced with; having faith in the Living God of the Bible whose promises are faithful and true, or relying on the man-made gods of Satan that promise much but deliver only death.

**Revelation 19:11, 16**
Then I saw Heaven opened, and a white horse was standing there.
And the One sitting on the horse was named Faithful and True.
For He judges fairly and then goes to war. On His robe and thigh
was written this title: King of kings and Lord of lords. (NLT)

**"I will dwell in them and walk among them.
I will be their God and they shall be My people."**
(2 Corinthians 6:16)

# *"Spirit Power"*

**Romans 8:6-7**
If your sinful nature controls your mind, there is death. But if the
Holy Spirit controls your mind, there is life and peace. For the sinful
nature is always hostile to God. It never did obey God's laws, and it never will. (NLT)

The only way anyone can refrain from following their sinful nature is through the Power of God, the Holy Spirit, because our nature to sin is just too powerful. Most people sin without really thinking about it because they don't know they are sinning. We have no choice in the matter of our birth and the sin nature attached to it, but the moment we begin to think for ourselves we begin to act upon our nature to sin. Although God created us with the sense of right and wrong, He also gave us the freedom to make our own choices, whether right or wrong. And it is these choices that not only determine our earthly lifestyles, but they also determine our eternal destiny as well. We all come into this world as sinners and we will all leave this world a sinner, and without the blood of Jesus we are condemned to die the sinner's death. The human will is much weaker than our nature to sin is, so sinning becomes almost as natural as breathing. Because sin seeks to satisfy our inherent carnal pleasures, we tend to do it even though we know the consequences are risky.

The curse of sin and death is indeed a mighty force to be reckoned with—one that is satanic driven and much too powerful for human strength alone. We must have the sovereign power of God the Father if we are to win the battles for our hearts and souls. We must have the indwelling of God the Holy Spirit to successfully fight the Enemy, and we need God the Son as our Savior. We should take advantage of the love that the Lord has for us, because He has broken the power of sin and the fear of death that holds us in bondage. There is no one more sovereign than the Almighty God of creation and there is no One more gracious and forgiving than our Lord God and Savior. And with the Power of the Holy Spirit, you have God completely on your side!

## A Whisper of Hope

**Be Mine, dear child…**for I love you with a love beyond your understanding. I gave you My life and I ask you for yours. You cannot stop the sin that you so love doing without the power of the Holy Spirit that is mine to give upon your salvation. Ask—and you shall receive!

**Galatians 5:16-18**
So I advise you to live according to your new life in the Holy Spirit. Then you won't be doing what your sinful nature craves. The old sinful nature loves to do evil, which is just opposite from what the Holy Spirit wants. And the Spirit gives us desires that are opposite from what the sinful nature desires. These two forces are constantly fighting each other and your choices are never free from this conflict. (NLT)

**For His Holy Spirit speaks to us deep in our hearts.**
(Romans 8:16)

# *"One Way Only"*

**Psalm 44:5**
Only by Your Power can we push back our enemies;
Only by Your Name can we trample our foes. (NLT)

The most dangerous battles we face, we face every day. They are battles for our hearts, minds, and the life of our eternal souls. It is impossible to avoid the ungodly living and brazen immorality that is taking over our world, for the evil of Satan is spreading like a wild fire. The satanic forces behind the media and world governments are forcing us to comply with its evil. These same satanic forces have also compromised the Church of our Lord God and Savior Jesus Christ, by twisting and distorting the absolute, inerrant Truth of God's Word. The Christian Faith is being changed right before our very eyes, in order to justify mankind's sinful behavior and sugar coat the cost of our disobedience against our holy God. The new age evangelists teach self love and prosperity, social justice and fairness, and there is no place called Hell, rather than proclaiming the absolute Truth about who our God is, who we are, and the eternal consequences of our rebellion.

There are many voices in this fallen world that sound good and seem well intended, but they are voices from Hell that will guide you down rather than up. The voices of this wicked world are smooth and sweet sounding, but they carry the sting of death my friends. Their only purpose is to lead you into the darkness until you cannot escape. Don't be fooled by the enemies of God, for there is only One God, One Way, One Truth and One Savior, and He is Christ Jesus our Lord God. There is only one path that leads to Heaven and it is definitely not one of the many paths that this dark world embraces.

## A Whisper of Hope

**Remain alert, My child...**for the world is full of lies and false hope; paths that will lead you in the wrong direction—paths that lead to Hell. But when you follow My Way and My Way only, I will lead you Home where you where created to be with Me. Stay clear of and remain alert to the slick lies of the Enemy, for they will trick you into Hell, slam the door shut and throw away the key. This is no lie!

**1 Timothy 4:1-2**
Now the Holy Spirit tells us clearly that in the last times some will turn away from what we believe; they will follow lying spirits and teachings that come from demons. These teachers are hypocrites and liars. They pretend to be religious, but their consciences are dead. (NLT)

**Jesus said to him, "I am the Way, the Truth, and the Life."**
(John 14:6)

# *"Ready in Peace"*

**1 John 3:28**
And now, dear children, continue to live in fellowship with Christ so that when
He returns, you will be full of courage and not shrink back from Him in shame. (NLT)

There can be little doubt that storm clouds are gathering over our world, signaling the return of King Jesus to oust all evil leaders and unrighteousness, to set up and govern the world, and to right all wrongs. This new millennium we are living in today will be short lived indeed, because God's prophecy is being fulfilled before our very eyes and throughout the world—a corrupt world that cannot survive another 1,000 years of mankind's foolish wisdom. The human race has excelled more quickly over the past 100 years than it has since man was created by God, and it is being manipulated by Satan to discredit and lead people away from God's Plan for man. There are many people who are oblivious to the real future of our world that is controlled by God. Most people who fear man-made annihilation of the world put their hope in some kind of miraculous intervention by a human savior. Some deny the existence of God and the eternal plans He has for His entire creation. There are others who don't look beyond their own lives and live only to please their sinful appetites.

The world's ways are foolishness and time is running out for the godless, because the Lord will not be mocked, nor will He allow His people to suffer much longer. The Lord has a sovereign Plan for man and His Plan is quickly coming into completion. So are you ready to face the Lord as you are? Have you made peace with God through the cleansing blood of Christ? Are you living the Lord's Way or the ways of this wicked world? Do you believe that Jesus Christ is our eternal Lord God in Heaven? Have you asked God for His forgiveness? Are you a born again Christian? These are all questions that must be answered correctly or you will suffer some horrible eternal consequences. The Lord does not force us to follow His Way, but when you don't, you can be sure that you will be held accountable for everything!

## A Whisper of Hope

**My Truth, dear child…**is anything but foolishness; it is a fair and concise warning. There are many lies, but My Word is the absolute Truth about life and death. Hold steadfast to these words of wisdom, for they will bring you everlasting peace. My Ways prevail and My Words are final.

**Titus 2:12, 13**
We should live soberly, righteously, and godly
in the present age, looking for the blessed hope and
glorious appearing of our great God and Savior Jesus Christ. (NKJ)

**These words are trustworthy and true…"Look, I am coming soon!**
(Revelation 22:6, 7)

# *"Less is Better"*

**John 3:30-31**
He must become greater and greater, and I must become less and less. He has come from above and is greater than anyone else. I am of the earth, and my understanding is limited to the things of earth, but He has come from heaven. (NLT)

In order to understand the things of God we must first get over ourselves and put life into its proper perspectives, especially when it comes to who the Creator is and who the created are. In reality, everyone who creates something is always greater than that which he has created; much like a potter is with whatever he is making with his hands. This simple analogy was developed by the greatest Designer of all time and it's absolute, especially when it comes to describing the relationship between God and His creation. Until we believe that it was our Almighty God who created everything that exists, we will continue to pursue and focus on our own greatness during our meager existence on this earth that is short lived at best. Thinking this way leaves little or no room for getting to know the One who gifted us with life. And if we are to experience the richness of life that God intended for us, we must first know our Creator and believe the simple how's and why's of life. For it is only then that you can rise above your meager human existence to live a godly and honorable life that glorifies God, who will in His own time, return the favor.

In order for us to live a godly life in humility, we must stop focusing only on what this created world can give or do for us, then we can use our limited time more wisely discovering the Truth. God is greater, bigger, and more powerful than His entire created universe combined. And even though we are incredibly small and seemingly insignificant in the vastness of God's immense created universe, He has chosen us above all else to share in the eternal glory of His Kingdom. It is not such a bad thing my friends, that you consider yourself lesser than, for when you do, you will surely rise above the insignificant greatness of this fallen world so you can walk and talk with our most incredible and amazing God, because He designed and planned it this way.

## A Whisper of Hope

**There is none greater than I...**For "I AM WHO I AM." There is no other who is able save you from eternal darkness. I am a just and holy God with whom you can safely invest your earthly life in; an investment that will last forever. When you humble yourself before Me, you will raise above the futility of human greatness and find your place in My Great Plan. Think less of yourself and more of Me, and start an amazing life-journey that only gets better.

**Jeremiah 18:3-6**
"Go down to the shop where clay pots and jars are made. I will speak to you while you are there." So I did as He told me and found the potter working at his wheel. But the jar he was making did not turn out as he had hoped, so the potter squashed the jar into a lump of clay and started again. Then the LORD gave me this message: "O Israel, can I not do to you as this potter has done to his clay? As the clay is in the potter's hand, so are you in My hand." (NLT)

**The person who has the power to bless is always greater than the person who is blessed.**
(Hebrews 7:7)

# *"Power of One"*

**Hebrews 10:23, 25**
Without wavering, let us hold tightly to the hope we say we have, for God can be trusted to keep His promise. And let us not neglect our meeting together, as some people do, but encourage and warn each other, especially now that the day of His coming back again is drawing near. (NLT)

In these last days our world is being consumed with deception and ravaged by unthinkable evil that has darkened the hearts of the many lost souls who have little hope. But not so for those of us who belong to Christ Jesus, because we know He is coming soon to end the madness and remove all ungodliness from our world. It is for this reason that we, the children of Light, should never withhold the saving Light that the Lord has so graciously shinned upon our own, once darkened lives. Now, more than ever before is the time to warn and encourage all peoples with the Truth about the fast-tracked, end-time drama that is being played out before our very eyes. We must share the only Hope there is for life; Hope that not only brings the peace of God into all the madness, but gives us the strength to persevere the onslaught of trouble and persecution that will continue to plague this world until that moment of the Lord's return.

Human beings do not have what it takes to stand alone against the powers of darkness and evil, but when we unite together in Christ as one righteous body, we have the Greater Power. Just as we need God's sovereign grace to live, so too, do we need the wisdom and power of the Holy Spirit to endure. For our gracious God takes no pleasure in the death of anyone whether they are righteous or wicked, but He desires all people to repent of their sinful ways and learn how to live a life that is worthy of God's honor. Lord Jesus has commissioned His disciples to proclaim the Good News of His saving Light and lead His lost and hopeless ones into the place of salvation and eternal life. There are many false prophets and wannabe gods of Satan who hunger for your soul and will eat you alive. And only the Spirit of God has the power to save and keep you free from the deadly jaws of the Enemy. And when we stand together in His Power my friends, we are one mighty force to be reckoned with!

## A Whisper of Hope

**Hold on firmly, My child...**for the ride is rough. The evil powers of darkness that are driving this world are well focused and relentless in their pursuit against Me. And it is only through My Power that anyone can escape the everlasting flame that burns forever and refuses to let you die and be consumed! Break free from the darkness and stand strong with Me in the Light!

**Ezekiel 33:11**
As surely as I live, says the Sovereign LORD,
I take no pleasure in the death of wicked people.
I only want them to turn from their wicked ways so they can live. (NLT)

**Be steadfast, immovable, always abounding in the work of the LORD.**
(1 Corinthians 15:58)

# *"Everything Good"*

**Proverbs 13:14**
The advice of the wise is like a life-giving fountain;
those who accept it avoid the snares of death. (NLT)

True wisdom comes only from the LORD our God, and every word of Scripture is God breathed and without error. Although the Bible was penned by human hands, every word is God inspired. Jesus, the Word of life, has been our connection to the heavenly realms since God created mankind. Wisdom speaks to us from the pages of the Bible; it was simply designed so people could understand the truth about life and death, to give us clear understanding and hope, to give us the how's and why's of life, and to give us the Truth about God and His Great Plan. One of the most important truths I have learned from the Bible is that everything good comes from our God in Heaven, while everything else comes from the bowels of Hell and Satan. All that comes down from Heaven is God directed and brings us true Light, while all that comes from the darkness below is Satan directed and enslaves us to evil. The wisdom from Heaven is both pure and holy and leads to eternal life, but the wisdom of this world is purely deceitful and evil and leads to eternal death. Man-made wisdom is flawed and foolish and causes a lot of confusion and doubt that can bring us into a mindless state of depression and utter hopelessness of heart.

Don't be fooled by the world's short-sighted wisdom my friend, because it is nothing more than flawed human speculation that can change on a whim and turn against you in a heartbeat. There is no absolute truth when it comes to human wisdom, nor is there much difference in good or bad, for it is all relative and now a personal preference. The world's wisdom is just pure Satanism and has many ugly consequences that are both costly and deadly, both in this life and in the next one as well. Do not be deceived by the smooth sounding ideology of this fallen world that always sounds good, but really isn't. Instead, be blessed with the Wisdom of God that never changes, can always be trusted, and promises not to leave you unsatisfied and disappointed. God's Word is infallible and true—words that will bring you into the very Presence of the Living God who created you.

## A Whisper of Hope

**To know eternal wisdom, dear child…**is to know Me. Man's wisdom is not only foolish, but is deceiving and deadly to boot. The world's foolish wisdom has one purpose; to draw you away from My Truth and suck you into its darkness. Your only Hope comes from above; not below.

**2 Timothy 3:16-17**
All Scripture is God-breathed and is useful for teaching,
rebuking, correcting and training in righteousness, so that
the man of God may be thoroughly equipped for every good work. (NIV)

**"Man shall not live by bread alone,**
**but by every word that proceeds from the mouth of God."**
(Matthew 4:4)

# "The Key"

**Psalm 119:7**
When I learn Your righteous laws,
I will thank You by living as I should! (NLT)

It's hard for a child to please their father without knowing what pleases him and what does not. The same holds true in our relationship with God, because if we don't know what pleases God the Father, our chances of pleasing Him are slim to none. But you must first believe that your Heavenly Father is real and then submit to His Truth and authority over your life. Then you must learn who God is and how to please Him by developing a personal relationship with Him, learning and understanding the purpose of life and where it's all headed. You must know the Truth and live for Christ if you want to find the Way that honors God. For when you desire God and seek His will for your life, He will draw you close and teach you everything you need to know, for when you know and do what pleases God my friend, you can be sure that His blessings will be Heaven sent and eternally pleasing to you as well.

The Lord God is gracious and loving; One who takes great pleasure in providing for those who are willing to step out in faith and live a God fearing life. He turns no one away, but we must be willing to receive the key that opens the heart to humility, submission, obedience, and righteous living. As a child of the living God we must seek His forgiveness and follow His Way with joy and thanksgiving in our hearts. It is by seeking God's Wisdom that you find life—a God driven journey that is worth any and all struggles this fallen life brings. You will never know the peace of God or the fullness of life until you know your Heavenly Father and follow His Way, because apart from God, your life-journey will become your worst nightmare and one that will never end if you refuse to wake up. There are many ways to please God, but none is better than shedding your old life of sin for a new life in Christ that not only pleases God, but is a pleasure for you as well.

## A Whisper of Hope

**I hold the Keys of life...**Keys that open doors of knowledge and wisdom and understanding—doors that open into Heaven. These doors are not secret and the keys are not hard to find, for they are all well documented and simple to understand, but are not so easy to use.

**Proverbs 8:32, 35**
"And so, my children, listen to me, for happy are all who follow my ways.
For whoever finds Me finds life and wins approval from the LORD." (NLT)

**And you will seek Me and find Me, when you search for Me with all your heart.**
(Jeremiah 29:13)

# *"Amazing Grace"*

**Galatians 2:21**
I am not one of those who treats the grace of God as meaningless. For if we
could be saved by keeping the law, then there was no need for Christ to die. (NLT)

It is only because of God's tender mercy, His amazing grace, and His perfect love that we have any chance of escaping the Final Judgment and the eternal condemnation that we all deserve. One of the reasons that God wrote the Ten Commandments was to show us how disobedient and sin-weak we really are; to show us how desperately we need His help. It is our fallen nature to love sin and rebel against the holiness of God. We would all fail miserably if it were not for God's intervention, for without the Savior we would all die in our sin and be eternally entombed in the darkness of Hell. It is simply impossible for us to live a sinless life even though the Lord created us in His own likeness. God sets a high standard because sin cannot be in His Presence. We needed a sinless Savior and so God came into the world. He became our sin and died our death. It is through the atoning blood of Christ Jesus that we are cleansed of all sin, clothed in righteousness, and saved by His amazing grace.

Although Jesus was born without the human sinful nature, He grew up fully human and had to deal with the same temptations to sin as we all do. And because He was able to live a sin free life, Jesus became the spotless, once and for all time, sacrificial Lamb of God, taking the sins of the world and paying the full price that was due. By hanging on a cross and shedding His blood, Jesus saved the world. He defeated sin and death and ascended into Heaven where He sits at the right hand of the Father pleading our case, and forgiving our sins. And even though we continue to sin and fall short of God's standard, we have the power of the Holy Spirit to help us overcome our sin addiction, and we have the forgiveness of Jesus when we fail. Treasure the gift of your salvation, rejoice in the amazing grace you received from God, and hold tightly to the blessed hope it brings. And let no day pass you by dear friend, without verbally proclaiming your deepest thanksgiving and praise to the Lord God your Savior who accomplished what you could have never done.

## A Whisper of Hope

**You cannot comprehend,** child...the love I have for you this side of Heaven. I hung on a cross and died a criminal's death to save you from your sin. You'll never know the extent of the wrath I took in your place. What I did, I did for you. My grace is sufficient and my mercy is just.

**Romans 8:1-2**
So now there is no condemnation for those who belong
to Christ Jesus. For the power of the life-giving Spirit has
freed you through Christ Jesus from the power of sin that leads to death. (NLT)

**We give thanks to You, O GOD, we give thanks!**
(Psalm 75:1)

# *"Nailed"*

**Galatians 5:24**
Those who belong to Christ Jesus have nailed the passions and desires
of their sinful nature to His cross and crucified them there. (NLT)

The decision to surrender your sin-filled, rebellious nature into God's transforming hands can be a slow and painful process. For many like myself, this decision was a last stand to make sense of this seemingly futile life that beats us up and ends in death. For others, it can be a near death experience that strikes the fear of the unknown into their hearts thinking that maybe there are consequences for living apart from God. But whatever the cause may be, it is a life changer for sure. Giving up the things of this world that feeds our compulsive nature to sin is something that we cannot achieve by the power of our own will. We need Someone greater than ourselves; Someone who has the power to help us overcome the death grip of sin that leads us on a dark journey into bowels of Hell—a journey that is imminent for all those who remain enslaved by the pleasures of sin.

Like all Christians before me, I had to bring my old sinful life to the Cross of Christ to be nailed there and put to death. It was then that I received the Power of the Holy Spirit, who gave me the confidence to plow forward in the heart wrenching battle to give up the sin that I depended on to ease my pain. It takes courage and discipline to stand against the dark powers that grip us in sin. It takes both commitment and sacrifice to learn and use the weapons God gives us to fight the everyday battles against the powers of darkness that seek to destroy us. It takes the sovereign Power and Wisdom of God to win the battles for our hearts and minds and souls. But it's when you nail that old life of sin to the cross of Christ Jesus that you will truly experience the amazing peace of God that comes from being saved from the bondage of sin and the grip of Hell. God did not create us to die, my friends; He created us to live forever! And you can live anew, if you would only die of old!

## A Whisper of Hope

**There is One Way...**dear child. You must nail your old sinful nature to My Cross. This single act of obedience will free you from the bondage of sin and the fear of death. It is only through Me that you will find the power to fight your nature to sin—the curse that Satan holds over you. Get it nailed to the Cross and live in Me.

**Colossians 2:13-14**
You were dead because of your sins and because your sinful
nature was not yet cut away. Then God made you alive with Christ.
He forgave all our sins. He canceled the record that contained the charges
against us. He took it and destroyed it by nailing it to Christ's cross. (NLT)

**We have the LORD our God to help us and to fight our battles for us!"**
(2 Chronicles 32:8)

# *"Give it Up"*

**1 John 1:8-9**
If we say we have no sin, we are only fooling ourselves
and refusing to accept the Truth. But if we confess our sins to Him,
He is faithful and just to forgive us and to cleanse us from every wrong. (NLT)

Everyone but Jesus is born into this world with a sinful nature, which is simply our rebellious nature to disobey God and His righteous will for our lives. Most of us tend to either ignore the Creator of life altogether or we simply deny His authority over our lives and carve out an existence of our own liking, disregarding most of God's laws. And as sinful people puffed up with selfish pride, we quite often become so consumed with our own pleasure seeking that we forget about God all together. We tend to follow our own dark misguided ways that go against the holiness of God and if gone unchecked, will pull us deep into the darkness of this wicked world unaware of the dire consequences. So for most of us, we eventually find ourselves so lost in the darkness that we become discouraged, confused, hopeless, guilt ridden, ashamed, and depressed. And it was in this lost state that I found myself (like many others) looking forward to the end of my story. But there is a wonderful Way to escape the darkness before your story ends, because if you don't find the Way out, you will find yourself trapped in a darkness that never ends.

To start your journey out of the darkness, you must first acknowledge your sinful ways and bring them to the Savior, Christ Jesus. For only God can forgive your sins and only His blood can cleanse you from all unrighteousness. Only Jesus can deliver us from our Hell bound journeys and give us a new eternal life in Him. It was an awesome feeling to unload the things I did and thought about in the darkness of this world; a lost and lonely life that rewarded me with a lot of guilt and shame, and a lot of sorrow and pain that would not go away. To find the Way out of the darkness and be freed from the bondage of sin and the fear of death, you must come boldly to the throne of our gracious God and Savior and bring all your sins with you, where He will forgive, forget and cleanse you white as snow.

## A Whisper of Hope

**Come to Me, dear child...**so I can lighten your load and give you rest. For there is nothing that I cannot carry, nor is there anything I cannot not forgive, for I AM God, the final Judge Advocate. I will remember your sins no more, and shield you under the shadow of My wings.

**Colossians 3:5**
So put to death the sinful, earthly things lurking within you.
Don't be greedy for the good things of this life, for that is idolatry. (NLT)

**Give your burdens to the Lord, and He will take care of you.**
(Psalm 55:22)

# "Heart of Truth"

**1 John 3:19-20**
It is by our actions that we know we are living in the truth, so we will be confident when we stand before the Lord, even if our hearts condemn us. For God is greater than our hearts, and He knows everything. (NLT)

In order to find the real reason for this life we must first seek the Creator and His absolute Truth. The most brilliant secular minds of the world would have you believe there are no absolutes in this ever changing universe that was created from a big bang, especially when it comes to what is true and what is not; to what is wrong and what is right. These dark minds of the world try to convince us that truth does not exist, because what is true today may not necessarily be true tomorrow; what is true for you may not be so for me. Therefore, the truth is what we want it to be; what makes us happy and feel good about ourselves. Unfortunately, this kind of man-made truth that sounds reasonable to most people, is nothing but a flat out lie created by the father of lies, the Devil.

If it's the truth you are seeking my friend, the place to begin is in the written Word of God, inspired by the Author of life and Creator of the universe. I believe the first truth you must grasp and hold firmly is that God is the Creator and He has all Authority over His creation. This is not only absolutely true, but it also sheds some much needed Light on the lies that this fallen world has forced upon us. The second absolute we must take seriously is that God holds us personally accountable for the way we live. Like it or not, the Lord is King and His Truth prevails. Without the absolute Truth, there would be no order to the chaos. It would be survival of the fittest, with no limits and no restraints. We would be dictated by the law of kill or be killed. Without God there would be no goodness in this evil world that denies the Truth. When we live and love like Jesus the absolutes of life are proven. Living God's infallible absolutes in faith = Everlasting Joy and Eternal living!

## A Whisper of Hope

**My Truth reigns, dear child...**and it never changes. There are many false truths that seem right on the surface, but they only lead into absolute darkness. Be in My Word and know how to live in the Truth!

**Isaiah 59:13-15**
We know that we have rebelled against the LORD. We have turned our backs on God. We know how unfair and oppressive we have been, carefully planning our deceitful lies. Our courts oppose people who are righteous, and justice is no where to be found. Truth falls dead in the streets, and fairness has been outlawed. (NLT)

**A God of truth and without injustice; righteous and upright is He.**
(Deuteronomy 32:4)

# *"World of God"*

**Psalm 119:15-16**
I will study Your Commandments and reflect on Your Ways.
I will delight in Your Principles and not forget Your Word. (NLT)

In order for us to intelligently follow any kind of precept for living, whether it is godly or worldly in nature, we must first weigh the choices we have, and then pursue the lifestyle we desire. There is also the matter of the heart—do we want it bad enough to fully commit ourselves. With that said, if you desire a godly lifestyle you must first surrender completely to God, admit your sins, receive God's forgiveness, and study His Word. If you do this the Lord will send you the Holy Spirit, who will help you understand the Truth so you can apply it to your everyday living. The precepts found in the Holy Word of God are timeless absolute Truths. When the Lord God takes the reins, He will guide you safely through this difficult life-journey, and you will know that you have made the most important choice of your life, for it's when you learn the absolute Truth and fully accept the Way of God that you are given a new and better life and the promise of an even better eternal life.

God loved us so much that He chose to personally come into our world and not only share His Truth with us, but He also paid the heftiest price of all to set us free from our bondage to sin and the fear of death so we could become all that we were created to be. Living a Christian life does not take the fun out of living as the world wants you to believe. Instead, it puts fun into its proper prospective and brings an everlasting joy unsurpassed by anything the world has to offer. Your new godly nature will no longer crave the instant gratifying pleasures of your old sinful nature, because your desire to please God will take precedence over everything else in your life. You will also be able to discern the pleasures and fun that God designed for us from the sinful cravings that this fallen world embraces. Godly living leads to abundant blessings, everlasting joy, and eternal life, while the world's ways leads to confusion, disappointments, and eternal darkness. The world of God my friends, is much better!

## A Whisper of Hope

**When you follow My Way...**dear child, you follow the Truth. Living in this world can be anything but enjoyable, but in the New Heaven, on the New Earth your eternal life will be everything enjoyable and so much more. Live this life with Me, and you will become a citizen of My world.

**Romans 8:6-8**
If your sinful nature controls your mind, there is death. But if the Holy
Spirit controls your mind, there is life and peace. For the sinful nature
is always hostile to God. It never did obey God's laws, and it never will.
That is why those who are still under the control of their sinful nature
can never please God. (NLT)

**For the Word of God is full of living power.**
(Hebrews 4:12)

# "Saving Wisdom"

**Proverbs 26:8**
Honoring a fool is as foolish as
tying a stone to a slingshot. (NLT)

All people do foolish things, but that does not necessarily make us a fool. It is when we continue our foolish behavior in spite of the consequences that defines the fool. For example, there are many people in this world who are indeed foolish, because in spite of all the evidence, they still deny the existence of God, who is our Creator, Provider and the only Savior we have. There is a tremendous difference between God's view of foolishness and that of mankind's. Foolishness to God is mans most brilliant wisdom, which is speculation at best, and if lived by leads nowhere fast and ends with eternal condemnation. To the world, the Christian life is foolish because we seek the Truth from above and entrust our lives to an Almighty God who raises the dead and promises everlasting life. The Wisdom of God is infinite and it never changes, while mans created wisdom is both short-sighted and limited, and it changes with the drop of a hat. God, in His infinite wisdom, created everything that exists and He knows everything there is to know. The world's wisdom is made up from fallen human beings who have limited knowledge because they are finite.

Foolishness is believing in the Big Bang and how mankind slowly evolved by crawling out of the ocean to form legs billions of years ago, even though God has been revealing the Truth about creation since the beginning of time. And those of us who have the Wisdom from above know that most of the world's wisdom is utter foolishness, especially when it comes to this life and death. This is why we must be careful who we follow into the grave, because it will determine our eternal destination. If you are not looking to God for your wisdom, you will suffer the eternal fate of all fools. Foolish people turn away from God to follow their own foolish ways. Don't waste what little time you have on the foolishness of this fallen world. Instead, seek first the Kingdom of God and then His Wisdom will be yours to discover!

## A Whisper of Hope

**Heed not, the ways of man, dear child...**for tragedy will surely follow suit. But when you heed the Wisdom from above, you become wise and your life will flourish. Your Heavenly future is found in My Wisdom, so be wise in Me.

**1 Corinthians 1:18-20**
I know very well how foolish the message of the cross sounds to those who are on the road to destruction. But we who are being saved recognize this message as the very power of God. As the Scriptures say, "I will destroy human wisdom and discard their most brilliant ideas" (Isaiah 29:14). So where does this leave the philosophers, the scholars, and the world's brilliant debaters? God has made them all look foolish and has shown their wisdom to be useless nonsense. (NLT)

**For the wisdom of this world is foolishness to God.**
(1 Corinthians 3:19)

# "Hope Renewed"

**Psalm 51:10**
Create in me a clean heart, O God.
And renew a steadfast spirit within me. (NKJ)

When I ponder the word renew, I think of taking something old and making it new. I also think of the New Year's resolutions that we make at the beginning of each new year to improve the things about our old life that aren't so good. To experience a renewed life we must recommit your resolutions each and every day, rather than just once a year. Because sin is our nature and we are prone to succumb to it, so we must rely on some One much greater than ourselves, and that some One is the Lord our God, Jesus Christ. Without the power of God backing us up our renewal will peter out and we go back to the old ways of sinning, which makes most of us feel like failures and we kick the can down the road for another year. But if you want to get rid of the habits that feed your sinful nature, you must begin with the transforming of your heart, for it's from the heart that true change really takes place. And it's only the Lord God who can transform your calloused heart of stone into a soft heart of flesh that is filled with compassion and love for others—a heart that truly honors and glorifies the LORD. Being creatures compelled by our habits, we must replace the old sinful habits ( that lead us into the dark presence of the Devil) with new godly habits that lift us up into the Light of the Living God.

If it's a renewed heart that you desire my friend, ask God and He will not only transform your heart, but He will take you on an unbelievable journey of an eternal lifetime. This life-transforming change does not instantly happen overnight, but gradually with steadfast faith and the daily renewal of your heart, mind, and soul. There are many worldly ways of renewing your life that may sound great for the time being, but they cannot give you everlasting life. But when you accept the transforming ways of the Lord, He will give you a new heart and a new life that is forever. So join God's Plan and come to the throne of God's amazing grace where you will experience the life-changing transformation that will give you a new heart, a new life, and renewed hope!

## A Whisper of Hope

**Surrender your hard heart, child...**and I will give you a new heart and a new start. The pull of this wicked world is much too strong for you to resist without Me. I did not create you to stand alone; it's not wise to even try, for many have tried and all have failed.

**Galatians 5:17**
The old sinful nature loves to do evil, which is just opposite
from what the Holy Spirit wants. And the Spirit gives us desires
that are opposite from what the sinful nature desires. These two forces
are constantly fighting each other, and your choices are never free from the conflict. (NLT)

**For as he thinks in his heart, so is he.**
(Proverbs 23:7)

# *"Heart Matters"*

**Proverbs 27:19**
As a face is reflected in water,
so the heart reflects the person. (NLT)

As fallen human beings living in a fallen world, we are all prone to follow our fallen nature to sin. We either do it without thinking about it or we consciously sin denying its consequences, but either way, we love the sin and will devise a way to indulge in it. The down side to our indulging is that we will eventually pay the eternal price for our indulgence without God's forgiveness and our repentance. It's because of our rebellious nature against the holiness of God that we develop a deceitful heart. We must, therefore, be ever so mindful of the desires of our heart, for it is from the heart that our desires for living begins—be it for God or against God. So, if we desire to change the direction that this sin loving world is leading us, we must first and foremost, look deeply into the condition of our heart. Because it is only through God's infinite power and wisdom and saving grace that we are able to experience a truly transformed heart and new life—one that loves God and all people.

No matter who you are or how strong you think you may be, you cannot fight the dark forces of evil on your own, because the power of sin over your heart and mind, is far too strong for your human condition to combat without the sovereign power of Christ Jesus. Satan reigns in this fallen world that can only satisfy the wicked desires of your heart; desires that are borne out of our sinful lusts for pleasure; desires that will draw you away from God and leave you in a darkness that never ends. Don't be one of the many who experience the final condemnation and eternal separation from God, for it will not be a pleasant ending to an already difficult life that you did not ask for. This is why our gracious God continues to reach out for every heart; not forcing His will on anyone, but giving everyone the precious time to change. So take it to heart my friends, and do not gamble with the LORD our God. Instead, step up while you still can, and trust Him to transform the sinful desires of your heart into godly desires that will drive you into the very arms of the Living God Himself.

## A Whisper of Hope

**Ask, dear child...**and I will give you a new heart—one that desires Me and all the goodness I offer. This world hates Me and all that is righteous. It will destroy your heart and lead you straight into Hell before you know it. So be ever so mindful to guard your heart, because it is from the heart that will determine your eternal destiny.

**Ezekiel 36:26-27**
And I will give you a new heart with new and right desires,
and I will put a new spirit in you. I will take out your stony heart of sin
and give you a new, obedient heart. And I will put My Spirit in you so
you will obey my laws and do whatever I command. (NLT)

**Blessed are the pure in heart, for they shall see God.**
(Matthew 5:8)

# "Truly Wise"

**Ephesians 1:7-9**
He is so rich in kindness that He purchased our freedom through the blood
of His Son, and our sins are forgiven. He has showered His kindness on us, along
with all wisdom and understanding. God's secret plan has now been revealed to us;
it is a plan centered on Christ, designed long ago according to His good pleasure. (NLT)

Incredibly, when the Lord God redeems us, He forgives all our sins, takes away the guilt and punishment for our rebellion, and provides us with the Holy Spirit to help us gain both wisdom and insight—two very essential ingredients that we need if we are to change from godlessness to godliness. The Bible is God's Story and it spells out everything we need to know about Him and His will for our lives, but it is the Holy Spirit who gives us the ability to understand it's true meaning and the strength to carry it out. Even those who have never obtained any academic degrees will gain the wisdom of God that surpasses even the most educated unbeliever. For as a believer you will understand the most absolute and basic truths and values concerning both life and death. You will know that God is the Creator of all things and that He is sovereign over it all and controls the course of history to coincide with His plans. You will know the reason that God created mankind and what the future holds for us. And as believers in Christ Jesus you will develop the mind of Christ with goals and priorities that rise above the limits of any and all earthly circumstances.

Such absolute knowledge escapes the minds of unbelievers because they tend to view the things of God as being either irrational or irrelevant, or they view God with total disdain or apathy. My dear friends, to know God and His revealed plan for His creation is easily found in the inerrancy of Scripture. And once you understand who God is, who you are, and what the future holds, your knowledge and acceptance will usher you into God's Kingdom and a share in God's amazing glory. Every day that our gracious God gives you on this earth is an opportunity to do His good will—to live a righteous life in praise and thanksgiving to God—a life that will honor Him, and one that will be lived for all eternity with the One who created it all for you!

## A Whisper of Hope

**My will, will be done, dear child...**you need not look any further than the pages of My Holy Book. For within those pages you will find all you need to know for now. Trust in me and believe. Do not follow the world's failed ways, for they are filled with deceit and darkness.

**2 Timothy 3:16-17**
All Scripture is inspired by God and is useful to teach us what is true
and to make us realize what is wrong in our lives. It straightens us out
and teaches us to do what is right. It is God's way of preparing us in every
way, fully equipped for every good thing God wants us to do. (NLT)

**But we can understand these things because we have the mind of Christ.**
(1 Corinthians 2:16)

# "Father's Son"

**Psalm 18:16, 28**
He reached down from Heaven and rescued me; He
drew me out of deep waters. LORD, you have brought
light to my life; My God, You light up my darkness. (NLT)

Not so long ago my life was drowning in a dark sea of self-pity and self-hatred; despising this cursed life and longing for an end to it all. I was sinking deeper into a dark depth of hopelessness that sin always brings into the lost and isolated life—sin that was pulling me closer to the edge of the abyss that dropped deep into an endless darkness. The very thought of living to an old age weighed heavily on my heart and was dragging me down a dark path of depression with utter regret of ever being born and becoming the vile person I had so not wanted to become. I was mad at God and disappointed in the world. I was intolerant of most people and I hated myself. But it was in this fallen state of mind and unbeknownst to me, I was in the very place that the Enemy of God wants everyone to be. There are no human words that can fully explain the unrelenting torment that darkness brings, especially when you feel trapped and forsaken. The best scenario I can give is like being tied up and falling into an unknown darkness that you know will end badly, and there is absolutely no escape from whatever horrors that are lurking in the deepest darkness that you are falling into.

Living in darkness is not how God created us to live, so He is faithfully reaching into the darkness to rescue us. We have a God who has a Divine Plan for our escape from the prison of darkness that many are locked away in. He is the Lord God Almighty. It is God the Father's Sovereign Plan. It is God the Son who graciously pulled it off. And it is God the Holy Spirit who takes care of the rest. This fallen world can only deliver more of the same darkness and death, but God can deliver you from the prison of Hell and give you life. The only Way is in the Father's Son.

## A Whisper of Hope

**I bring life saving Light, child…**that's what I do. I know the hopelessness that darkness brings. That is why the Father sent Me; to bring Light to you. You will always struggle in this dark world that wants to consume your soul, but it is in My Light that you are saved out of the darkness and given the peace and strength to see you through to the other side.

**2 Corinthians 4:4**
Satan, the god of this evil world, has blinded the minds
of those who don't believe, so they are unable to see the
glorious Light of the Good News that is shining upon them. (NLT)

**"I [Jesus] have told you all this so that you may have peace in Me."**
(John 16:33)

# *"Power and Grace"*

### 1 Chronicles 29:11, 12
Yours, O LORD, is the greatness, the power, the glory, the victory, and the majesty. Power and might are in Your hand, and it is at Your discretion that people are made great, and given strength. (NLT)

It is so important for people of the Christian faith to believe in the power and grace of our Almighty God, especially when it comes to receiving and using the resurrection power of God that is needed to overcome our sinful natures and take advantage of God's amazing grace. We must believe in the Word of God and keep it written firmly on our hearts, for when we live in Christ Jesus we have all the power we will ever need to overcome this sinful world and its wicked ways. There is absolutely nothing that our Lord God cannot accomplish through our lives in order to fulfill His will and bring about the completion of His ultimate plan of Salvation.. The Living God is the Creator and He is justly sovereign over His creation. Without the sustaining power of Christ there would be nothing but uninhibited chaos without purpose or end.

The Lord gives and takes away whatever fits into His perfect will. No matter how weak we Christians may feel, or how ill-equipped for His service we think we are, we can be sure that God is constantly working in and through us to accomplish great and awesome things for the future of His Kingdom to come. The death and resurrection of our Lord God, Jesus Christ, is the Way for every believer to receive the saving power and grace of God. Because Jesus lives on forever, we, too, will live on forever. Nothing, not even the powers of darkness that rule this evil world, can stand against the power and grace of the Almighty God. Our salvation and the promise of eternal life are protected by this uninhibited Power of God. And by knowing these simple, yet profound truths about the Lord and His plans for you, will bring such a joy and peace into your troubled heart that you will never again fall asleep in fear.

## A Whisper of Hope

**Know and believe…**in the Power that created the universe. I can and will accomplish all I have planned. And you, My dear child, can be a part of that plan. This world is powerless over you when you are in Me and I Am in you. You need not ever be afraid, for I have overcome this world for you.

### Ephesians 1:19-23
I pray that you will begin to understand the incredible greatness of His power for us who believe Him. This is the same mighty power that raised Christ from the dead and seated Him in the place of honor at God's right hand in the heavenly realms. Now He is far above any ruler or authority or power or leader or anything else in this world or in the world to come. And God has put all things under the authority of Christ, and He gave Him this authority for the benefit of the Church. And the Church is His body; it is filled by Christ, who fills everything everywhere with His Presence. (NLT)

**By His mighty power at work within us,**
**He is able to accomplish infinitely more than we would ever dare to ask or hope.**
(Ephesians 3:20)

# *"Fear and Life"*

**Exodus 20:20**
"Don't be afraid", Moses said, "for God has come
in this way to show you His awesome power. From
now on, let your fear of Him keep you from sinning!" (NLT)

The more we discover the incredible amounts of energy that make up our vast universe, the more we should consider and understand the incredible power that our Lord God possesses in order to have created it all and is now holding it all together in perfect unison; which should then, give us a great reason to fear God's infinite power. He could squash us like a bug with just a mere thought. With that said, Jesus has revealed that He will unleash the powers of the universe upon this earth and mankind. But we must also consider Judgment Day and what it will bring if we have no fear of God and live as if He doesn't even exist. Fear is a healthy human emotion—one of the many unique characteristics that the Lord has given us so that we could better prepared and protect ourselves from the things that threaten both our physical and spiritual well being. Anyone who claims to have no fear is either living in complete denial or they are mentally unstable. We should use our God-given fear wisely though, because the eternal consequences for how we live our lives are of the utmost importance.

Although God is loving and kind and compassionate and merciful and gracious, He is also Holy and perfectly Just. Our God has graciously shared with us how and why we should live by His Law and the consequences for both our obedience and disobedience. But the world has made God's justice so irrelevant that our disobedience is now okay, because everyone does it. People are now being taught that there are no consequences for our behavior beyond this life. This is not so dear friend, because God's justice is very real , just as the consequences of our behavior is. For those who refuse to fear God and the final consequences of their disobedience to His Law will live however they please, and one day God's wrath will bear down on them like a great ball of fire. The fear of the Lord is the beginning of all true wisdom. For fearing God and honoring His Way will not only save your own eternal life, but others will see the Light and follow suit. Fear and life should always co-exist in peace, because it will bring you into the full glory of God.

## A Whisper of Hope

**Godly fear is wise, child…**for it saves lives. Do not be afraid of Me, but fear the consequences of your sin. When you deny Me and ignore the Truth there is an eternal price attached to it. Fearing the eternal consequences of sin is wisdom at its best, for it draws you into My saving arms.

**Hebrews 12:28-29**
Since we are receiving a Kingdom that cannot be destroyed,
let us be thankful and please God by worshiping Him with holy
fear and awe. For our God is a consuming fire. (NLT)

**Fear of the LORD is the beginning of all wisdom.**
(Proverbs 9:10)

# *"Words for Life"*

**Jeremiah 15:16**
Your words are what sustain me. They bring me great joy and are
my heart's delight, for I bear your name, O LORD God Almighty. (NLT)

Not only do the words of our Creator hold the universe in perfect order so the earth is able to sustain life, but God's words are living words and they give us everything we need for living a healthy, righteous life that is pleasing to God and brings us much delight as well. For when we have the Holy Spirit living in our hearts, we are filled with a non-decaying, everlasting wisdom that comes straight from the One who creates and sustains all life—a Savior who personally saved us from self-destructing sin and eternal condemnation. When you surrender your life to the Lord, He will give you an eternal purpose with an everlasting destination. Our Infinite God is the only being who has always been, who is perfect in every way, and is the only One with whom we can totally rely on and trust with our very life. Every word of God is absolutely the undeniable truth and if faithfully lived day to day puts you on an incredible life-journey that you cannot possibly imagine. The Word of God will fill your troubled heart with everlasting peace and indestructible joy. God's Word brings truth where is none, hope when all is hopeless, and peace amidst the trouble. God's Word lights up our darkness, turns our fears into courage, and exposes our enemies for who they are. And no matter who you are or where you live or what you have done, and no matter how hopeless and dark your circumstances may be, God's Word has the power to change any life at any time. The Lord sustains and provides with perfection, and although this world is on the road to destruction, you can trust our Great and Faithful Lord God to get you Home where you belong.

## A Whisper of Hope

**Trust My Word…**dear child, for it will give you life. I have given you My Word because I love you. I don't want to see anyone waste away in the evil of this perverse world. I came to give you life to the fullest and it is through My Word that you will be set free from the decadence around you.

**Job 34:14-15**
If God were to take back His Spirit and withdraw His breath,
all life would cease, and humanity would turn again to dust. (NLT)

**He will take care of you. He will not permit the godly to slip and fall.**
(Psalm 55:22)

# "Living Waters"

**Psalm 36:9**
For You are the Fountain of Life,
the Light by which we see. (NLT)

I picture the Fountain of Life as an inexhaustible Source of eternally, refreshing, crystal clear, Living Water that sustains all life in a world that is perfect and without death. But in order to find this inexhaustible Source for eternal living, we must follow the inexhaustible Source of Light, for without Christ Jesus we could not find the path that leads to the Fountain of Life, because all there would be is darkness and fear, guessing and doubt; unaware that we are stumbling closer to a cliff of the abyss, only to fall over its edge with nothing to hang on to. Our incredible Creator is the Light and the Fountain who is the Source for human life as God intended it to be. Without Jesus there would be either nothing at all or what there is, would be nothing but random chaos without order or purpose. Without the Fountain of Living Water replenishing us in this life, our lives would be meaningless, self-indulgent, and fruitless—never satisfying and would ultimately end in darkness and despair. What a priceless, undeserved gift that our Lord has given us my friends; the gift of Amazing Grace, which flows freely from the Fountain of Life. Without this free flowing amazing Grace, the Fountain of Life could never be found. If you desire a fulfilling and meaningful life, you must drink from the Fountain of Life and bathe in the Light of the Son.

There are a few basic choices that we are all faced with and they are; goodness or evil, light or darkness, life or death, God or Satan. God gives us all an opportunity to freely choose one or the other; there is no in between and there are no gray areas. So, it would behoove you to choose wisely and choose quickly, because if you wait too long the choice could be made for you and that choice is one that you will forever regret and one that is final.

## A Whisper of Hope

**It is time to choose, My child...**because you do not know the hour that your time to choose will run out. The living water which flows from Me will sustain your life forever—a life that will know neither defeat nor despair, only victory and joy. Wait no longer, because if you do you may lose.

**Hebrews 1:3**
The Son reflects God's own glory and everything about Him represents God exactly. He sustains the universe by the mighty power of His command. (NLT)

**God is Light and there is no darkness in Him at all.**
(1 John 1:5)

# August

# "All Anew"

**2 Corinthians 4:16, 18**
That is why we never give up. Though our bodies are dying, our spirits are being renewed every day. So we don't look at the troubles we can see right now; rather, we look forward to what we have not yet seen. For the troubles we see will soon be over, but the joys to come will last forever. (NLT)

Since the beginning of time there has never been nor will there ever be a trouble-free existence in our world this side of Heaven. Since the falling away from God, man has sought to create an utopian world, but he has never succeeded and he never will. We are flawed people, living in a flawed world, and we are incapable of creating anything that is perfect—imperfectness can never create that which is perfect—it's simply not possible because it's one of God's many absolutes. God is the only One who can bring about a utopian world and when Jesus returns, He will do just that. Jesus will remove all evil and get rid of Satan and all unrepentant sinners. He will set up His Kingdom that will never end and bring total peace to our world. Our finite minds cannot even begin to fathom a peaceful world without wars and death—a perfect world without end.

The Lord tells us that nothing can compared to the Glory that God has planned for us, for the Lord is going to create a new Heaven, a new Earth, and an entirely new universe for us to enjoy with Him forever. We have a glorious Creator who promises to make our Christian lives worth all the trouble that living in this sinful world brings. The Living God wants His children to stay focused on the eternal consequences of this extremely short-lived life. So ask yourself these questions and then choose carefully, my friend: Am I only striving to gain what this sinful world offers, denying the eternal consequences? Or am I striving to live a righteous life, denying the world's self gratifying pleasures that last but a moment? The answer you give will decide the choice you make, and it will be the most important one of your earthly life as a finite human being with an eternal future, because the time you are allotted to answer and choose is not only extremely short lived, but how short it is, is uncertain as well.

## A Whisper of Hope

**Think eternally and carefully...**for you must choose Me or the world. You can either live in Me and wait for the eternal rewards I promise, or you can bathe in the pleasures of this sinful world and die in eternal darkness. It is your choice to freely make, dear child. Make it wise and make it soon.

**Revelation 21:3-4**
"Look, the home of God is now among His people! He will live with them, and they will be His people, God Himself will be with them. He will remove all of their sorrows, and there will be no more death or sorrow or crying or pain. For the old world and its evils are gone forever." (NLT)

**Yet what we suffer now is nothing compared to the glory He will give us later.**
(Romans 8:18)

# "Don't Be Fooled"

**Proverbs 10:23**
Doing wrong is fun for a fool,
But a man of understanding has wisdom. (NKJ)

Whenever we do anything that is contrary to the will of God, it's wrong and it's sin. And the reason we are so easily tempted into doing what is contrary to the will of God, is because we are inherently wrong doers by nature. We are a sinful, self-centered, and greedy people, who are easily convinced that bad is not all that bad and being good takes the pleasure out of living—the age old lie of Satan, who manipulates our sinful nature for his dirty work. The arch Enemy of God and his deceitfulness is more alive today than it has ever been and it's spreading at high speed through the internet. The evil lies of Satan are taking this world down a dangerous path that leads nowhere and ends in eternal death. You may think that the battles of good and evil are nothing more than manmade fabrications for a good story, but don't be fooled my friends, because the battles for our hearts, minds, and souls are very real and they are being fought in both the physical and spiritual realms.

These life and death battles are very real and very intense. Everyone faces these every day battles; battles for our physical and spiritual survival; battles that can bring us life or death; battles that will determine our eternal destination. Just as the physical world has always been ravaged by war, so, too, has the spiritual world been at war. Satan wants to destroy everything that is God's, but he knows his time is drawing to an end, and is working feverishly to take as many people as he can into the eternal burning Lake of Fire. But Jesus Christ personally paid for your freedom from sin and death and saved you, if you so desire, from eternal condemnation that is justly due. Our Lord God does not want anyone to be locked away in Hell forever. We know this because Jesus took it upon Himself to pave our Way to Heaven.

## A Whisper of Hope

**Believe the Truth, My child…**it will set you free from the lies that would otherwise bring you into eternal punishment. I have made eternal plans for you that are out of this world. Stay close to Me and you won't be fooled by the foolishness of this wicked world that wants your soul.

**Revelation 20:13-15**
The sea gave up the dead in it and death and the grave gave up the dead in them. They were all judged according to their deeds. And death and the grave were thrown into the Lake of Fire. This is the second death—the Lake of Fire. And anyone whose name was not found recorded in the Book of Life was thrown into the Lake of Fire.

**Dear children, keep away from anything that might take God's place in your hearts.**
(1 John 5:21)

# *"Glorious Day"*

**Isaiah 45:21, 22**
For there is no other God but Me—a just God
And a Savior—no, not one. Let all the world look
To Me for salvation! For I am God; there is no other. (NLT)

There is only One who has the right to claim all authority over everything all the time. Yahweh is His Name—the Great I AM is He—a glorious Living God who loves perfectly and unconditionally. He is called Faithful and True, always keeping His every promise! Because of His Sovereign Power and Majesty, those who live by His Name can pray with the utmost confidence and peace, because we know that His unlimited power and resources can change any circumstance, at any time, especially when it serves His Kingdom to come and His Glorious Plan for man. Because we have a merciful and forgiving God, He graciously makes right our wrongs and saves us from the dark and wicked things that seek to harm and destroy us. We have a Savior who saves us from our sin loving nature that brings death and eternal destruction. What we have in our awesome God my friends, is not just a fabulous God, but a Heavenly Father, a Saving Son, and a Powerful Helper who can do all things.

We have a God that is so much bigger than the immense vastness of the universe that you should live every moment of your life in total awe of His Presence, and be ever so thankful for all He has done. And when the Lord God becomes your personal Savior, let not your heart be troubled, for no matter what happens in this fallen world, you will never perish. Instead, you will live in eternal victory that brings life to the fullest. We suffer much pain in this fallen world and shed many tears over this difficult life, but when the time arrives to leave this world, we are immediately in the Presence of the Lord our God, Jesus Christ, His mighty angels, and the redeemed saints who have gone before you. What a glorious day that will be—one that has no end!

## A Whisper of Hope

**I Am God, dear child...**there is no other. I came into this world to reconcile our relationship, so you could live in My Presence forever. When you live in My Light, I will be your God and you shall be My child forever.

**1 Chronicles 29:11-12**
Yours, O LORD, is the greatness, the power, the glory, the victory, and the majesty.
Everything in the heavens and on earth is Yours, O LORD, and this is Your kingdom.
We adore You as the One who is over all things. Riches and honor come from You alone,
for You rule over everything. Power and might are in Your hand, and it is at Your discretion
that people are made great and given strength. (NLT)

**"O Lord, You are a great and awesome God!"**
(Daniel 9:4)

# *"Saving Power"*

**Psalm 60:11**
Oh, please help us against our enemies,
for all human help is useless. (NLT)

There comes a time in almost every human life when failure or defeat, or sometimes even death seems to be winning the battle—when the odds of victory are slim at best. It's during these private moments of quiet desperation that many deflated souls turn to the Living God; the only Hope there is. Our Lord God and Savior Jesus Christ, is the only One with the power to radically change any circumstance, no matter how impossible it seems—He is the only One who can do the impossible. Our fallen human abilities are not only very limited and short sighted, but are usually faulty as well. Whereas our Savior's abilities are unlimited, knows all future things, and is right 100% of the time. This world is beyond our control, and our survival is an everyday struggle, especially when it comes to the attacks from our most dangerous Adversary, the Devil. Whether it is physical or spiritual in nature, the battles of life will continue to rage on until the end of time. And if we are to be victorious against the world and Satan, we must tap into the Saving Power of God, because He is our victory.

But in order for us to claim our victory, we must believe that God is completely sovereign, in control of every circumstance, and that He is personally involved in the lives of His people. No human life is too insignificant for God's help, nor is it too broken for God to fix. And for those of us who know their Creator and call Him Father, we know He is always with us, providing and protecting; confident that our eternal lives are safely in His hands. The most difficult and enduring battles that confront us are not the battles for our short physical lives in this fallen world, but it's the spiritual warfare for our hearts, minds and souls—battles for our eternal lives. The evil powers of Satan are too much for us without the full armor of God. You cannot claim the victory that the Lord personally paid for apart from His saving Power and the grace of God.

## A Whisper of Hope

**There is much evil, dear child...**that you are not even aware of that is deadly to your soul. The world will tempt you and bribe you and even force you to follow its dark ways, but don't try to fight it on your own, for you will lose. Instead, put on My armor and let Me win the battles for you.

**2 Corinthians 10:3-4**
We are human, but we don't wage war with human
plans and methods. We use God's mighty weapons,
not mere worldly weapons, to knock down the Devil's strongholds. (NLT)

**I warn you to keep away from evil desires, because they fight against your very souls.**
(1 Peter2:11)

# "Full Ownership"

**Psalm 24:1**
The earth is the LORD'S, and everything in it.
The world and all its people belong to Him. (NLT)

Our triune God, without exception, is the final authority in all things and at all times. The buck stops with the LORD our God. Since the Lord created the earth and everything in it, it rightly belongs to Him and therefore, has the final word over all things all of the time. Because God is everywhere at all times, there is nothing seen or unseen that He is unaware of, nor is there anything that can elude His all consuming Presence. God is so big that neither space nor time can confine His being or limit His supremacy. He sees and hears and knows absolutely everything that goes on in His creation—nothing can hide from Him. With God there is no darkness, and everything is in His Light and visible for Him to see. He is our Father, Provider, Savior, Lord, King, Judge, Shepherd, Light, Word, Rock, Shelter, Lion, and the Lamb, and the list goes on.

In other words, God is Supreme—nothing trumps His sovereign will. If everything ceased to exist, only God would remain. He always has been and always will be, for only God is infinite. Every living organism on this earth depends on God for its very survival. It is only by His grace and good will that our every need is met. Our dependency on God is absolute, for without Him we would not exist nor could we survive if we did. We owe God for everything we have and don't have. Every ounce of thanks and praise that we could ever muster, would never be enough to pay the debt we own Him. The Author and Finisher of Life is absolute in everything. And when you understand and believe this my friends, you will fully trust in His Way and it will bring you great joy and peace while you wait patiently for His Promise to make all things new, including you!

## A Whisper of Hope

**All that exists belongs to Me...**you only share in its glory. I give you all that you need and sometimes more, for I Am the Rightly Owner and I do what I please. This may sound harsh to you now, but one day you will understand and experience all that I have for you and you will be amazed at My generosity.

**Acts 17:24-25**
He is the God who made the world and everything in it. Since He is
Lord of Heaven and Earth, He doesn't live in manmade temples, and
human hands can't serve His needs—for He has no needs. He Himself
gives life and breath to everything, and He satisfies every need there is. (NLT)

**Before the mountains were created, before You made the earth and the world,
you are God, without beginning or end.**
(Psalm 90:2)

# "Victory"

**Deuteronomy 30:3, 4**
Do not be afraid as you go out to fight today! Do not lose heart or panic.
For the LORD your God is going with you! He will fight for you against
your enemies, and He will give you victory! (NLT)

L iving in this fallen state we find ourselves struggling to survive in a world that is not always
user friendly, especially for those of us who seek to live a Christian life. As followers of
Christ, we must always be ready to not only fight for our faith and families, but for our hearts,
minds and souls when it comes from an Enemy that hates our Lord God, Jesus Christ. Every
single day we are faced against the deadliest and most dangerous Enemy of man: Satan and his
wicked world that embraces his evil ways. The world is being bombarded with so many lies from
the Enemy that we are literally being brainwashed into believing even the most absurd. These
confused people are falling for the age old lie that this life is all about satisfying the hungers of
our carnal flesh.

Satan is moving our world further away from God and His Truth, leading it down paths
that seem okay, but lead to eternal death and destruction. Our children are being taught to
rebel against the Truth of God, which is no longer applicable in today's modern world. Satan
is cleverly using the power of the media; newspapers, magazines, television, radio, Hollywood,
and the Internet to poison our minds so we can be led to slaughter, unaware of the eternal destination. Living in this evil world is an excruciating battle for truth that can only be found in
Christ. Never fear standing for the Truth that is absolute and eternal. Do not let your discouragement get the best of you, because the Lord God has promised victory to all those who fight
the good fight. Our Lord God is mighty to save.

## A Whisper of Hope

**Listen carefully, My child...** You can follow Me into victory and live, or follow Satan into defeat
and die. No middle ground; no gray areas. It's one or the other. You can choose the world and
loose or you can choose Me in victory.

**2 Timothy 3:1, 2, 4**
You should also know this...that in the last days there will be very difficult times. For people
will love only themselves and their money. They will be boastful and proud, scoffing at God...
They will betray their friends, be reckless, be puffed up with pride, and love pleasure rather
than God. (NLT)

**But thanks be to God, who gives us the victory through our Lord Jesus Christ.**
(1 Corinthians 15:57)

# *"Undeserved"*

**Matthew 5:7**
God blesses those who are merciful,
for they will be shown mercy. (NLT)

The Lord commands us to be holy as He is holy; to be other than; to set our lives apart from the ways of this fallen world; to show mercy when needed and to always be gracious. But because we live in a fallen world made up of imperfect, sin flawed people who are basically self-centered, showing mercy can often go by the wayside. There are some people who are just plain cruel and unkind, but most people become so self-focused that showing mercy is hardly an option, because living is all about them. God's mercy is not giving us what we deserve for our love of sin. Because of His great love for mankind, He has made the Way for us to escape what we deserve, for He knows we cannot earn what we don't deserve. By living in the Way, mercy becomes a fruit of the Spirit that lives in the hearts of those whose who belong to Christ Jesus. The Christian faith is grounded in the mercy and forgiveness that is offered to everyone. The unconditional love, mercy, and the amazing grace of God is what sets Christianity apart from all other world views and religions.

It is because of God's great love for mankind that He showed us His mercy by suffering and dying for our sins so we would be spared the final condemnation that every sin brings. It is by accepting this gift of God's mercy that we, too, are able to be merciful to others, especially to those who hurt us. We live in a world whose people are oblivious to this Truth and they are unknowingly on the road to their own destruction. For those of us who have received God's mercy, we must step up to the plate and be merciful to those who reject God's ways. We are to pass God's mercy on to others; one precious soul at a time. As the people of God's Church, chosen by Christ and called by His Name, we are commissioned to show mercy to all those who are in need of God's mercy. But even more important, we are commanded to show others the dire need that we all have for God's mercy and forgiveness for without it, we are forever separated from the King of Mercy and dead in our sin.

## A Whisper of Hope

**What you sow, My child...**so shall you reap. Be merciful to others, as I am merciful to you. When you show mercy to others, you are really shining My Light into their lives. Forgive others as I have forgiven you, because by forgiving those who hurt you, you are living in the Truth of My Light.

**James 2:13**
For there will be no mercy for you if you have not been merciful to others. But if you have been merciful, then God's mercy toward you will win out over His judgment against you. (NLT)

**For Your mercy reaches unto the heavens.**
(Psalm 57:10)

# *"Cushion of Peace"*

**Psalm 29:11**
The LORD gives His people strength. The LORD blesses them with peace. (NLT)

When you surrender to your Savior, many amazing things begin to happen, and one of these is receiving the incredible peace that comes with knowing that the One True God has forgiven all of your many sins, wiping your record clean, and clothing you in the righteousness of Jesus. It's knowing you will escape eternal condemnation and be adopted into God's Heavenly Family forever. Knowing and believing that you have the power and wisdom of God living inside of you will add to that peace and He will help you, especially during the inevitable storms of life that can completely destroy one's life. It is God's Sovereign Power that provides us with a peace that cushions our many falls in this difficult life-journey. Many people throughout the world are struggling just to stay alive in this godless world that is putting less and less value on human life. We live in sin, in fear of tomorrow, and in fear of death, and we do it while suffering much trouble, pain, and discouragement, which will continue to beat us down until we are dead. Because of the utter chaos and uncertainty that living in this fallen world brings, there is a desperate need to know that the God in Heaven is real, that He really cares, and He has promised to help us defeat this evil world, no matter what. Our Lord God and Savior cares about all peoples, and He can save our souls and bring His peace to anyone in this world that delivers only trouble and death.

There is but One Way to peace my friend, you must surrender your troubled life into the hands of the Savior and allow Him to heal your wounds, nourish your life, and bring peace into your troubled heart. You must simply trust Jesus and allow Him to do what only God can do; save your soul and give you peace. When you know and trust in the Prince of Peace, He will fill your heart, give you rest, and comfort your weary soul. You don't know what tomorrow will bring, but the Savior knows. You don't have the wisdom or strength to battle this evil world alone, but the Living God does. Living this difficult life without Jesus will make you crazy, depressed, sad, empty, lonely, frustrated, and you will be so anxious and fearful that you will never experience the joy of living. When you know that you will be with the Lord when you die, there is peace. When you know you will not share in the fate of Satan, there is joy. Make the Lord your Cushion of Peace and truly live.

## A Whisper of Hope

**Come, My child…**and I will give you My peace, a peace that endures all things of this fallen world. When you come to Me I will show you the Way to live. I will comfort your weary soul and lighten the burdens you were never meant to bear. Come to Me and live life to the fullest.

**John 14:27**
"I am leaving you with a gift—peace of mind and heart.
And the peace I give isn't like the peace the world gives. So don't be troubled or afraid." (NLT)

**LORD, You are my strength and fortress, my refuge in the day of trouble!**
(Jeremiah 16:19)

# "News Worthy"

**Psalm 98:1**
Sing a new song to the LORD, for He has done wonderful deeds.
He has won a mighty victory, by His power and holiness. (NLT)

Before the Lord rescued me from drowning in a sea of self-loathing and sin, the only songs I knew were of hopelessness and disdain for my existence in this miserable world. I was unable to see any good or lasting purpose to this short life. I was filled with confusion and plagued with depression. I had been duped by the lies of the world, believing this life was all about me and what makes me happy. But as I lived out this self-gratifying journey, I began to question the validity of the world's secular views that were shallow, short sighted, and quite meaningless when it was all said and done and then you die. So with this foolish wisdom as my guide, I lived out its plan and in time I began to realize that the world was lying and I was empty. I began seeking things that would numb the pain of living and the futility of it all. I wanted to drown out the hopelessness. Where was the joy in living? Why did I feel there was something more, and what was missing? What was wrong? Why was living so hard and futile? For all the hard work and pain and suffering, where did lead? What was the reward if there really was one? Maybe it was a little contentment, a bit of happiness now and then, but in the end was it really worth it? For no matter what I did or accomplished it was never enough to satisfy, nor did it fill the emptiness that wouldn't go away.

And then, out of nowhere, the Living God reached down from the glory of Heaven and pulled me from the muck of this sin-filled world and revealed what I had always longed for—the Truth and a worthwhile purpose with substance. And the Truth finally set me free from the lies of Satan and his world. God revealed the Good News of His forgiveness and redemption. He cleansed my wretched life with His righteousness and blessed me with everlasting hope. He gave me understanding of this dark world and taught me His eternal wisdom. He healed my wounds from many years of self-destructive living. The only two things this world can give you that lasts, is death and Hell. But our gracious and loving Creator can give you your heart's delight and it's eternal. This is Good News my friends. News that saves lives. News that is truly worth hearing and sharing.

## A Whisper of Hope

**I bring you Good News...**dear child, please listen. Don't let the world's news drown out the only Good News that makes this difficult life worth living. The news of this evil world corrupts. My News brings Truth. Worldly news brings death and destruction. My Good News brings life.

**Romans 6:6-8**
Our old sinful selves were crucified with Christ so that sin
might lose its power in our lives. We are no longer slaves to sin.
For when we died with Christ we were set free from the power of sin.
And since we died with Christ, we know we will also share His new life. (NLT)

**But we are looking forward to the new heavens and new earth He has promised.**
(2 Peter 3:13)

# "Seekers, Finders"

**Psalm 105:4**
Seek the LORD and His strength; Seek His face evermore. (NKJ)

Because the world is in a fallen state of sin against our Holy God, we must live in constant conflict with the Enemy, not only for our hearts and minds and the eternal life of our souls, but it is also an everyday battle just to stay alive. Everyone must face the very real and difficult reality of not knowing what the next moment will bring; unknowns' that can be good or they can be devastating realities that are beyond our control. So the best way for us to cope with these unknown realities, is we must face them with the Truth of God, for nothing can survive these tough realities without God's Sovereign Power and grace. Everything in the universe is dependent upon the Word of God to sustain it. There is no other God that has the ability to created life and provide all that is needed to sustain it. As finite human beings, we are weak in physical strength, small in stature, and powerless against the powerful forces of the universe, as well as the unseen forces of evil that enslaves most of this fallen world—an enslavement that is impossible to break free from without the infinite power and wisdom of our Almighty God and Savior, Jesus Christ. Many have tried throughout the ages and all have failed miserably, because the sinful flesh is weak and the power of sin is mighty and cleverly disguised as natural and good.

As fallen human beings most of us are easily sucked into believing the lies of this wicked world, which often confuse our God given desires with sinful desires that alienate us from God. And sadly many of these deceived people will suddenly find themselves eternally separated from the good pleasures of God and in a place of utter hopelessness and darkness forever. The best solution for facing the hard and confusing realities of this fallen life, my friends, is to seek the Truth in Christ Jesus, and do it before it's too late. Seek the Truth and learn why you were created. Seek the knowledge and wisdom of God and find true value in living. Seek God's strength and wisdom in everything you do so you can overcome this sin-filled world that is filled with every kind of evil. When you seek the Truth, you will find Jesus Christ. Seek His Face and seek His will, and find life everlasting.

## A Whisper of Hope

**Seek the Truth...**dear child, but be aware of the lies of this ungodly world. The world's truth may sound good now, but it in the end, it is only darkness, emptiness and eternal regret. But when you seek My Face, you will find Me, and I will open the eyes of your heart and lead you in the Truth that trumps everything of this world, for all Truth seekers are Truth finders.

**1 John 2:16-17**
For the world offers only the lust for physical pleasure,
the lust for everything we see, and pride in our possessions.
These are not from the Father. They are from this evil world.
And this world is fading away, along with everything it craves.
But if you do the will of God you will live forever. (NLT)

**Let Heaven fill your thoughts. Do not think only about things down here on earth.**
(Colossians 3:2)

# *"Infinite Eyes"*

**Proverbs 15:3**
The eyes of the LORD are in every place, keeping watch on the evil and the good. (NKJ)

There are people who believe in a higher being who created the universe billions of years ago and left it to evolve on its own accord. They believe this creator is an impersonal being who is far removed from creation, allowing it to exist by the laws of probability and chance. There are also people who embrace an array of manmade gods that were created by people who do the Devil's work. And there are many people who either deny the existence of a God altogether or they knowingly reject the LORD our God so they can worship the god's of their own choosing, or to indulge in the wickedness of this fallen world. But because this world is quickly coming to an end, our gracious God is calling us to wake up and see the Truth—that the Living God of the Bible is the only LORD God, who is perfectly holy and just, and is personally involved in the lives of everyone. He sustains and provides everything we need to live healthy and righteous lives now so we can enjoy the new Heaven and Earth to come. Our Creator is also our Savior, who died for the sins of the world to save us from going to Hell, for we are all born sinners and we will all die as sinners without His blood cleansing our sins.

The Lord watches over His creation, and you can be sure that His infinite eyes miss nothing. The Lord hears every word and every thought, and He knows every heart completely. The Lord sets the standards for living and provides the Power to help us live by those standards and yet, He forgives us when we fail. But sadly, most people will reject God's Way for their own way, and when they die in their sin an eternal price will come due. If knowing these things about the Living God makes you feel a bit uncomfortable my friend, it should, because if you think you can hide your sin, your thinking will condemn you. Will you continue denying the Truth, trying to hide your sin in the darkness of this world? Or will you come boldly into the Lord's Light as you are—broken, dying and in dire need of His saving grace. There is only one Way that will bring you Home; all other ways are foolish, short sighted, but worst of all they will deliver your death sentence. The Lord is always watching my friend, His eyes are on you, patiently waiting for your surrender.

## A Whisper of Hope

**I Am everywhere, My child...**nothing is hidden, because I AM an all consuming Light. My heart aches for those who try to hide their sin in the darkness of this fallen world hoping I cannot see. But even though they continue to hide from Me, I wait patiently for the chance to bring them Home.

**Isaiah 42:5**
Thus says God the LORD, who created the heavens and stretched them out,
who spread forth the earth and that which comes from it, who gives breath
to the people on it, and spirit to those who walk on it. (NKJ)

**Restore us, O God. Cause Your face to shine, and we shall be saved!**
(Psalm 80:3)

# "Pure Purpose"

**Psalm 116:12**
What can I offer the LORD
for all He has done for me? (NLT)

There was a time not so long ago, that all I could offer the LORD was nothing but a broken down shell of a man with an awful distaste for living. I disliked life, hated myself, and was tired of people. I was hopelessly lost in darkness and slithering down the road of destruction that had but one eternal destination; death. Even though I tried to do what I thought was right, I found myself doing what I knew was wrong. I wanted to live a good life, but I didn't know how. A true and meaningful purpose for life was always an unsolved mystery for me, for life was nothing but a lot of pain and heartache and then you die. But somewhere deep inside my heart I wanted to believe there was a special purpose for our existence; that my life was no accident. I had to know that my life mattered and had a purpose that was greater than me. Although I believed in the God of creation, I had no idea who He was or why He allowed this miserable life to continue.

Although God had given me many different opportunities to get to know Him and learn the truth, my heart was hard, and my sin was deep. But at just the right time and in just the right way, Jesus came into my life and not only saved me from dying in my sin, but removed the blinders from my eyes so I could get a clearer picture of the world around me; a revelation that changed the direction of my life-journey forever. The Lord gave me vision when I had none. He opened my mind that had long been shut. He softened my heart that was hard as a rock. He blessed me with hope that I never had. He replaced my foolish wisdom with His godly wisdom so He could use me in His Great Plan of Redemption. And for the first time, I found value in living, a wonderful purpose greater than myself, and I could now offer God something of value! He set me free from the power of darkness and unlocked the mysteries of life. Lord Jesus gave me a new life that will never end, and He can do the same for anyone, because Christ Jesus is the Savior of the World. What the Lord gives us is a true reason for living and a Heavenly mission with a pure purpose.

## A Whisper of Hope

**Your life, dear child...**no matter how hard it may be is a precious gift from Me. For without this life there can be no other. Receive this gift with a thankful heart and live in the ways I have given you, for when you do, you will be living for Me. I gave you My life—now give Me yours.

**Acts 17:24-25**
He is the God who made the world and everything in it. Since He is Lord of Heaven and earth, He doesn't live in man-made temples, and human hands can't serve His needs—for He has no needs. He Himself gives life and breath to everything, and He satisfies every need there is. (NLT)

**Give your bodies to God. Let them be a living and holy sacrifice.**
(Romans 12:1)

# *"Stayin' Alive"*

**John 15:4**
Remain in Me, and I will remain in you.
For a branch cannot produce fruit if it is severed
from the vine, and you cannot be fruitful apart from Me. (NLT)

It is absolutely essential for every Christian, no matter where they are in their walk with the Lord, to stay connected to God by daily prayer, Bible reading, and meditating on every Word of God. For it is by doing this that we receive the wisdom and power to overcome the decadence of this dying world that is closing in for the kill. This priceless, infallible Truth is the heavenly nourishment that feeds our hearts and minds so we can develop the God-like attributes that produce a good quality of eternal fruit that this dying world is so hungry for and so desperately in need of. And as we develop and share this life-saving fruit with the dying souls of the world, we must remain disease free and healthy. Like any fruit bearing plant, we need the Gardener to nourish our growth by pruning and removing the growth that is dead, not healthy, or growing in the wrong direction. God's care and pruning will encourage new growth that will yield a heavenly crop of eternal fruit. Without this everyday spiritual nourishing, the stems of our new life will weaken and the fruit that begins to develop will shrivel up and die, dropping away from the Branch to lie dead and rotten, ready for the Gardener to gather them up to be burned forever.

Without the Head Gardeners gardening skills, we are destined to fall away from the Branch and return to the world from which we came. There are many hungry and starving souls who will taste of God's heavenly fruit when the world's nasty food turns sour in their stomachs, but they will only get nourished enough to return to their old feeding habits once again. Don't be one of the many who will partake in God's heavenly fruit for awhile only to return to their worldly feeding frenzy, because when you do, you will have been better off never having tasted the heavenly fruit in the first place. Instead, eat your fill of God's fruit and bathe in the glory of His Son's Light, where you will receive goodness and mercy and grace, and be nourished by the fruit of His Word that will keep you staying' alive forever.

## A Whisper of Hope

**Remain connected to Me, dear child…**For when you do, you will thrive and be fruitful. But be aware of the false gardener, for he knows not the Way of the True Gardener. He will prune and shape you to death, for his thumb is black and his nourishment is evil. Feed on My every Word to remain healthy and stayin' alive!

**1 Peter 2:21-22**
It would be better if they had never known the
right way to live than to know it and then reject the
holy commandments that were given to them. They
make these proverbs come true: "A dog returns to its vomit,"
and "A washed pig returns to the mud." (NLT)

**Anyone who parts from me is thrown away like a useless branch and withers.**
**Such branches are gathered into a pile to be burned.**
(John 15:6)

# *"Living Anew"*

**1 Peter 1:23**
For you have been born again. Your new life did not come from your earthly parents because the life they gave you will end in death. But this new life will last forever because it comes from the Eternal Living Word of God. (NLT)

O ur Lord God and Savior Jesus Christ, tells us clearly in His own words that in order for anyone to be saved from eternal condemnation they must be born again and remade a new creation. The old sinful life must die and a new life in Christ must emerge. Experiencing this new life means that you have been accepted by God the Father, cleansed by the blood of the Son, and empowered by the Holy Spirit, who helps you in the renewing of your heart and mind until your transformation is complete and you are glorified with Christ in Heaven. It's incredibly amazing that after all of my dysfunction and years of rebellion against God, that He still cleansed my ugly past and created a new and better me with a glorious new life that will never end. It was not long after being born again that the reality of living forever hit me hard, because I had no problem accepting the renewing of my dysfunctional life in the here and now, but the thought of living forever appealed to me about as much as swimming with hungry sharks did. But as the Holy Spirit continued transforming my heart and mind, I began to understand that living forever in Heaven would be quite different than living in this troubled world.

The more I grow in the Lord, the more God reveals about Himself and His eternal Plan, and I now look forward to living with our God in Heaven forever. Lord Jesus will physically come again into this broken world, but not again as a Savior. Instead, He will return with fire in His eyes to eradicate the evil and all those who embrace it. And when Satan and his many followers are removed from the scene, King Jesus will establish His Kingdom on Earth until He creates everything anew. And even though we can never begin to imagine the wonders that living in a new universe on a new and perfect earth will bring, we have no problem imagining what it will be like living in a perfect body that will never grow old or die. We will never experience sin, sickness, pain, sorrow, and we will never be bored or disappointed. In other words, it will be perfect.

## A Whisper of Hope

**Trustworthy and true...**are My words to you. Eternal life is the gift I offer you; a gift that has been paid for in full. Receive this Good News with thanksgiving and praise, and share it with others while you still can. For My return draws nearer with each passing day, and when I come I will make good on My offer and give you all that I have promised and then some!

**John 1:12-13**
But to all who believed Him and accepted Him, He gave the right to become children of God. They are reborn! This is not a physical birth resulting from human passion or plan—this rebirth comes from God. (NLT)

**Jesus replied, "I assure you, unless you are born again you can never see the Kingdom of God."**
(John 3:3)

# *"Doers Listen"*

**James 1:22**
Prove yourselves doers of the Word,
And not merely hearers who delude themselves. (NASB)

W e cannot not truly call ourselves "children of the Living God" and expect the many blessings that our salvation in Christ Jesus brings without actually doing what the Word of God commands us to do, because thinking otherwise is not only foolish, but it's quite dangerous as well. It is delusional to think you can hear God's Word, and then knowingly disobey it without any consequences. It is clearly written in Scripture that there is a price to be paid for those who claim to hear the Word of God but go about their everyday lives as if they never heard it at all. On Sunday the Church is filled with people, who sit through the sermons to hear the Word of God, but their lives really never seem to change and sadly, they will spend their short lives here on earth going about the business of this fallen world believing their salvation is in the bag. And how terrible it will be on the "Day of Judgment" when they hear Jesus say; "I never knew you."

Only God and you know what's in your heart and mind. You cannot hide anything from the Lord. Because we are sinful, our hearts are filled with deceit and malevolence, and even though most of us know the difference between right and wrong, we still love our sin and it is easy to justify our motives. No one can overcome the sinful nature that holds great power over us, especially when we don't know and apply the Word of God to our everyday lives. It is impossible to do what is good and right without knowing what God deems as good and right. When you read the Word of God, and listen for His still small voice, His Truth will replace your flawed human ways with the righteous ways of God. And that my friend, will change you from being deaf and dumb to a listener and doer, and one day you will hear King Jesus say, "Well done, my good and faithful servant," rather than, "I never knew you."

## A Whisper of Hope

**Listen to My Word, dear child...**and do what it says. There are many voices in this fallen world that claim the truth is only what you want it to be. Don't be fooled, for there is only One Truth and only One Way to the Father in Heaven and eternal life. I Am that Truth. All else is from the source of all untruth and evil; the Devil—the Prince of Darkness.

**Matthew 7:21-23**
"Not all people who sound religious are really godly. They may refer to Me as 'Lord,' but they still won't enter the Kingdom of Heaven. The decisive issue is whether they obey My Father in Heaven. On judgment day many will tell Me, 'Lord, Lord, we prophesied in Your name and cast out demons in Your name and performed many miracles in Your name.' But I will reply, 'I never knew you. Go away, the things you did were unauthorized.' (NLT)

**"I give all people their due rewards, according to what their actions deserve."**
(Jeremiah 17:10)

# "Light Speaking"

**1 Kings 17:24**
Then the woman told Elijah, "Now I know for sure that you are
a man of God, and that the LORD truly speaks through you." (NLT)

C hristian people that have been transformed by the power of God do not have to perform miracles to prove they belong to God, because the change itself is the miracle. With the change, we become one with the Holy Spirit who speaks through us so the world will hear and hopefully believe. In the fallen state of sin and darkness that the world is consumed in, it's not easy living with the Holy Spirit as your voice and guide, because the world hates and denies Jesus Christ, who is the Lord our God and Savior. The world cringes at the very Name of Jesus and hates the goodness and power that goes before Him. Because of our condition, we are all born as children of wrath and it is only because of the sacrificial death and resurrection power of our Lord God that we don't all die as children of wrath. While God lived on the earth as a man, He set a holy standard for people to live by—standards that go against the grain of this world and its self-gratifying standards. When we truly receive the gift of salvation, we not only speak the Truth, but we also live by it.

There always has been, and there always will be deceivers who speak the words of God's truth to impress others and for their own personal gain. And with the power that Satan possesses over the world, these deceiver's can easily fool people who don't know the Lord, and it's absurd to think they can fool God, but they try anyways. You are either with God or you are against Him, for there is no middle ground. Being lukewarm, continually turning God on and off is a very dangerous game to play, my friends. When you truly belong to Christ Jesus, you will speak from your new heart and draw others into His saving Light by the power of the Holy Spirit. We may be tempted to go back into the darkness of this world, but you can be sure that if your heart is right, the Lord will keep you in the Light where you belong. Everyone falls short of the holy standards that God sets for us and it will remain so until Jesus creates everything anew. But for now, we have God as our Rock, the Son as our Hope, and the Holy Spirit as our Power, and when we live and love like Jesus, the world around us will not only watch and listen a bit more closely, but we will see some of the most unlikely people drawn into the Light that saves!

## A Whisper of Hope

**Live and love as I do, My child...**For when you do you will truly live. You cannot save yourself or anyone else, for only I can accomplish that. But what you speak and how you live can make a glorious difference in this fallen world that needs the Truth.

**Ephesians 2:1-3**
Once you were dead, doomed forever because of your many sins. You used to live just like the rest of the world, full of sin, obeying Satan, the mighty prince of the power of the air. He is the spirit at work in the hearts of those who refuse to obey God. All of us used to live that way, following the passions and desires of our evil nature. We were born with an evil nature, and we were under God's anger just like everyone else. (NLT)

**"I know all the things you do, that you are neither hot nor cold.
But since you are like lukewarm water, I will spit you out of my mouth!"**
(Revelation 3:15, 16)

# "Victory Stand"

**1 Kings 20:27**
Israel then mustered its army, sat up supply lines, and moved into
the battle. But the Israelite army looked like two little flocks of goats
in comparison to the vast Syrian forces that filled the countryside! (NLT)

The army that God has on this earth is small compared to the vast army that Satan has been building since the fall of mankind. From all outward appearances it seems like the army of Satan is winning, but in reality, God's army stands in victory. The Almighty God has His reasons for allowing the evil to flourish, but our Lord God is completely sovereign and in control of everything. It's true that we live in a world that is in rapid decline and the Church of Christ Jesus is fighting for its very life against the powerful forces of Satan, but Christians should never live in fear, because we are protected and provided the Way to stand victorious against all the odds. For at just the right moment, King Jesus will remove His Church from this wicked world and will unleash His wrath against those who stand with the Enemy. But until then, we must stay in the Lord and be aware of the Devil, because he can fool you into a comatose state of complacency that is both dangerous and deadly.

As a child of the living God you are battling against a world that is led by the Devil and evil forces of darkness. You must prepare yourself by putting on the full armor of God every day, because without it, you are easy game for the hungry jaws of Satan, who wants nothing more than to devour your soul and digest you into Hell. No matter how strong you may think you are, you are putty in the hands of Satan without the saving power of God the Holy Spirit. When you battle the dark forces of evil on your own, you will lose and join Satan, His fallen angels, and all unrepentant sinners into the eternal burning Lake of Fire forever. You cannot win the battle for your heart, mind and soul without the Power of God. And as a soldier in God's mighty army of saints, you will learn quickly that the dark forces of evil are putty in the hands of God.

## A Whisper of Hope

**To follow Me...**is victory in life and death. Although My human army is small, it has the power of the Creator. Satan's evil army is vast but short-lived, for the war will soon be over. Stand confident and courageous My child, for one day soon you will stand in victory and live forever in peace.

**Revelation 17:14**
"Together they will wage war against the Lamb, but the Lamb
will defeat them because He is Lord over all lords, and King over
all kings and His people are the called and chosen and faithful ones." (NLT)

**He will swallow up death in victory!**
(Isaiah 25:8)

# "Safe in His Glory"

**Proverbs 18:10**
The name of the LORD is a strong fortress;
and the godly run to Him and are safe. (NLT)

There is no better God to call on, nor is there any stronger arms for us to run into than the Lord Jesus Christ, because He watches over and protects all those who faithfully serve Him and are called by His Name. There is absolutely nothing that our Sovereign God does not see or know, because He is the Creator. He keeps the universe perfectly balanced, protecting our world from forces that could so easily annihilate our tiny planet. And our God will continue to protect us until the end of time when He creates everything new and perfect forever. The Father of Life hears every desperate cry for help. He sees every tear that falls from every eye that He so masterfully creates. He feels the very pain we feel, because He knows firsthand what real pain is. But our God also takes notices and delights in our laughter and joy, for it gladdens His heart when we are alive and vibrant in His glory. Although we cannot physically see our mighty and awesome God now, we can be confident that He is very much a part of our everyday lives and is constantly interacting on our behalf—even in the lives of those who refuse to believe in Him. Our Living God speaks to every heart, because the life of every person He creates is precious to Him.

This is who our gracious God is and always will be. And as a child of the True and Living God, I can truthfully say that until I became one with the Savior, I not only remained enslaved to this evil world, but the darkness continued to deceive my mind, decay my heart, and kept me blind from seeing the Truth. Until the living Spirit of God is dwelling in your heart my friend, you will never know the Truth about life or death, and will you never experience the joy of knowing what the Lord has planned for you in the eternal life that is coming soon. God does not want you to follow Satan and all the unrepentant sinners into the eternal Lake of Fire that burns forever. Instead, He would rather help you escape the coming inferno by becoming one with Him and live forever in His glory!

## A Whisper of Hope

**Don't listen to this world, My child...**for it is full of false prophets and lies, which will only lead you into the pits of Hell. Instead, be still and listen with your heart, for I speak softly with the words of life that will lead you safely Home with Me where darkness can be no more.

**Hebrews 1:3**
The Son reflects God's own glory, and everything about Him
represents God exactly. He sustains the universe by the mighty power of His command. (NLT)

**And fire came down from God out of Heaven and devoured them.**
(Revelation 20:9)

# "Look Carefully"

**Colossians 3:1-2**
Since you have been raised to new life with Christ, set your sights on the realities
of Heaven, where Christ sits at God's right hand in the place of honor and power.
Let Heaven fill your thoughts. Do not think only about things down here on earth. (NLT)

We live on this earth but a brief moment in time—a very short life that has no guarantees and could end at any given moment. This is one of the many reasons why it is so important that we learn the Truth; what is reality and what is not—what is true and what is false. We must know the difference because knowing the absolute Truth not only improves the quality of life in the here and now, but it also answers the many questions that are embedded in our hearts and minds. What lies beyond this brief life, if anything? Do our lives really matter or do we simply live and cease to exist. Is there another life awaiting us after this one? And if there is, are we held accountable for how we live this life? And if we are held accountable, then what are the consequences? These are very legitimate questions that require very truthful answers, because the truth about this short life and our imminent death is what sets us free from living in fear and doubt. If it's the Truth that you are looking for my friend, you must look to the Source of all truth—the Creator and Author of Life.

The Lord our God is both the Giver and Taker of all life, and He has graciously given us a truly clear picture about life and death, and what lies on the other side. By seeing the bigger picture, you can ask the Lord to plot a course that will navigate you safely through this difficult life-journey; one that will take you Home where you were meant to live forever with your Maker. It's extremely wise to focus on the longevity of God's life for you, rather than foolishly living for the moment. The Lord created you as a physical and spiritual being that will exist forever. As a created eternal being, you have been blessed with the ability to choose your eternal destination; you can be eternally glorified with Christ or eternally condemned with the Devil, or you can simply buy a lottery ticket and hope for the best. Be wise and seek the Truth so you can better prepare yourself for the end of this life. Be wise and be glorified with Christ.

## A Whisper of Hope

**Set your eyes on Heaven, dear child...**and live in peace. Don't let this fallen world dupe you into believing the lies of Satan, for they only bring you false hope and eternal darkness. Instead, set your eyes on the new and improved eternal life in Heaven and live accordingly.

**Psalm 103:15-26**
Our days on earth are like grass; like wildflowers, we bloom and die.
The wind blows, and we are gone—as though we had never been here. (NLT)

**Oh, remember that my life is a breath!**
(Job 7:7)

# *"God Power"*

**1 John 5:20**
And we know that the Son of God has come, and He has given us understanding so that we can know the true God. And now we are in God because we are in His Son, Jesus Christ. He is the only true God, and He is eternal life. (NLT)

There are many false gods in this world; some we cannot see, but many that we cannot. There are also many false truths that compete with God's Truth and they are fighting to control our minds, poison our hearts, and kill our souls. These false truths are flat out lies coming from the father of lies, Satan. The Devil is the most powerful and deadly Enemy of God. Satan wants only to deceive the world and destroy all that belong to God, especially His people and His children. Because of our inherent sinful nature and the excellent ability of Satan to deceive, it's quite natural for people to follow the evil ways of this cleverly deceived world. We tend to follow the ways that offer little or no resistance. We love ways that satisfy the sinful pleasures of our flesh. And unknowingly, these clever ways of the false truth cause us to slip into a darkness that is quite often difficult to escape from. All you have to do is watch the news to see how the entire world is now infected with more lies and wickedness than we can shake a stick at. The majority of the mainstream media, like the internet, television, radio, news papers, movies, books, music, magazines, computer games, and even many of the so called Christian Churches, are bombarding us with false truths that make it not only believable, but also very tempting and addicting as well; so much so that most of us take the bait without even knowing it. Satan is the evil Prince of Darkness who is leading much of what is happening in this fallen world; he is the driving force behind all the evil events that are drawing much of the world into deadly chaos.

The only hope you have of escaping the deadly traps of the Devil is through God's Truth; the Power of the Living God, Christ Jesus. It is by your belief and faith in the death and resurrection of Christ Jesus that you will escape the condemnation of eternal darkness in Hell. It is through the Holy Spirit living in your heart that you find the strength to overcome the temptations of this evil world so you can live and love like Jesus. If you want to beat the odds and escape the darkness my friend, turn off your computer, television, or radio and spend that time in the Presence of God.

## A Whisper of Hope

**I AM**...the only True and Living God. There is no other! I have the power to save you, the power to protect you, and the power to transform you. I AM the SAVIOR—the Way for you to escape the power of Satan. There are many voices in this world that are loud and convincing, but they lie. You must tune them out and listen to the Truth—the only Voice that can give you peace and life!

**Colossians 2:8**
Don't let anyone lead you astray with empty philosophy and high sounding nonsense that comes from human thinking and from the evil power of this world, and not from Christ. (NLT)

**Be careful. Watch out for attacks from the Devil, your great enemy.**
**He prowls around like a roaring lion, looking for some victim to devour.**
(1 Peter 5:8)

# *"Good is God"*

**Psalm 16:2**
I said to the LORD, "You are my Master! All the good things I have are from You." (NLT)

Even though it is politically incorrect to use the master-slave narrative to reference how most relationships work in this fallen world, it is in truth, a reality. Because whatever controls the way you live and think, is by definition your master. When people spend most of their time and energy trying to get what the world offers them, it controls just about everything they do—they become enslaved by it—it owns them. This same kind of relationship can also be applied to our life in Christ, for when you accept Jesus as your Savior, you become His because He paid the price for your redemption—He set you free from your slavery to sin and this evil world—He owns you. Even though God is the Creator and He owns everything, He gives us the freedom to choose our masters. We can choose Christ Jesus and live under Him, or we can choose the god of this evil world, Satan and be bound in sin. We can choose the Father of Life and live righteously, or we can choose the father of lies and live in sin. When you reject and rebel against God, you become A slave to your sinful flesh and you will spend your time and energy seeking to satisfy your lusts with the evil things of this dark world.

Unbeknownst to me, my master was Satan and I was enslaved by this fallen world for most of my life. I indulged in many of its sinful pleasures, because I thought this life was all I had, and what I got was what I deserved. But that has all changed because I learned the Truth. Jesus Christ has set me free from the power of sin that this world embraces. I am no longer controlled by my sinful lusts and the evil of Satan, for I now belong to Christ. I have discovered that all good things are from our God in Heaven and everything else comes from the Devil, who is the creator of all evil. With God as your Master, you will sleep in peace knowing that His goodness will be with you when you awaken. So who would you like for a master, my friend? The God who lovingly created you to live in His goodness forever? Or the god of this evil world who wants only the worst for you? Be wise and choose the God who died for your sins and cleansed you with His blood, so you could dwell in His goodness forever.

## A Whisper of Hope

**Listen closely, My child…**don't let this world enslave you with its evil pleasures that result in death. Instead, allow me to be the only Master you serve and I will shower you with goodness. Bondage to this world will only leave you empty, alone and afraid. But when you serve the Living God, the Lord and King of creation, you have everything!

**Romans 7:24-25**
Oh, what a miserable person I am! Who will free me from this life that is dominated by sin? Thank God! The answer is in Jesus Christ our Lord. So you see how it is: in my mind I really want to obey God's law, but because of my sinful nature I am a slave to sin. (NLT)

**How true it is that a servant is not greater than the master.**
(John 13:16)

# "No More"

**Romans 8:23**
And even we Christians, although we have the Holy Spirit within us as a
foretaste of future glory, also groan to be released from pain and suffering.
We, too, wait anxiously for that day when God will give us our full rights as
His children, including the new bodies He has promised us. (NLT)

N o matter where people live on this planet or what they believe in, everyone, both the good
and the bad experience the difficulties and hardships that living in a fallen world brings. No
one is exempt from the suffering that is as part of living as breathing is. Everyone faces challenging
obstacles that threatens their way of life, their health, and often their very lives. All human flesh
is destined to die and decay. We are all susceptible to disease, starvation, accidents, nature's wrath,
and are at risk of being murdered—realities we must face every day of our very short lives. We are
surrounded on all sides by the decadence of this fallen world and it causes most people to live in
fear, doubt, and hopelessness, because they know it is inevitable that something bad will eventually happen in their lives that will take what little happiness they may have found while trying to
survive in a world that wants their souls. The entire planet and all its living creatures suffer from
the effects of sin and the battles within—battles that can destroy our hearts and minds, and rob
the life from our souls.

When you are uncertain about the Truth and what lies beyond this short life, it leaves you
fearful, unprepared, and living in vain. Trying to survive in this fallen world where Satan reigns, and
do it in a body that is destined to die are real and very sobering realities that will remain the same
until the Day of the Lord's glorious return. But there is Hope amidst all of the difficult realities of
living in this broken world. And that Hope is in the Good News of our Lord God and Savior, Jesus
Christ—the Hope of knowing that no matter what kind of pain and suffering you are experiencing
now or will experience in the future, you have the eternal joy and peace that comes when you are a
child of the Living God. As God's redeemed child, you are never alone in any of your tribulations,
because God is always with you, helping you persevere with joy during your afflictions, because you
know that even if you die, you will live. With the promises of God planted firmly in your heart my
friend, you will survive even the worst that this fallen world can do—and live through it forever!

## A Whisper of Hope

**This fallen world...**promises you nothing but shallow happiness, fleeting pleasure, and fear of the
unknown. But I, your Lord God, promise you a new and better life now, and a perfect, eternal life
when this one comes to an end. It is certain you will suffer in this life, but when you live in Me your
suffering is short and one day, will be no more!

**Romans 8:21**
All creation anticipates the day when it will join God's children
in glorious freedom from death and decay. (NLT)

**Yet what we suffer now is nothing compared to the glory He will give us later.**
(Romans 8:18)

# *"Live in Love"*

**1 John 4:7-8**
Dear friends, let us continue to love one another, for love comes
from God. Anyone who loves is born of God and knows God. But
anyone who does not love does not know God—for God is Love. (NLT)

O ur Creator endowed us with the ability to love—one of the many godly likenesses that our God passed on to us. God's love is something we should never take for granted and something we should aspire to model our lives after. Because the Lord God loves us so much, He became a man with flesh and blood so He could be that final sacrificial Lamb that saved us from our self-induced eternal destruction. Being plagued with sin, most people tend to selfishly search for the kind of love that makes us feel good, rather than seeking out those who are unlovable and in desperate need of our love. We want to fall in love with that someone who will satisfy our need to be loved, but we usually look in all the wrong places and the love that we normally find is not the kind of love that draws us close to God. The Truth is my friend, that until you personally know God and experience His love you will never understand what it is to love or be loved. When God created man, He created us to love and glorify Him above all else, but instead, we fell into a sinful state of self-gratifying love.

We live in this fallen world believing that this life is all about ourselves; what makes me feel good and what edifies me in the eyes of others. When we fall for this lie and refuse to learn how to love as God first loved us, we will never experience the richness of life. We cannot learn to love from the world, because we are selfish by nature, self-centered by osmosis, and we tend to push to the front of the line. Love is humility, following the Lord Jesus, and personal sacrifice. I believe that happiness is best found when we are actively living and loving like Jesus. We owe the Lord much for saving us from eternal destruction, but all He asks for in return is that we live in love—for God and others. Because love is what this life is all about!

## A Whisper of Hope

**Love Me, my child...**and love those whom I love. For when you love others as I have loved you, you will truly know what it means to live. From My holy view of the world from the glory of Heaven, most humans are certainly not very lovable, but I have chosen to love My creation because I am Love!

**1 Corinthians 13:4-7**
For love is patient and kind. Love is not jealous or boastful or proud
or rude. Love does not demand its own way. Love is not irritable, and
it keeps no record of when it has been wronged. It is never glad about
injustice but rejoices whenever the truth wins out. Love never gives up,
never loses faith, is always hopeful and endures through every circumstance. (NLT)

**We love Him because He loved us first.**
(1 John 4:19)

# "Infinite Truth"

**Hebrews 2:1**
So we must listen very carefully to the Truth
we have heard, or we may drift away from it. (NLT)

In our fallen state of ungodliness it is easy to let the voices of this busy, sinful world drown out the Voice of God; Truth that brings joy to living—the Truth that saves our precious souls and brings us into the very Presence of the Living God. But in order to escape the deadly traps that Satan sets for us, we must stay connected to the Infinite Source of all Wisdom and Truth, least we find ourselves drifting aimlessly in an ocean of lies that promises our demise. It is dangerously unhealthy for our spiritual well being to become so comfortable in our salvation that we become lazy or negligent in the good things of God that protect us from the evil that is eating this world alive. We need God's strength and wisdom to keep us steadfast in our faith. If we are to fulfill the Great Commission of the Lord, we must first and foremost, stay connected to the Way, the Truth, and the Life and listen closely for the Still Small Voice that speaks softly to our hearts. We must study God's Word consistently and faithfully. We must love God and people as our motivation, for if we live for any other reason, we are only fooling ourselves, for God will not be mocked. We must be loyal to God and be everything He calls us to be while we live in this desperate world that cries out for redemption.

Satan and His delusional followers are working overtime in this desperate world to fool you into complacency or get you so wrapped up in your own spirituality that you fail to grasp the true message of Jesus Christ. This world will fill you with so much doubt that you will lack the confidence to act upon your mission for God. Not everyone is destined to do great deeds of faith that catch the eyes of the world, but we are called to live our lives for God and others—to love God and others, to sacrifice for God and others, and to do it one day and one soul at a time! It is never easy to live and love like Jesus, because we are infected with sin, weak in stature, and handicapped by our carnal flesh. But when you trust Jesus to be your Savior and have the power of the Holy Spirit, you can live and love like Jesus, casting His life-saving Light onto this dark and dying world.

## A Whisper of Hope

**Tune in to the Voice of Truth, dear child...**and listen closely to what I say. There are many voices in this dark world that spew nothing but lie after lie. Don't listen to them for they only lead to death and darkness. Instead, listen to the Only Voice that is Truth—Truth that is infinite!

**1 Corinthians 15:58**
So, my dear brothers and sisters, be strong and steady,
always enthusiastic about the Lord's work, for you know
that nothing you do for the Lord is ever useless. (NLT)

**Laziness lets the roof leak, and soon the rafters begin to rot.**
(Ecclesiastes 10:18)

# *"Humble Callings"*

**Ephesians 4:1-2**
Lead a life worthy of your calling, for you have been
called by God. Be humble and gentle. Be patient with each other,
making allowance for each other's faults because of your love. (NLT)

E very Christian has been called out of the darkness by God. He has called us to receive His own glory and goodness and to live righteous lives that bring Him honor and glory. Because the Lord has called us to be a beacon of light in a dark world, our lives must be transformed from ungodliness to the likeness of our God and Savior Jesus Christ, the everlasting Light of the World. Because we are self-centered and sinful by nature, this transformation must take place if we are to fulfill our humble callings. It's a cleansing that cannot be accomplished without the indwelling of the Holy Spirit. We must have the Transforming Power of God working in us and for us if we are to be the saving beacon of light that God calls us to be. We must become humble and righteous, living and loving like Jesus.

When we are called by God, most of us come lacking both humility and patience, because we live in a world that is all about self-gratification. Without the God's daily direction and power, the dark forces of Satan will pull you slowly back into the darkness from which you came. But when you are Spirit driven to the calling, God will teach you to be humble and patient before God and others. This will soften your hard heart so you can become gentle rather than harsh, understanding rather than condemning, patient rather than pushy, and you will have a willingness to love the unlovable instead of simply dismissing them. No one will achieve perfection this side of Heaven, but when you live for God and take His callings to heart, He will give you exactly what you need at the very moments you need it and you will successfully carry out His special callings for you. When He calls you my friend, there is no need to fear that you are not up to the calling. Just step out in faith and trust the Creator and Author of Life, because with God you can accomplish everything He calls you to do.

## A Whisper of Hope

**Come to Me when I call...** and I will transform you in ways that are worthy of My calling. Ways that will make a real difference in this fallen world that cries out to be saved. I will give you the wisdom and courage to shine My saving Light into this dark world. Listen, I Am calling, dear child.

**2 Peter 1:3**
As we know Jesus better, His Divine Power
gives us everything we need for living a godly life.
He has called us to receive His own glory and goodness! (NLT)

**Commit everything you do to the LORD. Trust Him and He will help you.**
(Psalm 37:5)

# "Final Word"

**Job 19:25-27**

But as for me, I know that my Redeemer lives, and that He will stand upon the earth at last. And after my body has decayed, yet in my body I will see God! I will see Him for myself. Yes, I will see Him with my own eyes. I am overwhelmed at the thought! (NLT)

If you lost everything; your family, your home, your business, your health, and your friends, would you curse God and blame Him for your troubles or would you stand firm in your faith and ask Him to give you understanding and resolve? Would you still love God and be a witness to His goodness, or would you turn against Him in hate? I'm not trying to diminish anyone's difficult circumstances nor am I implying that God will deliberately cause you to suffer such a loss, but just as Job suffered, we, too, may find ourselves thrown into dire circumstances that we don't understand—trials that will test our faith—trials that can bring us closer to God or drive us away. But it is usually this fallen world and Satan that single us out, attacking us in ways that bring great suffering into our lives. And this can cause us to either question the righteousness of our Holy God or doubt His power and sovereignty. But whether it is God's discipline, Satan's attack, this fallen world, or our own foolish mistakes, we must still live and deal with it. And until Jesus returns, life on this earth will continue to worsen and decay. Nothing is immune—all things will suffer.

But amidst all the pain and trouble, there is Hope, because the Redeemer has come and restored the broken relationship between God and man. The Son came in the flesh to shed His blood and sacrifice His life to cleanse our sins and set us free from the power of sin and death. Death and the grave could not hold our Lord God and Savior, Jesus Christ and He became the first of many to be resurrected from the grave and be given a glorified body that will never again suffer and die. And like Job, we know that our Redeemer lives, bringing all peoples hope for redemption. You have been redeemed my friend, but you must accept and follow your Redeemer, because without Him death will have the final word. It is a pure and undeserved gift from God to know that no matter what you have done in the past or how much suffering this wicked world has caused you; death will not have the final say. But until then, live in the Light of the Redeemer and let Jesus have His Way!

## A Whisper of Hope

**I Am your Redeemer, dear child...**the only One who can save you from destroying yourself. I came to save the world, and I did just that. And when you believe in Me and the price I paid for your sins; redemption is yours; no questions asked.

**Isaiah 53:5-6**

But He was wounded and crushed for our sins. He was beaten that we might have peace. He was whipped, and we were healed! All of us have strayed away like sheep. We have left God's paths to follow our own. Yet the LORD laid on Him the guilt and sins of us all. (NLT)

**But as for me, God will redeem my life. He will snatch me from the power of death.**
(Psalm 49:15)

# *"Unstoppable"*

**Job 42:1-2**
Then Job replied to the LORD; "I know that You
can do anything, and no one can stop You." (NLT)

I believe that knowing and accepting this absolute truth about the sovereign power of our Lord God and Savior is the beginning of life-giving wisdom. For without the solid foundation this truth brings, living in this world becomes confusing at best and filled with doubt. We cannot successfully navigate through this difficult life without a solid point of reference that is constant and reliable; One that keeps us on the right course and reminds us of who God is and who we are. We cannot possibly begin to understand the full measure of our existence, why things are like they are, and where it's all going, but we can start by learning God's true purpose and destination for mankind and the world He made for us to live in. Fact: God created man in His own likeness and for His glory. Fact: God is the Creator and owns everything in the universe. Fact: God does whatever God wants to do because He can! Fact: God has a Plan for man and He is the only One who can make it happen and the only One who knows when it will come into completion.

We have an Infinite Father in Heaven who wants the very best for every single person He creates; even those who continually deny and rebel against Him. We have an Infinite High Priest in Jesus Christ, who sits at the right hand of the Father in Heaven—the True and Faithful One who saved us from God's wrath and is successfully advocating on our behalf. And we have the awesome and Infinite Power of God the Holy Spirit changing hearts, saving lives, and bringing hope into a fallen world that is gripped in chaos and sin-filled rebellion against the Word of God. Our triune God wants no one to perish, and it is for this reason that He gives you a choice and a time to choose. And when you choose the only Way to God, He becomes everything you need for a glorious future filled with peace rather than pain. He becomes a Strong Tower; a Place of safety from the daily assaults of our enemies, a Place for comfort and healing, and a Place to find rest for our tired and battle weary souls. His Plan for you is unstoppable!

## A Whisper of Hope

**Take refuge in Me, My child...**and you will find complete rest, comfort, and unstoppable Power. I Am all you need to navigate your way through the dark and turbulent storms that are consuming this dying world. I Am the Light that will guide you Home, for I AM UNSTOPPABLE!

**Romans 11:33-34**
Oh, what a wonderful God we have! How great are His riches and wisdom and knowledge! How impossible it is for us to understand His decisions and His methods! For who can know what the Lord is thinking? Who knows enough to be His counselor? (NLT)

**The name of the LORD is a strong tower, the righteous run to it and are safe.**
(Proverbs 18:10)

# "Trustworthy"

**Isaiah 2:22**
Stop putting your trust in mere humans. They are as
frail as breath. How can they be of help to anyone? (NLT)

Trusting in your own limited human abilities or that of other limited human beings to do what only God can do is not only short-sighted and prideful, but terribly foolish as well. Relying on anyone but the Lord God to help you find the true meaning and purpose of life will leave you feeling confused, disappointed, and unsatisfied. Putting your dreams and hopes in a world that is rapidly approaching its demise may bring you a little satisfaction for a while, but when it's all said and done, will leave you even more empty than before. The confusion that human pride brings into this world is so misleading to people that they deny the existence of God and believe there is no such thing as absolute truth. The Devil has cleverly deceived this fallen world and led most people away from the Truth that tells us who God is, who we are in relation to God, and what God has planned for us! It is our Infinite God's will that will prevail, because He is in charge and always in control. There is nothing bigger or mightier than our triune God. God's Truth is absolute. His Word is the Final Authority. God Wisdom is infinite. His ways are always right and just. God can be trusted fully with anything and everything.

No one will ever love you as completely as God loves you. No one knows you better than the One who formed you in your mother's womb. There is no One greater for you to look up to than the King of the Universe—your Savior and Advocate. Our Lord God Jesus Christ, is the Perfect Sacrificial Lamb who died every sinner's death so you would be spared. There is no One more forgiving, more understanding, or more dedicated to saving your life than Jesus Christ, who not only gave you your life, but He gave you His life as well. The ways of this fallen world cannot be trusted for anything at any time. The Lord will not withhold any good thing when you belong to Him. He is your Father, your Savior, and your eternal Redeemer. Our Mighty God is, was, and always will be the most trustworthy.

## A Whisper of Hope

**I Am trustworthy, dear child…**so trustworthy in fact, that no matter what, you can put your entire life into My trusting hands. My Truth is always right and it will always prevail. And when you live in My Truth, you, too, will also prevail.

**Micah 7:7-8**
As for me, I look to the LORD for His help. I wait confidently for
God to save me, and my God will certainly hear me. Do not gloat
over me, my enemies! For though I fall, I will rise again. Though
I sit in darkness, the LORD Himself will be my Light. (NLT)

**Trusting oneself is foolish, but those who walk in Wisdom are safe.**
(Proverbs 28:26)

# *"A Time to Choose"*

**Galatians 2:16**
So we have believed in Christ Jesus, that we might be accepted
by God because of our faith in Christ and not because we have
obeyed the law. For no one will ever be saved by obeying the law. (NLT)

No human being has the power or ability to stand holy and blameless before the Most High Holy God of Creation. In order for anyone to stand holy and blameless before the throne of the Living God, they must be holy as God is Holy. And the only way to be holy in the eyes of God is through the holy covering of our Lord God and Savior, Jesus Christ. We are born sinners and we will die sinners, and without the blood of Jesus cleansing our sins we will suffer the sinner's death. There is no other Way for us to be holy, because our human nature is to sin first and hope for the best. Without the Holy Spirit dwelling in us, sin controls our lives. We cannot obey the Laws of God because we like to do what we feel like doing. Many people do not submit to God because of their sin-filled pride. Pride is why Lucifer, God's most powerful and beautiful angel, rebelled against God and was cast out of Heaven and will end up in the eternal Lake of Fire. It was the pride of Jewish leaders that led to the murder of the Son of God. It is your stubborn pride gone unchecked, that will be your ticket to Hell.

But how blessed we are to live in the Church Age, because our sins have been forgiven and our death penalty canceled. When you embrace your salvation through the sacrifice of Jesus, you have His perfect blood cleansing your sins, His death as your own, and His robe of righteousness to keep you holy. God created His Plan for man before the foundation of the earth was laid. And unlike the waves of the sea and human beings, God does not waver in His plans. God knows that it is impossible for us to survive without His sovereign power. He knows how weak in our sin we are and that we need His lifesaving blood. God has given us fair warning because He wants no one to perish. But God's Plan is coming to completion and it's time to choose, if you have not already done so. Don't wait to make your choice, dear friend—don't let our Holy and Just God choose for you, because if you do you will not be pleased with the outcome.

## A Whisper of Hope

**Choose Me, My child...**for I Am your only Hope. You can choose Me or not, but know this; if you choose anything but Me, you die. Let My death be yours and be resurrected into a new eternal life with Me.

**Romans 3:25**
We are made right with God when we believe
that Jesus shed His blood, sacrificing His life for us. (NLT)

**You must be holy because I, the LORD your God, am holy.**
(Leviticus 19:2)

# *"Most Holy One"*

**Isaiah 43:1, 2, 3**
"Do not be afraid, for I have ransomed you. I have called you by name; you are mine. When you go through deep waters and great trouble, I will be with you. When you go through rivers of difficulty, you will not drown! When you walk through the fire of oppression, you will not be burned up; the flames will not consume you. For I am the LORD, your God, your Savior." (NLT)

These Living Words of God from the Old Testament are as true today as they were back then. This incredible, life changing Truth is God's promise to everyone who belongs to Him. When we become a part of the Body of Christ (God's Church) we are no longer like a lone wolf who is hungrily searching to satisfy its appetites. For unlike the wolf we have a conscience will to choose and decipher what we want to feed on. But sadly, many of us like the wolf, feed on whatever satisfies the cravings of our sinful flesh no matter what, rather than feeding on every Word of God that nourishes our souls and saves our eternal lives. As sinful human beings living in a sin-filled world, we tend to spend more time searching for and feeding on the things that are both physically and spiritually unhealthy—worldly things that lead us away from the Truth. But when we surrender our lives to the Lord, He breaks the sinful instincts that hold us captive to our sinful appetites and we are given a new life in Christ. And with this new life we not only receive everything needed to survive this difficult life, but our spiritual hunger for God and eternity is being satisfied as well.

When we accept the sacrificial death of Christ Jesus as the price paid for our salvation, we rightly belong to God, because He personally paid the price that set us free from our bondage to sin and death. Your eternal life has been bought and paid for. I think the most incredible sensation I have ever experienced was when the reality hit me that I was truly an eternal member of the Kingdom of God—that I was now and forevermore a citizen of Heaven and a child of the Living God. You, too, can experience this awesome sense of truly belonging to the LORD God Almighty—the One who gave His life so you could keep yours forever. And as a child of God, you will receive an everlasting peace amidst all the chaos around you, an everlasting joy even in your deepest sorrows, and the courage to live in the face of death as a redeemed child of the Most Holy One.

## A Whisper of Hope

**Live in peace, My child…**because when you belong to Me you are safe. I Am the One who has set you free from this world driven by sin and Satan; a world that hates My very Name. When you hear My calling, it is best that you follow My voice, for I will lead you Home to streams of living Water.

**1 Samuel 2:2**
No one is holy like the LORD! there is no Rock like our God. (NLT)

**Obey God because you are His children.**
(1 Peter 1:14)

# "Heavenly Body"

**2 Corinthians 5:2-3**
We grow weary in our present bodies, and we long for the day when
we will put on our heavenly bodies like new clothing. For we will not
be spirits without bodies, but we will put on new heavenly bodies. (NLT)

Experiencing this life is indeed a wearing down process. Not only because of the troubles it brings, but also because our mortal bodies will eventually wear out and die. Because death is a reality in this fallen world, many children and young people will die before growing old. But for people who are singled out by God to live a long life, they will experience the not so fun aging process that affects both our physical and mental decline. When we live long enough to understand how this life works and begin to experience the natural breakdown of our dying bodies, it's quite normal to wish we could find a way to stay young forever. It is never easy growing old, because with aging comes pain and change, especially when our bodies begin to decline. This kind of change is never easy to accept, but the end result is one that we should look forward to when we are God's children. For those who are in the later stages of decline through the natural aging process, they will either go to the grave bitter and afraid of the unknown, or they will go in thanksgiving to God and looking forward to their new resurrected bodies that will be the perfect age forever.

The Lord God loves all human beings more than we will ever comprehend this side of Heaven. He knows firsthand the pain and difficulties that we face while living in this fallen world with a body destined to die. And for this reason God has personally made the Way for us to overcome the fear that the decadence of sin brings to both our bodies and the world we live in. And when we follow His Way, we are promised a glorified body that will never grow old and die, and we will live on a new earth that will follow suit. This is not a fantasy dream my friends, but a promise from the Infinite Living God who created us to be eternal. For the first man (Adam) failed and brought death and decay to everything. But the second Man (Christ Jesus) succeeded where Adam failed. And for those who die in Christ, they, too, will receive a glorified body that stays young and will never die.

## A Whisper of Hope

**A life lived in Me, child…**is one that is not lived in vain, for I know your pain. Although you must suffer for just a while, I promise you shall never suffer again. I paid for your new and perfect body and will make a new and perfect Heaven on earth for you to live in.

**Titus 3:4, 7**
But then God our Savior showed us His kindness and love. He saved us, not because of the good things we did, but because of His mercy. He declared us not guilty because of His great kindness. And now we know that we will inherit eternal life. (NLT)

**For the wage of sin is death, but the free gift of
God is eternal life through Christ Jesus our Lord.**
(Romans 6:23)

# September

# *"The Makers Plan"*

**Jeremiah 4:22**
"My people are foolish and do not know Me," says the LORD. "They are
senseless children who have no understanding. They are clever enough
at doing wrong, but they have no talent at all for doing right." (NLT)

Similar to God's chosen people Israel, is the United States of America. A Christian nation
created by God, to be used for God. America was founded on Judea-Christian values and
law, and became the most powerful and freest nation the world has ever known—a Christian
nation that would stand strong in defending personal freedom and the Truth of God's Word.
America has helped millions of oppressed, helpless people who would have otherwise died in
hunger, hopelessness, and suffered eternal death. America has spread the Good News Gospel
of Jesus Christ throughout the world and keeps freedom alive. America also helped bring the
scattered Jewish people Israel back into the land that the Creator gave them. But just as the
nation of Israel was drawn away from God by the power of Satan, so, too, is Satan poisoning the
minds of American and infiltrating God's Church. The powers of darkness are leading America
down the immoral pagan path of atheism and hate, leaving America weak and unprotected.
Satan has America in his grip.

We are taught to worship ourselves and we have become lovers of self and money. The
Devil's disciples are spreading deadly lies that Hell does not exist, that everyone goes to Heaven,
and the bad just ceases to exist. The Lord speaks of Hell more than He speaks of Heaven, because
He does not want anyone to suffer the eternal consequences of sin. Our Maker has created a
Plan that has cleansed our sins, healed its infection, and set us free from its eternal condemnation. The Lord's Plan will cure the world's evil infection, and His Plan is coming soon. And
when it's complete, you will either be in Heaven with the Living God, or you will end up in
the eternal Lake of Fire with Satan, the other fallen angels, and those people who have rejected
God's Plan. Don't die being fooled by the plans of this world my friend, for if you do, it has
eternal ramifications that cannot be reversed. Instead, invest in the Makers Plan, and live your
eternal life with God Himself.

## A Whisper of Hope

**Follow My Plan, dear child...**for when you do you will learn the Truth, and the Truth will save
your eternal life. Do not be foolish and follow the many plans of this world, for they all lead to
the very same place; a hellish place to spend eternity.

**Psalm 119:73**
You made me; You created me. Now give me
the sense to follow Your commands. (NLT)

**A wise person is hungry for truth, while the fool feeds on trash.**
(Proverbs 15:14)

# "Harbingers"

**Jeremiah 23:16-17**
"This is My warning to My people," says the LORD Almighty. "Do not listen to these prophets when they prophesy to you, filling you with futile hopes. They are making up everything they say. They do not speak for the LORD! They keep saying to these rebels who despise My Word, 'Don't worry! The LORD says you will have peace!' And to those who stubbornly follow their own evil desires, they say, 'No harm will come your way!'" (NLT)

These same warnings from God to His people Israel thousands of years ago are the same warnings to His Church today. Just as God's message to the nation of Israel was being falsified prior to the Church Age, so, too, is God's Word being compromised by many false teachers in our churches and our schools. The false hope found in manmade religion is leading the world and America down a very dangerous path that I call complacent secularism—thinking that everything will be just fine and things will correct themselves; that this is America, and it will always be America. This is not so my friend, for just as Israel turned their backs on God and suffered the dire consequences, so, too, is the Lord's anger burning against the detestable sins of America. How can He not be? We are losing our morality and turning away from God's righteousness to do whatever our sinful natures crave. We have, as a nation, legally sacrificed millions of our unborn children to be thrown away like garbage. We have slowly removed the Truth of God's Word from our homes and schools, from our governing, and sadly God's Truth is even being removed from our churches as well.

Many people will never know the Truth because their minds are being poisoned with lies and false hope. The future of this country and the world's freedom looks rather bleak. Can God save this country? Of course He can! Will He save America? His Word tells us not! So what can American Christians do for God, our country, and this dark world? We can live godly lives in our homes, in our schools, in our work place, and in our communities, but most importantly in our hearts. By living and loving like Jesus the world will see the powerful hand of God graciously at work. And amidst all the bad news that is consuming the airways and media, we must be steadfast in spreading the Good News of our Lord God and Savior, Jesus Christ and sound the trumpet of warning. We must not hide in the Truth we know. We must reach out to the lost and deceived. We must not hide God's Light from the world, we must shine it and sound the harbinger trumpet.

## A Whisper of Hope

**Listen closely, dear children...**to all the warnings I have so graciously given you.

**Ezekiel 33:3, 4, 6**
When the watchman sees the Enemy coming, he blows the alarm to warn the people. Then if those who hear the alarm refuse to take action—well, it is their own fault if they die. But if the watchman sees the Enemy coming and doesn't sound the alarm to warn the people, he is responsible for their deaths. They will die in their sins, but I will hold the watchman accountable. (NLT)

**"Return to Me, and I will return to you,"** says the LORD of hosts.
(Malachi 2:7)

# "Let It Go"

**Titus 2:12-13**
And we are instructed to turn from godless living and sinful pleasures.
We should live in this evil world with self-control, right conduct, and
devotion to God, while we look forward to that wonderful event when
the glory of our great God and Savior, Jesus Christ, will be revealed. (NLT)

Turning away from the godless lifestyles that this world embraces is never an easy task, because our nature to sin is much like gravity; it is a powerful force that holds us down. And the first step in battling the gravity of sin is to know what it is, recognize its source, and know the consequences it carries. Sin is any act of disobedience against the holiness of God. Sin came from the Devil and is therefore, evil in its nature. Sin caused mankind and the entire universe to be cursed with decadence and death. So we are not only born with the nature to sin, but we are also destined to die in our sin as well. But our merciful God created a great redeeming Plan through His Son—a Plan that sets us free from the power of sin, forgives all of our past, present, and future sins, and gives us eternal life when our earthly bodies die. Although God's Plan is simple, it is not an easy plan to act upon, because this evil world has poisoned our minds and hardened our hearts. We have been brainwashed into believing that the main purpose for living is to seek whatever makes us happy by attaining things that give us pleasure and make us feel good about ourselves. These are all lies my friend, for God created us for His good pleasure and to reflect His glory.

So don't be duped into following the smooth sounding lies of the godless world being led to Hell by Satan; lies that sound good and seem right for you, but in reality, are misleading and extremely deadly. Instead, listen to the Voice of God and discover your true purpose in living and where it all leads. God's Word will not only define your sinful behavior and its immediate affects, but also the eternal consequences. God's life saving Truth is a life-changing transformation that is not by any means, an easy transition to make, because most of us try to hang on to some of our sins like hanging on to a cliff for dear life. And letting go of our sins can sometimes feels like pulling healthy teeth that are well rooted in. But God can break you free from the sin that is holding you down and bring you into the saving Light of His Son, so you can bathe in His glory forever!

## A Whisper of Hope

**Follow the Way…**dear child, and I will break you free from the dark world of sin and lead you safely into the Light of My Glory forever!

**Ephesians 2:1-2**
Once you were dead, doomed forever because of your
many sins. You used to live just like the rest of the world,
full of sin, obeying Satan, the mighty prince of the power of the air.
He is the spirit at work in the hearts of those who refuse to obey God. (NLT)

**The Lord of hosts—He is the King of Glory**
(Psalm 24:10)

# *"Sweet Victory"*

**2 Timothy 2:21**
If you keep yourself pure, you will be a utensil God can
use for His purpose. Your life will be clean, and you will
be ready for the Master to use you for every good work. (NLT)

The sacrificial death of our God and Savior Jesus Christ was the final and complete atonement for mankind's rebellion against the LORD. We are now able to come into the very Presence of God to confess our sins, because the barrier between God and man has been removed. And He not only forgives us anytime we come to Him, but He also remembers them no more. We become a new creation, for the old life of sin is nailed to the Cross of Christ, and our lives are set free from the power of sin and the fear of death and we are able to be in a personal relationship with Him. And when these earthly bodies give up the breath of life, God will raise them from the grave and transform them into new glorified bodies that will never again suffer or die, and we will live perfect lives with God forever. But in return for this incredible gift, we must live in Christ so we can be used by God for the good of His Kingdom. We must continually bring any new sins before the Lord, because although the power of sin has been broken and our sins have been forgiven, our nature to sin remains with us until we go to be with the Lord forever.

But until that day we will not fully escape our nature to sin. So for now, we must rely on the Lord's mercy and His amazing grace. We must also rely on power and wisdom of the Holy Spirit's indwelling to help us live in repentance until our sanctification is complete, because without God, we are putty in the hands of Satan. Our human wills are far too weak to stand alone against the dark forces of evil that are eating people alive and creating total chaos in our world. From the moment we are conceived in our mother's womb this evil battle for life begins and with the first breath we take the battle intensifies for not only our physical survival, but for the condition of our hearts, control of our minds, and eventually, for where we spend the rest of our eternal lives. Although Satan is the god of this world for now, King Jesus is Lord over it all and is in control. Nothing escapes His knowledge and nothing can stand in His Way. Satan knows his fate and many will go down with him. But when you stand steadfast and strong with the Savior, the victory is sweet, it's pure, and it's lasting!

## A Whisper of Hope

**The victory is yours, my child…**if you so desire, because I have the sovereign power to set you free from the decadence of this dying world. You have at your disposal the same Resurrection Power that defeated My death and My grave—the Resurrection Power of God that brings sweet victory to those who love the Truth.

**Titus 3:4-5**
But then God our Savior showed us His kindness and love.
He saved us, not because of the good things we did, but because of His mercy.
He washed away our sins and gave us a new life through the Holy Spirit. (NLT)

**He is the eternal King, the unseen One who never dies; He alone is God.**
(1 Timothy 1:17)

# *"Behind the Darkness"*

**Ezekiel 12:2**
Son of man, you live among rebels who could see the truth if they
wanted to, but they don't want to. They could hear Me if they would
listen, but they won't listen because they are rebellious. (NLT)

C hristians are the minority in this evil world that reeks of sin and wickedness; a world that
wages war against the holiness of God; a world where evil is sacred and godliness is out dated.
We live in a world that is held captive by Satan's evil ways and is consumed with darkness. We live
in a world where truth is not relative and deceit runs ramped, and to lie is the norm. We live in a
world whose voices of darkness speak loud and often, poisoning our minds and killing our hearts.
The world's evil ways turn the Truth of God upside down and inside out; that bad is good and good
is bad, and right is wrong and wrong is right. We live in a world where the Almighty God has been
reduced to whatever or whomever we want Him to be. And because the world is in such a fallen
state of delusion, we find ourselves lost in a thick, dark fog that is getting thicker and darker by the
moment. Even though we have God's Light to help us navigate through this dark fog, the darkness
remains and so, too, does our struggle to survive. The war being waged against the Holy Church of
our Lord God and Savior, Jesus Christ, is an intense war that will rage on until King Jesus returns.

Satan and his army of followers are not only working overtime to deceive and enslave the world
to their ways, but they are also working deep within the Church, twisting the Words of God to suit
their agenda. They sugar coat the Truth in order to keep people from knowing the victory that is
in Christ Jesus alone. The Book of Revelation is one of the least read books of the Bible, because
Satan is spreading his lies that the Revelation of Jesus Christ is not only too hard to understand,
but is nothing more than a mythical fantasy with little value. But the last Book in God's story is the
last Book in the Bible for a reason, my friend. It's to show us the end of this evil world, and how we
can best prepare ourselves for that ending. King Jesus is Lord over creation, Commands Heaven's
army, and will return to earth in all His Glory to condemn all those who partake in its evil and to
reward the righteous. Christians know that evil will be eradicated forever by King Jesus. We know
the Hope we have in our Savior. Don't let this evil world convince you otherwise. Leave your rebellion behind and make the effort to learn and believe in the Truth, because without Jesus you will
be left behind in the darkness!

## A Whisper of Hope

**Turn from your rebellion...**and follow the path that leads to Me, your King and Savior. There are
many that speak against the Truth, but don't be sucked into their vile lies. Follow that Still Small
Voice that speaks to your heart, for I will lead you out of this dark world and Home.

**Revelation 17:14**
Together they will wage war against the Lamb, but the Lamb will
defeat them because He is the Lord over all lords and King over all
kings, and His people are the called and chosen and faithful ones. (NLT)

**For every child of God defeats this evil world by trusting Christ to give the victory.**
(1 John 5:4)

# "Slip and Slide"

**Proverbs 27:12**
A prudent person foresees the danger ahead and takes precautions.
The simpleton goes blindly on and suffers the consequences. (NLT)

There have been times during my new life-journey in Christ when I have caught myself slipping through the safety net of salvation and sliding into the sinful pleasures of this wicked world. It was through my slipping and sliding that I discovered how easy it is to misinterpret and misuse the grace that our loving God pours out on us. I also learned that overcoming my sinful urges is impossible without the power of the Holy Spirit. For He gives us the courage to surrender to the will of God every day and the wisdom to pray for what we cannot do. We must always be alert to the sin lurking at our door and rely on God's Power to keep it shut. Because of our sinful appetites, it can be so easy taking the bait and then justify our sin, especially when we know God is forgiving. As children of the Living God we cannot overlook the basic precautions that help keep evil at bay, for when we are complacent in our faith and blind sighted by our salvation, we become the simpleton and will suffer the consequences. Whenever I find myself slipping into those gray areas of right or wrong, it reinforces the reality that there is indeed an intense spiritual warfare being fought for the hearts and minds and of those who belong to Christ Jesus our Lord God and Mighty Savior.

Because we are all natural born sinners, you will always struggle with sin and give in, and it will remain so until your sanctification is complete and you are glorified in Christ Jesus. But until that day you must wear the armor of God, faithfully bringing your new sins to the Lord, and live in daily repentance. You cannot keep from sinning, but you have an arsenal of mighty weapons to use in the battle. You cannot escape the evil of sin on your own, because no matter how hard you try, you will sooner or later succumb to its power. Your human weakness to sin and reap the instant pleasures it brings, is far greater than your ability to resist. It is so easy to slip and then slide into the darkness of sin, but it's not so easy to escape from. Keeping evil at bay is a hard battle to fight, but with God the Holy Spirit living in your heart and His wisdom guiding the Way, He will lead you right through the pearly Gates of Heaven and into the glory that is yours in Christ Jesus.

## A Whisper of Hope

**Keep close, My, child…**for I am your Shield—the One who protects you from the Enemy, for when you trust Me, you are strengthened so you will be equipped for the battles ahead.

**Hebrews 10:35-36**
So do not throw away this confident trust in the Lord. Remember the great
reward it brings you! Patient endurance is what you need now, so you will
continue to do God's will. Then you will receive all that He has promised. (NLT)

**But the Lord our God is merciful and forgiving, even though we have
rebelled against Him.**
(Daniel 9:9)

# *"The Way Home"*

**Ezekiel 34:31**
"You are My flock, the flock of My pasture.
You are men, and I am your God, says the Lord God." (NKJ)

From the very moment God created mankind, He has always been with us. He has not left us entirely to our own demise, and He graciously sent a Savior to rescue us from our sin. And from the time that God the Good Shepherd began His ministry on earth, He has been diligent in His search and rescue, gathering the lost into His loving arms where He heals the deadly wounds, comfort the hopeless hearts, and leads us safely Home. The Lord sees clearly through the darkness that we can so easily get ourselves lost in and He knows how weak and helpless we are without Him. He knows that we meander in our brokenness, while sinking deeper into a darkness that devours our souls. And this world is filled with false shepherds, speaking false hope and deadly lies that are leading the lost into a grave of eternal darkness. There are voices of pride that tells us we are our own shepherds and can find our own way Home, though many have tried and all have failed. There are voices telling us there is no God, no right or wrong, and that this life is all there is. The airways of this world are filled with smooth sounding voices that promise the riches of the world when we follow its ways. We hear the voices of defeat speaking in our heads, gloating over our failures and telling us we are too lost to be found, too wounded to be healed, and too far gone to be saved.

But amidst all these satanic voices, is a Still Small Voice that stands apart from all the rest; One Mighty Voice that whispers nothing but the Truth. And the Voice is that of our Lord God and Savior, Christ Jesus, the only Good Shepherd and the only Way out of the darkness that is eating us alive. Because the barrier between God and man has been removed by the sacrificial death of His Son, we are no longer isolated from the Presence of God. And it is because of this onetime, selfless act of love and sacrifice that we are able to reconnect with God and receive the Holy Spirit, who comes to live in those of the Shepherd's flock—whose Voice is Faithful and True . If you are lost and live in fear for your life, you can trust the Good Shepherd to be the Lord of your life—the One True Voice you can recognize and trust. For with each one He finds, He washes them clean, heals their wounds, comforts their hearts, and then carries them Home. There is no greater Shepherd, nor is there a Voice more sweet. Jesus is the only Savior there is, my friend, and it is only through Him that you will find your way Home.

## A Whisper of Hope

**When I call you out of darkness**...I will call you by name and you will know My Voice. The world promises much, but nothing you can keep. I promise you life and a safe journey Home. The way of the world leads only to Hell, but the Way of My Voice leads into the glory of Heaven and eternal life.

**John 10:14-15**
"I am the Good Shepherd; I know My own sheep, and they know Me, just as My Father knows Me and I know the Father. And I lay down My life for the sheep. (NLT)

**There is only one God and no other.**
(Mark 12:32)

# "Shepherd's Call"

**1 Peter 2:24-25**
He personally carried away our sins in His own body on the cross so
we can be dead to sin and live for what is right. You have been healed
by His wounds! Once you were wandering like lost sheep. But now you
have turned to your Shepherd, the Guardian of your souls. (NLT)

Most people walk in the darkness of this fallen world and drift far away from their Creator. I spent most of my life wandering in this darkness; dazed, confused, and desperately searching for anything that would make some sense in a world that really made no sense. We are born into a realm of darkness that we cannot escape on our own, nor can we see what it's like on the other side. So the Good Shepherd, Lord Jesus Christ, left the Glory of Heaven to shine His Light upon this dark and dying world. Jesus also came to save the people of this fallen world from the final wrath of God and eternal damnation. Christ Jesus' meager entry and His glorious departure brought the Hope of Salvation for everyone. He freely surrendered His life and selflessly shed His blood as the final sacrificial Lamb of God. The Lord suffered excruciating pain and died a horrible death nailed to a wooden cross, which paid the full redemptive price for our sins and condemnation.

This incredible gift from our merciful God is a gift for everyone who will accept it and embrace it. We cannot save ourselves, so God did it for us. Jesus was the only One who could pay the price that was due for the sins of the world. The Good News tells us that we no longer have an excuse to stumble blindly through the darkness of this wicked world, searching for hope and finding none. Be courage and humble my friend, surrender to the Lord--the Shepherd of your soul, because Jesus is the only One who can save you from your sins, heal the wounds they inflict, and then safely bring you Home. You can faithfully trust the Good Shepherd, because the journey Home is not an easy one, but when you follow the Shepherd you are following the Living God.

## A Whisper of Hope

**Be silent, My child...**and listen to My calling, so I can save your soul and take you Home. The world is a dark place, but the Truth will light your Way and lead you out.

**1 Corinthians 2:12**
Now we have received, not the spirit of the world,
but the Spirit who is from God, that we might know
the things that have been freely given to us by God. (NKJ)

**Be still and know that I am God.**
(Psalm 46:10)

# *"God is With Us"*

**Hosea 14:9**
Let those who are wise understand these things. Let those who are discerning listen carefully. The paths of the LORD are true and right, and righteous people live by walking in them. But sinners stumble and fall along the way. (NLT)

The Lord has never left us to our own demise, even though we chose to live apart from Him. He knew we could never defeat the evil without Him. Throughout the history of mankind God has been directing and implementing His perfect Plan for Redemption. Nothing slips by our Sovereign God. He is always with us, guiding our ways for the good of His Kingdom. The Lord created us in such a way that we would always need His help, especially while we live in this evil world. God has graciously given us His written Word so that we might gain the wisdom to live wisely and righteously and walk in His ways. God also gave us His Son, who saved us from our sins and the condemnation that this evil world will suffer at the end of time. And in the greatest love, selflessness, and humility, our Lord God, Christ Jesus gave up His life so ours would not be lived in vain. And to help us achieve perfection, the Lord sent the Holy Spirit, who helps us accomplish what would have otherwise been impossible for us—overcoming the evil that hold us in bondage to sin and death.

The Lord God is not the supreme dictator who forces you against your will. Instead, He is your loving Father in Heaven, who gives you opportunities to choose the path of your choice. God allows you to make mistakes, which helps you learn from first-hand experiences. He gives you the mental capacity and the ability to research and weigh all the different options you have. He gives you the plain truth and the common sense to see how your choices will affect you and what the end results will bring. Most people choose to take the world's path, opting to go after those things that satisfy our selfish human desires, which unbeknownst to them, leads into a darkness that is difficult to navigate and eventually leads into the abyss. God's path, on the other hand, is brightly lit with the glory of the Lord and you can see clearly what lies ahead. You are able to choose the right path that is not only the best for you, but also for those around you. And by remaining in the Light of the Living God, you will gain personal access into God's Presence where He comforts you in your times of trouble, gives you the courage to stand firm in the right choices you make, and the solid guarantee that you will make it safely Home.

## A Whisper of Hope

**I Am with you always…**dear child. I do not slumber nor do I get distracted. I Am always there to help you in every way. I watch over you every moment of your life, even when you are walking away from Me. I love My children as a Father should. You are safely in My care…ALWAYS!

**Jude 24**
And now, all glory to God, who is able to keep you from stumbling, and who will bring you into His Glorious Presence innocent of sin and with great joy. (NLT)

**For you were once darkness, but now your are light in the Lord.**
(Ephesians 5:8)

# "The Glory of God"

**Isaiah 6:3**
Holy, holy, holy is the LORD Almighty!
The whole earth is filled with His Glory. (NLT)

There is no One more holy than our Lord God, nor is there anyone as mighty or glorious than He. We can get a glimpse of God's awesome Power and Infinite Glory by simply looking at the universe He created and the incredible precision and power it takes to keep it all in perfect order, even though the universe and everything in it is infected by death and decay. We should marvel at the glorious power of God's creativeness, but we should praise Him for His glorious resurrection power that transforms our lives. For born again Christians, we are miraculously transformed into a new creation who thinks, feels, and lives a new life in Christ. Our lives are changed from sinful, hateful and self-centered lives into righteous, loving, and selfless lives. We should stand in awe of His unconditional love and His unlimited mercy and grace, because God left the glory of Heaven to become a man of flesh and blood so He could die for our sins and clothe us in His righteousness. With His amazing gift of forgiveness, our rebellion against God has been fully justified and for those who are born again, we will be raised from the grave and given a glorious new body that will never die. And as children of the Living God we can look forward to sharing in the glorious inheritance of our Lord and King, Jesus Christ.

Only the Lord God has the power to create from absolutely nothing, give life back to that which is dead, and make all things new and perfect forever. The Lord God has built into our very human fiber the longings for eternal life, and a trouble free existence filled with joy and happiness. Our Lord God and Savior will come again my friend, to put an end to the evil in our world and to set up His Kingdom on earth until He creates everything anew. This sounds pretty farfetched to those who belong to this dying world that is far away from God. But when you know you have escaped the wrath of God and the sinner's death, you will praise the glory and goodness of God with everlasting joy in your heart. Eternal life is a boat you do not want to miss, because the boat you're on now will sink deep into the darkness of the abyss and lost forever!

## A Whisper of Hope

**Know the glory that is Mine, dear child...**and all the plans I have for you. All other plans are fleeting and futile. But the plans I have for My entire creation are so incredible that nothing in this world can compare. With Satan removed forever, life will be perfect and glorious!

**Revelation 20:1-3**
Then I saw an angel come down from Heaven with the key to the bottomless pit and a heavy chain in his hand. He seized the dragon—that old serpent, the Devil, Satan—and bound him in chains for a thousand years. The angel threw him into the bottomless pit, which he then shut and locked so Satan could not deceive the nations anymore until the thousand years were finished. (NLT)

**For He has rescued us from the one who rules in the kingdom of darkness.**
(Colossians 1:11)

# "Heavenly Harvest"

**Galatians 6:8**
Those who live only to satisfy their own sinful desires will harvest the consequences of decay and death. But those who live to please the Spirit will harvest everlasting life from the Spirit. (NLT)

We live in a fallen world where sin is as part of our human make up as breathing is. It is our nature to rebel against the holiness of God to satisfy the sinful lusts of our carnal flesh. Satan has managed to disguise the evilness of sin so well that most people don't even know they are sinning, for they see it as simply enjoying the life they were given. This secular, humanistic world has brainwashed most of the world's people with lies that have produced a great harvest of pain, suffering, violence, confusion, anxiety, depression, and a lot of death and destruction. The Devil has become the god of this evil world, who is taking a lot of deceived souls into the eternal burning Lake of Fire with him. Nothing in this world works the way it's supposed to work without its Creator's help and direction. Whenever we take God out of the equation, what is produced is nothing but evil, chaos, and destruction. There are many godless people who become successful and live in comfort without God's help or approval, but what they reap when their short life is over is never worth going to Hell for.

People who live only for the moment are short-sighted and foolish. To make the best of this short life my friend, you would be wise to seek God and learn why you are here and where you are going. Without knowing the Story of God you will be left in the dark and living in vain. Living only for this life is much like chasing the wind; not knowing from where it came or where it is going. But when your life is over and you find yourself in Hell, you will realize it's too late. When you surrender to the Author of Life and receive His gift of salvation, and the Holy Spirit will reveal the Truth and guide you safely into Heaven. With the wisdom and power of God you will live a life that is truly worth living—one that is pleasing to God, yourself, and to those around you. When living as a child of God, you will know how glorious the future is, which makes the future of the humanist world view look absolutely foolish and futile. Satan and his world can promise you nothing but fleeting pleasure and eternal damnation.

## A Whisper of Hope

**Do not follow this world, my child...**for it will lead you far from the Truth. Although it is your nature to sin, I will forgive your sins and give you a new nature that is pure. This life is short but the next one is not. Know Me and learn how to live this life so you can live in the next. Live godly now and partake in the Harvest of Heaven.

**1 John 2:16-17**
For the world offers only the lust for physical pleasure, the lust for everything we see, and pride in our possessions. These are not from the Father. They are from this evil world. And this world is fading away, along with everything it craves. But if you do the will of God, you will live forever. (NLT)

**A wise person is hungry for truth, while the fool feeds on trash.**
(Proverbs 15:14)

# *"Joy in Hope"*

**Luke 2:34**
Then Simeon blessed them, and he said to Mary, the baby's mother,
"This child will be rejected by many in Israel, and it will be their
undoing. But He will be the Greatest Joy for many others." (NLT)

Our Lord God, Jesus Christ, is not only the Greatest Joy we have in this dark and dying world, but He is also the only Hope we have. Jesus is the joy that our human hearts long. And we will never experience this True Joy if we reject Him to love this world that hates His very Name. Without this Joy living in our hearts and directing our lives, there is no real hope in this life or for the next—only false hope that is both deceiving and deadly. Without the Joy of the Lord this difficult life always gives us a false sense of security, is always lived in vain, and ends in eternal damnation. I know firsthand that living this life without the gift of salvation as your hope, will leave you hopeless and desperate for anything that would ease the pain and numb the hopelessness. Most people are searching for that one ray of light that would lead them out of the dark hopelessness that is consuming our lives—one ray of hope that would bring comfort to their fearful hearts and some much needed peace about this difficult life-journey we don't ask for. There is no one, nor is there anything from this flawed and wicked world that can satisfy the longings and joy we were created with.

Only the Living God can satisfy the longings we have for love, an eternal future, and the kind of lasting joy that would make this difficult life worth living. Nothing in the physical realm of this fallen world is able to give us anything that is lasting; only fleeting moments of happiness that quickly dissipate when the rush ends. This decaying world and all who belong to it will one day disappear, and it is only through the death and resurrection of our Lord God and Savior, Jesus Christ, that you are promised a new and perfect life in the new Heaven and Earth that will follow. When you have the hope of a perfect eternal life, you have everything to look forward to and nothing to lose. When you know that your sins are forgiven and justified by the death of our Savior, you receive the Greatest Joy possible. Without the Lord Jesus there is no hope and no joy my friend, only fear of what tomorrow may bring and dreading another day of futile living.

## A Whisper of Hope

**Come to Me, My child…** and I will give you the Everlasting Hope that brings a joy you have never known. Don't look to the world for hope, because it has none. Don't look to the world for joy, for it's not there. Your only joy is through the Hope you have in Me, your only Savior.

**Psalm 146:3-5**
Don't put your confidence in powerful people; there is no hope for you there. When their breathing stops, they return to the earth, and in a moment all their plans come to an end. But happy are those who have the God of Israel as their helper, whose hope is in the LORD their God. (NLT)

**Don't be dejected and sad, for the joy of the LORD is your strength!**
(Nehemiah 8:10)

# *"GOD I AM"*

**Genesis 41:16**
"It is beyond my power to do this," Joseph replied.
"But God will tell you what it means and will set you at ease." (NLT)

The Lord ,our God and Creator, is sovereign over everything. Nothing escapes His knowledge, His sight, nor does anything exceed His awesome power. And because God knows all things actual and possible, He knows all things from the past, the present, and all future things as well. God did not create the universe and everything in it just to leave it and let it evolve on its own. God has planned out the destiny of His creation, and thus, controls the course of time and all events. God has always been involved in the development of human history and is also personally involved in each and every human life. And even when we think things are totally out of control, we can be sure that the hand of God is busy directing all things for the good of His Kingdom to come. God is the Creator, Director and the Owner of all things. He is God and there is no one like Him! If we are to know and understand the Truth about our all knowing, all powerful, and ever present God and why we were created, we must go straight to the Source—to the Author of Life—to God Himself. For when we do, God will give us everything we need to know and will righteously direct our paths according to His will. When we have the Spirit of Truth living in our hearts, He removes the blinders from our eyes so we can see the true reality about life, death, and what is yet to come our way.

Every living thing, no matter where it lies in the food chain or what its significance is, needs the Living God my friend, and that includes you, no matter if you believe it or not. But in order for God to help guide you, you must believe in His sovereignty over everything. You must also surrender your will and entire life-journey into His care and control, and also trust Him with the circumstances of the world around you as well. And when you let God be God, you will receive His peace that will comfort your heart and mind as you live in Christ Jesus. Knowing the Truth and living God's Way rather than your own, is not an easy road to follow, but if you stick with God, you can be sure that your Creator and Savior knows what is best and He will do everything to get you Home safely. God is God and He can be nothing less than who He is.

## A Whisper of Hope

**I Am God, My child...**there is no Other. And you can trust Me with the course of your life, because I have great plans for you. The world will tell you otherwise, but don't be fooled, for the world will lead you down a very slippery path that seems right, but will end in tragedy. My path, if chosen, is always the right path to take; it is the path that never ends!

**Nehemiah 9:6**
You alone are the LORD; You have made Heaven, the heaven of heavens, with all their host, the earth and all things on it, the seas and all that is in them.
And You preserve them all. The host of Heaven worships You. (NKJ)

### And God said to Moses, "I AM WHO I AM"
(Exodus 3:14)

285

# "Life or Death"

**Proverbs 11:19**

Godly people find life; evil people find death. (NLT)

Even though we have no choice in being born into this world, God has blessed us with the gift of life and the freedom to choose how we live once we are mature enough to decide for ourselves. But along with this freedom to choose, is the reality that the decisions we make will not only determine what happens to us in this short life, but will also determine where we spend eternity. God created us just as eternal as the angels are, and so we should never take our freedom to choose lightly, because every choice we make is really a matter of life or death, either in this short life or the eternal one to follow—whether we live eternally in the Light of God's Glory or suffer in eternal darkness without Him. We don't know from one moment to the next what this fallen world will dish out and although God made our physical bodies uniquely resilient, we are easily killed. It's not easy staying alive in this dangerous world, nor is it easy to live righteously in an ungodly world that is cursed with death, captivated by sin, and is in short supply of mercy and grace.

Because of these truths, it is essential that you know the Absolute Truth about life and death and the evil that drives this wicked world. Without God's Truth we tend to make choices that satisfy our sinful nature, rather than following the eternal ways that God designed us to live by. Without the Lord God directing your everyday life, you are more apt to give in to worldly things that draw us away from God. Without the indwelling of the Holy Spirit, it's hard to discern what is true and what is not; what is right or what is wrong, or what is good and what is bad. The man made wisdom from Satan is brain washing people with border-line truth that has twisted God's Word so much that it is barely recognizable. Man's finite wisdom is purely speculative and utterly foolish when compared to the wisdom of God. For those who think they are wiser than our Creator and Savior, their foolish pride gone unchecked will lead them straight into the pits of Hell and sadly, they will probably take many others down with them as well.

## A Whisper of Hope

**Choose wisely, My child...**because the fool has no insight on the brevity of life or the longevity of eternity. Don't live just for the moment, because the next moment may end up being your worst nightmare. This life is extremely short-lived and goes by rather quickly, but the next one does not.

**2 Timothy 1:9-10**

It is God who saved us and chose us to live a holy life. He did this not because we deserved it, but because that was His plan long before the world began—to show His love and kindness to us through Christ Jesus. And now he has made all of this plain to us by the coming of Christ Jesus, our Savior, who broke the power of death and showed us the Way to everlasting life through the Good News. (NLT)

**Send out Your light and Your truth; let them guide me.**
(Psalm 43:3)

# "Saved by Death"

**1 Peter 1:6**
So be truly glad! There is wonderful joy ahead, even though
it is necessary for you to endure many trials for a while. (NLT)

No matter how difficult this life is for the Christian who is solid in their faith, they have the confidence and courage to look ahead to the glorious future God has promised. His promise of a new eternal life with Him gives us a joy that cannot be taken away. It is this inner joy of salvation that sets the Christian apart from the rest of the world. Unlike the billions of people who do not embrace this promise, Christians have the advantage of knowing the plans of God—plans that exceed anything from this fallen world, because we know that this fallen world and everything it embraces is quickly fading away and will one day disappear. Our Lord God and Savior Christ Jesus, knows firsthand how hard, cruel and wicked this evil world is, especially for those who are called by His Name. He knows what is like to be hated and persecuted. He knows all the slander and lies that we face. He knows what it's like to go without. He knows what it feels like to be hurt, brutally beaten, and nailed naked to a dead tree. He knows what it's like to suffer like no human has ever suffered, and die a godforsaken death. He was unjustly condemned to die a criminal's death and was punished by God for the sins of the world, yet He Himself lived a sin free life.

Our Lord God took on human flesh to die the death we all deserve; so we would be spared the sinner's death of eternal darkness and condemnation. It is so essential to our spiritual health that we rely on the Cross of Christ to save us from the wrath that we all deserve. We cannot save ourselves no matter how hard we try, because we cannot be good enough to stand in the Presence of our Perfectly Holy and Righteous God. When you live apart from the Living God, going with the flow of this dying world, you will never find the kind of joy and hope that helps you endure the calamity this world dishes out. You will become discouraged, disappointed, and left hopeless. But when you put your future in the hands of your Lord God and Savior—hands that were nailed through with rusty spikes, nothing from this fallen would will ever take your joy away, because you will know that the glory of Heaven awaits for those who die to self for the sake of Christ Jesus.

## A Whisper of Hope

**Don't be fooled, My child…**you cannot be good enough to receive the gift of salvation. You cannot live apart from Me and escape the condemnation that sin brings. Only My death and blood can save you from the eternal punishment you deserve.

**Romans 5:1-4**
Therefore, since we have been made right in God's sight by faith, we have peace with God because of what Jesus Christ our Lord has done for us. Because of our faith, Christ has brought us into this place of highest privilege where we now stand, and we confidently and joyfully look forward to sharing God's glory. We can rejoice, too, when we run into problems and trials, for we know that they are good for us—they help us learn to endure. And endurance develops strength of character in us, and character strengthens our confident expectation of salvation. (NLT)

**He paid for you with the precious lifeblood of Christ, the sinless, spotless Lamb of God**
(1 Peter 1:19)

# "Life in God"

**Ezekiel 18:30, 31**
"Therefore, I will judge each of you according to your actions, says the Sovereign LORD. Turn from your sins! Don't let them destroy you! Put all your rebellion behind you, and get for yourselves a new heart and a new spirit. For why should you die? I don't want you to die, says the Sovereign LORD. Turn back and live!" (NLT)

The Sovereign Lord God feels exactly the same today as He did back in the days of Ezekiel, because God never changes! Because He loves people above all His creation, He gives us a chance to repent and live today, just as He was doing back then! This is why He personally came to save His chosen people and the world. God gave Israel and the world the only Way to escape His wrath and eternal condemnation. He has woven into the very fibers of every human being, the desire to live forever. And because of this God given desire, most people fight hard to hang on to this short life as long as they possibly can, regardless of the pain and suffering it brings. God did not created us to die, but to live in fellowship with Him forever. But because sin has infected our world with death, all its inhabitants must die. So the Lord came to give us the Way to escape our second death, which is even more frightening than the first. And God's Church, the body of Christ, is the bearer of this Good News that not only saves us from a fiery end and eternal damnation, but gives us the guarantee that our earthly death is not death at all, but the beginning of a very long and perfect life.

God does not force us to listen to His message of Good News or accept His gift of salvation. Instead, He graciously gives us a chance to hear the Good News and make our own decision. Sadly, most people will reject the saving grace of the Cross of Christ so they can continue to indulge in their own ways and the sin they love. We have two basic choices: Heaven or Hell. You can choose God's Way or Satan's way. You can selfishly live this life your own way hoping for the best, or you can live God's Way knowing the best is yet to come. You can live in the darkness of this fallen world and follow the crowd, or you can live in the Light of the World and be transformed into His Likeness. You have been blessed with a free will and a sound mind my friend, use it wisely while it's still on the table.

## A Whisper of Hope

**Turn to Me, My child...**for I don't want to lose you forever. I want you to live and enjoy the glory of My Presence now and in the Home I am building for you—an eternal Home where there is no more pain or tears or suffering. But you must choose the Way I have provided, for it is the living Way!

**1 John 4:9**
God showed how much He loved us by sending His only Son
into the world so that we might have eternal life through Him. (NLT)

**His ways are everlasting.**
(Habakkuk 3:6)

# *Broken Chains"*

**Psalm 107:14**
He led them from the darkness and deepest
gloom; he snapped their chains. (NLT)

It is only through the power of God the Holy Spirit that anyone can escape their bondage to sin and the darkness that is consuming our world. Only the resurrection power of our Lord God and Savior can break the chains that hold us captive to the life-destroying evil that poisons our minds, hardens our hearts, and kills our souls—an evil that lurks in every dark corner of our lives, waiting to sink its deadly fangs into our sinful flesh. The only way to break the chains of bondage that Satan holds over his prey is through the nail scared hands of our Savior, whose death and resurrection has broken the chains of sin and the death penalty that it brings. Once the chains are broken, and you are led into the Light of the living God, you can live freely from the power of sin without fear for your life. Jesus Christ is the Truth that sets you free. There is no victory from sin and death without Jesus, my friend, it's simply impossible.

As prideful people, we can always fool ourselves and others by saying we can break our sinful appetites by hunkering down and not indulging in them. But without the transforming power of God the Holy Spirit, the evil from Hell will pull us back into its darkness and whisper what a failure we are. The sinful hungers of our carnal flesh are strong and our fallen human wills are fickle, but the power of God will always trump the evil powers of darkness. For no matter how deep the stain of your sins may be, the blood of Jesus can cleanse them all. Jesus is the power and the Way, and He knows what it takes, because He personally defeated the power of sin and death, and He offers it to you. But you must never give up and never lose faith, because even though the struggles are hard and the battles are tough, the victory over death is yours in Christ Jesus!

## A Whisper of Hope

**Take My nail scared hand, dear child**...and let Me lead you into the Light and away from the decay of this dark and evil world. I Am your only Way out, your only Hope for living in My glorious Light forever.

**Colossians 1:11-13**
May you be filled with joy, always thanking the Father, who has enabled you to share the inheritance that belongs to God's holy people, who live in the Light. For He has rescued us from the one who rules in the kingdom of darkness, and He has brought us into the Kingdom of His dear Son. (NLT)

**So Christ has really set us free.**
(Galatians 5:1)

# "Dark Times"

**2 Timothy 4:3-4**
For a time is coming when people will no longer listen to
right teaching. They will follow their own desires and will
look for teachers who tell them whatever they want to hear.
They will reject the Truth and follow strange myths. (NLT)

The time in which the apostle Paul is speaking is here; it has been for quite some time. We live in a fallen world that is driven by the evil one—a world that creates its own truth in order to justify its love for wicked things. We live in a world whose god is Satan and its people are being led into a darkness so deep and so dark that for many there will be no escape and no turning back. We live in a world driven by hate—a hate for our God and anything that is holy and righteous. It's a world that depends on its lies to spread its hate and division—a world that worships sin so much that it embraces even the most perverted acts of evil and justifies them as being good—acts that are despicable and disgusting to God and those who are called by His Name. In this world of immorality, anything goes as long as it feels good and makes you happy. This world has foolishly rejected its Creator and Savior, the Infinite Living God who created us with many of His triune attributes. But sadly, most people deny the Living God and their connection with Him to worship worldly gods that satisfy their evil cravings.

But amidst all this evil and ungodliness that our world is embracing, there is One Hope for those who long for what the world cannot give them. And that Hope is found in the Word of God, Christ Jesus; the Son who is shinning the Light of Truth into this dark world. He has lit the path for those who are desperately searching for a Way out of the evil darkness. The time for God to complete His redemptive plan for man is getting closer with each passing day. Jesus Christ saved us from eternal condemnation and death, but the Devil has fooled many a scholar, and in return they have deceived the world. But by putting your hope in the Cross of Jesus my friend, you will defeat the grave and live forever in a place where evil cannot exist.

## A Whisper of Hope

**It's time, dear child…**to follow Me, the Living God, your Savior. Only I can lead you safely out of the darkness of this evil world. All others lead to Hell. The world will tell you differently in a very convincing way, but I AM the only Way, the only Truth, and the only God—there is no Other!

**1 John 5:19-20**
We know that we are children of God and that the world around us
is under the power and control of the evil one. And we know that the
Son of God has come, and He has given us understanding so that we
can know the true God. And now we are in God because we are in His
Son, Jesus Christ. He is the only true God, and He is eternal life. (NLT)

**Fear only God, who can destroy both soul and body in Hell.**
(Matthew 10:28)

# *"Promised Peace"*

**Micah 4:3-4**

The LORD will settle international disputes. All the nations will beat their swords into plowshares and their spears into pruning hooks. All wars will stop, and military training will come to an end. Everyone will live quietly in their own homes in peace and prosperity, for there will be nothing to fear. The LORD Almighty has promised this! (NLT)

What an awesome change this will be for a world that has been at war with itself and its Creator from the very beginning. Mankind has been fighting and killing, cheating and stealing, slandering and suing one another since the beginning of time. But our Lord God and Savior put a plan in place to save us from the chaotic that sin brings to bring His righteous rule into our world where we will live together in peace and prosperity forever. Although many people have dreamed and tried to create utopia in this fallen world, every attempt has failed miserably, making matters even worse. But unlike the many failed attempts of utopia, we Christians know and can trust that Jesus, our King, will return to set up His perfect Kingdom on Earth. Jesus, the King of the universe, is also our God and Savior, and only He has the power to end the evil in our world.

Upon His return, King Jesus will reign in this world for a thousand years and there will be no more killing or wars, no disease or death, no suffering or pain, and absolutely no injustice at all. It will be a safe haven for every person, because Jesus will remove all unrighteousness before it can spread to others. And after His thousand year reign, Satan, the fallen angels, and those who have rejected Christ Jesus will be sent into the eternal Lake of Fire forever. And our God will create everything new and perfect for those who are faithful and called by His Name. God's promise of eternal life in a body that will not grow old or get sick makes this difficult life a whole lot easier to cope with. Knowing you will live in a perfect world without sin and evil is like a perfect dream that will come true. Utopia, as we understand it, is not even close to the incredible future that God has planned for His children.

## A Whisper of Hope

**It is true, dear** child...that I have a glorious future planned for all those who are called by My Name. I know it seems too good to be true, and maybe a little farfetched for your human mind to grasp, but nonetheless, it is true. And one day, in the blink of an eye, it will become a reality for you!

**Revelation 20:1-4**

Then I saw an angel come down from Heaven with the key to the bottomless pit and a heavy chain in his hand. He seized the dragon—that old serpent, the Devil, Satan—and bound him in chains for a thousand years. The angel threw him in to the bottomless pit, which he then shut and locked so Satan could not deceive the nations anymore until the thousand years were finished. Afterward he must be released for a little while. (NLT)

**Hallelujah! For the Lord our God, the Almighty, reigns.**
(Revelation 19:6)

# *"Honor and Respect"*

**Malachi 1:6**
The LORD Almighty says to the priests: "A son honors his father,
and a servant respects his master. I am your Father and Master,
but where are the honor and respect I deserve? (NLT)

When we become a born again Christian, we become a new person, dedicating our lives to God and His purpose, much like a priest does. We also become disciples of Jesus Christ—messengers of the Good News of Salvation through the death and resurrection of our Lord God and Savior. The message of forgiveness and eternal life is for everyone living on the face of this earth, and Jesus has given us the Great Commission to proclaim this Truth to the world. But as disciples and holy priests, are we living a new life of repentance and devotion to the Lord? Are our actions honoring and respecting our Mighty God and Savior? Do our lives reflect the kind of reverence and respect that God so rightly deserves? Our Lord God not only created us and sustains us, but He also saves our precious souls from eternal condemnation. As holy priests we must live righteous lives before God and the world, thanking and praising Him for His gracious provisions, especially His saving grace—the undeserved gift of salvation that saves us from eternal condemnation in Hell.

As a disciple you must stay connected to God, so you can know His will, stay repentant, and to be re-energized. We owe God our very lives, because He chose not to give us what we deserve, rather He chose to give us what we don't deserve. As Christians, we have a high and holy calling because we belong to God. He gave it all so you could have it all. Christ Jesus was not forced to become a man of flesh and blood and sacrifice His life for a wicked world. He gladly volunteered to take the sins and punishment of the world. The blood of Jesus is the only Way to forgiveness and eternal life. The Lord God is our Father, Provider, Healer, and our Source for eternal life. The least we can do is give Him our life in return, honor Him in our living, and respect His authority with our obedience.

## A Whisper of Hope

**Honor Me, child...**and I will honor you in return. Show Me respect and I will bless you richly. Live to please Me and I will guide you safely through this difficult live until you reach Home. You will fail Me from time to time, but I never forsake My children, nor will I ever stop loving you!

**Revelation 1:5, 6**
All praise to Him who loves us and has freed us from
our sins by shedding His blood for us. He has made us
His Kingdom and His priests who serve before God His Father. (NLT)

**And you must love the Lord your God with all your heart,**
**all your soul, all your mind, and all your strength.**
(Mark 12:30)

# "His Light is Pure"

**Matthew 6:22-23**
Your eye is a lamp for your body. A pure eye lets sunshine into your soul.
But an evil eye shuts out the light and plunges you into darkness. If the
light you think you have is really darkness, how deep that darkness will be! (NLT)

When God's children look purely upon the goodness of the LORD, letting the Son shine into their souls, they find peace and hope in difficult circumstances, because they know that no matter what, they are safely in His grip. But people who take in the evilness of this dark world are shut off from God's Light and if continued, slip even deeper into a darkness far removed from God. It is our fallen human nature to hide our sinfulness, which leads into a double life and worse. And the more evil we put into our minds and hearts, the darker our soul becomes, until it becomes so dark and deep that we can't see the way out. But when we cast our gaze upon the Lord with pure eyes, we always find Him; the Light of Life that helps us escape. But looking through evil eyes, we see nothing but darkness.

The sin that you enjoy for awhile may satisfy your evil lusts with its instant pleasure, but if it remains hidden, it will only lead to the three dire D's: Darkness, Death, and Decay. The world is infected with the wicked, evil ways of Satan—temptations that come straight from darkness of Hell—a darkness that destroys lives and kills the soul. The only Hope anyone has of escaping the evil that is consuming this world, my friend, is through the Light of God's saving grace found in Jesus Christ, the Light of the World. Without Jesus we remain blind and lost, searching for something to make us feel good, unaware that we slipping deeper into the abyss of darkness; that bottomless pit, called Hell. Don't be one of the many to deny or ignore the only Light that will save your eternal soul. The little and temporary pleasure that this fallen world are not worth the price you will eventually pay for it. And that price is the forfeit of your eternal life, forever separated from the Light of God's glory.

## A Whisper of Hope

**Be careful, My child...**for the world is filled with deceit—lies from the Enemy that will suck you into the darkness before you know it. Always live in the Light, looking through pure eyes. The darkness that is consuming this world cannot exist in the Light of God where you are safe.

**Romans 13:12**
The night is almost gone; the day of salvation will soon be here.
So don't live in darkness. Get rid of your evil deeds. Shed them like dirty clothes.
Clothe yourselves with the armor of right living, as those who live in the Light. (NLT)

**So be careful how you live, not as fools but as those who are wise.**
(Ephesians 5:15)

# "Remain Forgiven"

**Luke 21:34-36**

But take heed to yourselves, lest your hearts be weighed down with carousing, drunkenness, and cares of this life, and that Day come on you unexpectedly.
For it will come as a snare on all those who dwell on the face of the whole earth.
Watch therefore, and pray always that you may be counted worthy to escape all these things that will come to pass, and to stand before the Son of Man." (NKJ)

It is so amazing that the Almighty God of Heaven and Earth left His glory behind to give us fair warning about the coming wrath the He will unleash upon this evil world that is governed by the Prince of Darkness. Satan has been successfully deceiving mankind since the dawn of time and it will continue to be so until Jesus returns to rid the earth of evil and to set up His Kingdom. The warning clearly shows that we have a merciful and gracious God who created us to be His children forever, for He did what needed to be done to make it so. Unlike Satan and his band of fallen angels, God gives His people a second change to be redeemed and forgiven for our rebellion. The Lord loves His people, Israel, and all human beings above all His creation and He takes no delight when we sign the eternal lease for the eternal Lake of Fire with Satan and all his fallen angels.

Sadly there will be many who call themselves God's people and Christians who will be caught with their pants down when the Lord removes His Church and unleashes His deadly wrath upon this earth for seven dark and bloody years. Our God is a patient God who has given us gracious time to choose His Way or the Devil's way. When you choose God's Way you die to self and are born again in Christ Jesus, no longer living and thinking as the world does. Instead, you live and love like Jesus, because the moment of His return, you do not know. So remain alert, and stay free from the darkness. For a moment of pleasure is not worth the risk.

## A Whisper of Hope

**I provided the Way, My child...**because of My Great Love for you. Don't be tempted and fall for the lies of the Enemy who wants to destroy your life and kill your soul. Remain in the Light of My saving grace and all will be forgiven.

**Revelation 3:10**

Because you have obeyed My command to persevere,
I will protect you from the great time of testing that will
come upon the whole world to test those who belong to this world. (NLT)

**Do not be misled. Remember that you cannot ignore God and get away with it.**
(Galatians 6:7)

# *"Hot for Christ"*

**Revelation 3:19**
I am the One who corrects and disciplines everyone
I love. Be diligent and turn from your indifference. (NLT)

I f the Lord God did not love human beings like He does, He would have washed His hands of us a long time ago and we would all die in our sin and reap the ugly consequences. Because the Lord is perfectly righteous and just, unforgiven sin must be dealt with. But He is also a merciful and gracious God who is filled with love and compassion for people, sin and all. God was quick to respond to the sins of Adam and Eve, promising a Divine Savior who would crush the head of Satan and provide the Way back into His Holy Presence. And from that time forward, the Lord has been pursuing people faithfully, correcting and disciplining us when needed, because He wants no one to suffer the horrors of eternal condemnation. Since the death and resurrection of Christ Jesus, the Holy Spirit has been working in our world in order to wake us up to the truths about life and death, and Heaven and Hell. Since God's ways are far above our finite ways, we must humbly trust in the ways of the God who saved us. God's Way is best, no matter how unfair they seem to us.

Why God allows some to die young in their sins and saves others when they are old and sick is not our concern; it is not for us to know this side of Heaven. We must simply trust in God's sovereign plan for man and believe in the gift of salvation that He so graciously purchased for us. When we reject the infinite Truth of God for the false truths of this wicked world, we become deceived by blatant lies and led to make choices that we will regret. Trusting God's Truth and disciplined is a prerequisite to successfully navigating through this hard and dangerous life-journey. Surrendering your life to the Lord and accepting His death and resurrection as your own, is the key that unlocks the door to God's complete forgiveness, His gift of salvation, and a new godly life. With Christ Jesus you have the Way, the Truth, and the Life. He is the Saving Light for this dark and dying world, and He is the only One who can usher you through Heaven's door.

## A Whisper of Hope

**Be at peace, My child…**trust in the plans I have for you; plans for a future that is bright and full of life. My great love is unknowable, my compassion is beyond great, and My justice is perfect. Don't be indifferent to the plans I have for you, and always allow Me to lead the Way.

**Isaiah 55:8-9**
"My thoughts are completely different from yours," says the LORD.
"And My ways are far beyond anything you could imagine. For just
as the heavens are higher than the earth, so are My ways higher than
your ways and My thoughts higher than your thoughts." (NLT)

**But since you are like lukewarm water, I will spit your out of My mouth!**
(Revelation 3:16)

# *"Amazing Saving Grace"*

**Micah 7:7**
Therefore I will look to the LORD; I will wait for
the God of my salvation; My God will hear me. (NKJ)

I now fully trust in the Lord my God. I put my life into His hands each day He gives me the breath of life. And because Christ saved me from the eternal condemnation I deserve, I trust Him with my dying as well. And as this relationship deepens, I am able to see more clearly how He has used the many foolish mistakes I made to strengthen my faith and prepare me for the mission at hand. The Lord kept me from dying in my sin because He not only loves me, but wanted to use me in a unique way for the good of His Kingdom. We know the Lord God is in the people saving business because He did not create us to die; He made us eternal beings. Before God created us He had a redemptive plan in place, because He knew we would need it.

People need to know the truth about this fallen world and the reason it's so difficult to live in, impossible to rely on, and brings us death. Without the grace of the Living God, we are putty in the hands of Satan. Without Jesus we are caught in the Devil's web of lies while he sucks the life out of our souls. Everyone needs the Savior who came into our fallen world to rescue us from our sinful ways and save us from the eternal condemnation that we justly deserve. Every person living in this decaying world needs Jesus, because without His saving grace there is absolutely no way to receive eternal life. The Lord is always available, my friend, to help you escape the prison of darkness that awaits so many innocent and unsuspecting souls. The Living God is the only Savior for our eternal souls, even those who think they have fallen too far from His amazing, saving grace.

## A Whisper of Hope

**I listen closely, dear child...**for the cries of those lost in the darkness. I let no cry for help go unanswered. I AM GOD, the Savior for all who want to break free from this wicked world that seeks to kill the soul. You don't have to die, for I AM eternal life for you.

**Psalm 18:30**
As for God, His way is perfect;
The word of the LORD is proven;
He is a Shield to all who trust in Him. (NKJ)

**Because the Sovereign LORD helps me, I will not be dismayed.**
(Isaiah 50:7)

# "The Great Escape"

**Proverbs 5:22**
An evil man is held captive by his own sins;
They are ropes that catch and hold him. (NLT)

As people living under the curse of sin and death, it is our fallen human nature to sin first and worry about the consequences later. The evil in our hearts opposes the righteousness of God and has the power to hold us captive to our carnal flesh. While in this mortal body, we are prisoners to whatever controls the way we think and live. And until you know the Truth, you will never escape the power that sin has over your life and you will remain its slave, bound to a wicked world that is pulling you into Hell. When you are driven by your sinful desires, you mock the goodness of God, and every breath you take will lead you farther from the Truth and the harder it is to escape the darkness. The power of Satan and sin is the driving force behind our world and sadly, most people fall for it and get imprisoned by it. Many people who hear the Good News of Jesus Christ laugh at the absurdity of it all and pass it off as myth or fiction. Many will hear the Truth, but say it's not for them. Unfortunately, most people will continue to indulge in the pleasure of sin no matter what they hear, for satisfying the flesh in spite of the consequences is the way of the world.

But there are many discouraged people who are crying out for help and hoping to wake up from their nightmare of living in a hopeless world that can only offer them more of the same hopelessness. It is these truth seekers who will hear the Good News and take God's offer. They will sense that Christ Jesus is their only Hope of escaping the decadence of this dying world. They are tired of living in a world that promises much, hardly delivers, and will take it all way when they die. The only things we can count on from this world are lies, false promises, deception, disappointment, evil, sinful additions, immorality, temporary pleasure, death, and the full wrath of God when it's all said and done. Don't be a slave to Satan and this wicked world. Instead, come to the Lord just as you are and let Him break the chains so you can escape the darkness that is killing your soul. You don't have to die chained to your sins my friend, because you have a Savior and He can set you free.

## A Whisper of Hope

**I can break the chains, child...**and bring you into My Everlasting Light. I can free you from the darkness that holds you prisoner to fear and death. I can set you free from the powers of Hell and lead you into eternal life.

**Isaiah 50:10**
Who among you fears the LORD and obeys His Servant?
If you are walking in darkness, without a ray of light, trust
in the LORD and rely on your God. (NLT)

**Do not let sin control the way you live; do not give in to its lustful desires.**
(Romans 6:12)

# *"Your Sacrifice"*

**Psalm 116:12**
What can I offer the LORD
for all He has done for me? (NLT)

I n my humble opinion, and from the deepest depth of my heart and soul, I believe that the best thing a true believer can offer their Creator, Provider, Protector, Savior, Advocate, and Lover of their soul is their very life that He created and then saved from eternal death. Our holy and just God came to save the people of this wicked world from the darkness and damnation that is rightly deserved. And He did it by physically suffering, dying, and taking our punishment. Our Lord God, Christ Jesus, was murdered by religious thugs for crimes He did not commit. He did this to satisfy God's anger against His people who no longer followed His ways and a world that blatantly turned against its Creator. Our God is a Saving God and He has been more than patient with this evil world, which is probably more wicked than it was in Noah's days before He destroyed mankind with the flood. And yet, our Lord God has given this wicked world fair warnings and another escape route so that everyone (not just a select few) will have the chance to change their evil ways and avoid the destruction and eternal condemnation that is coming.

But this fallen world tells us a different story. It blames God for all the pain, suffering, sickness and injustice that appears to have no end—that God does not care and has left us to our own demise. But our merciful God is not at fault, my friend, it's because this wicked world is governed by evil and its people have turned away from God and chosen Satan instead. We cannot know the ways of God this side of Heaven, but we can know that the Lord is giving the lost and misinformed people of this fallen world more time to hear the Good News Gospel of Jesus Christ. But as God's redemptive plan draws to an end, there is still time to nail your sinful life to the Cross of Christ and be born again in Spirit and Truth. For with the blood of Jesus covering your sins, you will escape the terrible wrath of God that will be poured out upon this evil world.

## A Whisper of Hope

**I sacrificed My life for you, dear child...**now it's time to sacrifice your life for Me. I came to die for you, so you could live. I shed My blood to cleanse your sin and paid the price that belonged to you. I came, I died, and paid your debt!

**Romans 12:1**
And so, dear brothers and sisters, I plead with you to give your bodies
to God. Let them be a living and holy sacrifice—the kind He will accept.
When you think of what He has done for you, is this too much to ask? (NLT)

**"I assure you, unless you are born again, you can never see the Kingdom of God."**
(John 3:3)

# *"Victory Sings"*

**Exodus 15:2**
The LORD is my strength and song, and He has become
my salvation. He is my God and I will praise Him. (NKJ)

The LORD did not create us to be self sufficient, nor did He put us in a vast universe and then leave us to chance. We are a product of Gods marvelous creativity. We are living human beings created in His image, with a purpose and a place in God's Eternal Plan. We are created by God for God's glory. We have many of the same emotions, desires, and attributes of our Creator, but we lack His infinite wisdom and His sovereign power. So where we lack, the Lord takes up the slack. Our fate lies in the grace of our sovereign God, and if we are to experience any real peace in this life, we must know who the LORD is and why He created us. And then, with the knowledge that God has allowed us to have, we must believe in its Truth and live accordingly. Everything on earth is carefully monitored by God and is used for His good purpose, because He sees the entire picture from start to finish.

As finite human beings created by God, we can never fully know or understand God. But we can be sure that what He has allowed us to know and understand is enough. He wants us to know that without Him to sustain, provide, comfort, and save us, our souls would be lost to the Devil. Without our Lord God and Savior, Jesus Christ, our songs would be few and the victories nullified, but with Him the songs are many and the victory is sweet.

## A Whisper of Hope

**Knowing Me, dear child...**is knowing the Truth, and with it comes an amazing peace that will get you through the worst this world has to offer. For when you know the Truth, you know that what lies ahead is perfect and wonderful, with the songs of Heaven's Best.

**Colossians 3:16**
Let the words of Christ, in all their richness, live in your hearts and
make you wise. Use His words to teach and counsel each other. Sing
psalms and hymns and spiritual songs to God with thankful hearts. (NLT)

**Treasures of wickedness profit nothing, but righteousness delivers from death.**
(Proverbs 10:2)

# "Truth or Consequence"

**Psalm 36:1**
Sin whispers to the wicked, deep within their hearts. they
have no fear of God to restrains them. In their blind conceit,
they cannot see how wicked they really are. (NLT)

One of the best deterrents for not doing things you know are wrong, is fearing the consequences of being caught before you do it. Stiff penalties for breaking the law's of the land keep normal people from committing crimes, but those who have no fear of authority do whatever they feel like doing. The same can be said about breaking God's Laws. When we know what God requires of us and what our unrepentant sin brings to the table, we are more apt to doing what is good in the eyes of God than not. But when we don't know God, we always do what our evil nature desires, because there is no fear of the Lord. This world is so far removed from God that most people spend their entire lives sinning without knowing it. They live in the ways of this fallen world unaware of God's absolute truths. They blindly follow the lusts of their carnal flesh without really knowing how evil they are really living and how dire the consequences are until it's too late. What this world deems as right and good is, in the eyes of God, sin, which is punishable by eternal death if gone unforgiven.

I lived like so many people do; blindly living this life knowing little about God's absolute truth and not really concerned about the consequences. When we live without Truth or consequences, it's hard to discern right from wrong, or good from bad. When you believe this life is all about your happiness and success, the devil has you right where he wants you—denying God and not fearing His Truth. The key to understanding your life, is the fear of the Lord, for He is the One who gives you life and He is the only One who can take it away. Without the fear of eternal consequences, you will live however you please. When you don't have to answer to a Higher Authority, you become that authority. You become your own god, but one that dies. Living apart from God, my friend, is both foolish and deadly. Know the Truth, believe in it, and live by it, because that is real living.

## A Whisper of Hope

**Be wise, My child...**and fear the Lord your God, for only I can take away the life I gave you. It is wise to know the Truth and fear the consequences. There are many voices, but only One Truth. Living God's way will bring good consequences. Living anything else, will not!

**Romans 6:23**
For the wages of sin is death, but the free gift of God
is eternal life through Christ Jesus our Lord. (NLT)

**Your Word is Truth.**
(John 17:17)

# "One to Trust"

**Mark 9:24**
"I do believe, but help me not to doubt!" (NLT)

Although believing that God is real and alive is an important first step, there is so much more that we must know, understand, and accept in order to have a lasting relationship with our Lord God and Savior, Jesus Christ. Because we live in a world cursed with sin and death, most of us find it difficult to trust in anyone or anything without doubt and worry clouding our minds. And this is especially true when it comes to trusting some One we cannot see. It is our fallen human pride to be overly wary about everything. But in the scope of how large the universe is and how complex and intricate life and its very survival is, I have always found it very easy and quite natural to believe in our Creator God; One who is infinitely superior and far above our finite human ways. But when it came to trusting God with my life that was a different story, because I thought He didn't even know who I was, or even cared, and because of my suspicious fallen nature, I had no relationship with Him. Because this fallen world always fails to fully satisfy the desires of the heart, it lets us down time and time again, and most of us will come into our relationship with God with our guards up, ready to justify ourselves and defend our ways.

As imperfect human beings we usually expect the worst, because we want to protect ourselves from being hurt or disappointed again. But as the Lord draws us closer and closer into our relationship with Him, the more we learn about who He is and all He is doing. As our relationship deepens, our trust grows one day at a time until we are fully vested into His glorious Kingdom. There will come a day when most of your doubts and fears about the Lord God will vanish and be replaced with His peace. If the Lord God can create everything that exists out of nothing and hold it together in perfect order so we can exist, and if He can defeat the power of sin and raise the dead, and if He can save any sinful life, no matter how sinful it has been, and if He can transform the godless into holiness, then He is the One, my friend, that you should fully vest your trust in and never doubt!

## A Whisper of Hope

**Come close to Me, My child...**and I will give you an eternal life that is perfect and fill your heart with peace. The creator is always greater than that which he creates, therefore, you can rely on Me. You can always trust Me, for I Am always Faithful and True to My Word!

**John 12:35-36**
Jesus replied, "My Light will shine out for you just a little while longer.
Walk in it while you can, so you will not stumble when the darkness falls.
If you walk in the darkness, you cannot see where you are going. Believe in
the Light while there is still time; then you will become children of the Light." (NLT)

**Believe in the LORD your God, and you will be able to stand firm.
Believe in His prophets, and you will succeed.**
(2 Chronicles 20:20)

# "In His Grip"

**Numbers 14:9**
Do not rebel against the LORD, and don't
be afraid of the people of the land. (NLT)

Rebelling against God is to sin against His holy ways. We are living in rebellion whenever we ignore God and live anyway we want. But God is always with those who submit to His Authority. He is always there ready to help and guide us through this difficult life. We can trust our Creator and Savior, because He had a Plan in place to save us from our rebellion before He created us. The Lord commands us to be holy, but we cannot because our sinful cravings are stronger than our fallen wills. Our Holy God came to us as a man of flesh and blood to live a sinless life so He could become the final Sacrificial Lamb of God, taking away the sins of the world. The righteousness of Jesus is now our own righteousness, if we so desire. When we accept the death and resurrection of Jesus as our own, we become a new creation, clothed in perfection and justified by the blood of Jesus.

When you are one with the Savior, you need never fear anything or anyone again, because Jesus has defeated the worst and most dangerous enemies you have (sin and death). Your Savior has set you free from the evil power of sin and fearing the unknown. The powers of darkness are powerless against the holiness of God that is yours and nothing can take you away from God's mighty grip. One day all of the evil and darkness will be removed from this world, but until that day, my friend, walk with Christ Jesus and fear no one but the Author and Finisher of Life.

## A Whisper of Hope

**You will live in peace, dear child...**when you live in Me. Do not turn away in rebellion, for you cannot fight and defeat the Enemy alone. When you do you lose. You must depend on Me, instead of foolishly going your own way. Run into My arms and be saved!

**2 Corinthians 1:9-10**
In fact, we expected to die. But as a result, we learned not to rely on ourselves,
but on God who can raise the dead. And He did deliver us from mortal danger.
And we are confident that He will continue to deliver us. (NLT)

**But if you keep turning away and rebelling, you will be destroyed by your enemies.**
(Isaiah 1:20)

# October

# *"Forevermore"*

**2 Peter 3:13-14**
But we are looking forward to the new heavens and new earth He
has promised, a world where everyone is right with God. And so,
dear friends, while you are waiting for these things to happen, make
every effort to live a pure and blameless life. And be at peace with God. (NLT)

K nowing and believing this incredible promise from God gives us the peace of God, which
helps us endure the troubles of this fallen world and remain faithful in Christ. When
we accept the blood of Jesus as the atonement for our many sins, we are motivated to live the
life that God calls us to live. But because of our sinful nature, it is easy for us to let our guard
down and get sucked into the sinful pleasures of this evil world, which gets us down and discouraged because of our failure. But when we bring our sin to God, His forgiveness makes us,
once again, right with Him and we can feel safe and secure knowing that He keeps all of His
promises. Without the eternal promises of God, there is no hope, no peace, and no lasting joy
while living in this world that denies God and hates His Son.

We live in a dying world that is morally decaying. The only thing this fallen world can truly
promise and deliver is death and damnation, because the god of this world is Satan. When
all you have is from the world, you will lose it, because it will all be taken away when you die,
leaving you with no hope, only darkness and regret for the wrong choices you made. But when
you follow the Way of Jesus and are adopted into God's eternal family, you have His promise as
your hope and everything to look forward to. You have the Holy Spirit helping you live a pure
and blameless life in a world that is evil in its wicked ways. So where is your hope and peace, my
friend? If it's in this world beware, for your future is bleak. But if your hope is in the promises
of God, your life is forevermore bright!

## A Whisper of Hope

**There is no peace, dear child...** to be found in this immoral world that has strayed away from
Me. There are times when you may feel peace, but then this fallen world takes it away from you.
My peace is eternal. The world's peace is a false peace that dies with you.

**Isaiah 9:6-7**
For a child is born to us, a Son is given to us. And the government
will rest on His shoulders. These will be His royal titles: Wonderful Counselor,
Mighty God, Everlasting Father, Prince of Peace. His ever expanding, peaceful government
will never end. He will rule forever with fairness and justice from the throne of His ancestor
David. The passionate commitment of the LORD Almighty will guarantee this! (NLT)

**For all of God's promises have been fulfilled in Christ.**
(2 Corinthians 1:20)

# *"Our Only Hope"*

**1 John 1:9**
But if we confess our sins to Him, He is faithful and just
to forgive us and to cleanse us from every wrong. (NLT)

When we confess our sins (rebellion against God's holiness) to the Lord, we are admitting His authority over our lives, which is the way He created it to be. God is the One who creates us and the only One who can destroy us. And He is also the One who personally sacrificed His life to cleanse us from our sins that would have otherwise rendered a guilty verdict that carried the death sentence in the prisons of Hell; the eternal death penalty that forever separates us from God's Presence. Christ Jesus purchased this freedom from a certain death sentence with His blood. But the Lord does not force us to accept His gift of a not guilty charge, because He wants us to seek His righteous council instead. He wants us to know the Truth about how and why He sacrificed His life to save us.

Jesus Christ is our God in the flesh. He knows firsthand the punishment that unrepentant sin brings us. Because we are created by a perfectly Holy and Sovereign God, He is always faithful and is filled with all the mercy and grace that we need, especially when it comes to standing before Him on Judgment Day. God wants us in His family so we can share the inheritance that is in Christ Jesus. There is no better Advocate than the Son of God. He sits at the right hand of the Father pleading your case and covering your guilt. Jesus is defending you against the Accuser; the greatest Enemy of God and your soul. Let no one sugar coat your guilt against the holiness of God. Without the testimony of the Lamb of God as your Advocate, you are guilty as charged. He has the Final say and is perfectly fair in all His judgments. If you are found guilty my friend, it's forever. There will be no more chances, and no hope for parole.

## A Whisper of Hope

**Your only hope for acquittal, dear child...**is found in My mercy and grace. I can clear the record and wipe your sin slate clean, but you must confess and put your life in My hands. For when you do, you will stand blameless and pure on Judgment Day. I AM your only Hope.

**Romans 3:23**
For all have sinned; all fall short of God's glorious standard.
Yet now God in His gracious kindness declares us not guilty. He has
done this through Christ Jesus, who has freed us by taking away our sins. (NLT)

**We are no longer slaves to sin. For when we died with Christ we were set free.**
(Romans 6:6, 7)

# "Undeserved"

**Daniel 9:18**
We do not ask because we deserve help,
but because You are so merciful. (NLT)

Considering the dysfunctional ways of my sinful past, I understand why we don't deserve the Lord's help, nor do we deserve His forgiveness or salvation. When I surrendered my broken life to God, I nailed my sinful life to the Cross of Christ, and the Holy Spirit revealed the truth of what we do and do not deserve. I learned that without the mercy and grace of our Lord God and Savior, we are nothing but dust, blown away by the wind. Without our Sovereign God guiding our ways and renewing our strength, we stand helpless in our sin and hopeless in our future. And even though I hate the sin that I put to death, I still sin. Even after learning what our Lord God and Savior Jesus Christ did for me, both on and off the Cross, I still succumb to the sin nature in me. How incredible it is to have a God that is gracious and merciful and ready to forgive.

Although the power of sin doesn't have the control it once had over my life, I, like everyone else, will always fall short of God's holy standards. We are all born into this world as sinners and we will all leave this world as sinners. What separates all sinners, is the saving grace of our merciful God and the blood of our Savior, Jesus Christ. For those who accept God's gift of forgiveness and the sacrifice of Jesus, His righteousness covers all repentant sins. Because God is perfect, His mercy, grace, love, and justice are also perfect. God is the Creator. It is His creation and we are His as well. God has the right to set the rules that save us from the eternal destination we deserve. My eternal life has been spared and I owe it all to the mercy and grace of our Almighty God. If He had given up on me, I would now be serving out an eternal life sentence in a very hellish place, forever burning in my sin and forever separated from the glory of God and all that is good.

## A Whisper of Hope

**When I look upon My people...**it breaks My heart to see their foolish ways. I have such pity on those who live in darkness, for I keep calling and calling, hoping that they might hear the Truth and repent of their sinful ways. I Am Just and Merciful. I want no one to perish.

**Romans 3:26**
And He is entirely fair and just in this present time when He declares
sinners to be right in His sight because they believe in Jesus. (NLT)

**I myself no longer live, but Christ lives in me.**
(Galatians 2:20)

# *"True Order"*

**Romans 11:36**
For everything comes from Him; everything exists
by His power and is intended for His glory. (NLT)

When you haphazardly look at the order of creation without God the Creator, it is easy for us to get all puffed up in our human pride thinking that the universe revolves around us—that we are at the top of the food chain and in control of our own destiny and the destiny of others as well. But when you take a closer look at the order of the universe and the life God has created, you will discover a very precise and ingenious plan. The Master Creator designed everything that exists to fit perfectly together in an order that would preserve life on this very small orb in a universe that is so big it cannot be logically fathomed by the human mind. God's creation is too complex for human understanding, no matter how much we learn with our intellect. It would take an eternity and beyond to uncover the extent of God's glorious creativity. Although our ability to create is an endowment from our Creator, it is indeed very limited, and no man will ever be able to create even the simplest ingredient of the earth or the simplest form of life.

Without knowing the true order of creation, you will never know how you fit into the great scheme of the things that God has planned. You will be confused at best and your pride will blind you from the Truth. Human pride is nothing more than a deadly sin that comes from the king of all pride, the Devil. Thinking the universe revolves around you and this life is all about you is foolish and deadly. The LORD created everything that exists and without the power of His Word holding it all together we could not exist. What God created, He created for His glory in Christ Jesus, and for His good purpose. If you cannot accept the Truth and humble yourself before the One who sustains your life, you are lost and you are headed for a horrible life-journey through a terrible darkness that will never end. Learn your true place in God's order of things my friend, for He made you just a little lower than the angels for now, but one day, if you accept His majestic plan for you and His Creation, you will reign with the Lord and the angels will serve you.

## A Whisper of Hope

**You are Mine, dear child...**Everything you have is from Me. It is my choice to give you the breath of life; to sustain you. I love you so much that I made a way for you to be with Me forever. Don't believe the pride that is in you, for it will keep you from receiving all that I have for you. I AM God.

**Jeremiah 29:11**
"For I know the plans I have for you," says the LORD.
"They are plans for good and not for disaster, to give you a future and a hope. (NLT)

**Pride goes before destruction, and haughtiness before a fall.**
(Proverbs 16:18)

# "Blood and Faith"

**Romans 12:3**
As God's messenger, I give each of you this warning:
Be honest in your estimate of yourselves, measuring
your value by how much faith God has given you. (NLT)

As a Christian, I know that Jesus Christ is God in the flesh and the only True God. He left the glory of Heaven to save His people, Israel, and the rest of mankind from perishing into eternal darkness. I also know that I owe Him my life, for He reached down from Heaven and plucked me out of the darkness that was eating my soul alive. It was only by the mercy and grace of God that I am alive and able to share the Truth that has saved many from the pits of Hell. I take no credit for the good things God has done in my life. One of the most freeing things I have learned in my new life is; if we are going to compare ourselves with anyone, it should be Jesus Christ, because He became a man and lived by perfectly righteous standards that He calls us to live by. God doesn't want us to think of ourselves as any better or any less than anyone else in this fallen world, because no mortal human being is able to live up to the holy standards of Jesus. It is our fallen human nature to compare ourselves with other fallen people, but we are all in the same boat, paddling frantically to stay afloat with a sinking feeling in our gut, but hoping to be saved.

You probably think there are many better off, better looking, and better at everything than you are, but if they don't have the gift of salvation, they have nothing—only fleeting promises of a dying world and the eternal condemnation when it ends. But if you are an adopted child of the Living God, you have it all my friend. And when you are fully grown in Christ, He will have made you perfect in every way, for you will put on your glorious new body to live in the Light of God's Glory forever. To be confident in your faith, you must think of yourself as a redeemed child of the Living God, cleansed by the blood of Jesus and saved by the grace of God. Those who are alive cannot save themselves. The dead cannot bring themselves back to life. The lost cannot find their way through the darkness and the broken cannot fix themselves. We are all at the mercy and grace of the Living God.

## A Whisper of Hope

**I create all peoples, dear child...**in My Likeness, but I do not create people all the same. When you belong to Me, you are an equal part of One Body with many different parts. You are a part of My Body the Church, and I made you to be an intricate part of My Eternal Body. That is who you are!

**Ephesians 2:13**
But now you belong to Christ Jesus. Though you once were far away from God,
now you have been brought near to Him because of the blood of Christ. (NLT)

**He saved us, not because of the good things we did, but because of His mercy.**
(Titus 3:3)

# "God Filled"

**Psalm 145:16**
You open Your hand and satisfy
the desire of every living thing. (NKJ)

When the LORD created human beings, He created us with deep and eternal desires that only He could fill. Although everything depends on God to exist, all living organisms depend on God to sustain life, especially human beings. If you have the normal God given wits about you, you have longed for that one person or something that would be perfect in every way that would make you feel complete and satisfied. We also look for someone to love us in spite of our short comings. Many of us spend a lifetime searching for a soul mate that could ease the pain of living and comfort us when we are life-weary; someone outside of ourselves that would bring purpose and peace into our lives. And after a while many of us get discourage because we are unsatisfied, alone, empty, and losing hope of ever finding that someone. Sadly there are many of us who, out of desperation, settle for less and it leads us astray. We are spiritually needy creatures. We need understanding, forgiveness, and reassurance that all is well and we are not alone. We need love and that some One we can fully trust.

If you are feeling life-weary and alone, believing there is no one for you, I know how it feels, because I was once in that place after 55 years of life. I learned that we will never find that someone until you meet the One who carefully formed you in your mother's womb and gave you the breath of life. The Lord God of Heaven and Earth is the only One who can fill your needs—the emptiness that He created in your heart. Most people search the world for something that would complete who they are, but to no avail. Many people go to the grave empty, alone, bitter and blaming the God they don't even believe in. But there is One Person my friend that can fill your heart with everlasting peace, love, joy, and hope. Before you give up, let your God and Savior, Jesus Christ fill that void and you will know that your life is complete and is not in vain. There is no One as wonderful, as loving, as forgiving or more faithful. And if you truly search for Him, He will truly find you!

## A Whisper of Hope

**I AM the One you search for, my child...**Don't be fooled, for only I can satisfy the longings of your heart. I have given you everything you need to satisfy the hungers that you have for life. Do not be dismayed, because I Am coming for all those who know Me, and they will be filled with so much more than they can ever imagine.

**Isaiah 26:3**
You will keep in perfect peace all who trust
in You, whose thoughts are fixed on You! (NLT)

**Be filled with the fruit of your salvation—those good things that are
produced in your life by Jesus Christ.**
(Philippians 1:11)

# "God Fellowship"

**2 John 1:9**
For if you wander beyond the teachings of Christ, you will not
have fellowship with God. But if you continue in the teachings of
Christ, you will have fellowship with both the Father and the Son. (NLT)

As Christians, it is imperative that we rely on the indwelling of the Holy Spirit to help us discern the true Gospel of Jesus Christ from the many false gospels that are flooding the churches of this fallen world. The forces of darkness that manipulate the world are also infecting the body of Christ; the Christian people of His Church. Satan want us to believe his lies, which are very convincing if you are not in true fellowship with the LORD. Those who have rejected the Truth for the false truth are joining the fight against Jesus Christ and His Church body. The Devil wants to confuse and distort the Good News Message that true Christians stake their lives on. This is why we must have the Power and Wisdom of God planted firmly in our hearts and minds. We must stay closely connected to the Word of God so we can remain in fellowship with the Father and the Son through the Holy Spirit. We must remain strong and unmoving in our faith that Jesus is Lord and He is the only Way.

For thousands of years Satan has been putting a plan in place to copy the deity of God so He can oppose Christ and take the world by deceit. It is an imitation of the True God Head. In these last days, Satan will rise up in power and deceive the world into believing he is God. Don't be duped by the false gospels of the Devil, my dear friends. Instead, believe in the Truth of God's Word. For the Truth is reliable and does not change with the times. When you have a firm grip on the Truth, you do not need to fear the Enemy, for he is powerless in the Light of God's saving grace. When you belong to Jesus, you have an open door into God's Presence where you will find eternal fellowship with the Father, the Son, and the Holy Spirit. And with this holy combo you will have the wisdom of the Father, your salvation in the Son, and the power of the Holy Spirit—Satan loses, and you win.

## A Whisper of Hope

**I offer you fellowship, My child...**a relationship that will never fail you nor forsake you; one that you can count on in every circumstance, whether good or bad. It is our constant fellowship that keeps you safe and secure from the Enemy of our soul. Fellowship with Me and live!

**Romans 16:17-18**
And now I make one more appeal, my dear brothers and sisters. Watch out
for people who cause divisions and upset people's faith by teaching things that
are contrary to what you have been taught. Stay away from them. Such people
are not serving Christ our Lord; they are serving their own personal interests.
By smooth talk and glowing words they deceive innocent people. (NLT)

**You can't drink from the cup of the Lord and from the cup of demons, too.**
(1 Corinthians 10:21)

# *"Discovery"*

**Hosea 6:3**
Oh, that we might know the LORD! Let us press on to
know Him. Then He will respond to us as surely as the
arrival of dawn or the coming of rains in early spring. (NLT)

The LORD has revealed everything we need to know during our short life on this earth. We have a loving God who wants the best for all people. He has graciously given us the Truth, so we would know how to live and how not to live, and the consequences of our actions. He has given us the Perfect Plan for everlasting life and the Way to achieve it. We must put to death our old sinful life and be made a new creation in Christ Jesus. We must get rid of our evil ways for His righteous ways. When we surrender to His authority, we become one with the Holy Spirit. And only then will we have the power and wisdom to navigate safely through the darkness of this wicked world that is quickly fading away. When we know the Lord God and place all of our hope in Him, there is peace. We no longer have to worry about this fallen world or what the Enemy does, because no matter what happens, all of God's redeemed children have the promises of the LORD to back them up.

What a tremendous miracle it will be when the Lord God restores His creation to perfection, giving us a new body, a new Earth, a new Heaven, and a new universe, where we will spend an eternity discovering just how big and awesome our Living God really is. It is impossible to imagine what it will be like to physically see, touch, and hear the Lord speak, for He will explain the mysteries of life and who He is. God wants you to know Him as completely as humanly possible, so you will be prepared for eternity. Spend every day in His Presence, reading and studying His Word, because the Lord will give you the godly wisdom and knowledge to improve your quality of living in this fallen world. You would be wise to press on to learn all you can about the One, True God who knows all things. The Lord wants you to experience the best He has to offer. And when you begin to discover God my friend, your life will never be the same again.

## A Whisper of Hope

**You need only ask, dear child...**and I will reveal Myself to you. Although you cannot handle all that I Am in your current fallen state, I will resurrect you into a new glorified body that can. But for now, you must learn the basics, trust in My promises, and wait patiently for Me to bring you Home.

**1 John 5:19, 20**
We know that we are children of God and that the world
around us is under the power and control of the evil one.
And we know that the Son of God has come, and He has
given us understanding so that we can know the True God. (NLT)

**In just a short time, He will restore us so we can live in His Presence.**
(Hosea 6:2)

# *"Master Plan"*

**Psalm 129:2, 4**
From my earliest youth my enemies have persecuted me, but
they have never been able to finish me off. But the LORD is
good; He has cut the cords used by the ungodly to bind me. (NLT)

The deeper my relationship with the Lord becomes, the clearer I see my past and the better I understand this life. Prior to my relationship with the Lord, I didn't really understand anything about the nightmare I called life. Although I believed in an Almighty God and His Authority over our lives, I had no usable knowledge about God's character or why He created me. I was enslaved to the wicked ways of this world, and being led through this life like a steer to a slaughter house. But unbeknownst to me, God was using my enslavement to better prepare me for His good purpose. He helped me understand how sin so easily enslaves us and why we rebel against the righteous ways of God. I learned that this fallen world can easily manipulate anyone into believing its endless lies that lead us away from the Truth of God's Word and into a destructive lifestyle. And most importantly, I discovered that our Sovereign God allows us to make our own choices and then uses them, whether good or bad, to finish out His eternal Plan for all those who are called by His Name.

Our Lord God is the Master and He wastes nothing, especially when it comes to the lives of the people He chooses to be a part of His great Plan for man. Does this mean that God just uses us and we have no say? Of course not! But when you give your life to the Lord you can fully trust in the fact that He is perfectly holy and just and His righteousness is flawless. He cannot lie, nor does He ever deceive anyone. God also keeps every promise faithfully. I have experienced, the saving grace and, transforming power of God. And even though I sometimes wonder about some of God's methods, I know that everything He does and allows is for the good of His Kingdom to come, and the people who live and suffer for Jesus. If you are a slave to sin and this wicked world is leading nowhere but down, you have a Savior that can set you free and guide you Home.

## A Whisper of Hope

**Your understanding My child, is limited…**this is why you must trust in My infinite wisdom. I created this life and I use everything for My good purpose. I Am Faithful and True, and I lead no one astray. I am a gracious Master that wastes nothing.

**Romans 8:28**
And we know that God causes everything to work together for the good
of those who love God and are called according to His purpose for them. (NLT)

**But even if you should suffer for righteousness' sake, you are blessed.**
(1 Peter 3:14)

# *"God Says"*

**Zechariah 1:4**
This is what the LORD Almighty says:
'Turn from your evil ways and stop all your evil practices.' (NLT)

Everything we do in this life is recorded in the books of God, which will be open on the Day of our Judgment. God knows everything that is said, done, and thought. When people partake in the evil ways of this wicked world, God knows every detail and records it all. Nothing is hidden and all will be exposed. Throughout the ages, God has given us many warnings about the eternal consequences that sin and disobedience bring. God hates every kind of evil and sin because pure holiness is His nature. We must remember that God did not create the evil that is killing our souls and world. Lucifer, the fallen angel did. He chose to rebel against God and became the Devil, whom God named Satan. He is pure evil in the darkest sense, and his power is great. When you combine the evil power of Satan with the sinful nature of mankind, you have a fallen world that is saturated with wickedness and every kind of evil. The deceit of Satan is making our world a darker place, making it harder and harder for people to discern the evil from the good, which is making it harder to see the traps.

But there is coming a day when the Almighty God will unleash His anger upon the wicked people of this world and purge the evil. Everything in this world will suffer the vengeance of God's anger, for no one will be able to hide from it. If you want to escape God's fury, my friend, it would behoove you to surrender to the only One who can save you. Only the Son of God has the power to set you free from the evil that is consuming this world. The death and resurrection power of Jesus Christ is the only hope you have of escaping the final wrath of God. When you surrender to Christ, He will break the chains that hold you captive to sin and the evil of Satan, and you will be made free to discover the joy of God. For as an adopted child of the Living God, you are as pure and holy as Christ is pure and holy in the eyes of the LORD, and nothing can snatch you from His hands. That is real joy!

## A Whisper of Hope

**My warnings, dear child, are clear...**and easy to understand. The power of sin and death over your flesh is a powerful force to be reckoned with, but I have defeated them on your behalf. Do not ignore the Truth, because I AM the only Savior you have.

**Ezekiel 7:8-9**
Soon I will pour My fury to complete your punishment
for all your disgusting behavior. I will neither spare nor
pity you. I will repay you for all your detestable practices.
Then you will know that it is I, the LORD, who is striking the blow. (NLT)

**For evildoers shall be cut off, but those who wait on the LORD,
they shall inherit the earth.**
(Psalm 37:9)

# "True Warriors"

**2 Corinthians 11:14**
But I am not surprised! Even Satan can disguise himself as an angel of light. (NLT)

Satan is the master of disguise and deceitful lies. He blinds us with his evil ways and teaches us his dark arts. We live in a fallen world that is confused and desperately grasping at straws hoping to get lucky. Unfortunately, many will deliberately or blindly choose the Devil's straw of darkness and death and suffer the eternal consequences of their pick. Some will pick the middle straw that could bring them hope, but without a firm grasp on what it means they will lose their way, only to be fooled by the deceitful, smooth sounding lies of the false prophets who are far removed from God and the Truth. Satan and his many false prophets have tricked this fallen world into believing so many of his clever lies that it is difficult for most people to discern the difference between what is right and what is not. There will be a lot of unsuspecting, precious souls who will go to their graves completely fooled by the Devil and they will pay the eternal price for their foolish choices.

As children of the Living God, Christians must stay connected to God through the Holy Spirit, who has the power and wisdom that we don't have, which will help us decipher what is true and what is false. Without this vital connection on a daily basis, we are more likely to either question the authority of Scripture, or follow the voice of a very clever enemy. But by staying grounded in the Word of God with the Holy spirit as our Helper, we create a solid foundation that brings both peace and victory. The war against God is raging and the battle is hard. If we are to persevere with the faith and confidence that glorifies our Savior, we must be refreshed in His Presence, where we receive the strength and the courage to go back into battle for those who are unaware that a battle is even being fought. When we surrender our lives to the King, we not only become God's adopted children, but we become warriors, saints, and priests. If you join the fight my friend, you will one day rule and reign with the King of the universe, Jesus Christ—this is what we are being trained for!

## A Whisper of Hope

**Press on Christian soldier...**for the war is almost over. For when My recruitment has reached its allotted number, I will bring an everlasting peace to this war ravaged world. And it will remain that way until the day when I make everything new and eternal.

**2 Peter 2:1-3**
There were also false prophets in Israel, just as there will be false teachings among you. They will cleverly teach their destructive heresies about God and even turn against their Master who bought them. Theirs will be a swift and terrible end. Many will follow their evil teaching and shameful immorality. And because of them, Christ and His true Way will be slandered. In their greed they will make up clever lies to get hold of your money. But God condemned them long ago, and their destruction is on the way. (NLT)

**Don't be misled. Remember that you can't ignore God and get away with it.**
(Titus 6:7)

# *"Master Builder"*

**Psalm 143:10**
Teach me to do Your will, for You are my God. May Your
gracious Spirit lead me forward on a firm footing. (NLT)

Every person born into this fallen world is born with a sinful nature and it is this nature that wills us to do what we desire, rather than doing what God wants. It is our fallen human nature to sin first, and then think of ways that we can justify our sin. Sinning is far removed from breaking the laws that men set in place for us to follow, because sinning against our Holy God is more like rebelling against the One who has the ultimate Authority over us. Breaking the laws that other people make for us normally brings only temporary consequences if we are caught and convicted. But we cannot break the Law of God and get away with it, because the Lord knows everything we do and say and think. It is written in stone that all unrepentant sin brings a guilty verdict with eternal condemnation.

When we are summoned by the Lord to change our rebellious ways, we must surrender to Him as natural born sinners in need of His mercy and amazing grace. We must acknowledge that we are shamefully guilty of all our sins and deserve nothing less than condemnation for our lawlessness. We must ask Him to forgive and forget our rebellion and to make us right with God. And when we are truly sincere in this, He empowers us with the Holy Spirit so we can learn the Truth and be able to live within the boundaries He has set for us.

Don't be left behind in the dark, grasping for some solid ground and searching for a place to hide. Instead, surrender your life and will to the Lord, and you will be sure that for the rest of your life your total transformation is securely in His hands. God will never lead you astray nor will He leave you incomplete. Your sanctification will be the laying of a solid foundation on which you will build a strong working relationship with the Master Builder of the universe and life. We were not created to build our lives apart from our Creator. Do not miss the awesome opportunity you have to work with the Master Builder, because without His Perfect Plan, what you build will not pass the test of fire and it will burn to the ground with you in it.

## A Whisper of Hope

**You need My Help, child...**for the fire will destroy whatever you build without Me. Only I can show you how to build a lasting life with protection. Without Me your house will fall into the hands of the Enemy and burn. Stand apart from the world and stand with Me, for I Am the Master Builder.

**1 Peter 2:4, 5**
Come to Christ, who is the living cornerstone of God's temple.
He was rejected by the people, but He is precious to God who chose Him.
And now God is building you, as living stones, into His spiritual temple. (NLT)

**Listen to Me, My children, for blessed are those who keep My ways.**
(Proverbs 8:32)

# "Son of Man"

**Galatians 2:20**
I myself no longer live, but Christ lives in me. I live my life in this earthly body
by trusting in the Son of God, who loved me and gave Himself for me. (NLT)

It is through the sacrifice of the Messiah, that we are given the promise of a new and ever-lasting life. It is only by the resurrection power of God that we are able to nail our old lives of sin to the Cross of Christ, and be resurrected into a new and everlasting life in our Savior, Jesus Christ. Our saving God loves us so much that He gave the world His only begotten Son to die and take our punishment. The blood of Jesus cleanses all of our sins, His death becomes our own deserved death, and His resurrection becomes our hope. This selfless act of love bought our freedom from the power of sin and the fear of death, and we can now live in the Presence of our Holy God and Creator. The Living God who created you my friend, took upon Himself the sins of the world in order to save you from certain death and eternal destruction. He did this because He loves you unconditionally and knew that you could not save yourself. The power of sin and its consequences are way beyond our finite power to comprehend, to control, or to conquer without the Son of God.

Because our Lord God created us as eternal beings with both physical and spiritual natures, He knew that the consequences of sin would utterly destroy us. So He left the glory of Heaven to do what we could not do ourselves—die the sinners death, pay the sinners price, and then be resurrected into a glorified body that would never again die. And this undeserved gift will be passed on to those who believe and put their trust and hope in the Cross of our Savior. God wants no one to suffer the penalty of sin that His Son received for us, because He knows we are but dust in the wind without Him. All of us are weak and vulnerable in the face of temptations, and our God takes no joy in losing one single soul to a punishment that is perfectly just. Should you lose your eternal life to the darkness void of God's Light, it is lost forever my friend, and you will never again have the chance you have now to reconcile with the One who holds the key to your eternal life in His nail pierced hands.

## A Whisper of Hope

**I came, I died, and I rose again...**for you, My child. I did it out of love, I did it for you. You no longer have to die a sinner's death, because I died in your place. But don't try it alone, for if you do, you will truly die over and over and over again for all eternity.

**John 3:13**
For only I, the Son of Man, have come to earth and will return to Heaven again.
And as Moses lifted up the bronze snake on a pole in the wilderness, so I, the Son of Man,
must be lifted up on a pole, so that everyone who believes in Me will have eternal life. (NLT)

**Christ, our Passover Lamb, has been sacrificed for us.**
(1 Corinthians 5:7)

# *"God's Rescue"*

**Psalm 73:2**
But as for me, I came so close to the edge of the cliff.
My feet were slipping and I was almost gone. (NLT)

Much like the psalmist who penned these words, I, too, (like so many others) was almost over the edge of the abyss, but unlike the psalmist, I (like many others) was unaware of the danger or the need to be rescued. I knew little about the horrors that awaited me when I ended up in Hell. I just wanted to escape the pain and hopelessness of my life in this depressing world that made no sense. I could not conjure up a good or believable reason why I existed, or where it was all headed. I had heard rumors of how good Heaven would be and how only a few were actually good enough to get through the pearly gates. And even though Hell didn't sound so good, I thought how much worse could it be than living in this horrible world that thrived on violence, death, and the suffering that most of us go through? But as I was creeping closer to the end, I was rescued by a Savior, the same God who created me. The Good Shepherd literally reached down from Heaven and grabbed me before I went over the edge and into the abyss. He sent me a human angel to intervene in my self-destruction and then introduce me to Jesus, who began to pull me out of the darkness that was draining the life out of my soul. I was saved and redeemed in God's rescue.

Jesus Christ is the only Savior we have, for all others are cheap imitators who will trick you into taking the bait that Satan puts before us. These deceitful, clever traps of the Devil promise you much, but the lies are dangerous and futile, for they only lead into a horrible nightmare from which you may never wake up. How I thank our Savior for taking the punishment I so rightly deserved by dying the death He did not deserve. If you want to know the Truth about life and death and about Heaven and Hell there is no better place to start than on your knees with your hands raised high towards the heavens, praising the One who created you, then paid the price to save you. Christ Jesus is your only Hope for salvation. There are no other ways. These are the options my friend: God or Satan; life or death; God or the world; light or darkness; sin or righteousness; right or wrong. For with God there is no middle ground and no gray areas. You are either for Him or you are against Him.

## A Whisper of Hope

**Take My hand, dear child…**let Me pull you back into the land of the living. Once you were dead in your sin and slipping into the darkness. I came to rescue you from the darkness and to give you the eternal Light of everlasting life. Take My hand and hold on tight!

**Proverbs 18:10**
The Name of the LORD is a strong fortress;
the godly run to Him and are safe. (NLT)

**O LORD, You alone can heal me, You alone can save.**
(Jeremiah 17:14)

# *"The Word"*

**Isaiah 56:11**
It is the same with My Word. I send it out and it always produces fruit.
It will accomplish all I want it to, and it will prosper everywhere I send it. (NLT)

The wisdom of God's Word is infinite. It is always perfect and it never changes. It is always right and never leads anyone astray. It is always fair and just. It is absolutely true and nothing can stand against it. It is our lifeline to God and our only hope. God's Word brings life, not death. It saves, rather than destroys. It heals instead of wounds. It nourishes our lives and keeps us healthy. It is food for our souls and it makes us wise. It builds us up, instead of tearing us down. It is solid as a rock and stands firm in every storm. It endures all things. The Word of God is full of living power. It is sharper than the sharpest knife, cutting deep into our innermost thoughts and desires. It is a lamp for our feet and a light for our paths. It gives us understanding and joy. The Word of God never disappoints us, nor does it ever lie. It is always faithful and brings us comfort. It protects us from the Enemy and gives us peace. It is eternal. It cannot be disproved and will never be defeated. It will teach you about the One who created you and why you exist. It will show you how to make the best of what you have. It will show you the best way to live this life, and it will tell you what lies beyond this short life. It is the only Source for Truth. If you wanted to know how a car works and how to fix it when it is broken, the best person to give you that information is one who either makes them or fixes them. And the same also applies to our broken world and our broken lives. The Lord God created life and He knows everything about it, including how to fix us when we are broken. Living apart from the Word is both foolish and frivolous, for without the Word my friend, your short life will end badly and you will experience something far worse.

## A Whisper of Hope

**I gave you My Word, dear child…**so that you would know how much I love you. My Word is the only hope you have in this evil world that worships the dark things of Satan. I have given you My life and My blood to save you. Now give Me your life in return.

**John 1:1-5**
In the beginning the Word already existed. He was with God, and He was God.
He was in the beginning with God. He created everything there is. Nothing exists that He didn't make. Life itself was in Him, and this life gives light to everyone. The Light shines through the darkness, and the darkness can never extinguish it. (NLT)

**Your words are what sustain me. They bring me great joy and are my heart's desire.**
(Jeremiah 15:16)

# *"From Heaven"*

**Psalm 63:7-8**
I think of how much you have helped me; I sing
for joy in the shadow of Your protecting wings; I
follow close behind you; Your strong right hand
holds me securely. (NLT)

Without the saving grace of God as our hope and without the Holy Spirit as our Helper there would be very little to sing joyously about, because without the protection and strength of our Sovereign God, we would either be annihilated by the mighty forces of the universe or be totally consumed by the evil that has taken over our world. Without God's infinite wisdom and the eternal Light of His Son, we would be helplessly lost in the dark, terrified and uncertain about the future. Without the death and resurrection of Jesus Christ, we would all be victims of this evil world that is progressively going from bad to worse. Without Jesus, there would be no truth, no place for shelter, and no one to save us from the Enemy of our souls.

Our Lord and God is Jesus Christ. He is your only Savior and your only hope for life. He holds the power of life and death in His hands. Relying on anyone or anything else but the Living God is much like chasing the wind and expecting to find where it comes from and where it is going. Christ Jesus is the only Light you can trust in this dark world. When you run into the shadow of His wings, you will find rest for your weary soul, comfort for your troubled heart, and the strength to persevere whatever this evil world does. When you walk with Jesus my friend, you walk with confidence, because you know that nothing, not even the power of Hell can separate you from His love. This fallen world can only promise you a life of pain, suffering, and death. Nothing good comes from this world. The good things we have come only from above. What the world offers is straight out of Hell and ends up in Hell. What our Lord God offers is perfect and it lasts forever!

## A Whisper of Hope

**Weigh your options, child**...and you will find I AM the best for you. The life instructions I give are eternal and they do not change. When you live for Me, you live in the glory of My eternal Light. When you live for this world, you live in total darkness and one day it will consume you forever!

**Romans 8:11**
The Spirit of God, who raised Jesus from the dead, lives in you.
And just as He raised Christ from the dead, He will give life to
your mortal body by this same Spirit living within you. (NLT)

**If God is for us, who can ever be against us?**
(Romans 8:31)

# *"The Future"*

**Zephaniah 2:2-4**
Gather while there is still time, before judgment begins and your opportunity is blown away like chaff. Act now, before the fierce fury of the LORD falls and the terrible day of the LORD'S anger begins. Beg the LORD to save you—all you who are humble, all you who uphold justice. Walk humbly and do what is right. Perhaps even yet the LORD will protect you from His anger on that day of destruction. (NLT)

The Lord has always been faithful to warn the world about His coming judgments. He does not sugar coat the destruction that will befall the people of this fallen world who reject His righteous ways. God is being more than patient and long suffering for mankind because He wants no one left behind to suffer the terrible destruction and horror of God's final wrath. It will be a dark and frightening time for those who love this wicked world more than God. The death and destruction that God pours out upon this earth for seven years will be unlike anything the earth has ever experienced. The Word of God not only explains the terrible suffering that the entire world will experience, but He also tells us how we can escape the horror of it all.

The picture the Bible paints from the Old Testament prophets through the Book of Revelation gives us a pretty clear picture of how He will bring about the completion of His Plan for Man. We know the ending of this life is not good for those who reject the Living God, Jesus Christ, because they will spend eternity in Hell. But those who are called by the Savior's Name, will live forever in the glory of God's Presence. The Lord wants no one to be thrown into the eternal Lake of Fire with Satan and his fallen angels, because He gives most of us plenty of opportunities to accept His gift of salvation. Our Gracious God has given us glimpses into the future so we would know what to do in order to escape the last days of this evil world. Pay close attention to God's Word and take heed my friends, for it will save your life.

## A Whisper of Hope

**Look closely, My child…**for I have shown you future days. I have told you how My Story ends and when your eternal life begins. I have explained in detail what lies ahead for this fallen world, and how you can escape its destruction. It's a simple plan and one that I give you the power to follow.

**Ezekiel 33:11**
"As surely as I live", says the Sovereign LORD, "I take no pleasure in the death of wicked people. I only want them to turn from their wicked ways so they can live." (NLT)

**But You, O Lord, are a God full of compassion and
gracious long suffering and abundant in mercy and truth.**
(Psalm 86:15)

# *"God Sense"*

**Proverbs 2:7**
He grants a treasure of good sense to the godly. He is
their shield, protecting those who walk with integrity. (NLT)

We are adopted into God's family when we accept the death and resurrection of our Lord God and Savior, Jesus Christ as our hope and salvation. And as a child of the Living God, the indwelling of the Holy Spirit gives us the desire to learn the Truth about God, what this life is all about, and where it is all headed. When we know the Truth, we learn to discern the good from the bad, right from wrong, and the truth from lies. The Lord will tell us when to say yes and when to say no. He will show us His will for our lives and how to achieve it. He will help us live a godly lifestyle that will please Him and bring us real joy. And as we grow in our knowledge of God, we will develop an up-close and personal relationship with our Lord God and Savior, the King of the universe.

When you get tired of the lies and broken promises of this fallen world, you need to seek the absolute truth from God, for it is the only Truth. When you know the Truth you will desire to change from an ungodly lifestyle to a godly one. The Lord will show you the simple ways to achieve a new life that is pleasing to God—a life that is not always easy to live, but one that makes it worth living. You have a great incentive my friend, to live in the Way that God desires for you to live, because your reward will be everlasting life in the glory of God's Light. Through the wisdom of the Holy Spirit, God gives you the sense to stay clear of the things that will cause you to drift into the darkness that this fallen world loves and embraces. There are many paths that are set before us, but only one path will lead you to your eternal Home, built by the mighty hands of our Creator, Christ Jesus. The key to your eternal Home is held in the hands of the Master Builder, who will also usher you Home safely.

## A Whisper of Hope

**I offer you eternal life, dear child...**in a Home I am building just for you. I give you everything you need to get there, but you must remain in Me, because apart from Me, your sense is godless. Let Me be your guide and I will make sure you get Home safely.

**Isaiah 33:5-6**
Though the LORD is very great and lives in Heaven, He will make Jerusalem His home of justice and righteousness. In that day He will be your sure foundation, providing a rich store of salvation, wisdom, and knowledge. The fear of the LORD is the key to this treasure. (NLT)

**But You O LORD, are a shield around me.**
(Psalm 3:3)

# "God's Gift"

**Mark 7:15**
"You are not defiled by what you eat;
you are defiled by what you say and do." (NLT)

U nder the new covenant between God and man, we are saved by grace through faith in the good works of our Lord God and Savior, Jesus Christ. We or the Jewish people no longer have to live under the old law of the Mosaic covenant that God gave His people, Israel. But God's Law, the Ten Commandments, is for all people of this world to obey; no one is exempt. Although God's Law is good, simple, reasonable, and makes sense, it is not easy to keep because of our inherent sinful nature to rebel against God. So the Lord sent us a Savior that would put in place the new covenant of grace.

We are currently living in the Church age, with Jesus Christ as the head and Christians as His Body, so what we eat does not concern our Lord God. He is more concerned with our thoughts, words, and actions, because it is these things that defile the Body of Christ and if gone unchecked can darken the heart and kill the soul. We must rely on the Word of God to help us discern what is bad, false, and godless. We must control what we put into our minds, for it is our fallen human nature to choose things that satisfy the flesh rather than the God given desires of our hearts. We must understand the world around us so we can better prepare ourselves for the battles to come. We must keep our focus on God and the things which are eternal in nature. For when we fill our lives with Him, who bore the sins of the world, we are assured the victory that is in Christ Jesus. We cannot stand blameless and pure without the blood of Jesus covering our sins, but we can stand strong in our faith that Jesus is Lord and He is the One who keeps us pure and holy.

## A Whisper of Hope

**I came to save you, My child...**from the Law that you cannot keep; a law that always condemns. You should rejoice, for I accomplished what you cannot. My grace is always sufficient, for your good works are not.

**1 Corinthians 3:16, 17**
Do you not know that you are the temple of God and that the Spirit of God dwells in you? If anyone defiles the temple of God, God will destroy him. For the temple of God is holy. (NKJ)

**For the wages of sin is death,
but the gift of God is eternal life in Christ Jesus our Lord.**
(Romans 5:23)

# "Trust God"

**1 Timothy 6:17**
Tell those who are rich in this world not to be proud and not to trust
in their money, which will soon be gone. But their trust should be in
the Living God, who richly gives us all we need for our enjoyment. (NLT)

Everything of this fallen world is quickly fading away and will one day be replaced when the Lord makes everything new. Nothing from this evil world is trustworthy or true. We cannot rely on anyone but our Lord God and Savior Jesus Christ, for only He can save us from the destruction that is coming to this fallen world. We cannot take anything with us from this world when we die, only our faith in the promises of God. The Lord Jesus did not come into our world to condemn us or to make us feel good about ourselves, but to save us from our sins and show us how in need we are of His saving grace. He came to forgive our sins and promise us an eternal life as it was meant to be. This promise of living with our God and Savior forever is what gets us through this difficult life, because this world always lets us down and can only promise death.

The Almighty God is the only One we can trust, because all the promises of this dying world are also dying. The world we are now living in is temporary at best and it can only produce those things which are also temporary. And people who love this temporary world and its riches will eventually be destroyed and replaced with eternal riches. We were not created to live a temporary life focused on ourselves. Rather, we were created as eternal beings that would live glorifying the God who created us in His image, to live pure and holy lives, and to worship Him with our praise and thanksgiving. Don't be sucked into the lies of this evil world my friend, because if you do you will be sorry. And do not become so comfortable in the promises of God that you take your eyes off the prize that never stops giving.

## A Whisper of Hope

**You can trust all My Promises, dear child...**for they are not only good in every way, but they are also eternal. I Am the Infinite Lord of creation and I created you to be eternal. Therefore, all that I promise you is yours forever.

**Hebrews 6:18-19**
So God has given us both His promise and His oath. These two things are unchangeable because it is impossible for God to lie. Therefore we who have fled to Him for refuge can take new courage, for we can hold on to His promise with confidence. This confidence is like a strong and trustworthy anchor for our souls. It leads us through the curtain of Heaven into God's inner sanctuary. (NLT)

**See, God has come to save me, I will trust in Him and not be afraid.**

(Isaiah 12:2)

# *"God Power"*

**Proverbs 25:28.**
A person without self-control is as defenseless
as a city with broken-down walls. (NLT)

Man powered self-control is undependable and cannot be trusted because it will eventually give in and fail you miserably. Our human will power is flawed because we are born with a fallen, sinful nature that easily succumbs to the weakness of the flesh. And it is this inherent human weakness to sin that gives the Devil a strong foothold on our lives so he can slowly coerce us into the darkness where he reigns. Satan is a powerful force to be reckoned with and without the power of the Holy Spirit we are as good as dead, because without the protection of Christ, the powers of darkness can easily break through our weak defenses and overpower us. Without God, we are like the cities of old that had no walls to protect them from their enemies. And much like those vulnerable cities, our human defenses against the evil powers of darkness are weak at best.

If we are to keep the enemy at bay, we need the Presence of God at our side. If we are to control our urges to sin and our human nature to rebel against the righteousness of God, we need the indwelling of the Holy Spirit to help us stand strong in our faith so we do not fall prey to the powerful Enemy of our souls. There is no other way my friend. It is either God's Way, or the highway to Hell. Sin and death are the curses that Satan holds highly in esteem and Christ Jesus is the only One who can save you from them. The Lord came and defeated both sin and death for those who want more than this life can offer them. The Lord gladly took the full wrath of God for your sins. God came. God delivered. Now it's up to you to either accept His gracious offer to help battle the dark forces you cannot defeat, or try it on your own and lose the gift of eternal life with your Maker.

## A Whisper of Hope

**I came to save you, My child...**not to see you succumb to the powers that want you dead; eternally dead. I did all the suffering and dying so you would not have to. Now all you have to do is choose my way and live in the Light of My Truth.

**Psalm 97:10**
You who love the LORD hate evil. He protects the lives of
His godly people and rescues them from the power of the wicked. (NLT)

**Take heart, because I have overcome the world.**
(John 16:33)

# *"Almighty One"*

**Jeremiah 10:10**
But the LORD is the only true God. He is the
everlasting King! The whole earth trembles at
His anger. The nations hide before His wrath. (NLT)

E ven in this Church Age, the LORD still speaks to His people through many prophets, but He does not make it known when He pours out His anger upon this wicked world. Although God does not often speak in a voice we can hear, He does speak directly into our hearts through the Holy Spirit who dwells within us. The Lord God came the first time as our Savior, to save mankind from their sins and the condemnation that was deserved. But when He comes the second time, He is coming as the conquering King with fire in His eyes and a sword in His mouth to destroy His enemies who refuse to fear Him. It is true that Jesus Christ is our gracious and forgiving God who loves His creation, but we must not forget the power behind the One God who created all things. Although He came to do for us what we could not do for ourselves and to satisfy the anger of God, the Son will put an end to the wickedness of this world by burning it up with Hell's fire along with those who follow its evil ways. And God warns us that it won't be pretty, for there will be a lot of suffering, pain, blood and death.

Our Lord God and Savior, Jesus Christ is King and you need to fear His power. You need to let the Savior open your eyes to the Truth. You must respect the Power of God for it is infinitely more powerful than the entire universe that He created with but a Word. Although we have a loving God who is abundant in mercy and grace, we must also understand that the Almighty God will have the last say. Sadly, most people either deny the existence of the Almighty God or they completely ignore His sovereignty—they simply have no fear of the LORD. It is unwise my friends, to disregard the warnings from God. It would behoove you to heed those warnings if you have not already done so, because if you are living on this earth during the seven years of God's fiery wrath, there will be no place to hide from it.

## A Whisper of Hope

**My warnings, dear child...**are clear and easy to understand. It is true that I am the Savior of the world, but it is also true that I am also the Judge of the world; a just and righteous Judge that will pour out My judgment on those who defy My sovereign authority.

**Revelation 16:1-2**
Then I heard a mighty voice shouting from the Temple to the seven angels, "Now go your ways and empty out the seven bowls of God's wrath on the earth." So the first angel left the Temple and poured out his bowl over the earth, and horrible, malignant sores broke out on everyone who had the mark of the beast and who worshiped his statue. (NLT)

**Can't you see how kind He has been in giving you time to turn from your sin?**
(Romans 2:4)

# "The Foundation"

**2 Timothy 2:19**
But God's Truth stands firm like a foundation stone
with this inscription: "The Lord knows those who are His," and
"Those who claim they belong to the Lord must turn away from all wickedness." (NLT)

We know that God and His Truth are infinite because He tells us so. He tells us that He is perfect in every way, that He is perfectly holy and righteous and cannot tell us anything that is not true. Therefore, when we know and believe these truths about our Creator and Savior, we can trust that His Truth is always absolute and never changes. And if this the way it is, what better foundation is there to build one's life on than the Rock of our Salvation, Christ Jesus? The inscriptions found on the foundation stone (The Rock of Salvation) are found in the Old Testament; Numbers 16:5 and Isaiah 52:11 and they tell us who the Lord is and what He expects from His people. God's Word does not change with the times my friends, nor does it play favorites. It is solid to the core, it cannot be destroyed, and we can stake every breath we take on it.

When you truly belong to your Creator and Savior, Jesus Christ, and trust in the work He did for you by dying nailed to a piece of wood with rusty spikes, you are trusting the Cornerstone of True Life. And you can be confident that the Cornerstone of Life will stand strong and in place during all the turbulent storms of this life. You live in a fallen world that has been blindsided by God's most dangerous Enemy, the Devil and you need His help. The Good Shepherd knows His Sheep and they live in Him, for He is always there to protect and guide them Home. He knows each one by name and He knows them up close and personal. God's Cornerstone is strong and unbreakable. The world builds on many different cornerstones, but they are weak, and will be utterly destroyed and burned to the ground on the last day. Which would you choose to build your life upon? A cornerstone of straw and wood, or the infinite Rock of Salvation?

## A Whisper of Hope

**Choose your foundation wisely, My child...**for the storms of this life are many and they are furious, tearing down the strongest of this world. Build on the Foundation that is both infinite and eternal and your life will be protected by the Rock of Ages; the Cornerstone for Eternal Life.

**Ephesians 2:20-22**
We are His house built on the foundation of the apostles and the prophets. And the cornerstone is Christ Jesus Himself. We who believe are carefully joined together, becoming a holy temple for the Lord. Through Him you Gentiles are also joined together as part of this dwelling where God lives by His Spirit. (NLT)

**Come to Christ who is the Living Cornerstone of God's Temple.**
(1 Peter 2:4)

# *"The Servant"*

**2 Timothy 2:24-26**

A servant of the Lord must not quarrel but must be kind to everyone, be able to teach and be patient with difficult people. Gently instruct those who oppose the Truth. Perhaps God will change those people's hearts and they will learn the Truth. Then they will come to their senses and escape from the Devil's trap. For they have been held captive by him to do whatever he wants. (NLT)

Aservant of God shares the Good News with people who are slaves to sin and trapped in this dark and evil world that is headed for destruction. The good news is; they don't have to go down with the ship. The good news is; the Captain of the ship has already gone down for us and has come back to save those who want to be saved. This is the greatest news for those who are far removed from the Truth and are going down with their master the Devil. For many of the saved, born again Christians, discovering the Truth and seeing this life as it really is, is quite hard to keep secret, because they know there is a Way out the darkness that consumes our world and enslaves its people. When God reveals the Great Escape to us, we are blessed with real peace, hope and true joy, with the desire to share it with the many lost and hopeless souls who are blindly being led to their slaughter.

Many of these lost and desperate souls are crying out to the world for hope and peace and finding none, because the world cannot deliver what it does not know. They are people who are weary of the of the lies and being let down, and pointing these precious souls to their only Savior, Jesus Christ, is exactly what God wants all His servants to do, without shame and unafraid. There will be many opportunities to share the Good News but let the Holy Spirit take the reins and guide you in your new life-journey as a servant of the Lord. Allowing God to use you to do His will is always the best path to take. The job of the servant is to follow the Master's Way, and that is spending each day in prayerful submission, so He can teach you and strengthen you for the day ahead. The stakes are high as we watch this world quickly decaying. You are living in these last days of history for a good reason, my friends. So ask the Master, and it will be given to you.

## A Whisper of Hope

**I have saved you** child...and you are mine. I did for you what you could not do for yourself, now it is time for you to do a good work for Me. I will prepared you for the work ahead and I will give you the tools to finish the work. And know, I Am always with you even to the end of the age.

**Romans 1:16-17**

For I am not ashamed of this Good News about Christ. It is the power of God at work saving everyone who believes—Jews first and also Gentiles. This Good News tells us how God makes us right in His sight. This is accomplished from start to finish by faith. As the Scriptures say, "It is through faith that a righteous person has life" (NLT)

**Look at the proud! They trust in themselves and their lives
are crooked; but the righteous will live by their faith.**
(Habakkuk 2:4)

# *"Praise God"*

**Psalm 95:1-2**
Come; let us sing to the LORD! Let us give a joyous shout
to the Rock of our Salvation. Let us come before Him with
thanksgiving. Let us sing Him psalms of praise. (NLT)

No matter what a person's circumstances are, if they dig deep enough into their hearts they will find something good worth praising and thanking God for, and there are many people who do. But there are more who will refute this truth, because of their unbelief in God and the dire circumstance they find themselves in, but unbeknownst to them, it is the Truth. For they do not understand the reality that they are eternal beings and without this brief life there would be no new life in the new Heaven, on a new Earth; void of sin, pain, and suffering and living with our physical God Jesus Christ forever. There are many people who think their lives are anything but worth thanking God for, especially a God who seems to have forgotten them. But their sufferings will end and not be in vain if they would only believe and trust in the saving grace of the Lord God, Jesus Christ.

Before I accepted the saving grace of God, I found little good about this world or my sufferings. And it wasn't until the Lord opened my eyes to the Truth of who He is, what He has done, that I discovered just how good God really is, in spite of this suffering world. We have an awesome, loving, merciful God, my friends. We all have an opportunity to persevere this hard life for Jesus, trusting Him to make all things right when it's all said and done. All believer's will receive a perfect new body that never gets sick or dies or lacks anything good, and the will live forever in a perfect world where nothing bad happens and life just gets better and better. Praise God!

## A Whisper of Hope

**Your life, My child...**is a precious gift and should not be taken for granted, but savored. No matter what befalls your way, when you believe in Me, trust My Way, and persevere in My Name, I will make all your pain, disappointment, and sorrow right. I Promise.

**Revelation 7:12**
Amen! Blessing and glory and wisdom and thanksgiving and honor
and power and strength belong to our God forever and forever Amen! (NLT)

**But You O LORD my God, have snatched me from the yawning jaws of death!**
(Jonah 2:6)

# "Eyes of Light"

**Luke 11:34**
Your eye is a lamp for your body. A pure eye lets sunshine into your soul.
But an evil eye shuts out the light and plunges you into darkness. (NLT)

Some will say that the eye is a window into the soul, because as created human beings we learn much by what we see, for it is then stored in the brain. We also learn with our ears and that, too, is stored in our memory banks. Children see and hear their parents do things and often follow suit. Even as adults we often pattern our lives after those we look upon. What we read, watch, listen to and associate with, shapes our character and determines how we live our lives. What is focused on is what controls us. Those who focus on the world and its fallen ways live their lives to please themselves and to look good in the eyes of other people. We live in an evil world that blinds the eye, prohibiting the saving Light of the Son from entering our souls. And the darker the persons soul, the more likely it is that they will be led like a lamb to be slaughtered through the darkness that leads into an even deeper darkness that is; eternal death. But those who focus on God are being filled with the Son Light of eternal Life that pleases, honors, and glorifies God, and He honors and glorifies them in return.

Satan has darkened the hearts and minds and souls of most people, who are just trying to survive the chaos. The world and its unseen evil forces are hardening hearts and poisoning minds with lies and trash that are leading most people away from God and deeper into a darkness that only gets darker. But there is hope, for there is still time to get out before it's too late. The Son is still shining brightly for those who want to find the Way out. A open eye will let the Son Light in my friend, and it is pure and safe and will lead you straight into the arms of Jesus, where He will heal your wounds, comfort you soul, give you peace, and carry you safely Home.

## A Whisper of Hope

**See the Light, dear child?...**it is still shinning through the darkness of your world. Let it navigate you through this dark and evil world that is not your Home. There is yet, much more life to be lived when My Light is shining through your eyes.

**2 Corinthians 4:4**
Satan, the god of this evil world, has blinded the minds of those who don't believe, so they are unable to see the glorious Light of the Good News that is shinning upon them. They don't understand the message we preach about the glory of Christ, who is the exact likeness of God. (NLT)

**May the LORD lift up His countenance upon you and give you peace.**
(Numbers 6:25)

# *"His Kingship"*

**Mark 15:2**
Pilate asked Jesus, "Are you the King of the Jews?"
Jesus replied, "Yes, it is as you say. (NLT)

Although Jesus is telling us the absolute truth, there is so much more to be said about His infinite Kingship. Jesus is not only the King of the Jews, but He is also the King of creation. This King is our Lord God and Savior. He is the Eternal King, the King of ages past, the King of the present age, and the King of future ages. He is the King of Heaven and the King of Earth. He is King of the Universe. He is King of the living and the King of the dead. Jesus is not only King over all things, visible and invisible, but He is the Infinite King—the One True God who has always been and always will be. He is the only infinite being and always will be the only One. He creates everything, holds it all together, and has the power to make it all disappear. If there was nothing at all, there would be King Jesus.

The King is God Almighty in the flesh. He is God the Father, Son, and Holy Spirit. He sustains all that exists. He gives life to everything living and is their sole Provider. Without Him nothing would exist. The King is Final Judge, Jury, and Executioner. He is the Savior of the world. He is the Master Builder and the Cornerstone of His Church. He is the Rock of Salvation and the foundation for life. He is the Protector, Shelter, and the Comforter of our souls. He is Healer and He is True and Faithful. He is the Mightiest Warrior. He is the Lamb and the Lion. He is the High Priest, He is the Lord of lords, and the King of all kings. He is an all consuming fire. He is the Light of the world, the God of Israel, the Bridegroom, and the Bride. This is the King my friends, who owns your life and the only One whom you should worship and fear. But He is also your Friend, my friends.

## A Whisper of Hope

**I know who I AM, dear child...**But who do you think I am? If you believe I AM is your King, you will be with Me in Heaven. If you do not believe that I AM, who I AM, then you must choose another King. I have given you My Word, My life, and My Name, and now I AM giving you time.

**Exodus 3:14-15**
God replied, "I AM THE ONE WHO ALWAYS IS. Just tell them, 'I AM has sent me to you.'" God also said, "Tell them, The LORD, the God of your ancestors—the God of Abraham, the God of Isaac, and the God of Jacob—has sent me to you. This will be My name forever, it has always been My name, and it will be used throughout all generations.

**For who is God, except the LORD? And who is a Rock, except our God?**
(Psalm 18:31)

# *"Father Knows Best"*

**Deuteronomy 8:3**
So obey the commands of the LORD
by walking in His Ways and fearing Him. (NLT)

Our God demands our obedience, and the Father knows best—He knows the only safe way to live in this fallen world. Our God creates people because He wants everyone to fully experience the joy of living. Although this leg of our eternal life-journey is quite difficult for most, God promises us that it won't always be this way. He personally came down from Heaven to tell us how to deal with this brief stay on earth and how we can escape its darkness. God came to shine His Light of Truth upon us, which would carry us through to the other side. Satan has spread his darkness so thick in this fallen world that most people will never find their way through it. They will never know the Father's Way, nor will they escape the darkness. When Moses gave Israel the Mosaic Law it was not only designed to save the people as a nation, but it was also designed for their personal health; to keep them safe, clean, and alive. It was also designed to show them their dependence on God. When we follow what the Father knows best, we experience a life filled with satisfaction, joy, and eternal hope.

God also tells us that fearing Him is the beginning of all true wisdom. It only makes sense that we should fear the very One who created us, because the Creator is always greater than that which He creates. The Lord has already destroyed the entire human race except for one small family and He will destroy most of the human race again before the end of this age. Only those who accept His gift of salvation will survive. When the Lord God pours out His wrath upon this world, there will be no place to hide and if you are not protected by the Lord, you will suffer in the most horrible ways imaginable. If you do not fear God my friend, it would be wise to take the time to learn why you should, for the Truth, when discovered, will save your life.

## A Whisper of Hope

**I love all people, dear child…**that is why I came and I died; to save My creation. I AM not only a loving Father, a merciful Savior, and a gracious Helper, but I AM also a perfect and fair Judge. Those who rebel against Me without remorse and repentance will receive what they deserve. But those who know that the Father knows best, will receive the best of the Father!

**1 Peter 4:17**
For the time has come for judgment, and it must begin with God's
household. And if judgment begins with us, what terrible fate awaits
those who have never obeyed God. (NLT)

**Don't be impressed with your own wisdom. Instead, fear the LORD
and turn your back on evil. Then you will gain renewed health and vitality.**
(Proverbs 4:7-8)

# *"Judge Jesus"*

**Psalm 75:7**
It is God alone who judges; He decides
who will rise and who will fall. (NLT)

For the time being, we are stuck living in a fallen world with other fallen people that is headed for a fallen ending. We live in an age that is quickly coming to an end; an age where wrong is right and bad is good. There is little justice and there is little we can do about it. But amidst all the upside down and inside out morality that has consumed our world, we can be sure that Judge Jesus will have the final word. If you are frustrated with the direction that you, your country, and the world are headed in, you need to give that frustration to the Lord and let Him deal with it. Allow God to give you the peace that one day soon, He will return to make things right, to judge fairly, and give people what is due. Your part is to trust Judge Jesus, for He is the One who is in charge. You must believe that He is the Sovereign God and in absolute control of His creation.

Jesus does not want you to worry or resent the wicked and immoral people who prosper and get away with their evil ways. He sees and knows everything they do, and they will be judged fairly and get what they deserve. But the Lord wants His followers to spread the True Gospel Message, so that those in rebellion against His Way will have a chance to escape the eternal consequences of their rebellion. Without this chance, they will blindly follow the world into eternal death and destruction. The world will be judged fairly and you can be sure that when it's all said and done, those whose sins are forgiven will receive the Crown of Life from Judge Jesus in His court, and on the last day of this earth. And they will all be pardoned and redeemed.

## A Whisper of Hope

**I AM, dear child, the Perfect Judge...**And I am coming soon to judge the world. No one will be judged unfairly. I cannot be paid off, nor do I play favorites. All people will receive what is due. Those who wear My Robe of Righteousness will receive eternal life; all others will be sentenced to the eternal prison found in the Lake of Fire.

**Revelation 19:11**
Then I saw Heaven opened, and behold, a white horse. And He who sat on him
was called Faithful and True, and in righteousness He judges and makes war. (NKJ)

**The day will surely come when God, by Jesus Christ will judge everyone's secret life.**
(Romans 2:16)

# "Pure Eyes"

**Titus 1:15**
Everything is pure to those whose hearts are pure. But
nothing is pure to those who are corrupt and unbelieving
because their minds and consciences are defiled. (NLT)

This wicked world begins brainwashing us as soon as we open our eyes and can see the world around us. And we remain this way until the Lord intervenes and opens our eyes to the Truth. It is the god of this world, Satan, who is behind all of the evil lies that are turning people away from the Truth of God, which is leading them into a godless lifestyle that opposes everything is good and pleasing to God. The Devil is the most powerful and dangerous Enemy God has, and he despises the very name of Jesus and everything that is associated with Kingship. The Devil is so clever that most people are not even aware that they are living a life of sin, because if the world says it's okay, then it's okay. There is nothing pure or good about this evil world that is leading people so far away from the Truth that many of them won't learn about their eternal death and destruction until it is too late for them to change their minds.

My dear friends, everything that is pure and holy comes from our God in Heaven. And when we accept the death and resurrection of Jesus as our hope and salvation, we are inviting Him to live in our hearts, so that we, too, become pure and holy as we slip into His robe of righteousness. And with this new Hope, He will open our pure and hopeful eyes so we can see clearly the corruption that is destroying lives and killing souls. And we can then, help others who are being deceived by the deadly lies of this evil world. Let God's Truth cleanse your mind and soften your heart so you can see purely the road ahead.

## A Whisper of Hope

**Let Me give you a clean heart, My child...**One that is soft and pure. This evil world hardens hearts, poisons minds, and defiles lives. But I can change all that and give you a pure heart that loves Me and others—a heart of compassion, mercy, and grace—much like Mine.

**2 Timothy 2:22**
Run from anything that stimulates youthful lust. Follow anything that
makes you want to do right. Pursue faith and love and peace, and enjoy
the companionship of those who call on the Lord with pure hearts. (NLT)

**Every word of God is pure:**
**He is a shield to those who put their trust in Him.**
(Proverbs 30:5)

# *"Ready or Not"*

**Luke 12:39-40**
Know this: A homeowner who knew exactly when a burglar was coming would not permit the house to be broken into. You must be ready all the time, for the Son of Man will come when least expected. (NLT)

We must be prepared and always ready for Jesus to return for His Church. You do not want to be caught with your pants down, and then be left behind to suffer the Lord's anger against this fallen world led by Satan. In order to escape this mass destruction you must live in repentance as if it could happen in the twinkling of an eye. You must be sober and be fully aware of God's Plan and what you are doing. Any people living in this world who fail to heed the warnings that have been given will suffer greatly and die without the Lord's protection. Jesus Christ came in the flesh to warn and save us from His wrath and He put the world on notice—that when the right number of people have accepted the gift of salvation, He would remove them and unleash His wrath.

You must surrender to the Lord and let Him protect you from your enemies who want to destroy your life and break any connection that you may have to God so they can kill your soul. No one knows how long they have to surrender and change their ways before they die and miss the chance. No one knows the future like our God does because He creates the future. And no one but the Lord knows the day and hour of His return. It is better to be ready at all times. The warnings from our God should not be taken lightly, because where you spend your eternal life is at stake. Don't wait to change your ways my friend. Do not gamble with God, because you will lose everything if you do.

## A Whisper of Hope

**Be ready child…**I have given you fair warning, because I want no one left behind. Don't believe the lies of this lying world, for it will soon perish with all those who love it and fail to changes their evil ways.

**Revelation 16:15**
"Take note: I will come as unexpectedly as a thief! Blessed are all who are watching for me, who keep their robes ready so they will not need to walk naked and ashamed." (NLT)

**So stay awake and be prepared,
because you do not know the day or hour of My return.**
(Matthew 25:13)

# November

# "Deadly Idols"

**Jeremiah 51:18-19**
Idols are worthless, they are lies! The time is coming when they will all be destroyed.
But the God of Israel is no idol. He is the Creator of everything that exists, including
His people, His own special possessions. The LORD Almighty is His Name. (NLT)

Anything and everything in this world can be made an idol; something or someone we
worship and believe can help us get what we want. Most idols become gods to people.
All idols are manmade and evil in nature, because the Devil is behind them all. Many people
allow these idols to control them; how they think, act, and live their lives. And sadly, many will
take their idols to the grave with them and when the end of time comes, they and their idols
will be destroyed forever.

Everything about this world is temporary and when we make an idol from this world our
god and depend on it, it's not only a bad idea, but it's a deadly idea as well, because all an idol
does, is it separates us from the One who gives us the breath of life. The LORD God is the only
One we should worship, put our hope in, and trust with our lives, because anything else is like
playing with fire that will one day burn us up. God came to save His people, Israel and then the
world, and to start His Church, and no idol can pull that off! It is foolish dear friend, to worship anyone but the Lord, because if you do, you will be signing your death warrant to boot.

## A Whisper of Hope

**Do not trust, dear child...**the false idols of this godless world. For they only deliver eternal
destruction. Listen to the only God there is, for I AM who I say I AM—the One who created and
saved you from this foolish, wicked world. Trust Me.

**1 Corinthians 8:19, 20, 21**
Am I saying that the idols to whom the pagan bring sacrifices are real gods
and that these sacrifices are of some value? No, not at all. What I am saying
is that these sacrifices are offered to demons, not to God. And I don't want any
of you to be partners with demons. You cannot drink from the cup of the Lord
and from the cup of demons, too. (NLT)

**We all know that an idol is not really a god
and that there is only one God and no other.**
(1 Corinthians 8:4)

# *"The Nourished"*

**Matthew 13:22**
The thorny ground represents those who hear and accept the Good
News, but all too quickly the message is crowded out by the cares of
this life and the lure of wealth, so no crop is produced. (NLT)

As flawed human beings it is easy for us to get excited, but soon after the excitement begins to fade into doubts, impatience and then ends up going by the wayside. And the same can be said for many who hear the Good News of Jesus Christ; they are excited at first, but the sin within and evil powers of darkness re-emerges and begins to choke out their new faith of hope. This often happens when their new found faith has not had enough time to be nurtured and grown in the proper environment. The Good News Gospel of Jesus Christ is life-changing news that gives each person a fresh perspective on life, the absolute Truth about the world around them, and the hope of an eternal life in Heaven. But people who reject the Saving grace of God do not have a very bright future before them, because after all the struggle and pain and heartbreak that this life brings, their lives will have been lived in vain.

In order for the Good News to make a real difference in your life, you must commit everyday to nourishing your faith by spending time with the Lord; learning the Truth, growing in knowledge, and praying for replenished spiritual stamina in the face of the Enemy. It's when you get lazy and fail to follow through with these nourishing steps that the excitement fades, the old sinful nature hungers, and the demon of doubt enters into your heart and leaves the door open for the Enemy. Your faith cannot survive without the power of God. You cannot defeat your enemies without the Holy Spirit in your heart. You cannot save yourself, escape the power of sin, or defeat the Devil on your own. But with God, you can do all three and survive the storms.

## A Whisper of Hope

**Let Me nourish you, My child...**with My wisdom and strength. The world hates Me and all My children, and it can poison your faith with lies and doubt. If you stay close to Me, you will grow and be fruitful. When you live in Me, I will live in you and see you through to the other side.

**Mark 4:3-9**
"Listen! A farmer went out to plant some seed. As he scattered it across his field, some seed fell on a footpath, and the birds came and ate it. Other seed fell on shallow soil with underlying rock. The plant sprang up quickly, but it soon wilted beneath the hot sun and died because the roots had no nourishment in the shallow soil. The other seed fell among thorns that shot up and choked out the tender blades so that it produced no grain. Still other seed fell on fertile soil and produced a crop that was thirty, sixty, and even a hundred times as much as had been planned." Then Jesus said, "Anyone who is willing to hear should listen and understand!" (NLT)

**A good tree can't produce bad fruit, and a bad tree can't produce good fruit.
A tree is identified by the kind of fruit it produces.**
(Luke 6:43, 44)

# *"Follow the Leader"*

**Psalm 100:3**
Acknowledge that the LORD is God.
He made us and we are His. We are
His people, the sheep of His pasture. (NLT)

There is no better Leader to follow; no better Shepherd to stay close to than our Lord God and Savior, Jesus Christ. This passage of Scripture is an awesome truth—one that we should repeat to ourselves at the beginning of every new day that He gives us. Following the Leader of life is no game, for this life is the only chance we get to follow the right Leader. Whether we sing out this truth or whisper it in private, it is pleasing to God when He hears His people acknowledge Him. He commands us to have no other gods aside from Him. And for those of us whose only God is the LORD, we know that God is with us 24/7, watching our backs, guiding our ways, and giving us everything we need for godly living. And this brings us the peace and courage to boldly proclaim our God to the world.

Accepting the Lord as Savior will change your life in such an amazing way that both praising and worshiping Him will come as natural as breathing does. It is far wiser to pick the Creator and the Author of life to follow than anything He has created, because the Creator is always the One Greater and Wiser than anything He creates. God is Sovereign and in control of everything, and when you have the knowledge of who He is, what He has accomplished and what He promises to do, you gain the confidence and faith that will get you through this short, difficult life and Home where you belong. Without the Shepherd my friend, you will never find your way Home. Humble yourself at the foot of the Cross and accept His saving grace. For there is no One better, no One mightier, and no One wiser than the Good Shepherd.

## A Whisper of Hope

**I AM LORD, dear child...**the only living God and the only One who can lead you safely Home—the eternal Home that I made for you to live with Me forever. There are many false shepherds, many false prophets, and many lies, but there is only One LORD.

**Revelation 7:17**
For the Lamb who stands in front of the throne will
be their Shepherd. He will lead them to the springs
of living water. And God will wipe away all their tears. (NLT)

**But those who trust in idols,
calling them their gods—they will be turned away in shame.**
(Isaiah 42:17)

# *"The Forgiven"*

**Titus 3:7**
He declared us not guilty because of His great kindness.
And now we know that we will inherit eternal life. (NLT)

Because our gracious Lord God and Savior died naked, nailed to a dead tree and received the eternal punishment that we deserve (a task that no One else could have accomplished), we are now offered to receive His robe of righteousness and stand blameless before the Throne of God. Christ Jesus died for the sins of mankind; sins and rebellion against the Most Holy One who created us. And because of His selfless act of love and sacrifice, we have the incredible opportunity to share in the Glory of His eternal inheritance. Our Savior is our Advocate in Heaven, declaring forgiven sinners not guilty, even though we remain sinners.

This forgiveness, if accepted, is the most awesome gift that you will ever receive. So, it is only right that you, who have accepted this incredible gift of total forgiveness, give the Lord the glory and honor that is due. And the best way you can do that, is by godly living, loving the unlovable, and letting the world know about His saving grace. You must live to please God. You must live a life of repentance. You must let the transforming power of the Holy Spirit change the way you think, speak, and act. And even though you cannot live a sinless and perfect life this side of Heaven, you have the peace of God knowing that one day you will.

## A Whisper of Hope

**Be not afraid, My child...**for I have saved you from your sin. You no longer have to fear death, because I died the death you deserve. Your crime has been paid for and you have been set free. You have been forgiven.

**1 Corinthians 1:8**
He will keep you strong right up to the end, and
He will keep you free from all blame on the great
day when our Lord Jesus Christ returns. (NLT)

**So we praise God for the wonderful kindness**
**He has poured out on us because we belong to His dearly loved Son.**
(Ephesians 1:6)

# *"Revealed Mysteries"*

**Daniel 2:20, 22**
Praise the name of God forever and ever, for He alone has all wisdom
and power. He reveals deep and mysterious things and knows what
lies hidden in darkness, though He Himself is surrounded by light. (NLT)

Until we believe in the sovereignty of our Lord God and Savior, and until we believe He knows all things and sees all things, we will never experience life as it was meant to be lived. Nor will we have the opportunity to experience the peace of God knowing there is much more to this life and our death than meets the eye. When we discover the truth about who our Creator is and why He created us, the discovery changes our lives in ways that are so surreal, that it can be hard to wrap our minds around. And knowing that nothing is hidden from the eyes of God will be one of the most, if not the most humbling experience of this mysterious life. And when, for the very first time, God reveals something we never understood before and He makes it so clear and simple, we will scratch our heads and wonder how in world we missed it.

When you know the Lord, you will learn to trust Him with the deepest, most inner feelings you have and feel comfortable doing it, because you know He already knows and nothing surprises Him. God is only One you need ever fear. He is a Perfect Father. He takes care of His children and provides them with everything they need. The Lord protects the earth from being destroyed by the vast unknown universe that could snuff us out in a heartbeat. He keeps the cosmos in perfect tune by the power of His Word. But the most revealing truth about our God is His love and compassion for all of us, no matter what. His love and devotion to you is most revealed when you understand what He personally sacrificed in order to save you from everlasting Hell.

## A Whisper of Hope

**When you know Me, child...** I will reveal the mysteries of this life to you. For there is no better Authority to learn from than the One who created these mysteries. When you remain in Me, I will remain in you. You can trust My Word and believe in My promises.

**1 Corinthians 2:7-9**
The wisdom we speak of is the mystery—His plan that was previously hidden, even
though He made it for our ultimate glory before the world began. But the rulers of this
world have not understood it; if they had they would never have crucified our glorious
Lord. That is what the Scriptures meant when they say, "No eye as seen no ear has heard,
and no mind has imagined what God has prepared for those who love Him. (NLT)

**Then you will be filled with the fullness of life and power that comes from God.**
(Ephesians 3:19)

# "Best High"

**Lamentations 3:37-39**
Can anything happen without the Lord's permission? Is it not the
Most High who helps one and harms another? Then why should
we, mere humans, complain when we are punished for our sins? (NLT)

If we are to know what this life is truly all about, we must look to the very beginning of its creation. And it is our LORD God who started it all—it was His idea and His plan. He created us in His image so we could fully enjoy the eternal life He created us with. He made us to live in close fellowship with Him, so we could learn the incredible mysteries of His Glory and Being. Unlike our infinite God who has always existed, we are finite, hand created beings that are very limit in our nature, whereas, God has no limitations whatsoever. He has seen the entire picture that He created and directs from start to finish, and it all reflects His glory. Without understanding these basic truths, all we do is busy ourselves, running about doing this and doing that, going here and going there, but without a real concrete plan in place, especially the plan that extends beyond this life.

It is the Lord who designed our entire existence and it is He who holds our destiny in His hands. It is the Lord God who decides who will live and who will die. He will choose who He disciplines and who He does not. Although we have a free will, it is God who has the final word. God does not need us to help Him along. But we must understand that He disciplines us because He loves us. And being our Heavenly Father, He knows what is good for us and what is not. He does not enjoy seeing anyone of us suffering like we do, but it is a bi-product of sin and decadence. Without our Sovereign Guide, we would all be totally lost in our sins, and enjoying every minute of it. We would be blind and unaware of the dire consequences of our seemingly, mindless actions of self-indulged pleasure. If you are living anyway you like my friend, without knowing the Lord, you would have been better off being an animal, for they have no conscience nor are they created to be eternal.

## A Whisper of Hope

**You must trust Me, dear child...**when I discipline you it is for your own good and the good of My Kingdom. When you live in humble obedience I will guide and protect your every step, even when you veer off course and I must correct you. I do it because I love you.

**Hebrews 12:5-6**
And have you entirely forgotten the encouraging words God spoke to you,
His children? He said, "My child, don't ignore it when the Lord disciplines
you, and don't be discouraged when He corrects you. For the Lord disciplines
those He loves and He punishes those He accepts as His children." (NLT)

**Those who live in the shelter of the Most High
will find rest in the shadow of the Almighty.**
(Psalm 91:1)

# "Saving Robe"

**Hebrews 2:11**
So now Jesus and the ones He makes holy have the
same father. That is why Jesus is not ashamed to call
them His brothers and sisters. (NLT)

Our Lord God and Savior Jesus Christ has made it possible for anyone, no matter how far
away they are from the righteousness of God, to be totally forgiven, cleansed by the blood
of Jesus, and be adopted into the Eternal Family of God. This incredible Gift should never be
taken lightly, because it is an awesome privilege to be called the son or daughter of the Living
God, and the brother or sister of the Son of God, Jesus Christ—the Savior of the world. Jesus
suffered and died for the sins of the world, and became the First One of the Family to be resurrected from the grave and into eternal life. To be holy as the One True God is holy, is amazing,
because every man, woman, and child in this world is born with a sinful nature that desires the
things that defile the holiness of God. Most of us go about our everyday lives rebelling and sinning against the holiness of God without even knowing it. It's a wonderful blessing to mankind
that the righteousness of Christ Jesus can be ours, when we surrender our condemned lives to
God and receive His Robe of perfect standing.

Receiving the gift of forgiveness and eternal life means you are a vested member of God's
Holy Family. You become the adopted child of the Living God, and receive your citizenship
of Heaven. You are filled with the Holy Spirit. You gain access to God and learn the Truth
about this life and the one to follow. You will learn to discern what is true and what is from the
Devil. You will discover the glory of God the Father, God the Son, and God the Holy Spirit.
You will recognize His amazing grace and His just mercy. You will desire to live as God wants
you to live, and He will bring you safely into the eternal life that He has planned before the
world began. You have a God, friend, who is so wise and powerful that He spoke creation into
existence, created life, and saved you from an eternal existence of utter darkness. Run to Him!
Slip on His Robe and be holy!

## A Whisper of Hope

**I offer you My robe, dear child...**one that covers you completely with My righteousness.
Without it you will stand naked and ashamed to be judged for your sins. But I have paid the price
so you would not have to. So come naked and ashamed to Me now and escape My Judgment!

**Luke 12:2**
The time is coming when everything will be revealed; all that is secret will be made public.
Whatever you have said in the dark will be heard in the Light, and what you have whispered
behind closed doors will be shouted from the housetops for all to hear. (NLT)

> **So let us come boldly the throne of our gracious God. There we will
> receive His mercy, and we will find grace to help us when we need it.**
> (Hebrews 4:16)

# *"Close and Safe"*

**Hebrews 3:12**
Be careful then, dear brothers and sisters.
Make sure that your own hearts are not evil
and unbelieving, turning you away from the
living God. (NLT)

Because our fallen world is filled with all kinds of evil and wickedness, and because we come into this world with a sinful nature that loves to rebel against God, we soon develop an evil heart that is world hardened, selfish, prideful, and unbelieving. We become doubtful, skeptic, and self reliant. We begin to think ourselves as a god, judge, and executioner. But all that beings to change when are born again in Christ Jesus through His death and resurrection. We become a new creation filled with the Holy Spirit who begins transforming our hearts and minds away from the world and helps us fend off the power of sin. But because our transformation cannot be completed while we live in corruptible bodies, we must be diligent in our relationship with the Redeemer, so He can protect our hearts and minds from this evil world that tries to pull us back into its terrible darkness of sin and unbelief.

We need the power of God and we need it every day, because our fallen human nature is weak and unable to stand on its own. The evil in our world is gaining more ground and power every day and it's imperative that Christians cling tightly to Truth of God, who keeps us free from its evil and the power of sin. If the Lord is calling you out of the darkness, go my friend, for once you are living in the Light of God's saving grace, you will be safely lead through the darkness and be transformed into the person that you where created to be—a child of the Living God. Your life may not be made any easier, but you can be sure that the Lord is always near, ready to rescue you in your times of trouble.

## A Whisper of Hope

**Listen closely, My child...**when I call you out of the darkness that is killing your soul. Sometimes My call is soft, sometimes it is not, but calling My lost ones is what I do, for you must follow My Voice so I can save you from the evil powers of darkness that will drag you down into the pit.

**Ephesians 5:16-17**
Make the most of every opportunity for doing good
in these evil days. Don't act thoughtlessly, but try to
understand what the Lord wants you to do. (NLT)

**With my whole heart I have sought You;**
**Oh, let me not wander from Your commandments!**
(Psalm 119:10)

# *"Place to Rest"*

**Hebrews 4:9-10**
So there is a special rest still waiting for the people of God.
For all who enter into God's rest will find rest from their
labors, just as God rested after creating the world. (NLT)

Although we know the Lord is preparing a special place for His children to forever rest from the labors of this difficult world, He also wants us to know that He is our place of rest right now in this life. We live in a busy world that demands much from us, with many decisions to make and much labor to be done. Our days and nights can be filled with worry, concerns about tomorrow and regrets for yesterday's debacles. But even though we know we need the time to rest and refresh our strength or this life's business will take its toll and we either wear down or break down, we still fail to heed God's wisdom to rest. We need the Lord's rest, not only for our weakened body's sake, but to renew our hearts, minds, and souls as well. We were not made to live without God.

I know there is no better Place to rest than in the arms of our Lord God and Savior, Jesus Christ. Just being in the Lord's Presence brings rest for both your tired body and your weary soul. In the renewing Presence of the Living God you find healing and restoration for your brokenness. You find comfort knowing that your Savior is always close at hand, watching over you like the Good Shepherd He is. He gives you strength to persevere in your troubles and the courage to face any new ones. What an awesome Place you have to rest from life, my friend. For without Him there is no true rest, especially from the demands of this busy world filled with evil. When you take the time to rest in the Lord, you can be sure that you will come out stronger and wiser than when you entered into it. For the renewing is either life changing, life saving, or both!

## A Whisper of Hope

**Rest in Me, dear child...**for your burdens are heavy and sometimes overwhelming. When you rest in Me I will take those burdens from you and give you My Peace, which will comfort your soul and quiet your troubled heart. I AM your infinite Resting Place and Burden Bearer.

**Psalm 16:8-9, 11**
I know the LORD is always with me. I will not be shaken, for He is right beside me. No wonder my heart is glad, and I rejoice. My body rests in safety. You will show me the Way of Life, granting me the joy of Your Presence. (NLT)

**He heals the brokenhearted, binding up their wounds.**
(Psalm 146:3)

# *"God the Great"*

**Psalm 105:1**
Give thanks to the LORD and proclaim His greatness.
Let the whole world know what He has done. (NLT)

Everyone in this world has something to be thankful for, some more than others, but nonetheless, thankful. We should never hesitate admitting our gratitude for the opportunity to experience life, no matter how difficult our circumstances are, for without this short life there can be no eternal life. The prerequisite for receiving the perfect life in a perfect world with our perfect God that never ends, is surviving this hard life and dying in the arms of Jesus. It is not easy living this life with or without our Lord God and Savior Jesus Christ, but when we live without Him, this hard life only gives us the death sentence. But when we live with Him, following His Way, we receive the gift of eternal life. The world does not want you to know this Truth, because the leader of this world, the Devil, wants to take as many of us to Hell as he can. Satan does not want us to even know who the perfect sacrificial Lamb of God is, because Jesus is the One who defeated the sin and death that is Satan's signature.

The LORD our God, in all His Greatness, knew before He created the world that we would fall away from His Holy Presence, and that we would not be able to recover from our fall on our own without His holy intervention . And because He is a great and mighty, He took all of our sins and punishment and they died with Him on the Cross. Our Great and Mighty God made us, saved us, and has provided the prefect Plan for us to survive this life so we could live the life He created us to live. Our Lord God Jesus Christ is the only Hope you have dear friend, for defeating this world so you can joyfully move on to the perfect world that He is preparing for you. Thank Him for life and then rejoice!

## A Whisper of Hope

**Be ever so thankful, My child...**for the life I have given you. But you must live in My Way if you are to survive in this world gone bad. I promise to get you through this life and into the Perfect Place of Rest. The Place where you will always be happy and thankful!

**1 Peter 2:22-25**
He never sinned, and He never deceived anyone. He did not retaliate when He was insulted. When He suffered, He did not threaten to get even. He left His case in the hands of God, who always judges fairly. He personally carried away our sins in His own body on the cross so we can be dead to sin and live for what is right. You have been healed by His wounds! Once you were wandering like lost sheep. But now you have turned to your Shepherd, the Guardian of your souls. (NLT)

**Now wherever we go He uses us to tell others**
**about the Lord and to spread the Good News like a sweet perfume.**
(2 Corinthians 2:14)

# *"Soul Safe"*

**Hebrews 6:17, 18**
God also bound Himself with an oath, so that those who received the promise could be perfectly sure that He would never change His mind. So God has given us both His promise and His oath. These two things are unchangeable because it is impossible for God to lie. (NLT)

F rom the moment sin entered into God's Story, He made an oath and promised us a Savior, one that would save us from our sin and banishment from God's eternal Presence—that one day we would walk in His Presence once again, and to live in a personal relationship with Him forever. He kept His promise by sending His Son, Jesus Christ, to die the death we deserved, to cleanse our sins with His holy blood, and to remove the barrier that made it impossible for us to be with our God, at anytime or anywhere. And we are now waiting for the Lord to come and finish His Plan, so we can physically live with Him forever in our newly created bodies, eternal Home, and New Earth. This is the Promise of God that keeps our souls safe and our hopes alive.

But to be a part of His glorious Kingdom to come you must embrace His every Word and every promise as the absolute Truth, not just those words or promises that suit your agenda. You must get rid of your own interpretations and learn to fully trust the Lord with every area of your life. Our Lord God did not come as your Savior to please Himself or because He had to. He did it because He gave an oath and made a promise, and God cannot break an oath or fail to live up to His promises any more than He can tell a lie or claim He doesn't exist. You have a loving God my friend, One who loves you so much that He refused to let you suffer the eternal consequences of your inherent sinfulness and the rebellion you live in against His righteousness. Never doubt God's love or His commitment to save your soul, because He did it before you ever knew you needed it or that He did it.

## A Whisper of Hope

**You can stake your life, child...**on the promises of My Word. Do not gamble your life away by trusting in the world for your future, because this world and those who trust it, do not have a very encouraging future. Only My children have a hope and a future.

**Isaiah 43:11-13**
"I am the LORD, and there is no other Savior. First I predicted your deliverance, I declared what I would do, and then I did it—I saved you. No foreign god has ever done this before. You are witnesses that I am the only God," says the LORD. From eternity to eternity I am God. No one can oppose what I do. No one can reverse My actions." (NLT)

> **Without wavering, let us hold tightly to the hope**
> **we say we have, for God can be trusted to keep His promise.**
> (Hebrews 10:23)

# "Fair Warning"

**Luke 21:34-36**

Watch out! Don't let Me find you living in careless ease and drunkenness, and filled with worries of this life. Don't let that day catch you unaware, as in a trap. For that day will come upon everyone living on the earth. Keep a constant watch. And pray that if possible, you may escape these horrors and stand before the Son of Man. (NLT)

Here is yet, another gracious warning from our Lord God and Savior Christ Jesus. Our God has given us a very clear picture about the future end of this fallen world, because He wants no one to be caught off guard and left behind to suffer the horrific ending of the Devil's reign over this world. As a matter of fact, Jesus left the glory of Heaven to suffer and die what we deserve. And because Lord Jesus is God in the flesh, His death justified our rebellion and His resurrection from the grave into a glorified body that would never suffer or die again, became our Hope. For the resurrected Jesus is now advocating our justification before the Father in Heaven and the Accuser has lost his case against us and we are set free from the Devil's grip and the sting of sin, if we so choose.

This clear message from Jesus is a warning to live every moment of your life justified by the blood of Jesus, to live everyday in repentance, and to walk in the Light of God's Truth, because He does not want to catch you with your pants down. Our Lord God and Savior has been warning us since the beginning of time. Christ Jesus personally came into this wicked world to save it from the destruction it deserves. He came to give us a new eternal life in Him, that would help us while we are struggling through this short life. God has written His Message in a way that everyone could understand—that in the time it takes the eye to blink, the end will begin. Don't be one of the many my friend, who will suffer on that great and mighty Day of the Lord, for your options will have run out.

## A Whisper of Hope

**Don't let Me catch you sleeping, dear child...**unless you are sleeping in the grace of My mighty arms. All those who are caught off guard will pay the price for not heeding and embracing My many warnings. Be wise, be on watch, and always be ready, for I will come when least expected.

**1 Corinthians 15:52**

It will happen in a moment, in the blinking of an eye, when the last trumpet is blown. For when the trumpet sounds, the Christians who have died will be raised with transformed bodies. And then we who are living will be transformed so that we will never die. (NLT)

> **For you know quite well that the day of the Lord will come unexpectedly, like a thief in the night.**
> (1 Thessalonians 5:2)

# "Times Out"

**Ezekiel 12:23**
Give the people this message from the Sovereign Lord:
"The time has come for every prophecy to be fulfilled." (NLT)

Although this message from the Lord was given to God's chosen people Israel, before their captivity and exile into Babylon, the same message is still speaking loud and clear to anyone who will listen. We have a gracious and patient God, but His Word is true and His prophecy is kept. We know through God's Word found in the Scriptures, that all but one of God's prophecies, excluding the revelation of Jesus Christ, have been fulfilled. Only the LORD our God knows the day and hour that the ending will begin. And it is for this reason that we must be prepared at all times, and keep sharing the Good News Gospel that salvation through the Son is for everyone. We see a world gone mad and getting madder every day. We see people not concerned with anything but themselves and this short life. We see the world's ways being implemented into the minds of our children, who will grow up believing that this life is all we get, and it's all about getting whatever we can get while we can get it.

The beginning of all wisdom my friends, is to fear the LORD our Almighty God, Judge, and Savior—the One who holds your destiny in His hands. Without this reverent fear, you will go about this life doing whatever you feel like doing as long as it makes you feel good. When you believe there are no real consequences for your behavior after this life is over, you will promote your godless living to others and you will all end up living life wildly and spinning out of control. You will ignore and probably mock the One who created you, tried to save you, and will be your final Judge. But the LORD will hold you accountable for mocking His Authority. God has graciously given you the time and the warnings to prepare. God didn't have to do this, but He did because He loves you, my friend.

## A Whisper of Hope

**Know what the future holds, My dear child...**I will be glad to tell you, because I am its Creator. Once you know the Truth, you will discover how much I love you and how I long to be your God now and for all eternity. You can live now or later, it's up to you!

**1 Peter 1:17**
And remember that the Heavenly Father to whom you pray
has no favorites when He judges. He will judge or reward
you according to what you do. So you must live in reverent
fear of Him during your time as foreigners here on earth. (NLT)

**I am the Alpha and the Omega—the Beginning and the End.**
(Revelation 21:6)

# "Gods or God"

**Psalm 106:20**
They traded their glorious God for a statue of a grass-eating ox!

Most people are not sure how they were created or who created them. They do not know the glorious God who made them, so they are not aware of the incredible future He has planned for them. This world is drifting away from its only God, looking for other gods in all the wrong places and for all the wrong reasons. Our world is a haven for godless living. People worship anyone or anything that excites them. Sadly, the world is controlled by the Devil's lies, who preys upon the lost and uses their sinful nature to lure them into the darkness. And as the world slips deeper into darkness, it is easy to picture God as the enemy, making this the most dangerous lie of all. For it was God who left the glory of Heaven to suffer shamefully, to shed His life's blood innocently, and to die carrying the sins of the world with Him to the grave, so we could fully enjoy the eternal life He created in us.

God does not want you to trade Him in for the many temporary pleasures that the false gods of this wicked world offer you, because they are both really bad for you and will end up destroying your chances of living the perfect eternal life God has planned for you. He does not want you to suffer the terrible wrath that He, the slaughtered, innocent Lamb of God, will send down upon this wicked world that is destined for death and destruction. The only hope you or anyone has to escape God's fury, is to make the LORD God your only God and worship Him as Creator, Provider, and Savior. Get rid of those man-made gods that were designed by the Devil to bring you death.

## A Whisper of Hope

**Come into My Light, child...**and see the truth about this dark world that detests every good thing from Heaven. Don't be fooled by the lies, because they are from the Devil, and are deadly for sure. Live in Me the true Light of eternal life and the only real God of gods.

**1 Corinthians 8:5-6**
According to some people, there are many so-called gods and lords, both in heaven and on earth. But we know there is only One God, the Father, who created everything and we exist for Him. And there is only One Lord, Jesus Christ, through whom God made everything and through whom we have been given life. (NLT)

**I know now that the LORD is greater than all other gods.**
(Exodus 18:11)

# *"Judge Jesus"*

**Ezekiel 18:30**
"Therefore, I will judge each of you, O people of Israel,
according to your actions," says the Sovereign LORD.
"Turn from your sins! Don't let them destroy you." (NLT)

This Truth from thousands of years ago is not just directed at the people of Israel anymore, but it is now for the Church and the entire population of the world. The old covenant between God and His people Israel, has been replaced with the new covenant of saving grace that the Jewish people and this world have not yet accepted, but the Christian Church has. It still holds everyone accountable for how they live and think, but no amount of good works or money or the blood of animals will do us any good on Judgment Day. Our only hope is in the blood of Jesus and His saving grace. Those who have not been cleansed by the blood of the final sacrificial Lamb ,will suffer the eternal consequences for their unforgiven sins; a punishment you would be wise to avoid. But those of us who have been born again in the death and resurrection of Christ Jesus, are Now clothed in His robe of righteousness, and we will escape the final judgment, but receive the eternal inheritance that is in Christ Jesus.

The Lord honors the surrendering hearts of sinners who live a life of repentance, loving Him and living in His Way. But without the sacrificial blood of the Son covering your sin filled life, you cannot stand holy in His Presence to receive His grace when you need it. No amount of good deeds or words will be accepted without the blood of the Lamb. But by His blood, all sins are forgiven and forgotten, and you can finish this life living in the Spirit. For He will transform your sinfulness into a godliness that is pleasing in the eyes of God and reflect His Glory. It is no longer about us or how good we can be or anything else, it is all about the glory and grace of the Lord our God and Savior, Jesus Christ.

## A Whisper of Hope

**Surrender, My child...**for you are weak and flawed. You cannot change your sinful lifestyle without Me. And without My robe of righteousness covering your naked shame and guilt, you will die of exposure. And the consequences are not pretty when you die naked and ashamed. I invite you to slip on the Robe of forgiveness and receive the crown of life!

**Hebrews 9:14, 15**
For by the power of the eternal Spirit, Christ offered Himself to God as a
perfect sacrifice for our sins. That is why He is the One who mediates the
new covenant between God and people, so that all who are invited can receive
the eternal inheritance God has promised them. For Christ died to set them
free from the penalty of the sins they had committed under that first covenant. (NLT)

**He paid for you with the precious blood of Christ,
the sinless, spotless Lamb of God.**
(1 Peter 1:19)

# "Anew Way"

**Hebrews 9:11, 12**

So Christ has now become the High Priest. He has entered that great, perfect Sanctuary in Heaven, not made by human hands and not part of this created world. With His own blood—not the blood of goats and calves—He entered the Most Holy Place once for all time and secured our redemption forever. (NLT)

Our Lord God and Savior, Jesus Christ is the Final Sacrificial Lamb of God—no other blood needs to be shed for the sins of man. The death and blood of our Savior satisfied God's anger and we have been cleansed. This Good News clothes us in the righteousness of Christ and provides the Way to Heaven and everlasting life. Under this saving grace of God, no other blood sacrifice is needed. The old system of sacrifice found in the Law of Moses was only a shadow of the things to come, paving the Way for our sins to be forgiven once and for all time.

But there is yet another sacrifice needed; it is the living sacrifice of putting to death your old sinful life by nailing it to the Cross and being resurrected into a new creation who lives in the Power of the Holy Spirit. There is no other Way. Once forgiven this Way, always forgiven. No longer do you need to struggle alone with sin and the powers of darkness, because you have the Spirit in your heart to give you everything you need. When you accept the gift of forgiveness and salvation from the Lord, you are cleansed and holy. In Christ you are made perfect, without Him you are guilty.

## A Whisper of Hope

**Surrender, dear child...**and let My death be yours. I paid the price for your sins so you would not have to. All that is needed is your living sacrifice—putting to death your old life of sin to become a new creation in Me—forever cleansed and robed in Righteousness.

**2 Corinthians 5:17, 18**

What this means is that those who become Christians become new persons. They are not the same anymore, for the old life is gone. A new life has begun! All this newness of life is from God, who brought us back to Himself through what Christ did. (NLT)

**May you always be filled with the fruit of your salvation—those good things
that are produced in your life by Jesus Christ.**
(Philippians 1:11)

# *"Blind Rebellion"*

**Ezekiel 12:2**
Son of man, you live among rebels who could see the truth
if they wanted to, but they don't want to. They could hear
me if they would listen, but they won't listen because they
are rebellious. (NLT)

We live in a very evil world that is filled with people whose blatant purpose is to rebel against the righteousness of the LORD God. It is a world that embraces the evil ways of Satan, a world of many gods, and most of its people worship everything but the God who created it. It is a world that listens more to the voices from Hell than the Voice of Heaven. The sad thing about these billions of people living the gift of life is that most of them do not know why they exist or the God who created them. Most people living in this dying world have no clue to who God is and what He has done for them. Most people have been indoctrinated into believing in the false gods that meet their expectations, unaware that they are being led into a life of dark deception and if gone undetected, will surprise them with a deeper eternal darkness from which there is no escape.

As a Christian, you must learn to live in this evil world fighting for your godly life. You must, with the power and wisdom of the Holy Spirit as your guide, be able to see, hear, and understand the decadence around you. It is through your faith in Christ that you overcome this decadence and become the salt and light for the lost people in this dark world. You know the Truth and it must heard. You must speak by the Spirit of God who overpowers the voices from Hell. You must speak out against this rebellion and plant the seeds of hope into the hearts of the blind and hopeless. Exposing the lies that are blinding the lost souls of this dying world and pointing them to their Savior is the goal, anything less is worthless and anything else is hopeless.

## A Whisper of Hope

**I Am the only Truth, My child...**I Am your only Hope. There are many false gods that can only promise you lies and a false sense of hope. The voices from Hell are loud and convincing, but My voice brings peace and comfort while this world continues to decay.

**Psalm 95:6-7**
Come, let us worship and bow down. Let us kneel
before the LORD our Maker, for He is our God. Oh
that you would listen to His voice today! (NLT)

**Evil people seek rebellion, but they will be severely punished.**
(Proverbs 17:11)

# *"Life Way"*

**Hebrews 10:19-20**
And so, dear brothers and sisters, we can boldly enter Heaven's Most Holy Place because of the blood of Jesus. This is the new life-giving Way that Christ has opened for us through the sacred curtain, by means of His death for us. (NLT)

This is truly Good News for those who find themselves lost and hopeless, and just trying to survive in this uncertain world that is getting more dangerous and unpredictable by the day. We can see our world is spinning out of control with no real solutions on the horizon; only more destruction, death, and disaster after disaster. But there is hope and there are people who have hope for a bright and perfect future that is guaranteed by the Lord. Who are these people? They are God's adopted children, the Church of Jesus Christ. We are no longer separated from God, because the sacrificial death of the final and perfect sacrificial Lamb, Christ Jesus ,removed the sin barrier that keeps us apart from God. Our sins are removed and replaced with the righteousness of Christ so we can enter into the Presence of God at anytime and anywhere. We can bring our sins, concerns, troubles, and anything else to God and He will forgive our sins and give us what we need. The Lord gives us the peace and strength that helps us through this difficult life, because we know there is nothing that can keep us from God and the eternal life He purchased with His blood.

It is an honor and a blessing to enter into the Most Holy Place of God's Presence without having to kill an innocent animal to do it. And this final forgiveness is not just for a select few, but for any humble sinner who nails their old life of sin to the Cross of Christ and be resurrected a new, redeemed child of the Living God. Whenever a forgiven sinner comes into the Presence of the Lord, they can come boldly just as they are and not fear God's rejection, for their nakedness and shame is covered with Jesus' robe of righteousness. When you know for sure my friends, that you will not die infected with sin and suffer the eternal consequences, you will live with the peace of God in your heart and the death and resurrection of Jesus as your hope.

## A Whisper of Hope

**Come boldly and unafraid, dear child...** and I will forgive all of your sins once and for all time. I will remember them no more. Come as you are, but come humble. For I have a soft spot for the humble, but not so with the proud.

**1 John 1:8-9**
If we say we have no sin, we are only fooling ourselves and refusing to accept the truth. But if we confess our sins to Him, He is faithful and just to forgive us and to cleanse us from every wrong. (NLT)

**But the Lord our God is merciful and forgiving,
even though we have rebelled against Him.**
(Daniel 9:9)

# "It Ain't Easy"

**1 Corinthians 7:17**
You must accept whatever situation the LORD has put you in
and continue on as you were when God first called you. (NLT)

When you become a born again Christian, you become a child of the Living God, but your life is not instantly transformed and made easier. Rather, the transformation can be very slow and painful. Many experience attacks from the Enemy of our souls that actually make our transformation even more difficult and our circumstances even worse. This life never magically improves overnight, nor does living necessarily get any easier when you become a Christian, But what it does do, is it opens your eyes to the real Truth about who God is, who you are, and where it's all headed. When you know the Truth about this difficult life, the struggles begin to make sense. Once we begin to know why our world is in this terrible state of flux, we can live in faith that God is in control and He knows what He is doing. We have God's wisdom and strength to get us through the storms. And we grow in confidence that the One who saved us from our sins and Hell will be with us always.

It is so important for God's children to live in the Light of His Truth; to remain connected through the means He has given us. We are in a furious spiritual warfare that is not only being fought in the physical world we live in, but in the heavenly realms as well. And this is why we must rely on our Sovereign Lord God to help us fight the battles we cannot win without Him. God wants us to not focus so much on the problems of this life, but on Him; the One who is in charge and has all the answers. This is how we maintain our steadfast faith that God is who He says He is and that He always comes through for those who call Him Father. We may not always agree with His ways, but we can always count on His perfect results.

## A Whisper of Hope

**Follow Me, My child...**and I will lead you safely through this temporary life and into the glory of Heaven. But you must remain close and fully aware of the dangers around you, because the Enemy lurks around in his darkness like the evil demon he is.

**Romans 1:16-17**
For I am not ashamed of this Good News about Christ. It is the power of God at work, saving everyone who believes—Jews first and also Gentiles. This Good News tells us how God makes us right in His sight. This is accomplished from start to finish by faith. As the Scriptures say, "It is through faith that a righteous person has life." (NLT)

**The Lord is a Shelter for the oppressed,
a Refuge in times of trouble.**
(Psalm 9:9)

# "Patient God"

**Isaiah 30:18**
But the LORD still waits for you to come to Him so He can
show you His love and compassion. For the LORD is a faithful
God. Blessed are those who wait for Him to help them. (NLT)

The LORD is our God and Savior. He is the only Living God. He has proven to the world over and over again that He is not only actively involved in the history of mankind, but He is also very much involved in the personal lives of everyone, especially the people who call to Him for help. God has shown the world His amazing mercy and grace, and His faithful love and compassion. God is the One who provides everything we need for both our physical and spiritual survival. He protects our world from within as well as from far away. We have an all powerful, all knowing God who happens to love people above all other things He has created. He created everything in such a way that His creation that would always need Him. But unlike the rest of His creation, He created us in His image and to live with Him for eternity.

God knows we are a needy people that need Him for both our physical and spiritual lives. We are physically and spiritually flawed and weak in stature, and it doesn't take much to end our lives. The Lord did not create us to die, and He wants everyone to be His eternal children. The LORD is perfectly holy and just, and He has been more than gracious with our sin and wickedness to date. He is a patient God and gives us many chances to give up our evil ways so we can receive His forgiveness and redemption. God Almighty wants you to be His child, my friend. He wants to save you from self-destruction and eternal condemnation because He loves you. And you can trust that He will continue calling you until the end of time!

## A Whisper of Hope

**Call to Me, My child...**while there is still time. I Am your Helper as well as your Savior. I created you so you could enjoy the glorious gift of eternal life. I can help you overcome this evil world and become My eternal child.

**Isaiah 41:13**
I am holding you by your right hand—I, the LORD your God.
And I say to you, "Do not be afraid. I am here to help you." (NLT)

**Wait patiently for the LORD. Be brave and courageous.**
(Psalm 27:14)

# *"God's Reign"*

**Psalm 89:14**
Your throne is founded on two strong pillars—righteousness and
justice. Unfailing love and truth walk before You as attendants. (NLT)

For the time being, the Lord our God rules from His throne in Heaven. He is in total control of every aspect of His creation. He knows about every little detail found in the entire universe, including all the comings and goings of every living creature, regardless of its size or importance. The Living God of the universe is perfect in every way. He is the essence of holiness and everything He says and does is goodness in the purest form. His justice is pure and simple, never unjustly condemning or unjustly rewarding. Everyone is guilty of sinning against the holiness of God and we all deserve to be punished, but our Sovereign Lord has shown how much He loves us by dying in the flesh and suffering the wrath due to mankind. This is our God.

God tells us that His attributes never change. His righteousness is always the same. We can always depend on God to be God, because He can be nothing else. Trusting God in all things is the only pathway to peace in this world that embraces everything that God is not. It is impossible to trust in a world that changes with the drop of a hat. The flawed and imperfect ways of fallen world is fickle at best. It moves back and forth, and up and down like the waves of the ocean. And not only that, the ways of man are evil and wicked and it is our very nature to rebel against the very God who created us. It is not wise my friends, to trust this dying world as your hope and future, because it will one day burn up with all those who worship it!

## A Whisper of Hope

**I AM Holy, child...**I Am righteously just and fair in all I do and say. I never create anyone and then leave them on their own. Sometimes it may seem this way, but I came to your world and died your death, so you could reign again with Me.

**Revelation 15:2-4**
I saw before me what seemed to be a crystal sea mixed with fire. And on it stood all the people who had been victorious over the beast and his statue and the number representing his name. They were all holding harps that God had given them. And they were singing the song of Moses, the servant of God, and the song of the Lamb: "Great and marvelous are Your works, O Lord God, the Almighty. Just and true are Your ways, O King of the nations. Who will not fear, O Lord, and glorify Your Name? For You alone are Holy. All nations will come and worship before You, for Your righteous deeds have been revealed." (NLT)

**Man is unstable in all his ways.**

(James 1:8)

# "Wholly Family"

**Hebrews 12:6-7**
For the LORD disciplines those He loves and He punishes those He accepts as His children. As you endure this divine discipline, remember that God is treating you as His own children. Whoever heard of a child who was never disciplined? (NLT)

B eing adopted into God's Holy Family is no small matter, either for us, or for our Lord God and Savior Jesus Christ, who died a horrendous death in order to bring us back into this holy relationship between God and man. God created a man and woman to populate the earth to be a part of His family forever. And if it had not been for God's unconditional love, mercy, and grace, all of us would have remained in our rebellious state, lost in darkness, living anyway we want, ignoring the eternal consequences, and then paying the ultimate price for our rebellion. Before Jesus' sacrifice we all lived lawlessly as children of wrath. But the Lord had a plan and chose to give us an opportunity to become a member of His holy eternal Family.

Those of us who have been adopted by the Living God should never let a day go by without praising Him for His gracious kindness and great generosity, for without Him we would be forever separated from His goodness. If not for God's unconditional love for people we would only live to die as a child of wrath. Our Loving God wants a big family my friends, the bigger the better. When He calls you to be a part of His incredible eternal family, listen and accept His offer. For you will reap the inheritance that comes with your adoption. Don't miss out on this chance of an eternal lifetime, even though you must suffer for a short while.

## A Whisper of Hope

**I AM and always have been a Family, dear child...**And I created you in My image to also be family and even though sin has come between us, I have made a Way for you to be adopted. Don't refuse this generous offer because the alternative is eternally not so good at all.

**Romans 8:15-17**
For all who are led by the Spirit of God are children of God. So you have not received a spirit that makes you fearful slaves. Instead, you received God's Spirit when He adopted you as His own children. And we call Him Abba, Father. For His Spirit joins with our spirit to affirm we are God's children. And since we are His children, we are His heirs. In fact, together with Christ we are heirs of God's glory. But if we are to share His glory, we must also share His suffering. (NLT)

**With all my heart I will praise you, O Lord my God.**
(Psalm 86:12)

# "Holy in Peace"

**Hebrews 12:14**
Try to live in peace with everyone, and seek to
live a clean and holy life, for those who are not
holy will not see the Lord. (NLT)

Trying to live peacefully with a world that has never known peace is a difficult task to perform, even for the most peace-loving people. Being asked to live in peace with a world filled with angry people is a hard pill to swallow for even the most kind and loving person there is. And trying to live a righteous life in the midst of all kinds of evil is a very dangerous mission, because we not only live in a world that hates the very Name of Jesus Christ, but it also hates anyone or anything that is associated with Him . We live in a world blinded from knowing the Truth about who the Living God is—a world that denies His deity and Truth so they can continue living in the darkness of their sinful pleasures. It is a difficult challenge to live in the Light of God's Truth, and it cannot be done successfully without the power of the Holy Spirit dwelling within us and surrounding us with His protection, wisdom, and strength. It takes the Power of God to pull this off, and pull it off we must, because the Lord commissions us to live in the Light so the world will see and know that the Lord is God, that we belong to Him, and His will will be done.

If God's children are to defend the absolute Truth that the Lord God is sovereign, righteous, and in control of this out of control world, we must know who we are fighting for, who we are fighting against and why we are fighting in the first place. We must be fully vested in God's Plan for man and we must stand steadfast and faithfully in the face of evil that surrounds us every day—a mission that requires the infinite Power of God backing us up. Every living soul needs the only Savior this world has. Every breathing person needs Jesus, because without Him, there can be no peace. Without the Father, Son, and Holy Spirit as the foundation for your life, the dark and evil powers from the depths of Hell will swallow you up in a heartbeat and forever separate you from the glory of God!

## A Whisper of Hope

**You can do anything, My child...**when you do it in Me. I Am the Lord your God and with Me you can escape your bondage to sin and defeat the power of death. With Me there is peace and godliness. When you live in Me there is eternal life with Me.

**2 Timothy 1:9**
It is God who saved us and chose us to live a holy life. He did this not because
we deserved it, but because that was His plan long before the world began—to
show His love and kindness to us through Christ Jesus. (NLT)

**Turn away from evil and do good. Work hard at living in peace with others.**
(Psalm 34:14)

# *"Prevailing Justice"*

**Ezekiel 33:18-19**
For again I say, "When righteous people turn to evil, they
will die. But if wicked people turn from their wickedness
and do what is just and right, they will live." (NLT)

The LORD is the One and only Living God. He is supreme in His being and His sovereign reign is over everything, both the visible and the invisible. The Lord is perfectly just and is always right. No one or anything trumps the Power of God. God's character and attributes cannot change and His holy nature is perfectly just. But we also have a God who is filled with love and compassion, who is both merciful and gracious when dealing with the people He created in His image. We must also know that God will not be mocked or compromised in anyway. He loathes all evil and unrighteousness, and He is a fair Judge. No matter how good or righteous we may think we are, when we turn away from God to participate in the evilness of this wicked world, God's justice will prevail. Make no doubt about it, the Lord is against all those who are evil and two faced and they will pay a price for their sneaky double mindedness.

It is impossible to pull the wool over God's eyes. You cannot say one thing and think another thing without Him knowing. You cannot be good during the day and then slink into the darkness of night to satisfy the sinful lusts of your flesh and hide it. You are naked before the Lord 24/7, and one day you could be held accountable for our every word, thought, and action against God's ways. You are either with God or without Him. You are either for Him or against Him. With God there are no gray areas and no double standards. You are either His friend or His enemy. The Truth, my dear friend, you cannot live a secret life apart from God and get away with it, for God's Perfect Justice will prevail on that Glorious Day of His return.

## A Whisper of Hope

**Do not try to hide, dear child...**nor try to take advantage of My grace, for My Way cannot be compromised and everything you do and say will be exposed in My Light on Judgment Day. Don't gamble your life away. Instead, live in the Light for all to see.

**Isaiah 56:1, 2**
"Be just and fair to all," says the LORD. "Do what is right and good,
for I am coming soon to rescue you. Blessed are those who are careful
to do this. And blessed are those who keep themselves from doing wrong." (NLT)

**Just and true are Your ways, O King of the saints.**
(Revelation 15:3)

# *"Sin is Evil"*

**James 1:14-15**
Temptation comes from the lure of our own evil desires.
These evil desires lead to evil actions, and evil actions lead to
death. So don't be misled, my dear brothers and sisters. (NLT)

We live in a fallen world that reeks of evil. It was evil that separated us from God and brought sin into our hearts, and if gone unchecked, not only controls our lives, but will forever separate us from God. As natural born sinners we love to sin even when we know it's detestable in the eyes of God. We come into this world with a sinful nature, and as we grow and experience the world around us, we are indoctrinated into believing that sin is whatever we see it as being. This is not the Truth, for sin is evil and it has a hefty price tag attached to it. The Devil is the evil ruler of this world and he has enslaved most its inhabitants without them even knowing it. The Devil has fooled much of the world into believing that traditional godly values are old fashioned and take the fun out of living.

You cannot escape the bondage that sin has over you if you are unaware or misinformed about it. The world would have never known the Truth unless our Lord God and Savior, Jesus Christ had not intervened on our behalf. We would be hopelessly lost in this dark world of sin with no way to escape. Christ Jesus became a man of flesh and blood to die and suffer the penalty for your sins so you, if you wanted to, could escape the horror it brings. Jesus came to break the chains of bondage. He gave you His Word, His blood, and you no longer have an excuse to continue indulging in the sin you love. The choice is yours, my friend. Do you want to escape your bondage to live a God honoring life, or do you want to continue in your sin, enjoying its pleasure while it lasts and then spend eternity regretting your choices?

## A Whisper of Hope

**Seek the Truth, My child...**for it will truly set you free from the love of sin and the fear of the unknown. I chose to come to you. I chose to save you from death and I chose you to be a witness to My Glory and Goodness. With the Truth there is life and pardon, without it you will die condemned.

**1 Corinthians 10:13**
But remember that the temptations that come into your life are no
different from what others experience. And God is faithful. He will
keep the temptation from becoming so strong that you can't stand
up against it. When you are temped He will show you a way out so
that you will not give in to it. (NLT)

**You, who love the LORD, hate evil. He preserves the souls of His saints.**
(Psalm 97:10)

# *"Unleashed"*

**1 Timothy 2:1-3**
I urge you, first of all, to pray for all people. As you make your requests, plead
for God's mercy upon them, and give thanks. This is good and pleases God our
Savior, for He wants everyone to be saved and to understand the Truth. (NLT)

The Lord calls us to pray for all peoples throughout the world, especially for those who suffer at the hands of the oppressive and those who have never heard the Good News Gospel of Jesus Christ. This Good News brings much needed hope into lives that have little hope. God loves all people in ways that our finite minds can never know. Our loving God takes no pleasure in seeing people suffer but He wants the world to know that our suffering does not have to be in vain. And it is the prayers of saints that can make the difference between life or death. The Lord answers prayer and it is through the power of prayer that we can help support God's plan of redemption while He softens hardened hearts and opens the eyes of the blind.

Our prayers for the lost souls of this dark and dying world are an important part of who we are as children of the Living God. And with our prayers is our commission to spread the Good News that forgiveness and salvation is for all peoples throughout the world. When it is all said and done, it is the sovereign power of the Lord that changes lives and saves souls, but it's an awesome thing when the prayer bearer sees God's answered prayer at work in the lives of those they have been praying for. Our relationship with God cannot thrive without prayer. We cannot successfully be guided through this difficult life without conversation with the Lord. For when we try going it alone and ignore God, we either end up making a big mess of things, or we hurt ourselves or the people we are trying to help. The power of prayer dear friend, can unleash the Power of God.

## A Whisper of Hope

**Talk to Me, dear child...**You can come to Me at any time and any place, because I came, I suffered, and I died to remove the barrier between us. You are My voice and My Light for this dark world that chooses not to listen. Our relationship is a key ingredient, our communication a must.

**1 Peter 3:12**
The eyes of the Lord watch over those who do right,
and His ears are open to their prayers. But the Lord
turns His face against those who do evil. (NLT)

**Devote yourselves to prayer with an alert mind and a thankful heart.**
(Colossians 4:2)

# *"Good Living"*

**James 3:13**
If you are wise and understand God's ways, live a life
of steady goodness so that only good deeds pour forth.
And if you don't brag about the good you do, then you
will be truly wise. (NLT)

Tue and absolute wisdom comes from One Source only, the LORD, our God, Creator, and Savior. He created all things, and is our Source for everything. If you want true wisdom, all you have to do is go to the Source. If you want to know the best way to live, go to the One who created life. No question is too difficult for God, or a mystery too mysterious. God always has the correct answer that is perfect, and it comes at just the right moment in time for those who humbly asks and expect an answer. The Lord has sent many prophets over the ages to give us His Wisdom. He also personally came into our world to help us understand His Wisdom— Wisdom that brings life, rather than death—Wisdom that changes lives from hopelessness and doubt to lives filled with hope and truth—Wisdom that tells us how to live this life with peace and confidence.

Mans flawed wisdom comes from the Devil and our sinful nature. It is pride that tells a man that he knows better how to live than God does. We can see the evidence of this flawed wisdom of man by the state our world is in because of man's denial of God's Way. We cannot rely on manmade wisdom because it is not only conjecture and in flux, but its source is flawed and does not come from the Creator, but from that which He created. Man's wisdom is made up, unreliable, and self serving. Man's wisdom scrambles about like a disturbed nest of ants, frantically running about in all directions hoping for the best results. God's wisdom, on the other hand, is first hand, purpose driven and leads to good living. God's wisdom brings peace amidst the chaos. God's wisdom is your only chance for a good life now, and a perfect one later. And you can trust that it never changes and will get you Home!

## A Whisper of Hope

**My Wisdom is best, dear child...**I share it to bring goodness and truth into this fallen world that is filled with evil and vile lies. I came to give you a hope and a future in My goodness, so you could, in return, share it with those who are without God and know no goodness.

**Psalm 33:4-5**
For the Word of the LORD is right, and all His work
is done in truth. He loves righteousness and justice,
the earth is full of the goodness of the LORD. (NKJ)

**Trust in the LORD always, for the LORD GOD is the eternal Rock.**
(Isaiah 26:4)

# *"Best Way"*

**Lamentations 3:31-33**
For the LORD does not abandon anyone forever. Though He brings grief,
He also shows compassion according to the greatness of His unfailing love.
For He does not enjoy hurting people or causing them sorrow. (NLT)

Our God is first and foremost, a Holy God. One that is perfect in every way. He is never unjust nor is He ever unfair. He never leads anyone into anything that is less than righteous. But there are times when the Lord disciplines His children for their wrongs, but He does this because He is our loving, eternal Father who wants to transform our sinful lives into righteous lives. He disciplines, we learn. And it is these invaluable lessons and righteous truths, that awaken our souls and save us from the eternal condemnation that is justly due for our vile conduct against our Holy God.

Many people, like myself, spent much of our lives believing that God is a mean, angry, and unjust old coot that sits on His throne in Heaven watching all the chaotic messes we create for ourselves, laughing at our stupidity, and looking forward to punishing us for not obeying His rigid, fun killing rules that are impossible to keep. But many of these same people, much like I did, learn the truth about a different kind of God after we surrendered our struggling lives to the Lord in search of truth and peace. We learn that our God really loves all people unconditionally and deeply, because He left the glory of Heaven to become a mere human being so He could die our death. Once you begin to understand the true nature of God and why He saved us, the fog is lifted and you will see more clearly who God is, who you are, and why this world hates Him.

## A Whisper of Hope

**My Way is best, dear child...**all others are in vain. The world's ways will lead you away from the Truth and into the darkness. I came to you from the glory of Heaven, to do what you could not do for yourself. Trust in the Best Way and you will live forever!

**Revelation 15:3, 4**
Great and marvelous are Your actions, Lord God Almighty. Just
and true are Your ways, O King of the nations. Who will not fear,
O Lord, and glorify Your Name. For You alone are Holy. (NLT)

**We have been made right in God's sight by the blood of Christ.**
(Romans 5:9)

# "Rejoice"

**Psalm 118:24**
This is the day the LORD has made.
We will rejoice and be glad in it. (NLT)

Whenever a new day is given to us, it is because we have a gracious and merciful God. As for the children of God, we should be glad and rejoice, because we know that the One who holds our lives in His hands is not yet finished with us in this short life. Our mission is not yet complete. For those who ignore God and live as they please, they, too, should rejoice, because God is giving them another day to change their way, and be adopted into His Family. God does this because He puts the highest value on all human beings. Everyone born into this difficult life should really trust God no matter what their circumstances may be, because He is the One in charge. There are many reasons to begin each new day with thanksgiving to God, because without His sovereign control over creation and without His special love for mankind there would be no reason to rejoice, no life to enjoy, and absolutely no hope after this life is over.

If you are one of the many who take this life for granted, or you wake up dreading the day to come, or you feel like a victim of circumstance and there is no way out, you don't know the Living God who created you and personally saved you from living this life in vain. Without the Lord God Jesus Christ, you will have no true understanding about life or the purpose for your existence. Without Jesus you will be grasping at straws and hoping to get lucky. And after too many wrong straws drawn, you will simply give up, hoping the end will really be the end. Living this difficult life without the hope of Christ Jesus, is like living dead—no hope for tomorrow, no hope for the next day, and no hope when this life is over. Without Jesus my friend, there is simply no hope in living or in dying.

## A Whisper of Hope

**There is reason to rejoice, child...**for when you live in Me, your life will never end and it will only get better. You need not worry about this dangerous world, because in Me, you are safely in My mighty hands. Be glad that I AM who I say I AM.

**Psalm 31:7**
I am overcome with joy because of Your unfailing
love, for you have seen my troubles, and you care
about the anguish of my soul. (NLT)

**Always be full of joy in the Lord. I say again, rejoice!**
(Philippians 4:4)

# *"Glory Gift"*

**1 Peter 1:4**
For God has reserved a priceless inheritance for
His children. It is kept in Heaven for you, pure
and undefiled beyond reach of change and decay. (NLT)

What an incredible promise this is for all those who have been adopted into God's eternal family. Because of this promise, all of our sins have been forgiven, we are justified by the blood of Jesus, and are granted the legal rights to an incredible, everlasting inheritance. A share in the glory of our Lord God and Savior Jesus Christ is an amazing gift, one that our finite minds cannot really grasp the totality of. But we can fully trust that whatever this undeserved inheritance is, it will be out of this world and indeed glorious. Through God's Word we get a partial picture of this inheritance in our eternal life in the new Heaven and Earth that will replace the old. And this information is just enough to give our inquiring minds a taste of the wonderful future to come, and that hope will help us get through the many difficult circumstances that living in this world brings. And it also helps us keep motivated to live a godly, righteous life in the here and now.

Our gracious God tells us throughout the Scriptures, that He is the only True, Living God, and that we can fully trust in His every Word and Promise. When we fully entrust our lives to the LORD God, our Heavenly Father, there comes a peace of heart and mind of the believer that surpasses anything this world has to offer, because this world and everything in it is quickly fading away. We must understand that this priceless gift of an inheritance is a piece of the glory that is Christ Jesus' alone, but it is being reserved for God's children as well. If you have embraced and accepted this incredible gift, honor the King with a righteous life filled with thanksgiving and praise. If you have not, it would be wise to look into it while you can, before the offer runs out.

## A Whisper of Hope

**I came bearing good gifts, dear child...**The undeserved gifts of eternal life and a share in My inheritance. You need not bring anything to the table, but a sorrow-filled, repentant, and humble heart and your love and praise for your God and Savior.

**Colossians 1:11, 12**
May you be filled with joy, always thanking the Father,
who has enabled you to share the inheritance that belongs
to God's holy people, who live in the Light. (NLT)

**I want you to realize what a rich and glorious inheritance**
**He has given to His people.**
(Ephesians 1:18)

# December

# *"Nowhere to Hide"*

**Proverbs 28:13**
He who covers his sin will not prosper, but whoever
confesses and forsakes them will have mercy. (NKJ)

It is wise to believe that our Sovereign God knows and sees all things, even the most inner secrets of our hearts and minds, because thinking we can hide anything from our all knowing, all seeing God is frivolous and foolish. No one can successfully serve two masters( sin and God) and get away with it, especially when One is omnipresent. We cannot enjoy the pleasures of our sin hoping to cover it up with our good works, because our God will not be mocked or manipulated. When we set our minds to it, we can fool other people most of the time, but not so with God. The best and wisest way to live this life is to always be upfront and honest with the Lord, because He is the One who holds our destiny in His hands. For the Lord God accepts everyone with a humble and contrite heart, but He rejects all those who are too wise to confess and too proud to submit.

You cannot fight your fallen human nature without God and win, even if you give it your best shot, because your human flesh is weak and the urge to sin is natural. Unless you have the power of God through the indwelling of the Holy Spirit you will fail. Without God's help you will continue in our secret love affair with sin, thinking you have the upper hand. But when you surrender to the Lord my friend, He will give you the victory over the power of sin and you will no longer have to live in shame and guilt. Jesus forgives and forgets and then empowers you to be holy as He is holy.

## A Whisper of Hope

**Hate your sin, My child...**and love the Forgiver. Don't try to hide in the darkness of your sin, for in Me, there is no darkness. Rather than trying to hide your sins from Me, bring them into the Light and be honest. It will bring My mercy and grace into your brokenness.

**1 Peter 3:12**
The eyes of the Lord watch over those who do right,
and His ears are open to their prayers. But the Lord
turns His face against those who do evil. (NLT)

**The LORD is close to the brokenhearted,**
**He rescues those who are crushed in spirit.**
(Psalm 34:18)

# *"Come Home"*

**1 Peter 3:18**
Christ also suffered when He died for our sins once for
all time. He never sinned, but He died for sinners that
He might bring us safely Home to God. (NLT)

The fact that our glorious God and Savior loved us so much that He became a man of flesh and blood so He could suffer, bleed, and die for our many sins, is an incredible Truth and an awesome blessing. Because without God's intervention there would be no hope of salvation for anyone. We would all get a well deserved guilty charge and an eternal life sentence in Hell with no hope for parole. What a sorrowful state of mind we would be in if this extremely short-lived life with all its pain and suffering and hardships was all we had. What an incredible waste of precious souls it would be if we had to live in this difficult life for nothing more than death and eternal punishment. Our God has not only warned us about the cost for living however we want, ignoring His Law and righteous ways, but He has also paid the price for our disobedience. In this modern age of man we can watch the whole world in real time and see the damage that godless living inflicts. We clearly see the decay of morality, godly living, and the family, and yet we continue to make matters worse.

Why would our betrayed God want to save such a rebellious and wicked people from the terrible fate we have justly earned by loving our sin more than Him? Why does the Almighty God continue to allow mankind to continue mocking Him right to His Face, yet does not completely destroy us, but gives us ample opportunity to turn from our sins and redeem our lives? Never doubt God's love for you my friend, for He voluntarily suffered a bloody death, nailed naked to a piece of dead tree to save you from the agony of dying over and over again for all eternity. God created you to live with Him forever in a perfect world. Don't miss out on His offer to personally guide you safely Home, because the alternative is not pretty at all.

## A Whisper of Hope

**Allow Me, My child...**to be your Everything, for when you do, you will surely be glad you did. For I created you to live with Me, forever and in sweet peace. This world is not the end for My children; it is only the beginning of a very long and perfect life to come.

**2 Corinthians 5:4-5**
Our dying bodies make us groan and sigh, but it's not that we
want to die and have no bodies at all. We want to slip into our
new bodies so that these dying bodies will be swallowed up by
everlasting life. God Himself has prepared us for this, and as a
guarantee He has given us the Holy Spirit. (NLT)

**For if we are faithful to the end, trusting God just as firmly
as when we first believed, we will share in all that belongs to Christ.**
(Hebrews 3:14)

# *"The Joy of Jesus"*

**1 Peter 4:19**
So if you are suffering according to God's will, keep
on doing what is right, and trust yourself to the God
who made you, for He will never fail you. (NLT)

No matter who you are or where you live on this sin infected earth, you will suffer. No human is immune from the pit falls of living in a world that has turned away from its Creator. Because mankind decided to live apart from God's influence, human suffering is as much a part of living as breathing is, because with sin and rebellion there come consequences. All people experience sickness and poor physical health, whether it's from disease, natural disasters, accidents, or the aging process. We also experience a variety of emotional sufferings like sadness, regrets, disappointments, and depression, which also takes its toll on the quality of life. We may escape some of these sufferings for a while or simply die at a young age, but inevitably we will all suffer greatly as we live into the later years. Pain and hardship is a reality of life, some experience more than others, but nonetheless, suffer we must until our earthly body can no longer support this difficult life.

So you know that suffering and disasters and dying is just the way it is. But do you know that you are only a decision away from making this short stretch of your life-journey worth all the pain and suffering that it brings? Well, when you belong to the Almighty Lord God and Savior, Jesus Christ and accept His sufferings and death as your own, the sufferings you experience in this life will be replaced with a glorious new life that makes any sufferings in this life a very small price to pay. This gift from God is indeed a life-changer, for when you know you have the forgiveness of God and His promise of a perfect, eternal life sharing in His glorious inheritance, which you cannot possibly begin to imagine, it puts a whole new light on living this difficult life. With Christ Jesus dear friend, your suffering will turn to a joy so deeply rooted in your heart, that even the powers of Hell cannot strip it away from you.

## A Whisper of Hope

**I know this life is hard, dear child...**but live in Me and I will make up for all the sufferings you must face. I will not only get you through to the other side with joy, but I will bring you peace and comfort in your sufferings until that time. Trust Me!

**Philippians 3:9, 10**
But I trust Christ to save me. For God's way of making us right with
Himself depends on faith. As a result, I can really know Christ and
experience the mighty power that raised Him from the dead. I can
learn what it means to suffer with Him, sharing in His death. (NLT)

**May you be filled with joy, always thanking the Father, who has enabled you to share the inheritance that belongs to God's holy people, who live in the Light.**
(Colossians 1:11)

# *"Good Endings"*

**Daniel 5:23**
But you have not honored the God who gives
you the breath of life and controls your destiny. (NLT)

Those people who have been deceived into believing the many deadly lies of the "Big Bang" theory as the reason for their existence are being lead down a very dark path that drops into the abyss of total blackness and regret—an eternal existence without ever seeing the light of day again. This is not a good ending my friends, but it's an ending that many have already chosen and fallen into, and many more are still yet poised to follow suit. Our gracious and loving God has done everything, short of making us His robotic puppets, to teach us the Truth, show us the Way, and warn us of the dire pit falls that disobedience and rebellion bring; ways that dishonor and disclaim the One True God who gives us the breath of life. But in this fallen world that is dominated by the dark and evil forces of Satan, the lies about our beginnings still prevails and many deceived souls have carelessly taken the bait and are foolishly being lead into a darkness so black, that it is impossible to get out.

Our Lord God is not being unreasonable when He calls us to honor Him and His Way. Because the reason He wants us to know the Truth is because He knows what is best for us. God is the only One who knows everything, past, present, and future. He knows what is good for us and He knows what can destroy our lives. God has gone out of His Way to give us the Truth that can save our souls from eternal condemnation. He does not have to do anything, but He has chosen human beings as His special creation and all He wants us to do is to love, honor, and live in His Way—with love being the Key to good endings!

## A Whisper of Hope

**I don't force you to honor Me, dear child...**because I honor your every decision. When you live in the Way I have provided for you, the results are much better for you than for Me. I created You and I know what is best. In most cases, you do not.

**1 Chronicles 16:25-27**
For the LORD is great and greatly to be praised; He is also to be
feared above all gods. For all the gods of the peoples are idols, but
the LORD made the heavens. Honor and majesty are before Him;
strength and gladness are in His place. (NKJ)

**Do not imitate what is evil, but what is good.**
(3 John 11)

# *"Ways and Means"*

**Psalm 119:137-138, 142**
O LORD, You are righteous, and Your decisions are fair. Your
decrees are perfect; they are entirely worthy of our trust. Your
justice is eternal, and Your law is perfectly true. (NLT)

For those of us who believe that the Living God of the Bible is the Creator and Author of
life, we also know that He created us in His image, and that we can fully trust in the Word
of God as the Absolute Truth. We can proclaim the Truth because dishonesty is not a part of
God's perfect character—He cannot lie, because otherwise, He could not exist as God. Because
the power of sin has corrupted our hearts and minds, we cannot always discern what is true
and what is not. Because of our inherent nature to sin first and think about it later, we tend
to look at the righteousness of God as a way to take the fun and pleasure out of life—that the
righteousness of God is unfair and out dated. Because sin blinds us from seeing the Truth as it
really is, many of us struggle with God's ways because they are foreign to us and we are a rebellious, self-centered lot who are filled with pride and good at trusting no one, not even ourselves.

But all this changes when we surrender to the Creator of creation and understand that He
is the One who created us in His image so that our lives would reflect the glory of who He is.
He did not create us to be puppets that would need to rely on His every movement, but to live
as free agents of His righteousness so we could enjoy all that He has provided for us. For the
time being we must deal with this fallen world and our sinful natures, but it won't always be
this way, because our Savior has conquered the power of sin and death once and for all and we
now have the resurrection power of our Lord God to help us do the same. If we can trust our
God to save our eternal lives from pits of Hell, we can trust in all His ways here on earth as well.

## A Whisper of Hope

**Come to Me, My child...**and I will take away the confusion and give you My peace. The world's
ways are twisted and degenerate and they only lead to more uncertainty. But you can trust in
Me, for My ways are perfect, righteous, and fair. They can be nothing less.

**Jeremiah 23:5, 6**
"For the time is coming," says the LORD, "when I will place a
righteous Branch on King David's throne. He will be a King who
rules with wisdom. He will do what is just and right throughout
the land. And this is His name: The LORD Is Our Righteousness. (NLT)

**"Hallelujah! Salvation is from our God.**
**Glory and power belong to Him alone. His judgments are just and true."**
(Revelation 19:1, 2)

# *"Believe It"*

**1 John 1:1, 2**
The One who existed from the beginning is the One we have
heard and seen. We saw Him with our own eyes and touched
Him with our own hands. He is Jesus Christ, the Word of life.
He is the One who is Eternal Life. (NLT)

It is sometimes hard for us to understand why our Infinite, Almighty LORD God, the Creator of Heaven and Earth, lowered Himself to become a mere mortal man like ourselves. Especially, so He could suffer in such a horrible, shameful way and then die a criminal's death in our place. This single act of unconditional love not only saved our eternal lives, but also changed the course of time as well. The resurrection of Jesus into a glorious new body that would never again experience suffering or death also became our own resurrection if we so desire. This Good News my friends, is the Truth that gives new meaning to our lives. For when we have the kind of hope that tells us we will be resurrected from the grave of this earth, to receive a glorious new body that will never again suffer or die, gives us an incentive to do what is good and pleasing in the eyes of God; the One who made it all possible.

But don't be fooled, for there is a price that we must yet pay even though our salvation has already been bought and paid for in full. And the price you must pay will cost you your old life of sin, for it must be nailed to the Cross of Christ, where it can no longer live and reign in your midst. For it is only then, that we become a new creation in Christ Jesus, and it is this new person, whose sins are covered by the blood of Jesus, that receives the Crown of Life from the Eternal One who has always been and always will be. Without our Lord God's sacrifice and death there would be no forgiveness, no glorious resurrection, and no eternal life. But with this undeserved gift we must also sacrifice and die as well—reemerging as a child of the Eternal King.

## A Whisper of Hope

**I died so you could live, My child...** To give you new life in Me. Nothing about this life I have given you is easy, but living in Me will make it worth its trouble in gold. For when you are in Me, I, too, Am in you and I AM the Infinite, Eternal One.

**Colossians 3:3, 5, 10**
For you died when Christ died, and your real life is hidden with Christ
in God. So put to death the sinful, earthly things lurking within you.
In its place you have clothed yourselves with a brand-new nature that
is continually being renewed as you learn more and more about Christ,
who created this new nature within you. (NLT)

**Those who say they live in God should live their lives as Christ did.**
(1 John 2:6)

# "Father in Son"

**1 John 2:23-24**
Anyone who denies the Son doesn't have the Father either. But
anyone who confesses the Son has the Father also. So you must
remain faithful to what you have been taught from the beginning.
If you do, you will continue to live in fellowship with the Son and with the Father. (NLT)

God's Word tells us clearly that the Father and Son are One. Our Almighty God walked upon the face of this earth as a Man of flesh and blood, named Jesus Christ; fully God, and fully human. We will never fully understand the essence of our triune God this side of Heaven. But we can trust that Jesus Christ is the Living God; our Creator, our Savior, and our eternal King. He absorbed into His body the sins of the world to suffer the death and punishment that we deserve for all our detestable sins against the Most Holy God of creation. If you cannot believe that Jesus Christ is LORD, God in the flesh, and that He is the only Way to eternal life, then you have either been duped, or you are living in denial of the Truth so you can take pleasure in your sin. This world denies Christ, it denies the Living God, and it denies that His Word is the absolute Truth. And the world my friends, seems to have a death wish, because without the Father and the Son and the Holy Spirit as One God, there is only darkness in the future. Without LORD God leading our ways, healing our wounds, and forgiving our many sins, we waste this life by living in fear, worry, doubt, guilt, shame, and a sense of hopelessness and futility when we could be living in peace and thanksgiving and joy for the gift of salvation.

For the people who deny the triune God of the Bible, this difficult life with its few pleasures will not be worth the price they will pay when this life is over, because the price for denying the Living God is eternal death, which will not be a pleasant way to spend the rest of eternity. For an eternal life without the glory of God is absolute darkness and isolation, dying over and over again. But for those of us who believe in the Word of God, we will be walking hand and hand with the Creator and the King of the universe in a real close and personal relationship forever. Our suffering in this short life is nothing compared to the glorious inheritance we will receive for the rest of eternity. By embracing the Father and Son my friends, you will receive the Holy Spirit to live in you while you wait for Him to come and take you Home.

## A Whisper of Hope

**There is only One God, My child...**and I Am He. I Am your only hope in this life if you want to escape the consequences that living apart from Me brings. I created you and I died for you, and I have eternal plans for you that are out of this world.

**1 Corinthians 12:4-6**
Now there are different kinds of spiritual gifts, but it is the same Holy Spirit who is the Source of them all. There are different kinds of service in the church, but it is the same Lord we are serving. There are different ways God works in our lives, but it is the same God who does the work through all of us. (NLT)

**God the Father chose you long ago, and the Spirit has made you holy.
As a result, you have obeyed Jesus Christ and are cleansed by His blood.**
(1 Peter 1:2)

# *"Freely Alive"*

**1 John 3:24**
Those who obey God's commandments live in fellowship
with Him, and He with them. And we know He lives in
us because the Holy Spirit lives in us. (NLT)

If you say you are a Christian, but cannot curb your appetite for sin, you do not have the Holy Spirit helping you control your sin addiction. If you say you love God but you do not obey His laws, you do not have the Spirit of Truth living in your heart. If you say you believe that Jesus Christ is the Light and Savior of the world, but continue to live in the darkness, you are only fooling yourself, for it is the Holy Spirit who gives us the desire to live in the Light of God. You cannot serve the gods of this wicked world and be a child of the Living God. When you follow the gods of this world, you cannot faithfully serve our God in Heaven. And you cannot expect to receive the blessings of God when you are living in darkness, satisfying your own sinful flesh, and without God's blessings you have nothing to bless others with. When you are living your life just for you and ignoring the One who created you, you are living far away from the Father, the Son, and the Holy Spirit, and living in close fellowship with the Devil and the gods of this evil world.

We live in a world that is far away from its Creator. We live in a world filled with hate, greed, and self love. We live in a world that denies the deity of Christ Jesus, and worships a vast array of manmade gods that promise much, but delivers only death. Living in this world is a very dangerous proposition for all people, because without God's cover of protection we are easy prey for those who want to eternally harm us. The only wise option you have my friend, is receiving the gift of salvation through the blood of Jesus Christ and the power of God through the indwelling of the Holy Spirit. Because without God safely guiding you through this difficult life-journey, you will not make it to Heaven! It is not easy staying on the path of righteousness that God calls us to travel on, but with the blood of Jesus as your cover and the Holy Spirit as your Strength, this fallen world holds no power over you—you are free and alive and safe!

## A Whisper of Hope

**Fellowship with Me, dear child...**is life. Without it, there is only a meek existence and false hope. Do not be fooled by the gods of this wicked world, because in them there is only darkness and death. They promise much, but what they deliver is dark in nature and leads only to your demise.

**Philippians 3:7-8, 9**
I once thought these things were valuable, but now I consider
them worthless because of what Christ has done. Yes, every
thing else is worthless when compared with the infinite value
of knowing Christ Jesus my Lord. For His sake I have discarded
everything else, counting it all as garbage, so that I could gain
Christ and become one with Him. (NLT)

**Dear children, keep away from anything that might take God's place in your hearts.**
(1 John 5:21)

# "Privileged"

**1 John 5:18**
We know that those who have become part of God's family
do not make a practice of sinning, for God's Son holds them
securely, and the evil one cannot get His hands on them. (NLT)

Being an adopted child of the Living God has many incredible privileges. One of these privileges is the power to control our sinful nature. For we are not only forgiven, but we are also given the means to live a new life through the power of the Holy Spirit. When we come to the Lord humble and broken, admitting our sinful rebellion, He doesn't leave us forgiven, alone, and helpless amidst the evil that controls the world around us. Rather, He opens our eyes so we can see the true difference between God's Way and the world's ways and then gives us the power to change. Jesus did not suffer and die nailed to a cross to satisfy God's anger against mankind only to abandon us, but to walk with each one of us through the steps of a total transformation that makes us a new creation—a process that not only requires the resurrection power of God, but our full commitment as well.

It is not only an incredible privilege to be a part of God's eternal Family, but it is the only way that helps me through this difficult life-journey with a heart filled with peace, joy, and the hope for better things to come. I understand that loving the ways of this fallen world for the few pleasures that can make you feel good in the moment is rather futile, because after the thrill is gone you are right back where you were before, with a future that is unknown and looking quite bleak. Be of good sense my dear friends, accept the unconditional offer of being adopted into the greatest Family in existence. Give up your life of sin and darkness and be empowered to live righteously in the glorious Light of God's saving grace. Don't be sucked into the pleasures of deception and then, one day, find yourself in Hell without a plan or a hope of escaping, because there is none for either.

## A Whisper of Hope

**Come as you are, My child…**and I will take you in, cleanse you from your sin, clothe you in My righteousness, and give you a new life—one that is not only better for you now, but a life that is also forever. Come into My eternal family just as you are and I will transform you into perfection!

**Galatians 4:4, 5-6, 7**
God sent His Son to buy freedom for us who were slaves to the law,
so that He could adopt us as His very own children. And because you
Gentiles have become His children, God has sent the Spirit of His Son
into your hearts, and now you can call God your dear Father. Now you
are no longer a slave but God's own child. (NLT)

**Light shines on the godly, and joy on those who do right.**
(Psalm 97:10)

# *"One God"*

**Hosea 4:11, 12**
Alcohol and prostitution have robed My people of their brains.
Longing after idols has made them foolish. They have played
the prostitute, serving other gods and deserting their God. (NLT)

All peoples belong to God because He makes us and gives us the breath of life. He sustains our lives and gives us everything we need. We belong to God much like a child belongs to their father, and He wants everyone to understand and believe this truth. God loves us so much that He gives us a free will and the ability to make sound judgments and intelligent decisions. But the Devil has taken us into the realm of darkness, sin, and rebellion; deceiving us into believing that we are gods and have the power to do whatever we like and without accountability, believing that it is God who is the real enemy and He does everything He can to disclaim our godhood. Many of the people in this world do believe they are gods, while others believe in many gods, and we can see how the decadence of this way of thinking is killing our world. We see how man made wisdom (foolishness) has poisoned the hearts and minds of its people, and they are being led down a path of self destruction, false hope and godless living. And we see that most people are either too busy lusting after worldly things, or they are simply too busy just trying to stay alive to see the grace of God.

The sinful desires of the flesh blind us from seeing the Truth and finding the joy of the Lord that is in His amazing grace. Instead, unbeknownst to most, they are seeking to fill the emptiness that only God can fill. And because they know so little about the One who created them, they try to fill their emptiness with things that do not last—things that are here today, but soon fade away—things that have no eternal value whatsoever. If you are there and do not know the One who created you and then saved you, it would behoove you to do so, because ignorance or pride or any other excuse will not stand on the final day of God's judgment. It is foolish to ignore all of God's gracious warnings. It is extremely foolish to follow this dying world that is killing its babies, mocking its Creator and following the Devil. Do not contribute to your own demise and that of the worlds, my friend, by acting like a godless god, because you will be destroyed!

## A Whisper of Hope

**I made you, dear child...**but not to control you. You can choose to follow anyone or anything you please. But you need to choose wisely; use the God given sense and intelligence that I gave you, for your choices will either lead you to life or death; into the Light or into the darkness.

**Jeremiah 10:14-15**
Compared to God, all people are foolish and have no knowledge at all.
They make idols, but the idols will disgrace their masters, for they are
frauds. They have no life or power in them. Idols are worthless; they
are lies! The time is coming when they will all be destroyed. (NLT)

**The wise shall inherit glory, but shame shall be the legacy of fools.**
(Proverbs 3:35)

# "God's Power"

**Proverbs 11:7**
When the wicked die, their hopes all perish,
for they rely on their own feeble strength. (NLT)

As finite, mortal human beings who rely on our Creator to survive in this vast, untamed universe that threatens our very existence every moment in time, we are relatively powerless in our quest to fight both the unseen evil forces and ones we can see threatening our lives. Neither our physical bodies nor our limited intelligence has what it takes to overcome these powerful forces that are far greater than the limited power God has given us. We are God dependent and a God needy people because He created us this way, and it is this absolute law of creation that we cannot dispute or ignore with a any sense of confidence. Our Sovereign God alone has the infinite power to save us from ourselves, the evil powers of Hell, or anything else in the universe, no matter how powerful or how impossible it may be. Nothing trumps the power our Almighty Creator.

Our Lord God has given us just enough power to fight the everyday challenges that come with living in this fallen world, but when it comes to protecting ourselves from the forces of the universe or the everyday battles for our hearts, minds and souls, we do not have a chance without the protection or infinite power of our Almighty God. For those who fight their sinful nature and the evil forces of darkness without God's help, they will simply lose or realize their mistake when it's too late. For once we breathe our very last breath, so, too, do our opportunities to call out to the Lord to help us fend off the powers of darkness that want only to kill our souls. God's power is the only Way to win the battle of life, so be wise my friend, and don't compromise.

## A Whisper of Hope

**Without My Sovereign Power, dear child...**you are easy prey for those who want to kill your soul. But with My Power, I will not only protect you from the Enemy, but I will give you the desire to do good, rather than that, which is harmful and often deadly.

**Luke 10:17, 18-20**
"Lord, even the demons obey us when we use Your name." "Yes," He told them, "I saw Satan falling from Heaven as a flash of lightning. And I have given you authority over all the power of the Enemy, and you can walk among snakes and scorpions and crush them. Nothing will injure you. But don't rejoice just because evil spirits obey you, rejoice because your names are registered as citizens of Heaven." (NLT)

**We have the LORD our God to help us and to fight our battles for us!**
(2 Chronicles 32:8)

# "Solid Rock"

**Psalm 125:1**
Those who trust in the LORD are as secure as
Mount Zion; they will not be defeated, but will
endure forever. (NLT)

There is no One more trustworthy than the LORD our God. He is the Rock of our salvation that cannot be shaken. He is as solid as an iron mountain that cannot be moved. Whenever we put our trust in Him, we can rely on His every Word and feel absolutely secure in the Truth of His glorious Light. For when you truly belong to the LORD, nothing will ever be able to snatch you from His mighty grip—His love for you can never be weakened—His commitment never shaken. When the storms in the sea of life are unleashing their fury upon you, thrashing you about like a paper doll and you are gasping for one last breath, you will be able to still your heart and be sure that your Savior is near and your life is safely in His hands. He is there to calm the sea with His peace and pull you into His loving arms to comfort your fears, clothe you in new strength, and get you safely to the other side where you and He can rejoice and set sail again on your life-journey Home.

No matter how we have rebelled against our God, or how long we have lived without Him, He is our everlasting Forgiver and Redeemer. He never turns a humble soul or a troubled heart away from His saving grace, for as long as we have the breath of life, He is with us. He never gives up searching for those who are lost at sea, gasping for life and grasping for something to hang on to that will keep them afloat until help arrives, so they won't be swallowed up by the raging storm and sink deep into the depths of the dark unknown where many have been lost before. With the Lord as the captain of your life-journey, when the seas get rough and throw you about, there is no need to fear, for the Savior is always near!

## A Whisper of Hope

**I Am, dear child...**your solid foundation...upon which you should build your life. I Am the Rock of your eternal life; the Way that is never shaken nor broken. If you want to experience the life-journey that I have prepared for you, follow Me, you will be so happy you did!

**2 Samuel 2-3**
The LORD is my Rock, my Fortress, and my Savior; my God is my
Rock, in whom I find protection. He is my Shield, the strength of
my salvation, and my Stronghold, my High Tower, my Savior, the
One who saves me from violence. (NLT)

**I will lie down in peace and sleep, for you alone O LORD, will keep me safe.**
(Psalm 4:8)

# *"The Way"*

**Hosea 14:8**
"Stay away from idols! I am the One who looks after
you and cares for you. I am like a tree that is always
green, giving My fruit to you all through the year." (NLT)

Anything that takes the place of God in your heart will leave you incomplete, unsatisfied, and longing for more. When you trust this world to give you the desires of your heart rather than your Creator, you are foolish, short-sighted, and one day you will regret it. Only our infinite Lord God knows what is best for us. We all desperately need the Living God, because we are finitely mortal, weak in stature, and inherently flawed with sin, self-pride, and death. We tend to blindly follow our sinful nature to satisfy the desires of our flesh, because we are either ignorant in the ways of God or we don't care what lies beyond this short life. But in due time and unbeknownst to those who live apart from God, this world and all the things they idolize will eventually let them down and bring them down. The ways of this fallen world are all directed by the Devil and his evil counterparts, and when combined with our sinful desires becomes a deadly trap for sure. This evil world has hardened many hearts and caused much havoc in the lives of ordinary people who were just searching for happiness and something that would fill the emptiness and give them peace.

God created each of us with an emptiness that only He can fill. God created us with desires that only He can satisfy. But since the Devil introduced evil and rebellion into our world, it is the sin within that causes us to lust for things rather than God—evil things that pull us away from God. And without God's Truth we are gullible and easily fooled, and will blindly follow our sinful nature into the grave. Even when we know God but fail to follow His righteous ways, our hearts harden so hard that our lives become nothing more than a mockery of the authority of God, and that my friends, is not a very good place to be. The Best Way is also the only Way to Heaven and it is found in Christ Jesus.

## A Whisper of Hope

**I Am not only the Best Way, dear child...**I Am the only Way Home. All others are false in their premise. It was I who put eternity in your heart. It was I who wove the longings for God into your very being. Only I can fill the emptiness that yearns to be filled. Let Me fill you completely.

**Matthew 6:31-33**
So don't worry about having enough food or drink or clothing. Why be
like the pagans who are so deeply concerned about these things? Your
Heavenly Father already knows all your needs, and He will give you all
you need from day to day if you live for Him and make the Kingdom of
God your primary concern. (NLT)

**There is no one like the God of Israel. He rides across the heavens to help you.**

(Deuteronomy 33:26)

# "Heart of God"

**Joel 2:13**
Return to the LORD your God, for He is gracious
and merciful. He is not easily angered. He is filled
with kindness and is eager not to punish you. (NLT)

As sin flawed people living in a sin filled world, our vision is clouded, our hearts are hardened, and we overlook our God, and fail to see this wicked world as it really is. We are more prone to focus on the temporary things that this world falsely promises, rather than on the eternal things that our God truthfully promises. We are taught, not only to think that we deserve everything we want, but it is our right to have it. But when we don't get it, we are more apt curse God for our misfortune and blame this unfair life for not coming through. But God is not the problem, He is the solution. Our Lord God left the glory of Heaven to became a man so He could cleanse us of our sins and give us eternal life. The Lord God not only gave us His life's blood, but He gave us His written Word to explain how this life works, and to warn us about the pit falls of living without Him. Our gracious and merciful God has shared His infinite wisdom, not to punish us, but to save us from this sin filled world.

Our God cannot lie, and He never does anything less than righteous. God is our Creator, Provider and Protector. He is an eternal Father to His children. He tells us the absolute Truth and we can stake our eternal lives on it. Our Sovereign God observes all the goings on in the world and He directs everything towards His good will and His Plan for man. Our Lord God and Savior, Jesus Christ, helps us through this difficult life with His Holy Spirit. He helps the humble who are poor in spirit and strengthens the righteous who are fighting for their lives. But for the proud and arrogant, He usually allows the laws of sowing and reaping to bring them to their knees in search of the Truth. Our LORD God is good, honest, and just. He loves you as if you were His only child. The Lord desires to share His goodness and glory with you—goodness that is yours forever if you so desire.

## A Whisper of Hope

**I desire good things for you, My child...**Although I disapprove of your sin and allow you to feel the pain of its consequences, I do not like to see you hurt or discouraged. I want what is best for you in the long run and will continue to watch over you and do what I can to help you.

**Isaiah 44:21, 22**
I, the LORD, made you, and I will not forget to help you.
I have swept away your sins like the morning mists. I have
scattered your offenses like the clouds. Oh, return to Me, for
I have paid the price to set you free. (NLT)

**God is wise in heart and mighty in strength.**
(Job 9:4)

# "Living Through Death"

**Revelation 2:17**
"Anyone who is willing to hear should listen to the Spirit
and understand what the Spirit is saying to the churches.
Whoever is victorious will not be hurt by the second death." (NLT)

Jesus Christ is our Lord God and Savior; the One who defeated sin and death for us because we are incapable of doing it on our own. He accomplished what we cannot. He became our sin and was victorious over its sting by becoming the first to be resurrected from the grave. All people are cursed with sin and death. We all sin and we all die because of our sin—a very real reality that we must all face someday. If we are not taken out early in life, we can count on our bodies growing old, wearing out, and finally dying. God made man from the dust of the earth, and so shall we return in this present fallen state. But we don't have to decompose in the darkness of the grave forever, for there is Good News for those who embrace the death of the Sacrificial Lamb of God as their own. The child of God grew into a man to die for the sins of mankind—so that whosoever believed in the death and resurrection of Christ Jesus our Lord would escape the second death of eternal condemnation. But for those who have rejected the saving grace of Jesus' death, Judgment Day will be a dreadful day indeed, for every non-believer will be raised from the darkness of their grave to face the Lord and give a full account for how they lived their lives, and then be thrown into the eternal burning Lake of Fire.

There are only two basic choices you can make in this first leg of your life-journey. You can choose to live in the Light of God's saving grace, or live in the darkness of this dying world. You can trust Jesus with your life and live forever, or you can trust in the many gods of this evil world and forever die. You can choose to take up your cross and follow Jesus to receive the Crown of Life, or you can choose to indulge in the sins of this wicked world while you can, and hope that God does not exist. In the light of these choices my friends, there is only One Choice that is wise. The Lord God, your Savior, has graciously given you the opportunity to choose, but only in this life.

## A Whisper of Hope

**I give you a choice, dear child...**a time to choose how to live this life. It is not an easy decision to make amidst the many voices of this fallen world that want your soul. All I ask is that you study your choices carefully, weigh your options, and choose wisely—for your very life is at stake.

**1 John 5:11**
For there are three who bear witness in Heaven: the Father,
the Word, and the Holy Spirit who bears witness, because the Spirit is truth.
And this is the testimony: that God has given us eternal life, and this life is in His Son. (NLT)

**"If the righteous are barely saved,
what chance will the godless and sinners have?"**
(1 Peter 4:18)

# *"Son Shine"*

**Matthew 3:8**
Prove by the way you live that you have really
turned from your sins and turned to God. (NLT)

There is more to salvation than mere words. We must have the indwelling of the Holy Spirit to help us transition from a lifestyle of sin and self-gratification to a lifestyle of godly living and self sacrifice. We need the power of God to help us fight the battles for our hearts and minds; battles waged by the dark forces of evil that want to pull us away from God and His protection. Satan is indeed, a dark and powerful force to be reckoned with and he is too powerful, too clever, and too evil for our finite human strength, our fallen human will, and our limited human knowledge. We do not stand a chance against the Devil in our current fallen state. We need Jesus or we will lose.

As a child of God, we develop the desire to please Him. But we soon discover that it is much easier said than done, because living a godly life is not a part of our sinful nature, nor does it coincide with the ways of this wicked world. It is impossible to live in God's Light at the same time you are living in the darkness of this wicked world. You may fool other Christians for a while, but God will not be mocked. When you are truly God's child, you will spend everyday in His Presence, learning to live in this evil world reflecting God's Light into its darkness. And as you shine, your life becomes a picture of total transformation. Those who know you will see the amazing changes taking place, and they, along with many others, will be drawn to you wanting to know what you know that they do not. The Lord wants His children to shine in this dark world whose people are lost without even knowing it.

## A Whisper of Hope

**When you belong to Me, dear child...**the changes that others see in you will be your testimony to Me. You need not prove your heart to Me, but the world needs to see My good work in you, for I Am the only Way to everlasting life.

**Deuteronomy 30:10**
The LORD your God will delight in you if you
obey His voice, and if you turn to the LORD
your God with all your heart and soul. (NLT)

**"Now return to Me, and I will return to you," says the LORD Almighty.**
(Malachi 3:7)

# "Judgment"

**Amos 5:20**
Yes, the day of the LORD will be a dark and
hopeless day, without a ray of joy or hope. (NLT)

Although God banished mankind from His Holy Presence, He would not leave it that way. He saw how weak and helpless we were in our sin and provided the Way for us to overcome that weakness and come back into His Presence, saving us from judgment and eternal condemnation. The Lord God clothed Himself in humanity so He could live and die for this world filled with sin and hopelessness. He came as a child and grew into manhood. He graciously suffered the same worldly afflictions that we all suffer as human beings, but as a man, He did not sin and was able to bear the sins of the world and the punishment that was justly due. Jesus Christ not only came as our Savior, but He came so we would see, know, and experience God's love and compassion, His mercy and grace, and His sovereign power over creation. Jesus came the first time as the God Promised Messiah, but He also came to warn us about His second coming.

When Jesus returns to this world, He will come bearing the scars of His crucifixion. He will come with fire in His eyes and with a vengeance the world has never seen. He will come riding on a great white horse with His army of saints and angels to put an end to the evil and corruption that has been decaying our world since the fall of man. King Jesus will remove the evil from our world and He will set up His Heavenly Kingdom on Earth where He will reign with an iron rod. God's people will live in peace and prosperity for one thousand years and after that, the final Day of Judgment for all those who rejected His saving grace. When Jesus returns it will indeed be a fearful and horrible day for the unsaved—a day that I would encourage you to opt out on.

## A Whisper of Hope

**As My return draws near, dear child...**come back to Me so I can protect you from the wrath to come. I want no one left behind to suffer the fate of this evil world. I would much rather pull you out of the wrath to come and keep you safe.

**Revelation 16:15**
"Take note: I will come as unexpectedly as a thief!
Blessed are all who are watching for Me, who keep their
robes ready so they will not need to walk naked and ashamed." (NLT)

**"Look the Lord is coming with thousands of His holy ones."**
(Jude 14)

# "Warning!"

**Revelation 3:18**
Because you obeyed My command to persevere,
I will protect you from the great time of testing
that will come upon the whole world. (NLT)

The great and terrible time of testing is drawing near. The Lord could, at any moment, snatch up His Church and unleash His anger upon this world that hates Him. We lost our world to Satan and it has been in decline and decay since that very day, but the Lord has numbered its days. Although we do not know the day or hour, God has been gracious enough to give us many signs in the heavens and many messages that are written in words that we can read and understand. Many of these warnings have come straight from the mouth of God when He walked upon this earth, so it is very important that we understand who our God is, because although He is a saving God, He plays no favorites aside from His people Israel. The Lord is perfectly divine in both His character and kingship, which makes Him perfectly just and right in everything He does. He cannot and will not let the unrepentant sinners go unpunished, for if He did He would not be who He claims to be. Instead, He would be a liar and a fraud and that is simply not possible, because God can only be God. He is true to His Word and you would be wise not to believe otherwise!

The way Lord Jesus is going to protect His Church (Christian believers) from the seven years of His wrath being poured out upon this evil world is by simply taking us to live in the present Heaven until it is over. And this is where we will remain until we return with the King to set up His Kingdom on Earth forever. But until this time of great testing we have the Holy Spirit and the promises of God as our hope. If you are living in the Light of God's saving grace you are forgiven and protected. But if you are not, you should heed the warnings that have been graciously revealed to you by your Savior. They are not hearsay, nor are they mythical. They are absolutely true!

## A Whisper of Hope

**Live in Me, dear child...**and I will live in you and protect you. Do not live in the world, for it cannot protect you from the fire of My testing. But for those who belong to Me, I have already taken their testing and have set them free from harm.

**Daniel 12:1-3**
At that time Michael, the archangel who stands guard over your nation, will arise. Then there will be a time of anguish greater than any since nations first came into existence. But at that time every one of your people whose name is written in the Book will be rescued. Many of those whose bodies lie dead and buried will rise up, some to everlasting life and some to shame and everlasting contempt. (NLT)

**Since everything around us is going to melt away,**
**what holy, godly lives you should be living.**
(2 Peter 3:11)

# *"Grace and Favor"*

**Jonah 3:10-4:2**
When God saw that they had put a stop to their evil ways, He had mercy on them
and didn't carry out the destruction He had threatened. This change of plans upset
Jonah, and he became very angry. So he complained to the LORD about it. "Didn't
I say before I left home that you would do this, LORD? That is why I ran away! I
knew that you were a gracious and compassionate God, slow to get angry and filled
with unfailing love. I knew how easily you could cancel Your plans for destroying
these people. (NLT)

There are some things our Lord wants us to learn from these God inspired words of
Scripture, living words that will help us in this difficult life-journey that is not so easily
understood. One of the things God wants us to know is His character, that He is a living God
who is filled with mercy and grace and compassion for all people, including pagan Gentiles. The
Lord wants us to know that He is a sovereign and patient God—a God of second chances and
One who is all knowing, all seeing, and in control of His creation. God has given the people of
this world chance after chance to change their wicked ways and return to Him so He can teach
them how to live. Our God wants us to be gracious and merciful as He is, because we tend not
to be so gracious or merciful to others. Instead, we like to condemn others for their wicked ways
while overlooking our own sinful ways. We tend to compare ourselves with those who are far
away from God when we should be comparing ourselves with the likeness of Jesus Christ. The
Lord wants us to understand, respect, and fear His authority over our lives and all creation—
that it is by the Power of His Word that we even exist. It is because of His mercy and grace that
He gives us the chance to change our evil ways and turn to Him. God is still giving us time—
time we should use wisely while we still live in this time of His gracious favor.

## A Whisper of Hope

**Waste not a moment, dear child...**for you know not the hour of your time's end. Use godly
wisdom, rather than your limited earthly wisdom. My wisdom is meant to save, rather than to
deceive. Come to Me and I will teach you how to live forever.

**1 Thessalonians 5:8-9**
But let us who live in the Light think clearly, protected by the
body armor of faith and love and wearing as our helmet the
confidence of our salvation. For God decided to save us through
our Lord Jesus Christ, not to pour out His anger on us. (NLT)

**For the Word of God is full of Living Power.**
(Hebrews 4:12)

# *"Making Change"*

**Micah 6:6**
What can we bring to the LORD
to make up for what we have done? (NLT)

Although this is a great question, I believe the greater question is this: what can we bring to the LORD for what H<u>e has done?</u> I believe we can answer both of these questions much in the same way, with the latter question being a bit more pressing for us now that we are living towards the end of the church age. What our Lord God and Savior has done, He did for every living person in the world. The Lord became our sin and has given us the glorious, undeserved gift of eternal life. This once in a lifetime gift is wrapped in forgiveness, bound in the ribbon of protection and secured with the bow of salvation. This glorious gift is one that is easy enough to accept, but not so easily secured, because what the LORD really wants from us is our undying love, selfless commitment, and total submission—qualities that are really foreign to us in our current fallen state.

The LORD calls us to sacrifice our old life of sin—out with the old and in with the new; cleansed by the blood of Jesus and resurrected a new creation. It looks easy on paper, but it takes the Power of God to pull off, because our sinful nature is too deeply rooted for us to fight on our own. There are always enjoyable sins that are so hard to let go of that we often hang on to them as long as possible, trying to justify their power over us. Change is never easy and it always requires sacrifices we don't necessarily like, but are needed if we are to live in God's Light. We owe God for sacrificing His life for us, but He won't force you to accept His sacrifice. But when you do, He will help you make the change from loving sin to loving Him. Without Jesus' death there would be no forgiveness and no eternal life. We would never know who the One who created us is, nor would we have His joy and promise to get us through this difficult life and to the other side.

## A Whisper of Hope

**Dying to self is a sacrifice, My child...**one that only I can help you with. The power that sin holds over you is powerful, but its power has been broken by Me. I not only defeated its power but I defeat its sting as well. And I can do the same for you.

**Romans 12:1-2**
And so, dear brothers and sisters, I plead with you to give your bodies
to God. Let them be a living and holy sacrifice, the kind He will accept.
When you think of what He has done for you, is this too much to ask?
Don't copy the behavior and customs of this word, but let God transform
you into a new person by changing the way you think. Then you will know
what God wants you to do, and you will know how good and pleasing and
perfect His will really is. (NLT)

> **You must display a new nature because you are a new person,**
> **created in God's likeness—righteous, holy, and true.**
> (Ephesians 4:24)

# *"Pride is Sin"*

**Habakkuk 2:4**
Look at the proud! They trust in themselves, and their
lives are crooked, but the righteous will live by their faith. (NLT)

Pride, in layman terms, is a soul killer. Pride is the root that grows deep into our sinful nature. It is pride that tells us, we are gods; that we are in control. Pride tells us that we are better than others. Pride causes us to hunger for the forbidden; those things that can secretly satisfy the pleasures of our carnal flesh. It was the pride of God's most beautiful and powerful angel, Lucifer, that tempted him to rebel against the LORD God Almighty and lose His righteous standing in Heaven. Pride is a self-adornment disease that decays the soul and destroys our relationship with God and those around us. The pride that lurks within, hangs on to its crown of deception at all costs, for pride cannot lose face in the eyes of others, especially those who are below its kingly standard. But the saddest thing about the disease of pride is that its misguided, self-indulging ways blind us from seeing the glory of the LORD. Pride will lead us down a dark path of self-induced destruction that separates us from the saving Truth that is found in the death and resurrection of Christ Jesus, our Lord God and Savior.

Don't let the terrible sin of pride rule in your life my friend, instead, see yourself as a humble servant of the Lord, dedicated to doing what is right, not what makes you feel good. See yourself as a child of the Living God and open your heart and mind to His life saving Way. Look at everyone as better than yourself, and most importantly compare yourself only to Jesus Christ. For He is your creator and he creates all people in His likeness and in the same way. So be of humble heart and live ever so faithful in your thanksgiving to the Lord who graciously gives us every good thing.

## A Whisper of Hope

**Be of humble spirit, My child...**and I will draw you near to Me. I will show you how to walk upright and holy without letting it go to your head. I made you to walk with Me as My child, just as I made all those around you. Be humble and contrite and be all I created you to be for Me.

**Romans 12:3**
As God's messenger, I give each of you this warning:
Be honest in your estimate of yourselves, measuring
your value by how much faith God has given you. (NLT)

**"God resists the proud but gives grace to the humble"**
(James 4:6)

# *"Soundly Safe"*

**Zephaniah 2:3**
Beg the LORD to save you—all you who are humble, all you who uphold justice. Walk humbly and do what is right. Perhaps even yet the LORD will protect you from His anger on that day of destruction. (NLT)

Those of us who believe that God's Word is literal and true, know that the LORD is going to put an end to the evil in this world and destroy all godless people. We also know that we are living in the "Last Days." We know that the One who saved us is going to meet His Church in the sky to usher us into the present Heaven, where we will celebrate the Great Wedding Feast—the final union between the Church (the bride) and the Jesus Christ (the Bride Groom). King Jesus will rescue His bride from the wrath of God. The death and devastation brought on by God's mighty wrath will be so horrible that many will want to die, but can't. The suffering of those who refuse Christ Jesus will be like never before in the history of mankind. What the Bible tells of the Final Days of God's Wrath will seem mild when it is all said and done. But we have reason to praise and thank God, because He has made a Way for anyone to escape the heat that is about to come upon this wicked world; something you would be wise to avoid at all cost.

The Church of Jesus Christ, is not a building where people gather once a week so they can feel good about themselves in spite of their sin. It is not an organization or corporation that takes your money and deals in justification. The Church, my friends, is made up of true believers who have been born again as children of the Living God. They are sinful people who recognize their need for a Savior. They are people who were once lost in the darkness, but have found the Way out. They are repentant sinners that have sacrificed their old lives of sin for a life of righteous living. They are being made a new creation in Jesus Christ They are people who were once deceived but now they know the Truth that has set them free from the power of sin and the fear of death. If you have made the decision to live in Christ Jesus, He is living in you and your life is now on a sound foundation and your salvation is safely in His hands.

## A Whisper of Hope

**Just ask, dear child...**and I will save you from the destruction that is imminent for those who deny Me. Most people in this world disbelieve in the wrath of God to come, because they do not know Me. So they continue to live in darkness, loving their sin more than their Savior. Do not follow suit!

**2 Thessalonians 1:7-9**
And God will provide rest for you who are being persecuted and also for us when the Lord Jesus appears from Heaven. He will come with His mighty angels, in flaming fire, bringing judgment on those who don't know God and on those who refuse to obey the Good News of our Lord Jesus. They will be punished with everlasting destruction, forever separated from the Lord and from His glorious power. (NLT)

**Return O LORD, deliver me! Oh, save me for Your mercies' sake!**
(Psalm 6:4)

# "When the Thrill is Gone"

**Proverbs 30:8, 9**
Give me neither poverty nor riches! Give me just enough
to satisfy my needs. For if I grow rich, I may deny you and
say, "Who is the LORD?" And if I am too poor, I may steal
and thus insult God's holy name. (NLT)

We have a gracious God who delights in giving us good things. He is a faithful giver, especially to His children. The LORD is the One who created and provides everything we need. Without His generous provisions mankind would not survive. Our Creator did not create us and then leave us on our own. Instead, God gave us the wisdom and the desire to depend on Him for our survival and to enjoy our lives. Prior to Adam and Eve's eviction from Eden, they were fully satisfied with the good things God had given them. But since that eviction day, mankind has become self-focused and greedy. There are people who have received much thanking only themselves and God is the furthest thing from their minds. And there are those who have very little and they blame God for their misfortune. This is not right, because no matter what we have, we should be thankful for our lives, because without this life there can be no eternal life, and for this reason alone, we need to give God all of our thanksgiving and praise.

When the Lord God is not a part of our lives, we are easily duped into believing that the world is our provider; that mother earth is our God and it is up to us to take what we can. When we pursue only worldly things that have no eternal value, they quickly get old, and as the thrill fades, we begin looking for more of the same. When the Lord is not in the forefront of your life-journey, you are living in vain my friend. When you refuse to acknowledge God as your provider, you are inviting the Devil into your life, and when your sinful nature partners up with the Devil, the darkness will consume your soul. But when you humbly rely on the Lord to provide, He will give you exactly what you need, when you need it, and it will satisfy the desires of your heart.

## A Whisper of Hope

**You need Me, child...** You will perish without Me. On your own you will not only work in vain, but the darkness will swallow you up. But when you rely on Me for everything, you will receive more than you can ever imagine.

**2 Chronicles 16:9**
The eyes of the LORD search the whole earth in order to
strengthen those whose hearts are fully committed to Him. (NLT)

**Yes, a person is a fool to store up earthly wealth**
**but not have a rich relationship with God.**
(Luke 12:21)

# *"Our Advocate"*

**Zechariah3:1-2**
Then the angel showed me Jeshua the high priest standing
before the angel of the LORD. Satan was there at the angel's
right hand, accusing Jeshua of many things. And the LORD
said to Satan, "I, the LORD reject your accusations, Satan.
Yes, the LORD, who has chosen Jerusalem, rebukes you. (NLT)

The children of God have the greatest Defender in the universe. Jesus Christ is our advocate who sits at the right hand of the Father pleading the cases that Satan brings against us in an attempt to discredit God and steal our souls. Although Satan is the greatest accuser of all time, he is no match for Jesus Christ who crushed the serpents head. Jesus humbly came into this evil world to put Satan's power over man to shame and to set us free from our fear of death. Christ Jesus shed His life's blood for our forgiveness. Jesus paid the price we could not and defeated death. Satan's power has been broken and God's children are free. Satan knows his days are limited and he is putting up a horrific battle to take as many unsaved people into the eternal Lake of Fire as he can. Satan is our mightiest foe and should never be underestimated. He will stop at nothing to prove God wrong and he will do anything to destroy you.

When we commit our lives to God we are under His care and control and He becomes many things for us. He becomes a wise and loving Father, One who leads us down righteous paths, guides our every godly step, and teaches us His Holy Way. The Lord becomes our Protector, our Defender and our everyday Savior, protecting us from our enemies, defending our right standing, and saving us from our enemies. He also becomes our Refuge—a Place we can run to for safety and comfort, a place we go for forgiveness, encouragement, and peace, because we know He is always with us. The King of kings and Lord of lords, my friends, is also your Advocate and if that doesn't bring you a great sense of peace, then you don't know the God who saved you.

## A Whisper of Hope

**I Am your Savior, dear child...**and as your Advocate, your slate is wiped clean. It is not in your best interest to defend your sinful nature alone, because Hell's Accuser is crafty in all his deceitful ways. This why you need the Truth standing with you.

**1 John 2:1-2**
My dear children, I am writing this to you so that you
will not sin. But if your do sin, there is Someone to plead
for you before the Father. He is Jesus Christ, the One who
pleases God completely. He is the sacrifice for your sins.
He takes away not only our sins but the sins of all the world. (NLT)

**The LORD is good. When trouble comes He is a Strong Refuge.**
(Nahum 1:7)

# "A Saving Birth"

**Isaiah 9:2**
The people who walk in darkness will see a
great Light—a Light that will shine on all who
live in the land where death casts its shadow. (NLT)

Our Sovereign God loves everyone He creates. He loves us far above anything else in creation. So much so that He refused to leave us living in the darkness that sin has cast upon our world without a way out. God knows how helpless we are without Him; that we are easily pulled into this darkness that hardens our hearts and kills our souls. Before the day of man's first sin, the Lord had a Plan that would save us from our sin and the darkness of the grave—a Light that would shine brightly and bring us Hope. Without the Light of God's Son there would be no life, only darkness. Without God's Light we would be stumbling through the darkness, hopelessly lost, and living in constant fear. Without His Saving Light we would all end up falling into the eternal abyss that has no bottom. Without Jesus there would be no forgiveness, no redemption, and no joy.

At the right moment in time, our Savior came into the world—for a child was born to us, a Son is given to us. And the government will rest on His shoulders. These will be His royal titles: Wonderful Counselor, Mighty God, Everlasting Father, Prince of Peace. His ever expanding peaceful government will never end. He will rule forever with fairness and justice from the throne of His ancestor David. The passionate commitment of the LORD Almighty will guarantee this! (Isaiah 9:6-7) The LORD clothed Himself in humanity, bringing hope to all who would listen and believe. God so loved the human race that He personally saved us from certain doom. We have reason to rejoice my friends, not only during the Christmas Season, but every day of the year, for the Savior has come.

## A Whisper of Hope

**I came into the world, My child...**born as you are born and grew as you grow. I put on a human body to save you from your bondage to sin and death. I have broke the chains that once held you captive and arranged a stay in your death penalty for eternity.

**John 12:44-46**
Jesus shouted to the crowds, "If you trust Me, you are really trusting
God who sent Me. For when you see Me you are seeing the One who
sent Me. I have come as a Light to shine in this dark world, so that all
who put their trust in Me will no longer remain in the darkness. (NLT)

**Let us be glad and rejoice and honor Him.**
(Revelation 19:7)

# "Blessed Babe"

**Revelation 22:16**
"I, Jesus, have sent My angel to testify to you these things
in the churches. I am the Root and the Offspring of David,
the Bright and Morning Star." (NKJ)

Our Lord God and Savior, Jesus Christ came to us just as God had promised; a Babe born to a virgin, in a stable, and wrapped in the swaddling clothes of a servant. Jesus was the long awaited for Messiah, the One who would set Israel and the world free from the evil masters that controlled our existence; Satan, sin, and the fear of death. The Savior came to not only save us, but to expose the Enemy as well. He came as a Light for the lost—a Shepherd for His people. Jesus came to do for mankind what no One else could do. He came in love and filled with mercy and grace and power to fix the human race debacle. Jesus knew that without His sacrificial blood, we would have absolutely no chance of standing justified before Him on the Day of Judgment. Our world that Satan stole would be unrecognizable without Jesus—it would be a world consumed in the darkness of evil with no way out.

And there is really Good News to proclaim; Jesus is alive and the world has His life-saving Light. We are no longer trapped in the darkness of evil that consumes our world—we can get out! We can put on the robe of righteousness that Jesus purchased with His life's blood. We can now live in the Son's Light and experience the joy of the Lord. You have been given an incredible gift and to reject it is the worst decision that you will ever make, because you will never know the One who created you—the One who personally clothed Himself in a mere human body to save you from eternal destruction and to crown you with eternal life.

## A Whisper of Hope

**I am always with you, dear child...**when you belong to Me; even in your darkest hour, I am there. I loved you before I created you and I gave My life so that I could raise from the grave and bless you with eternal life. I saved you for Me.

**Luke 2:11**
"For there is born to you this day in the city of David a Savior,
who is Christ the Lord. And this will be the sign to you: You will
find a Babe wrapped in swaddling clothes, lying in a manger." (NKJ)

**All the world will know that I, the LORD, am your Savior and Redeemer.**
(Isaiah 49:26)

# *"Glorious Day"*

**Zechariah 9:16**
When that day arrives, the LORD their God will rescue
His people just as a shepherd rescues his sheep. They
will sparkle in His land like jewels in a crown. (NLT)

What a glorious day it will be when the Lord returns to rescue His people from this evil world—the day when He comes with the fire of vengeance in His eyes to rescue His people and put an end to the evil in our world. The Lord takes no pleasure in the death of anyone, but His justice must take place and reign throughout the land. No unrepentant sinner will be spared; they will pay the price for their sins. Those of us who have put our hope and trust in the blood of Christ as our sin payment in full, we are in safe keeping until King Jesus returns to make all things right. But for those who love their sin more than God, their day of reckoning is close at hand and they will pay the price and be condemned. Their sentence will be final and it will be eternal. They will share the Lake of Fire with Satan, which is far removed from the glorious new heavens and earth!

What a glorious day it will be when we are able to live in the Presence of our Holy God. We will slip into our glorious new bodies that will be perfect in every way. We will never again be separated from the Glory and goodness of God. We will never grow old and die. We will never be sick or get hurt, and sadness and tears will be no more. The new heavens and earth will be our Home and they will be so incredibly beautiful that the old will never come to mind. What awaits God's children in the future is beyond our finite comprehension, but the Scriptures explain all we need to know for now. Put your life in the hands of God my friend, become a part of the Greatest Escape in the history of mankind, one that puts the great Red Sea escape to shame.

## A Whisper of Hope

**Come to Me, dear child...**and I will give you rest. Come into My arms and let Me wipe away your tears. Let Me whisper in your ears the words of hope that will comfort your weary soul and bring My everlasting peace into your precious heart.

**2 Corinthians 4:4**
Satan, the god of this evil world, has blinded the minds of those
who don't believe, so they are unable to see the glorious Light of
the Good News that is shining upon them. They don't understand
the message we preach about the glory of Christ, who is the exact
likeness of God. (NLT)

**But the day of the Lord will come as unexpectedly as a thief.**
(2 Peter 3:10)

# *"Light Cleansing"*

**1 John 1:7**
But if we are living in the Light of God's Presence,
just as Christ is, then we have fellowship with each
other, and the blood of Jesus, His Son, cleanses us
from every sin. (NLT)

L iving in God's Light is a far cry from living in the darkness that most people are trapped in and don't even know it. Living in darkness is just another way of saying that you are indulging in the evil, sinful things that separate us from the goodness and glory of God and His Light—that you would rather live for the moment, enjoying the pleasures of the flesh rather than living for God in righteousness. Most people who live in darkness cannot give up their sinful ways, nor do they really care about what lies beyond this short life. It is our fallen human nature that leads us into this darkness and in many cases, it kills us before we can get out. This life is short and before we know it (if we make it that long) we are old and wondering where the time went. And without God's Light we are also left wondering if this life is all there is, and if it is, what a cruel joke it has been. Most people spend their busy lives just trying to survive without much thought of death until it hits close to home, and then they only ponder it for a bit before putting it on the back burner for another day.

The Light of the World has been shinning for over 2,000 years and is still lighting the Way in this dark world today, even though its future is looking bleaker every day. The dark forces that rule our world have tried their best to put out this Great Light and have failed miserably. The Good Hope that God's Light brings into our dark world has the power to transform even the darkest life into one that is like a bright shining city on a hill, glowing for all the world to see. The Saving Son Light of God is the only Light that can resurrected what is dead. He is the only One who can give us a new life that far exceeds anything this wicked world can promise. Step into His Light my friend, and bask in its healing Power. For when you do, you will wonder why you waited so long!

## A Whisper of Hope

**Step into the Light, My child...**and forever be changed. Your life will take on a new meaning and it will never end. You will see this world as it truly is. The darkness that surrounds you will never again hold you captive to its evil ways. You will be free!

**Isaiah 5:18, 20**
Destruction is certain for those who drag their sins behind them,
tied with cords of falsehood. Destruction is certain for those who
say that evil is good and good is evil; that dark is light and light is
dark, that bitter is sweet and sweet is bitter. (NLT)

**God is coming to destroy your enemies. He is coming to save you.**

(Isaiah 35:4)

# *"Lies bring Death"*

**Genesis 3:4-5**
"You won't die!" the serpent hissed. "God knows that your
eyes will be opened when you eat it. You will become just
like God, knowing everything, both good and evil." (NLT)

This is the oldest recorded lie in the history of mankind. When this lie was whispered to the
first man and woman they fell for it, hook, line, and sinker, and it changed the course of
time for mankind. Being cursed with sin, Adam and Eve and their descendants could no longer
live in the Presence of their Holy God and were banned from the Garden of Eden. Although it
is well within God's sovereign power to make us worship and love Him, He chose to create us
with a free will to choose to love and follow His ways or not. But because of God's great love,
mercy, and grace, He had a Plan that would bring us back in His Presence. Because of the blood
of Jesus, we can be cleansed of our sins and be in His Presence once again. And then one day,
physically live with our Creator, Savior and King in a new Heaven on Earth with a glorified
body that will never again be exposed to evil and sin and its power to enslave and decay—we
will be God's holy people and He will be our Holy God forever more.

But in this life we must continue to be on our guard, because the lies of the Devil are still
lurking in the darkness, ready to deceive, destroy, and kill our souls. It still amazes me that the
Lord would forgive and wipe our slates clean after all the wicked things we do and think. Oh
the patience God has while watching us indulge in the evil that is totally disgusting to Him,
and yet He is so full of mercy and grace and love in spite of our wicked ways. Our Lord God
and Savior has the Power to save any life no matter how wicked or evil it is. He not only has
the Power but He has the love to save as many of us as He can. Never doubt the love of God
my friends; for it can save you no matter what you have done. Jesus is calling you softly with
whispers of Hope and nudges of love.

## A Whisper of Hope

**Listen closely, dear child...**for My whispers of hope. They can bring you out of the cold and
into My warm embrace. I have vowed to save My children and bring My vengeance against the
wicked and evil. Come close and I will draw you near to Me—forevermore!

**2 Thessalonians 2:9-10**
This evil man will come to do the work of Satan with counterfeit power and
signs and miracles. He will use every kind of wicked deception to fool those
who are on their way to destruction because they refuse to believe the Truth
that would save them. (NLT)

**A false witness will not go unpunished, and he who speaks lies shall perish.**
(Proverbs 19:9)

# *"Glorious Heaven"*

**Isaiah 57:1-2**
The righteous pass away; the godly often die before their
time. And no one seems to care or wonder why. No one
seems to understand that God is protecting them from the
evil to come. For the godly who die will rest in peace. (NLT)

For people who are committed Christians, trusting in the blood of Jesus as the Christ, God promises that the moment we breathe our last breath in this life we will instantly be with the Lord forever. This promise is rooted in the Scriptures and we can trust it fully. What a cruel joke it would be if this life was all there is—that we go through all the pain and suffering and anxiety just to die and rot in the grave. The lies that this life is all there is or there are no consequences, is from the Devil and its infection has spread throughout the world. It has caused us to live in greed, taking what we can while we can, and doing it anyway we can, regardless of the consequences. But this short life is just the beginning of a very long life, and what we do in it has a great bearing on the next. There are many views about the afterlife and many people are easily fooled by the deceitful traps that give a false sense of hope. These lies are deadly, for if we take them into the grave, it's too late to change our minds.

As a believer in God and His amazing redemptive Plan to save man, you cannot afford to second guess God's motives, especially when it comes to who lives a long life and who does not. You must simply trust Him in everything. When you doubt our Sovereign God, you can be easily be pulled into the deadly traps of Satan, that are not easy to escape from. But when you belong to God and become His child, nothing will be able to snatch you from His Mighty Grip and you can rest assured that when you awaken from this life's sleep you will be in the Glory of Heaven with Jesus and that my friends, will be a glorious place to be.

## A Whisper of Hope

**The moment you become My child...**you become a citizen of Heaven and you are not left on your own to defend your citizenship. I will carry you in My arms right through Heaven's Gate. With Me, dear child, you will always sleep in perfect peace.

**1 Thessalonians 4:16-18**
For the Lord Himself will come down from Heaven with a commanding shout,
with the call of the archangel, and with the trumpet call of God. First, all the
Christians who have died will rise from their graves. Then, together with them,
we who are still alive and remain of the earth will be caught up in the clouds to
meet the Lord in the air and remain with Him forever. So comfort and encourage
each other with these words. (NLT)

**"When I awake, I will be fully satisfied, for I will see you face to Face."**
(Psalm 17:15)

# *"Peace Light"*

**Psalm 56:13**
For You have delivered my soul from death. Have
You not delivered my feet from falling, that I may
walk before God in the Light of the living? (NKJ)

There is one thing that human beings do quite well and it's living blindly in this dark world. We tend to stumble around in the darkness searching for the easiest path to a victorious life. But sooner or later we discover that without the proper lighting and guidance, all paths but one are a dead end. And after dead end after dead end many of us simply give up our search for the good and happy life that ends so quickly. And when we give up it can get really dark and awfully lonely. And the darker it gets, the lonelier we are, and the lonelier we get the darker it becomes. And when we are dark and lonely, it is so easy to simply lose our appetite for living and focus on the final dead end. But this short life-journey doesn't have to dead end in darkness and despair, for when we embrace the Light of God, our paths get brighter and brighter, and we are never alone.

Most people will never find their way out of the darkness because they don't know they are living in darkness. Many people choose to remain in the darkness because they love their sin too much. Some are afraid of the Light and fear it is just another dead end. But many who are exposed to the Light of God's amazing grace will walk down this new path and discover a whole new meaning with a whole new purpose. And even though their lives don't always get any easier, they know their Guide will get them safely through to the other side. There will be plenty of challenges on this path to Heaven and when the darkness of the world is beating at the door of your heart to get back in, your Savior is right there to keep that door shut so you can continue safely on your way. And the moment you step out of this life and into Heaven you will instantly know that it was well worth the difficult journey.

## A Whisper of Hope

**Receive My Peace, dear child...**and your deepest needs will be fulfilled. I, the Prince of Peace, will pour Myself into your neediness, for My abundance and your emptiness are a perfect match. My Peace will live and grow in you forever.

**Hosea 14:9**
Let those who are wise understand these things. Let those
who are discerning listen carefully. The paths of the LORD
are true and right, and righteous people live by walking in
them. But sinners stumble and fall along the way. (NLT)

**Peace I leave you. My peace I give you.**
(John 14:27)

CPSIA information can be obtained
at www.ICGtesting.com
Printed in the USA
FSOW02n0717051215
14033FS

9 781498 438476